CANADA IN SPACE

CANADA
IN
SPACE

LYDIA DOTTO

FOREWORD BY
MARC GARNEAU

IRWIN PUBLISHING
Toronto, Canada

CANADIAN CATALOGUING IN PUBLICATION DATA
Dotto, Lydia, 1949-
Canada in space

Includes index.
ISBN 0-7725-1657-X (bound). ISBN 0-7725-1559-X (pbk.)

1. Astronautics-Canada-History. 2. Astronautics- International cooperation. 3. Outer space- Exploration-Canada. I. Title

TL789.8.C3D67 1986 629.4'0971 C86-093455-1

1 2 3 4 5 6 7 8 93 92 91 90 89 88 87

Published by Irwin Publishing Inc.

DESIGN: Artplus Limited/Brant Cowie

To my mother and father,
Assunta and August Dotto,
to whom I am forever grateful for never telling me
that girls aren't supposed to be interested in science

and

to the Canadian astronauts:
Roberta Bondar, Marc Garneau,
Steve MacLean, Ken Money, Bob Thirsk
and Bjarni Tryggvason

To my mother and father,
Assunta and August Dotto,
to whom I am forever grateful for never telling me
that girls aren't supposed to be interested in science

and

to the Canadian astronauts:
Roberta Bondar, Marc Garneau,
Steve MacLean, Ken Money, Bob Thirsk
and Bjarni Tryggvason

Contents

By Marc Garneau

There
could not have been a greater contrast.
My wife watched very nervously
as I prepared to launch into space
while my children behaved as if they
were at a carnival.
My wife understood that these were still early
days
in the conquest of space
while my children had the idea that
the whole operation was an exciting
but routine event—no big deal!

Of course my wife was right. The space age has only just begun,
complete with triumphs and tragedies, major strides and setbacks,
and Canada is part of it all. To many Canadians, it has been a
pleasant surprise to discover that their country is way up there
along with the big players, aggressively pushing back the
frontiers of space, and leading the pack in many areas.

Undeniably, interest in space is growing. Our children's
generation sees itself intimately involved with the colonization of
space and many young Canadians dream of going up there
themselves. And so the time is ripe for us to examine how Canada
became involved with space and where it plans to go in the years
ahead.

Since my flight aboard the shuttle Challenger, I have had many
opportunities to tell Canadians first-hand about the magic of space
and about the personal experience of orbiting planet Earth.
Occasionally, I have also been able to discuss the subject on a
more technical level and to delve into the underlying economics.
But unfortunately, there never seems to be enough time to tell
people more than a part of the whole story. I normally get to

spend an hour or two at most with groups that have enough interest and curiosity about space fo fill a day's worth of questions.

So I've often felt the need for a comprehensive account of Canada's involvement in space — both a detailed look at the people and events behind some of our recent space triumphs and a scan of the drawing board to see what may be next. *Canada in Space*, written by Lydia Dotto, one of Canada's most respected science writers, fulfills that need.

Lydia brings to life some of the most memorable events of my own selection, training and flight and examines our nation's future space presence, all the while mixing in the right dose of technical detail to please the scientist in us all.

ACKNOWLEDGEMENTS

Writing
this book has been
challenging in many ways,
but perhaps the greatest challenge
has been trying to stay abreast
of the dramatic events
in the manned space program
during the past two years.
Since most of the events discussed in this book
had not even happened when I began writing it,
I had to depend to a great extent
on personal interviews
with people in the middle of the action —
which generated some 200 hours of tapes.
I owe these people a great debt of gratitude for being so generous
with their time when the last thing they needed was one more
thing to do. This book could not have been written without their
co-operation.

I want to thank, first and foremost, Canada's six astronauts:
Roberta Bondar, Marc Garneau, Steve MacLean, Ken Money,
Bob Thirsk and Bjarni Tryggvason. They were unfailingly
helpful despite the many extraordinary demands on their time and
energies during this unique period in their lives. The same is true
of Karl Doetsch of the National Research Council's Space
Division, the first director of the Canadian Astronaut Program.

The co-operation and assistance of other officials in the Space
Division and in the NRC public affairs office was
also vitally important and much appreciated. I would like to thank
Bruce Aikenhead, Bernard Poirier, Parvez Kumar, Garry
Lindberg, Clive Willis, Wally Cherwinski, Estelle Dorais and

John Wildgust for the information they so helpfully supplied, and for assistance in organizing interviews over a two-year period.

For invaluable assistance in staying abreast of developments in Canada's space station program, I owe special thanks to Karl Doetsch, Jim Middleton of Spar Aerospace Limited, and Mac Evans, director-general of the space policy sector of the federal Ministry of State for Science and Technology. I would also like to express my appreciation to Doug Watt of McGill University for his assistance, and to thank Chris Trump, vice-president of Spar Aerospace Limited, for his encouragement.

Writing a book of this sort puts quite a strain on an author's budget and I would like to gratefully acknowledge the financial support of the Canada Council, the Ontario Arts Council and the Public Awareness of Science and Technology Program of the Ministry of State for Science and Technology. These funds made it possible for me to devote my energies to this challenging project almost on a full-time basis and to retain the services of my research assistant, Pippa Wysong, who deserves a medal for her uncomplaining assistance in transcribing nearly 200 hours of taped interviews and for myriad other research tasks.

I would also like to thank my editors, Greg Ioannou of the Editorial Centre, and John Pearce, Donald G. Bastian and Elizabeth Wilson of Irwin Publishing Inc., for support and encouragement and for their always helpful handling of my manuscript. And I would like to sincerely acknowledge the help of my friends, Eleanor Sawyer, Joan Hollobon and Kay Rex, who provided a life-support system and the kind and soothing words an author always needs.

Brief sections of this book have appeared previously, in a slightly different form, in *Quest* magazine and the *Globe and Mail*.

"We Have No Downlink"

A_t
T + 1 minute and 13 seconds,
everything changed.
It happened in the time it takes
a heart to beat.
At 11:39:13 a.m. EDT
on January 28, 1986,
in a breathtaking flashfire
of exploding hydrogen and oxygen,
the space shuttle Challenger,
streaking toward the heavens
at 318 kilometres an hour,
was blasted to bits, taking with it seven lives,
more than two billion dollars in high-tech machinery, one quarter of an already hard-pressed shuttle fleet and, possibly, the dream of permanent human habitation and industrialization of space before the turn of the century, at least for most of the Western world.

It was not supposed to be an unbelievable thing. Many people within and close to the space program had said many times that such an accident was bound to happen sooner or later — and believed it — and yet still watched with horrified disbelief as flaming debris, trailing billowy white streamers of smoke and condensed ice particles, rained down for nearly an hour from a cold, impossibly blue sky into the Atlantic Ocean.

The lingering pall gave grisly, graphic emphasis to the bewildered observation of shaken flight director Jay Greene, who said: "It just stopped."

Stop it did — so suddenly and with so little warning that the NASA commentator, monitoring a computer console rather than the TV screen, briefly continued his recital of flight information after the explosion had occurred: "One minute, 15 seconds, velocity 2900 feet per second, altitude nine nautical miles, down range distance seven nautical miles." He paused for a moment, then said: "Flight controllers here looking very carefully at the situation." Another pause, as a series of asterisks marched across his screen, indicating a loss of data from the spacecraft. "Obviously a major malfunction. We have no downlink." A longer pause and then the first official confirmation of an unalloyed disaster, delivered in an eerily calm monotone: "We have the report from the flight dynamics officer that the vehicle has exploded."

The unprecedented tragedy occurred just as the manned space program was reaching its first quarter-century. Coming after two years of impressive gains in the space shuttle program, it created a most paradoxical situation: missions to retrieve and repair satellites in space had featured many risky but successful space walks by astronauts; now the worst had happened — a shuttle and its crew were lost. The green light to proceed with building a permanently manned space station had been given and now shuttle flights were suspended. Industrial and scientific interest in space research was finally beginning to pick up serious momentum and access to the microgravity environment was all but lost.

On the technological side, tremendous advances have been made in the quarter century since Yuri Gagarin orbited the earth in 1961 — astronauts have walked on the moon and rescued disabled satellites; unmanned probes have landed on Venus and Mars and have had close encounters with comets and with the giant gas planets of the outer solar system; satellite communications and remote sensing of the earth's resources from space have become multi-billion-dollar businesses; the space shuttle had begun to do its job as a workhorse vehicle for ferrying humans and equipment into space and back; human beings have worked in space for months at a time. Perhaps most significantly, many young people today think seriously, and in personal terms, about living and working in space; to them, it is an oppportunity no longer considered the epitome of the unattainable.

The political and social climate surrounding the space program has changed less dramatically in the past 25 years. The United States and the Soviet Union, still vying for technological — and implied political — superiority, strive separately for permanent human habitation of space. The space program is still used for political purposes and is still routinely criticized as a giant technological boondoggle, and as a waste of taxpayers' money that could be better spent fighting poverty and pollution on earth. But there are new developments as well; perhaps the most important of these is the prospect of weapons being placed in orbit, with much-debated implications for the stability of peace on earth.

This book is about some of these developments, but it is not, and cannot be, an exhaustive examination of all aspects of the international space program. Its perspective is structured by two main guiding principles:

• *It focusses on the present and the future:* There are already many excellent histories of the space program; this book tries to avoid covering old territory. In general, historical events are dealt with only when necessary and only in enough detail to provide a context for the current and projected activities that are the focus of this book.

• *It is about the manned space program:* This book is primarily about human beings living and working in space, and about the symbiosis between humans and machines that makes possible the permanent human habitation of this fundamentally alien environment. Four major elements of the manned program are examined — the space shuttle; the space station; the role of the astronauts; and, finally, the scientific, commercial and industrial activities that are likely to be supported by the space station infrastructure. In the Canadian context, this entails an examination of the Canadian astronaut program; the development and role of the Canadarm aboard the space shuttle; and Canada's scientific and technological involvement in the shuttle program and the U.S./international space station. For the most part, unmanned programs — such as communications and remote-sensing satellites and planetary probes — are not examined in any great detail, although they are interesting and important in their own right. The focus on the manned program in this book reflects the

3

fact that this is a field in which activity has increased dramatically during the past five years and one that will dominate the space program to the turn of the century — technologically, financially and politically. Certainly there are critics within the space science community who wish this were not so, but the fact remains that it *is* so and thus it merits exploration.

It should be noted that this book was written during a two-year period that represented perhaps the most rapid evolution of the manned space program to date — a period in which some of the most dramatic events in the human conquest of space have occurred. It has been like shooting at a moving target. Although every effort has been made to anticipate the trends of the next two decades, this effort has been fraught with all the usual pitfalls one expects while crystal-ball gazing. This book might best be viewed as a snapshot of the manned space program as it stood poised on the brink of the next major migration of the human species, and of the political and economic climate in which it has struggled for existence and growth.

Two further aspects of this book should be pointed out:

• *It has been written largely from a Canadian perspective.* However, given the increasingly international nature of the manned space program, and the fact that so much of the Canadian program is inextricably linked with the U.S. program, the manned space programs of United States and Europe are necessarily discussed in considerable detail. On the other hand, this book does not attempt to provide a detailed analysis of the Soviet space program, about which comparatively little is known and with which Canada has had little involvement.

• *This book does not examine military uses of space in detail.* This is a subject that has already been, and doubtless will continue to be, the subject of many other books. The discussion in this book is restricted to only a few aspects relevant to the major themes of the book — for example, the much-debated question of whether the U.S. civilian space station project will play any part in the militarization of space.

Finally, the reader should know that this book is based on three underlying premises: (1) that the U.S./international manned space program will persevere despite the setback of the Challenger accident; (2) that, on balance, it is a good thing that human beings

4

are moving into space to live and work and (3) that this move will ultimately result in both tangible and intangible benefits for humanity as a whole that will justify the investment of money and effort.

The first and second points rest on the assumption that meeting a great challenge and pushing ourselves to the limits provided by our environment — even in the face of failure and tragedy — is one of the finest expressions of the human spirit. This tends to be a matter of faith or personal philosophy; either you believe it or you don't. The third premise will be proved or disproved in time and at a considerable cost — in money, in human effort, and in human lives. The arguments will rage on as to whether the returns are worth the investment, but perhaps, in the end, we will discover that the doing of it is ultimately more important to us than the material rewards we are likely to gain.

The Challenger Seven thought so:

"When you find something you really like to do and you're willing to risk the consequences of that, you probably ought to do it."
— Commander Francis Scobee.

"I wanted to fly. I can never remember anything else I wanted to do but fly. To tell you the truth, it's been wonderful."
— Pilot Michael Smith.

"You launch, not knowing what is going to happen. And that is the challenge you have to take. Without doing that, one would never accomplish the work one sets out to do."
— Mission specialist Judith Resnik.

"Just opening the door, having this ordinary person fly, says a lot about the future."
— Citizen-observer, teacher Christa McAuliffe.

"If they sold tickets, I'd be the first to buy one."
— Payload specialist Gregory Jarvis.

"If we feared danger, mankind would never go into space."
— Mission specialist Ellison Onizuka.

"The true courage of spaceflight is not sitting aboard six million pounds of fire and thunder as one rockets away from this planet. True courage comes in enduring…persevering, the preparation, believing in oneself. You can only become a winner if you are willing to walk over the edge."
— Mission specialist Ronald McNair.

CHAPTER ONE

Canada's First Astronaut Flies

The
white room
is the last outpost
before entering
the space shuttle.
It sits, small and box-like, at the end of
a 20-metre-long passageway
known as the orbiter access arm,
a swing arm
that extends out to the shuttle
from the launch tower
45 metres above the ground.
The white room is aptly named.

It is ruthlessly clean and everything is symbolically white: the walls, the floor, even the clothing of the "close-out" crew, the efficient, mostly silent group of men and women who assist shuttle crews into the spacecraft — their last face-to-face contact with the outside world until the end of the mission. The only shock of color in the white room comes from the vibrant blue flight suits of the astronauts and the brightly colored patches on their arms. On one suit, this October morning, the patches are red, white and black — the Canadian flag on one arm, the Canada wordmark with maple leaf on the other. For the first time ever, the official mission patch, worn by all seven crew members, carries the symbol of a foreign country — a tiny Canadian flag.

It is 5:01 a.m. EDT, October 5, 1984, and the patches, along with the man who wears them, are about to disappear into the hatch of the space shuttle Challenger. For the Canadian journalists and space program officials watching on closed-circuit TV at the Kennedy Space Center in Florida, this is the moment of truth, when, suddenly, it all becomes real. For 35-year-old Navy Commander Marc Garneau, the arrival at the launch tower, the ride up the elevator, the walk down the orbiter access arm and the ministrations of the close-out crew all mark a psychological passage from fantasy to reality. As he enters the spacecraft, the countdown clock reads T-1 hour, 41 minutes and 18 seconds. In about two hours, Garneau will become the first Canadian to fly in space. He has been an astronaut for just ten months.

As Garneau settles himself in to wait for the launch, shuttle watchers gather in the pre-dawn hours, in anticipation of the scheduled 7:03 a.m. liftoff. The pitch dark shrouding the Kennedy Space Center is broken by sweeping search lights, which bounce off the low-lying clouds scudding over the launch pad. Challenger, glowing brilliantly in the light, is visible for miles along the isolated stretch of swampy coastline of northeast Florida. The surrounding highways and waterways are lined with people in campers, cars and boats who have staked out prime vantage points. The crowds are not as large as they once were; shuttle launches, occurring about once every two months, are considered almost routine by many people — a situation fervently welcomed by the U.S. National Aeronautics and Space Administration after the program's troubled early days. Not surprisingly, though, the Canadian contingent here is larger than usual, comprising about 130 journalists milling around the press site and about two dozen VIPs, representatives of the Canadian government, industry and universities flown in by special charter from Ottawa. Tom Siddon, the first science minister in the newly elected Progressive Conservative government, is in attendance but reports circulate through the press corps that Prime Minister Brian Mulroney declined an invitation to the launch. The significance, if any, of this is not immediately apparent, but it prompts inevitable speculation that Canada's involvement with the manned space program, not yet even off the ground in the literal sense, might already be earmarked for the chopping block, another victim of the new government's vigorous cost-cutting. It's the only downer of the morning, though, and not enough to dampen the irrepressible excitement among Canadians at the Kennedy Space Center.

Meanwhile, both of Canada's national TV networks are preparing for live broadcasts from temporary open-air studios facing the launch site. They huddle, like poor relations, in the shadow of the permanent buildings housing the three American networks. Veteran American journalists are indulgently amused by the almost childlike enthusiasm and sense of importance of the Canadians, but they are nonetheless helpful to the Canadian reporters, most of whom are neophytes struggling for the first time with NASA's well-oiled but intimidating public affairs operation. As with a sports event or a papal visit, the Canadian networks have arranged for experts to provide color commentary — in this case, two of Garneau's colleagues, Canadian astronauts Roberta Bondar and Bob Thirsk. Thirsk, who was designated the backup astronaut for this flight, finds the watching bittersweet; he had trained alongside Garneau for months, and, until perhaps a few days before launch, could have stepped into his shoes — if not necessarily his flight suit and helmet — had Garneau for some reason been unable to fly. But now the countdown had dwindled from weeks to days to hours. After watching on the TV monitors as Garneau entered the spacecraft, Thirsk commented that his colleague "really looked like all the training had been done, the pressure was off and he was going to enjoy this. The last seven months have been very intense; it was a short time to prepare for a space flight." He added, rather wistfully, "I knew almost exactly to the minute what Marc would be doing. We've been through many simulations; we had a dry countdown that went right up to T-5 seconds. But when he goes in the hatch, you know that this time they're going to close the hatch and ... it's different."

Ken Money, another of the Canadian astronauts, was assigned to provide support for the print media on launch morning and the other two members of the Canadian astronaut team had non-media duties. Bjarni Tryggvason accompanied Garneau's wife, Jacqueline, and her two children as they observed the launch, following a long-standing NASA tradition of providing astronaut escorts for the families of flight crew members. Steve MacLean was in Mission Control at the Johnson Space Center in Houston, providing technical support for one of the mission's Canadian experiments, which was scheduled to occur about eight hours after launch; he thus remained the only one of the five who had never seen a shuttle launch.

Along with the American members of his crew, Garneau had flown in from the Johnson Space Center, where the astronauts are based, to be quarantined in the crew quarters at the Kennedy Space Center for three days before the flight. On their arrival at

KSC, there was the usual media scrum and the usual, unsurprising responses: "I'm Marc Garneau, the fortunate Canadian who gets the chance to go up in the shuttle on Friday. I'm very excited, needless to say, and really looking forward to the mission." For the previous two months, Garneau had been working intensely alongside his American colleagues at both JSC and KSC, familiarizing himself with the shuttle and rehearsing virtually every minute of the mission. Now the last three days were to be spent quietly — resting, relaxing, perhaps marshalling psychological resources, and spending time with family. During a barbecue on the beach the day before launch, Garneau visited with his wife, Jacqueline, and his parents, Jean and André Garneau, who had undergone medical tests beforehand to ensure they would not give the quarantined crew any show-stopping infections. Simone and Yves, Garneau's 8-year-old twins, were not present; NASA bans children from the final farewells because, as one official put it, they're "notorious for picking up and spreading germs." However, Garneau collected seashells for his children as he strolled on the beach reflecting on his plans for the future. His mother found him "terribly calm, serene." His father, a retired Canadian Army general, said of his son: "He's a military man and he knows it's a job." The astronauts' families were spirited away by NASA officials with only a minute's warning to preclude long, teary goodbyes. "I think it was better like that," conceded Jacquie. She had time only for a quick "I love you" and, in response, Garneau told her not to worry. They had one more chance to talk on the phone late Thursday afternoon, the day before launch, when Jacquie told him to "break a leg."

For Garneau, the early evening hours of Thursday were a time of somewhat reluctant reflection. He was anxious to get a good night's sleep and had been wondering all day if he'd be too worked up. In fact, when he retired around 7 p.m., he lay awake in bed for more than two hours. "It took me a while," he admitted later. "Normally, it takes me about five minutes." His mind was filled with random thoughts — *what are you going to do during the two hours you're sitting inside there? Are you going to get cold feet? Is there something you can think about to keep your mind busy? Have I gotten myself into something I really want to do?* His concern with being able to fall asleep that night was more than just an understandable desire to be well rested for the extraordinarily demanding day he was facing. There was an underlying psychological factor: the preoccupation with performance and with control of external events that seems to come naturally to the kind of people who end up as astronauts. Garneau couldn't help wondering how his six colleagues were faring. Two were veterans: Commander Robert Crippen (known as Crip), embarking on a record fourth mission, and astronaut Sally Ride, who was flying for the second time. The other four — Jon McBride, Kathy Sullivan, David Leestma and Paul Scully-Power — were rookies like himself. *"Are they all in their beds right now sleeping?"* Garneau thought as he lay awake. And then: *"If I'm not sleeping, I hope they're not sleeping. I wonder if Sally, who's done this before, is any more relaxed the second time."* As it turned out, he was happy to have managed about five hours of sleep, which signified to him that "I've got this thing under control."

Garneau was awakened just before 3 a.m. After washing and shaving — not only his face, but patches on his chest for electrodes that would record his heart rate during the launch — he joined the others for the launch morning breakfast. There was the traditional large cake, iced with a replica of the mission patch. This was the first shuttle crew to have two women and the patch featured the male and female gender symbols. The crew members were dressed in "civvies" for breakfast, not in their regulation blue flight suits, because, as Garneau wryly remarked, "you don't want to get jam on it before you leave." He was hungry — "My appetite ... is one of the things that rarely suffers" — but, being only too well aware of his propensity for motion sickness, he opted to play it safe and settled for dry toast. Aware that he would be sitting on the launch pad for at least two hours, and possibly longer, he also limited himself to a single cup of coffee.

As usual, a NASA photographer was in attendance to record the event for posterity. Garneau admitted it was a bit disconcerting to have "cameras in your face while you were eating your porridge," but the crew was grateful not to have to contend with the press at this point. The mood was rather subdued. "Everybody's their typical sort of sluggish at breakfast time. Nobody is on top at a quarter to three," Garneau recalled. "There's a feeling of unreality about the whole thing: This is really the morning; it's not rehearsal anymore." He was conscious of watching Crippen and Ride because they'd been through this before; they appeared to him to be "more mellow" than the rookies, but careful not to rub it in. "They could be nauseatingly cool and relaxed, but I think they sort of subdue that on purpose so that we all feel the excitement."

After breakfast, the crew dressed in their flight suits and emerged from their quarters in the Operations and Checkout Building shortly after 4 a.m. As they negotiated the walkway toward the astrovan, they received a send-off from media representatives and NASA workers; Garneau, bringing up the rear looking happy and (at least outwardly) relaxed, spotted a few familiar faces and cheerfully gave a "thumbs up" before boarding the van for the 14-kilometre ride to Launch Pad 39A. The van, a camper, was a recent acquisition, purchased by NASA to accommodate the increasingly large shuttle crews. The seven-member crew of 41-G was the largest to date.

Escorted by security cars and helicopters to ensure that no unforeseen traffic tie-ups would cause delays, the van reached the pad in about 25 minutes. Garneau recalls that, despite the imminence of the great adventure, the crew's mood was still rather subdued; "quiet jokes and very casual chit-chat, nothing heavy." A quick ride up the elevator deposited them in the white room. Still mindful of the two-hour wait in the spacecraft before launch, Garneau used the washroom and waited his turn. The four who were to sit on the flight deck — the upper part of the shuttle's crew compartment — went first: Commander Crippen, pilot-astronaut McBride and mission-specialist astronauts Sullivan and Ride. Garneau was next; now helmeted, he shook hands with a white-coated technician (who remarked: "See you when you get back.") and crawled on hands and knees through the circular hatch into the Challenger. His only thought at that point was "to be as co-operative as possible, because you hate to be the one who's holding things up." David Leestma and Paul Scully-Power followed in short order and, by about 5:30 a.m., the crew was settled.

Garneau's seat was located in the mid-deck, the lower section of the crew compartment, near the hatch of the airlock that astronauts use to leave the shuttle during space walks (called EVA — for "extravehicular activity"). He was more lying down than sitting, with his back to the ground and his knees up. A quick communications check with the ground to ensure that he was plugged in properly and then there was only the waiting and the "creeping butterflies." It was a situation, Garneau later acknowledged, that permitted feelings of fear to surface for the first time: "It's a long time to sit there with basically nothing to do. You suddenly realize that you're here for the real thing now." In this, he was being rather more frank about his feelings than astronauts usually are; generally they are cautious about admitting to apprehension of any kind, since this doesn't fit the image. Before the flight, Garneau commented: "People often ask me if I get afraid at the thought of what could go wrong. I'd be less than normal if those thoughts didn't occasionally cross my mind — especially when I think of what would happen to my family." He added, "It doesn't unduly concern me."

The countdown had proceeded smoothly throughout the night, without even the minor hitches that had dogged most previous flights. The low clouds lingered overhead, but did not pose any serious threat. (The weather had to be appropriate for a landing as well as the launch, in case an immediate return, known as a "return to launch site abort," was required for emergency reasons.) About an hour and a half before launch, the crew received the final weather briefing, including a report from chief astronaut John Young, who was monitoring weather patterns above the launch site from the shuttle training aircraft. NASA was also keeping a close watch on other aircraft in the vicinity; on several occasions, private pilots had penetrated the restricted zone around the site and once actually caused a launch delay.

Now the pace really starts to pick up. Although the countdown clock reads T-1 hour, it is actually one hour and 20 minutes to launch; this example of NASA's rather arbitrary time-keeping methods accommodates two built-in "holds" of ten minutes each to allow for last-minute trouble-shooting if needed. None is required for this flight — the countdown is proceeding "as written" — and the clock comes out of the last hold at T-9 minutes. Most of what follows now happens too fast for human beings to handle, so the automatic launch sequencer, the ground-based computer, assumes control. At T-7 minutes and 30 seconds, the orbiter access arm, the passageway that had remained in place against the shuttle's entry hatch as a means of emergency escape, is retracted, but it can be swung back into place in 30 seconds if need be. For the next seven minutes, all spacecraft systems, fuel tanks and rocket boosters are rapidly checked and readied to perform by the sequencer. "You get the feeling the shuttle is coming alive," Garneau says. Finally, at T-31 seconds, if all is well, control is handed over to the shuttle's five on-board computers.[1] This is breath-holding time; the computers can stop — and several times have stopped — the launch within that last half-minute, detecting trouble and neutralizing it within milliseconds, before human beings can even comprehend that trouble is brewing.

But there is no trouble this morning and, at T-6.6 seconds, the computers start to fire the shuttle's three main engines. As the engines build up thrust, the shuttle strains mightily against the holddown bolts that anchor it to the launch pad and, among the watchers, there is a palpable, almost physical, effort to will the vehicle off the ground. Finally, the clock reaches T-0; with the main engines now nearly at full thrust, the two solid rocket boosters are ignited, the holddown bolts are blown and Challenger lifts off the pad on a plume of brilliant yellow-white smoke that transforms the pre-dawn darkness into daylight. The dazzling visual display is only part of the experience; the thunderous roar of the rocket boosters shakes the ground, vibrating right through the bodies of those watching from the viewing area, about six kilometres away. Within 20 seconds, the spacecraft enters the clouds, suffusing them with a warm golden glow as it vanishes from view. The presence of the clouds magnifies the rapid machine-gun effect that peppers the crowd as the shuttle rolls on its back and heads out over the ocean. The smoke plume lingers over the launch pad, now tinted a translucent pink from a bright red sun poking its nose over the horizon.

Those inside the shuttle tend to feel like they have a tiger by the tail — they're along for the ride, come what may. Sally Ride has commented that there is "an overwhelming sense that you have no control over what is happening." It was the noise and vibration and being "enveloped by the experience" that Garneau remembered long after.

For those watching, it was 30 seconds of total sensory assault — an almost tactile experience and, for most, a very emotional one. It is not unusual to see a few teary-eyed people in the crowd and even veteran launch observers never fail to find the experience moving. ("It's better than sex," observed one.) For many of the Canadians watching — the other five astronauts, space program officials, the media, Garneau's family — the launch of flight 41-G had an added emotional impact simply because it carried a man who was not just the first Canadian to fly in space, but a friend and colleague, a father, husband, brother or son. Garneau's mother crossed herself twice and buried her face in her husband's shoulder, murmuring "I can't believe it." André Garneau put his arm around his wife. Garneau's brother Philippe exclaimed as he hugged his mother: "Wasn't that something else!" Philippe was not exactly a model of detachment as he reported live to a Montreal radio station: "Oh my God, look at the light! It's unreal. My hands are clammy; I'm shaky; I'm still short of breath." British-born Jacqueline managed to apply some of the famed English cool to the event, but it was still "the most thrilling, exhilarating thing I have ever seen." She admitted that she hadn't slept at all the night before, adding that she was relieved but "emotionally quite exhausted."

With the liftoff of 41-G, Canada became the fourteenth nation to put a person in orbit[2] and Garneau joined the ranks of a select group, then numbering less than 200 people, who can truly call themselves astronauts because they have flown in space. The press immediately dubbed him the "half-million-dollar man" in reference to the $500,000 Canada spent preparing for the mission. (Actually, the government did not have to pick up the entire tab; since NASA had invited Canada along for the ride, the U.S. space agency contributed its services in training Garneau and Thirsk during the last two months before the mission.)

For the other five Canadian astronauts, the launch triggered complex and mixed emotions. They'd bonded into a close-knit team in the year they'd worked together and they were excited for Marc. Bondar, who shared an office with Garneau, said she felt "it was like a brother going up." At the same time, however, each one could not help but wish that he or she had been the one selected for this ride; Bjarni Tryggvason said he would find the shuttle launch even better "when I'm sitting in it." The astronauts were only too conscious that, as things stood then, there were just two more flights confirmed for Canadian astronauts, both more than a year away. If it turned out that that was all there would be, at least three of them would never fly at all. It was a possibility they all clearly had great difficulty coming to terms with, given the intensity with which they had all been focussing on the goal that had consumed them for the past year — and most especially on the morning they had witnessed the first of their group embarking on the dream they all shared. If this mission went well, the prospects for other flights, perhaps even on the U.S./

international space station in the early 1990s, would be greatly improved; but so many other things were involved — not the least political and financial factors over which they had no control — that there was no realistic way of telling, at the time, whether more than two opportunities remained.

And so, as he watched Challenger disappear in a cloud of incandescent smoke, Ken Money "felt like yelling, 'Wait for me, Marc!'" Money was a unique case. As an expert in the physiological adaptation of the human body to zero gravity, he had been involved with the U.S. manned space program for nearly 25 years and had seen three potential opportunities for space flights, including this one, elude him. Even so, the good-natured Money said that Garneau was more qualified for this flight because it involved engineering and physics experiments as well as life sciences experiments. "I would have liked to have done it — and I could have done it — but I think Marc is better qualified to do the overall thing than I am." At 49 the oldest of Canada's astronauts, Money was conscious that time was eroding his chances of realizing his passionately held dream of flying in space. He believed that one of the two subsequent flights might well be his last chance. "I think almost surely there is a future for Canadian astronauts beyond the next two [flights], but if it isn't until 1993, then I'll probably be out of the running."

It took Challenger about 8 1/2 minutes to achieve orbit. About two minutes into the ascent, the solid rocket boosters shut down and were dropped off to fall into the ocean, where they would be recovered to be used again. The shuttle was then riding on its three main engines. Should any of them quit or fail to achieve full thrust, thereby compromising the shuttle's ability to reach the desired orbit, various emergency landing contingencies had, as usual, been planned. Depending on the nature of the failure, this could mean a return to launch site (RTLS) abort, with a landing back at the Kennedy Space Center strip; a trans-Atlantic (TAL) abort, with a landing at a designated strip in Europe; or, if there was enough juice to obtain low orbit, "abort once around" (AOA), which would take the shuttle to the California landing strip at Edwards Air Force Base. None of these emergency procedures had ever been used and none was required for flight 41-G, which continued in textbook fashion and established itself 351 km above the earth on schedule about 45 minutes after launch. It was in what is known as a "high inclination" orbit; that is, inclined to the equator as far as 57 degrees of latitude north and south. This was unusual — shuttle flights normally stayed closer to the equator — and it was fortuitous for Garneau because it enabled him to observe many parts of Canada during the mission.

The moment the main engines stopped firing, the crew experienced weightlessness or what is commonly called zero gravity.[3] It was not the first time they'd experienced it, since part of their pre-flight training included flights on an aircraft flying a roller coaster pattern that produces zero-G in brief episodes of less than 30 seconds; but Garneau recalled that the onset seemed much more sudden on the shuttle — and, of course, it didn't go away within 30 seconds. Garneau also experienced the "puffy face" syndrome reported by other astronauts, caused by a shifting of fluids to the upper part of the body. Knowing his susceptibility to motion sickness, he moved rather gingerly at first, thinking: *"Move my head — how's that feel? OK, now take it easy, nobody hurry."* He knew that, if he were going to be affected, it was most likely to happen in the first few hours. As it turned out, he did not get sick at all during the flight, but he commented later that "I felt fragile at the beginning and I think, if I'd wanted to, I could have made myself sick." Studying motion sickness was one of the life sciences experiments Garneau was to perform — he would later try, unsuccessfully, to make himself sick — but in the early hours of the mission, he was more concerned about coping competently with zero-G and performing his assigned duties in getting the shuttle mid-deck ready for the first day of operations. The first order of business was to remove and stow the seats in the mid-deck and to remove helmets and boots. New astronauts tend to be all arms and knees in zero-G, he observed wryly, and "you don't want to kick somebody in the face."

One of Garneau's most memorable moments occurred when he moved to the side hatch — the small port-hole that is the only window on the mid-deck — for his first look at the earth from space.[4] "That first view is spectacular. That's something you've been dreaming about seeing for the longest time. The thing that struck me was how crystal clear the colors were. I was expecting there would be a sort of haze due to pollution or moisture in the air." Later, he would reflect that he was never more conscious of the earth as a whole planet, as the place that human beings call home. From space, it has the look of "a friendly place — that's where we came from." It made him all the more aware that Challenger, in contrast, was "a fragile cocoon — a few panes of glass, a little bit of aluminum, a hull holding us in."

Flight 41-G was the thirteenth shuttle flight[5] and Challenger's sixth. It cost about US$180-million and boasted several firsts — the largest shuttle crew, the first to include two women, the first space walk (EVA) by an American woman and, of course, the first Canadian. In the cargo bay was a full complement of payloads and experimental equipment, most designed for remote sensing of the earth's climate and environment. They included:

Earth Radiation Budget Satellite (ERBS): a satellite to measure the amount of solar energy absorbed in different regions of the earth and the amount of thermal radiation emitted back into space (hence the term "radiation budget"). These heating patterns play a major role in the circulation of the earth's atmosphere and therefore are important in understanding weather and climate.

Stratospheric Aerosol and Gas Experiment (SAGE II): located on the ERBS satellite, SAGE was designed to monitor the global distribution of aerosols (small particles) and gasses in the high atmosphere to help scientists study the impact of human activities and natural events (such as volcanic eruptions and dust storms) on climate and environmental quality.

Measurement of Air Pollution from Satellites Experiment (MAPS): an instrument to monitor carbon monoxide in the atmosphere as part of a study on the environmental impact of industrial activity.

Large Format Camera: the first mapping camera to photograph the earth from space was bigger, more stable and contained more advanced optics and electronics than its airborne predecessors. At an altitude of 300 km, it can take a picture of something the size of a single-family house. The large pictures are used for resource and mineral exploration, geological studies, environmental monitoring and map making.

Shuttle Imaging Radar (SIR-B): an instrument that transmitted microwave radar pulses toward the earth and measured the returning signals to produce "radar snap-shots" — detailed photograph-like black and white pictures of the varied terrain below. Different surfaces produce different "signatures." In fact, the first image produced by SIR-B was one of Montreal that showed such fine details as bridges, farms and a racetrack. One unique advantage of the radar system is that it can take these pictures in virtually any weather or sunlight conditions. The images would be used for a wide variety of scientific studies in geology, cartography, oceanography, vegetation studies and archeology.[6]

Orbital Refuelling System (ORS): a system to demonstrate for the first time the techniques needed to refuel satellites in space. The ORS consisted of two tanks located in the shuttle cargo bay, one empty, the other full of satellite fuel, a highly toxic and corrosive substance called hydrazine. The objective was to transfer the fuel from one tank to another, simulating what would be done with a spent satellite. However, none of the satellites then in orbit or being built were designed for refuelling, since they lacked the necessary access valve. Therefore, the ORS test called for a three-hour space walk by David Leestma and Kathy Sullivan[7] to install a valve assembly and hook up a linking device — essentially a siphon hose — between the two tanks to permit fuel to flow between them. (The shuttle happened to be on one of the northerly legs of its orbit when the two went out and, as he emerged into the cargo bay from the shuttle's airlock hatch, Leestma observed: "Looks like Canada.")

"Getaway Specials": these are drum-shaped cannisters that are tucked into nooks and crannies in the cargo bay and can be purchased relatively cheaply by companies, universities, schools and even individuals who want to fly experiments on the space shuttle. On flight 41-G, these included: the first "space art" project, sponsored by Arizona sculptor Joseph McShane, who used vacuum deposition techniques to coat glass spheres with gold, platinum and other metals; a zero-gravity fuel test; various materials processing experiments, including the production of metal alloys and crystals; a study of seed growth; an amateur radio transmission experiment; and a test of the effect of cosmic radiation on microelectronic circuits — a matter of considerable concern to those anticipating the long-term use of computers in space.

All of the Canadian experiments aboard flight 41-G were conducted by Garneau inside the spacecraft.[8] There were ten of them in three major categories: space technology, space science and life sciences. Like everything else in the space program, they had promptly been reduced to acronyms. Collectively known as

19

CANEX (for "Canadian experiments"), they included SASSE, VISET, SPEAM, OGLOW and ACOMEX.

SASSE — the Space Adaptation Syndrome Supplementary Experiments — comprised a set of half a dozen life sciences experiments designed to help scientists better understand the effect of weightlessness on the human body. Most of the tests focussed on space motion sickness, disorientation and the sense of body position in zero gravity; they were a continuation of long-standing research efforts in this field by Ken Money and physiologist Douglas Watt of McGill University. Watt was the principal investigator of the SASSE experiment on flight 41-G and was responsible for ensuring that Garneau was trained to perform the tests. Garneau did the tests in three sets for comparison purposes — once on earth before the flight to obtain "baseline" information, then in space, and again on earth within an hour of returning from space. These tests are discussed in detail in Chapter 5.

The second set of experiments that Garneau performed related to the machine vision system being developed by the National Research Council to enhance the capabilities of the Canadarm, the shuttle's Canadian-built remote manipulator arm. VISET — the Space Vision System Experiment Development Test — was intended to test certain aspects of the system, which is designed to provide the operator of the arm with precise and rapid computerized information on the relative position, orientation and motion of the arm and the payload it is trying to grab. It's expected that the SVS will make arm operations faster, safer and more accurate, particularly with the very large payloads likely to be handled in the future. These experiments and the development of the space vision system are discussed in more detail in Chapter 6.

Another Canadian experiment on 41-G, the Advanced Composite Materials Experiment (ACOMEX), was designed to determine the extent to which certain lightweight, non-metallic materials deteriorate in space. To study this phenomenon, samples of various materials were attached in narrow strips to the Canadarm, which was extended to expose the materials in the direction of the shuttle's flight for a total of 36 hours. Garneau observed and photographed the samples at regular intervals during the flight. This experiment is discussed in greater detail in Chapter 8.

Two further experiments in space science were included in Garneau's checklist: OGLOW and SPEAM. OGLOW (for "orbiter glow") refers to a reddish glow that develops on some shuttle surfaces in space. During the 41-G mission, Crippen maneuvred the shuttle so that Garneau could photograph the glow on Challenger's tail using a 35mm camera with high-resolution optical filters (which permit pictures to be taken at different wavelengths of visible light) and an image intensifier (which magnifies visible light). The experiment was intended to provide clues to the nature and cause of the glow, which is believed to result from interactions between the shuttle's surfaces and the tenuous upper reaches of the earth's atmosphere. There was concern that the glow might interfere with measurements taken by optical instruments in the shuttle cargo bay. Garneau's photos demonstrated that it should not pose problems for a Canadian instrument called WAMDII (Wide Angle Michaelson Doppler Imaging Inter-ferometer), a remote-sensing device that measures winds and temperatures at altitudes between 80 and 300 km, which is expected to fly on a shuttle mission after flights resume. Garneau's photos did show something unexpected — that the glow became patchy when the shuttle's thrusters were firing. It's also still a mystery why the glow has been brighter on some missions than on others; as a result, a follow-up experiment is planned for the second mission of a Canadian astronaut, which will be flown by Steve MacLean.

Garneau also used the camera to photograph the earth's atmospheric glow at night (since Challenger orbited the earth every 90 minutes, there were 16 "nights" every 24 hours) and the southern aurora. He was able to obtain unprecedented pictures of the aurora during the mission because a severe solar storm pounding the earth with radiation triggered spectacular auroral displays over both poles.

The final item on Garneau's scientific agenda was SPEAM — Sun Photometer Earth Atmosphere Measurements — sponsored by the Atmospheric Environment Service of Environment Canada and York University. The photometer, a hand-held instrument that measures solar radiation at several wavelengths, is used in studies of atmospheric conditions and pollution. Garneau's first objective was to "calibrate" the instrument — i.e., determine its absolute accuracy. On earth, sunlight is scattered or absorbed by dust, moisture, pollution and acidic haze, but it is difficult to estimate the extent to which this happens with great precision; pointing the photometer at the sun from the shuttle, which flies above most of the earth's atmosphere, eliminates virtually all atmospheric interference with the measurements, providing a necessary basis of comparison with readings taken on earth.

Garneau was also to point the photometer at sunrises and sunsets, when the sun could be viewed through the earth's atmosphere — measurements intended to help assess the effect of water vapor and other gasses on the chemistry of the earth's ozone layer and to contribute to research on the climatic effects of the cloud of volcanic dust injected into the atmosphere by the eruption of the Mexican volcano El Chichon in 1982. However, capturing sunrises proved tricky; it was difficult to estimate exactly where on the horizon the sun would pop up and consequently aiming the photometer accurately was a challenge. In contrast, obtaining sunset measurements was relatively easy; Garneau simply followed the sun down as it disappeared over the horizon. As a result, he took more sunset measurements than originally planned to make up for some of the sunrise data that could not be obtained.

An astronaut's mission timeline — the schedule of things to do — is usually a workaholic's dream. Garneau's was no exception. "One of the the things we did was to make sure that Marc wouldn't suffer from boredom at any time," Karl Doetsch, then head of the Canadian astronaut program, commented dryly. Garneau's first weekend in space was the Canadian Thanksgiving holiday and there was joking speculation as to whether Garneau, technically a civil servant, would receive extra pay for working a long weekend. (The answer was no. Being in the military, Garneau was not paid overtime — nor did he receive hazardous duty pay — but he joked that he could probably qualify for eight days of "casual air duty.") Of his eight days in space, about 65 hours were devoted to the tasks painstakingly honed during months of pre-flight training and outlined in detail in his scientific checklists. In addition, Garneau had his share of housekeeping duties aboard the shuttle — everyone took turns preparing meals, for example — and there were public relations responsibilities as well, such as an in-flight news conference on the fifth day. Like all the other crew members (although to a lesser extent), Garneau was thrown off his schedule by the trouble-shooting needed to fix a continuing series of minor and major problems with other experiments unrelated to his work. For example, the SIR-B radar initially refused to work properly — it couldn't be stabilized or pointed in the right direction — and later there were problems in getting it to fold into three and latch down properly in the cargo bay. The drive mechanism on an antenna in the cargo bay, used to relay data to the ground, failed and could not be properly pointed.[9] Human error and technical difficulties caused problems with a communications satellite used to send data to earth. The solar panels on the ERBS satellite at first refused to unfold, until Sally Ride literally shook them loose using the Canadarm. Icing problems with Challenger's water boiler caused the temperature inside the spacecraft to reach more than 30° C.

Although none of the problems threatened flight safety and most were successfully solved or worked around, they did consume large amounts of precious crew time and forced the work schedule to be changed a record 102 times. The problems had a domino effect on all crew members; for example, trouble-shooting the communications problems caused the EVA by Sullivan and Leestma to be rescheduled to a later day, which affected Garneau because the lengthy preparations for the space walk took up most of the mid-deck area where he did his SASSE experiments. In other cases, Garneau needed to be able to take pictures of a specific geographic point (e.g., sunset) or a specific field of view (e.g., moon-free and dark) and "finding the right window wasn't always an easy task," said Doetsch. "There were many more maneuvres [of the shuttle] than had been pre-planned." And, because there were six other people, all trying to go about their own business in the cramped quarters, "he couldn't necessarily move to the window that was best suited. Garneau was kidded as the astronaut most known for whipping from one spaceship window to another looking for sunsets." At one point, Canada requested a special shuttle maneuvre to allow viewing through the side hatch window on the mid-deck, which had special optical qualities — a request that NASA accommodated. For all the difficulties, however, Garneau managed, by dint of sheer hard work, to complete virtually all of his scientific objectives, Doetsch said. "We had devised the whole thing so that blocks of it could be moved around. All the primary objectives were completely satisfied. We gave him more than could probably be reasonably expected. He carried out an astonishingly high proportion of the work."

Of course, Garneau wasn't left to juggle the in-flight contingen-cies alone; much of the rescheduling affecting him was done on the ground, not only by NASA's controllers, but by a support team of Canadians. The team, led by Doetsch and Bruce Aikenhead, program manager of the Canadian astronaut office, and including the principal scientific investigators of the Canadian experiments and the other five Canadian astronauts, put in long hours in one of the customer support rooms in the Mission Control building. This was one of the many "back rooms" that support the flight controllers; it was equipped with video monitors, computer consoles and communications channels that enabled the ground team to babysit virtually every minute of the mission. However, the Canada ground team was not allowed to speak directly to Garneau over the air-to-ground communications loop — that is a privilege generally reserved for the "capcom" (a NASA astronaut in Mission Control whose responsibility it is to communicate with the crew) and, on occasion, the U.S. president and the media. Therefore, messages to Garneau from the Canadian ground crew had to be conveyed by voice via the capcom or by telex from Mission Control to a teletype machine aboard the shuttle.

Messages from Garneau were infrequent and succinct, particularly during the early part of the mission. The Canadian media quickly became impatient with Garneau's devotion to scientific duty, since it deprived them of the quotable quips and personal anecdotal material in which they were most interested. His first report, on the evening of his first day in space, went like this: "I'd just like to let you know I've completed all the objectives today." Full stop. The first TV picture Canadians saw of Garneau in space came on Sunday, October 7, the third day of the mission. He could be seen sitting in the mid-deck, blindfolded and pointing his small flashlight, performing one of his SASSE experiments. As this image appeared on the screen, the capcom asked if Garneau could say a few words because "folks back in Canada would like to hear how it's going." Commander Crippen responded: "Right now he's going through one of his Canadian experiments. I'm afraid it might be a little bit difficult." Later, Canadian reporters asked flight director John Cox whether Garneau could be "prodded into saying something." Cox, who clearly did not belong to the "prodding" school of flight direction, responded mildly: "Anytime he wants to say something, we'll be happy to hear it." As the silent routine continued through the first few days, the media began to remark on Garneau's "laconic manner," his "terse messages filled with scientific data" and his "bone-dry recital of his daily chores." He was described as a "shy workaholic" and reportedly was dubbed "the Right Stiff" by U.S. reporters. The Canadian reporters began urging him to "phone home" — despite explanations by space program officials that crew members are not encouraged to clutter the airwaves with unnecessary chatter. "You don't say anything that is not essential," Doetsch told the press at the time.

Garneau's wife Jacquie took his silence philosophically even though Saturday, the second day of the mission, was their eleventh wedding anniversary. She sent him a message via Mission Control, agonizing over what to say, since it might become public. "I wondered whether to be humorous and ask, 'Marc, where are you?' " she said later. "But instead I sent a romantic message that's private." However, Mission Control, apparently also concerned about the privacy of communications, reportedly cut a good portion of the message. In response, Garneau conveyed a belated happy anniversary to his wife.

Conversations between the crew and Mission Control were not entirely restricted to "bone-dry recitals" of technical detail, however. On Monday morning — Thanksgiving Day for Garneau, though not for the American crew members — the flight controllers wished him a happy holiday. Their taste in wake-up music included the theme from *Flashdance*. One morning, Sally Ride responded with the message: "This is the 41-G crew. We're not in right now. If you leave a name and number, we'll get back to you." Later in the week, Garneau responded to the wake-up call in French: "This is a recording. Thank you for calling. Our lines are all busy. Please hold on for a few moments and someone will answer you." It was a bit too much for capcom John Blaha, whose plaintive comeback comprised about equal amounts of Texas twang, fractured French and bafflement: "Je ne comprends pas. Parlez-vous anglais, s'il vous plaît?"

The ordinary tasks of daily life aboard Challenger required as much organization as the work schedule did. With the largest crew ever to fly aboard the shuttle living and working for eight days in two areas no roomier than a small kitchen and the cockpit of a 747, Garneau allowed that things were "a bit cozy. It reminds me of a submarine." Of course, zero gravity helps considerably in this situation: "You have to remember that the ceilings and walls become usable space." For example, astronauts often sleep in sleeping bags attached to the walls, although some merely float, tethered by a cord around their wrist or ankle. Garneau didn't even bother with a tether; he simply found a corner and shut his eyes. As Kathy Sullivan observed: "Marc has recently been seen just kind of floating through the mid-deck at will, all night long."

"Some other people made complicated arrangements," Garneau said. "I'm very comfortable sleeping any old place." Of course, he didn't end up where he started out, since he inevitably floated free around the cabin. "You close your eyes in one place … and you eventually wind up somewhere else. And you bounce off things. You're not going to bump in fast, but very, very softly. I'm sure I bounced off things without waking up."

Another image that never fails to amuse audiences on earth is the sight of two astronauts working side by side but upside down with respect to each other, or the sight of the entire crew "sitting down" to a meal together, with bodies going every which way on all available surfaces. Despite the cramped quarters in the mid-deck, where meals were prepared and eaten, Crippen preferred the crew to share their mealtimes — part of the bonding process that helps a crew to function harmoniously in space. Most foods, other than beverages, do not have to be specially restrained in zero-G; surface tension, stickiness or sauces and gravies usually keep them in place well enough to allow them to be eaten normally with a spoon or fork. Garneau had some 70 food items and 20 beverages to choose from, including scrambled eggs and sausage, cream of mushroom soup, shrimp cocktail, steak and broccoli, cookies, puddings, strawberries and raw vegetables. A film from the mission showing Garneau, with a wide grin on his face, spinning a carrot in zero-G always elicited the biggest laughs from his audiences. (He once commented wryly that he couldn't resist doing this, despite the fact that his mother always told him not to play with his food. Later, a young boy wistfully asked him: "Were you allowed to play with your food a lot?" To which Garneau responded: "As much as you want, but if you make a mess you have to clean it up." Children always seemed fascinated with the subject of eating in zero gravity. Garneau was once asked: "After you eat something, would you get a stomach-ache from floating around?" He responded: "When you eat, it's just like on the ground. The food makes its way down your throat into your stomach and once it's in your stomach, if there's any room for it to float around in there, it probably does float around. It depends on how big your stomach is, but you don't really notice it. It's the same with liquids. A lot of people have asked whether the food comes back up, but it doesn't. It seems to be held down there.")[10] Happily surprised that zero-G was evidently not going to make him sick, Garneau, like most astronauts before him, found he enjoyed the experience: "It was great fun just to fool around in weightlessness. It was a ball."

Despite the full workload and the disruptions caused by rescheduling, Garneau did have some leisure time, much of which was spent looking out the windows. He was able to observe Canada for about 20 minutes out of each 90-minute orbit, when the frequent cloud cover permitted. "As a Canadian, I took every opportunity at looking for different views of Canada. The view is absolutely extraordinary," he said. "One realizes that one is very lucky to be a Canadian and to have as beautiful and vast a country as ours is." (After the mission, he would gently remind awe-struck youngsters — who often seemed to think he'd been exploring the intergalactic reaches with Captain Kirk — that he was "only really 120 miles away from Canada.") On Friday, October 12, the city of Kingston flashed its lights in salute to Garneau as he flew overhead at 6:16 a.m. Garneau, who had been alerted to the event the day before by telex from Mission Control, later radioed his thanks from space: "I just wanted to convey my appreciation to the people of Kingston ... for flashing their lights as we passed over. Can you relay that on to them please?"

One of the major requirements of the astronaut job is public relations — a duty that follows a crew into space, even into the midst of a mission jam-packed with scientific experiments and technical troubles. And so it was with 41-G. The in-flight news conference occurred on day five, October 9. All seven crew members were crammed into the mid-deck in front of one of the fixed-position cameras, all wearing shorts in deference to the 30-degree cabin temperature and resembling, in the words of one journalist, "a can of anchovies." The first question went to Crippen but the second was for Garneau — from his own brother, Philippe, who was covering the mission for the Montreal-based Telemedia Radio Network. First in French[11] and then English, Philippe asked Marc to give his impressions of the launch. "There was a lot of noise, a lot of vibration and my heart doubtless was beating very quickly," Garneau responded in French. "I was a little bit afraid," he admitted, a fact that the press did not fail to pick up. In English, Garneau added that it was the "utmost fantastic short trip I've ever taken."

The questions were, for the most part, predictable and unremarkable — mostly some variation of the only questions most of the media seemed to know how to ask Garneau: "How did you feel?" and "What are your impressions?"[12] Among his strongest impressions were the views of earth; he reported that he was in awe of what he observed every time he looked out. "Every time we go over Canada, I'm generally stuck at the window, having a look out there ... It's absolutely fantastic." One reporter asked why he'd been so tight-lipped in his conversations with the ground because "we know you're not shy." Garneau answered: "I'm just trying to keep it short because, from my naval background, I know it's not a good thing to keep babbling on." And, though none of the reporters had yet asked him about the scientific experiments, he added that they were on schedule and giving some good results.

The funniest part of the press conference was in the segments involving connections with two overseas sites — Australia (the birthplace of Scully-Power) and Indonesia. One of the Australian journalists confused Sally Ride and Kathy Sullivan[13] and asked Ride if she were looking forward to becoming the first American woman to walk in space. Sullivan, who in fact would be doing the EVA, quipped: "Well, this is the other Sally..." before describing preparations for the walk. And when she was subsequently asked how long she would be outside, she passed the hand mike to Ride and said: "Kathy will answer that." Whereupon Ride observed in a deadpan manner: "Kathy will be out there about three hours."

But the biggest laugh was provided by the inability to connect with Indonesia at all. In the middle of this ultimate in high-tech teleconferences, several unsuccessful attempts to establish the link culminated in the reception of a dial tone and a recorded message saying that the call could not be completed as dialled and that the caller should "hang up and dial your operator." Everyone, including the seven astronauts, cracked up.

On October 12, the last day before landing, the astronauts had another caller — U.S. President Ronald Reagan, who, during his four-minute message, remarked: "I'd like to say hello to Canada's fine astronaut ... With all there is to do on this mission, I know that Crip appreciates having three strong Canadian arms." (The third being, of course, the Canadarm.) Prime Minister Mulroney had again apparently distanced himself from the mission by declining an invitation to join Reagan in speaking to the crew. Mulroney had appeared with the crew at a ceremony in Washington about a month before the mission and he had sent best wishes to Garneau on the first day of the flight, telling the press at the time that he felt envious of Garneau's experience. News reports just before the launch indicated that the PM would participate in the in-flight conversation, but an aide was later quoted as saying this was in error. In any event, when the time came, Mulroney was nowhere in evidence. The explanation offered by his office was that he didn't want to upstage Garneau, who "is there on his own merit and deserves the credit." NRC officials later said they'd been told that Mulroney was just too busy, preoccupied as he was at the time with picking his first Cabinet from among large numbers of newly elected MPs. Among the media, speculation continued that Mulroney, who had made no secret of his determination to cut government spending, was keeping his distance so as not to appear to be committing himself to further Canadian involvement in the U.S. space program.

On October 13, after 132 1/2 orbits of the earth, Garneau returned to the Kennedy Space Center, to the landing strip just a few kilometres from the launch pad from which he'd departed on a column of smoke eight days, five hours and 24 minutes before. Aboard Challenger, preparations for landing began a few hours before the "de-orbit burn" — the engine firing that would kick the shuttle out of orbit and on its way home. All equipment and personal effects had to be carefully stowed to ensure nothing would break loose and cause any damage during the re-entry. Then some of the astronauts strapped pressure garments around their lower bodies to prevent blood from rushing to their legs with the return of gravity, possibly causing blackouts. The de-orbit burn occurred about 805 km east of Perth, Australia. This manoeuvre pitches the shuttle into a high "nose-up" attitude so that the black thermal tiles will take the brunt of the extreme heating — temperatures greater than 1200°C — caused by slamming into the atmosphere at nearly 26,000 km/h or about 25 times the speed of sound. The G-forces increased to about one and a half times normal gravity on earth — not a difficult thing to handle ordinarily — but after eight days in weightlessness, it seemed even stronger to Garneau, who said he felt "very, *very* heavy. You feel like you've had a whole bunch of weight pressed down on you for about 15 or 20 minutes prior to the landing, so you're quite tired when you finally land. You aren't quite sure whether your muscles are going to get you up." Strapped into his seat in the mid-deck, he could only see a little of what was going on through the small side hatch window. During re-entry, he could see a yellow-orange glow; "You know there's fire and brimstone out there. There's some vibration at different points and Crip would always come on — he's the coolest guy I've ever heard — and say 'Oh, don't worry about that, it's just this and this happening.' Apart from this heaviness, it's a bit like just a very long commercial airline re-entry."

The shuttle's re-entry path crossed over the northern Pacific Ocean, across central Canada and the U.S. and culminated in a U-turn out over the Atlantic that lined it up with the runway at KSC. It touched down at 12:26 p.m. EDT. Unlike the runways at Edwards Air Force Base, which run off into a hard-packed dry lake bed providing several extra miles of landing room, the 4600-m KSC runway is in the middle of a swampy wildlife area. Bob Crippen likes to remark that "NASA built a moat around it and filled it with alligators to give you an incentive to land on the runway." For all that, Crippen was glad to be able to touch down in Florida. On two of his previous three flights, he'd been forced by weather to divert to Edwards and, for several days during the 41-G mission, it looked like Hurricane Josephine would cause a deterioration in Florida's weather sufficient to send Challenger there again. This was something NASA wanted to avoid as much as possible because it put a crimp in its pitch to its customers about the shuttle's efficiency; a landing in California added about a week to the turn-around time needed to get the shuttle ready for another launch. Crippen, however, did have to pay a price for success, as Mission Control informed him when he touched down: "Congratulations, Crip. You landed at KSC, but the beer's been sent to Edwards."

The crew remained inside the shuttle for about half an hour. A flight surgeon boarded Challenger to give the crew a quick once-over, while ground crews did the same with the vehicle, ensuring there were no leaks of dangerous gasses. Then the seven emerged into the bright Florida sun, walking down the steps onto the red carpet laid out for them. Garneau, the second last to come out, stood for a moment with hands on hips, looking well and satisfied. He was a bit wobbly as he tried to regain his one-G legs after more than eight days in weightlessness. He remarked afterwards that, having weathered the expected peril of motion sickness while in zero-G, he had not entirely anticipated the difficulty he experienced with the heaviness of one-G. Getting up from his seat literally "brought me down to earth," he said. "When I got up, I thought I was going to faint."

Garneau had about five minutes to greet his wife, who had flown back to Florida from Houston for the landing, before the doctors pounced on him. Jacquie found him a little disoriented: "He asked where the children were, when he knew for weeks that they would wait in Houston." Karl Doetsch, Roberta Bondar and Doug Watt were also waiting in the crew quarters building. Doetsch said that Marc seemed "serene — a person who had done what he wanted."

"He looked terrific," Bondar said. "He was very confident and just beaming all over. I went out and gave him a big kiss. They didn't smell half as bad as they said they were going to."

Nevertheless, the crew went off for much-needed showers and then submitted to the hovering NASA medics for about half an hour. After that, Bondar and Watt ran Garneau and Scully-Power through the SASSE tests yet again. It was important that they be tested before they had a chance to re-adapt to earth's gravity and especially before they got on the plane that would take them to Houston, since another flight might affect the validity of the data. (Ken Money and Bob Thirsk had gone to Edwards to run the tests in case Challenger landed there.) Garneau and Scully-Power went through their paces quickly and efficiently; after so much practice, "they were real pros at it," Bondar said. But earth's gravity did take its toll; they had trouble with some exercises, especially deep knee bends with their eyes closed.

A few hours after landing at KSC, the crew and their entourage were aboard two NASA aircraft on their way to Houston, where about 100 people, including family members, space program officials and, of course, the ever-present media, were impatiently waiting in the midst of a gathering thunderstorm. One of the planes was a jet, the other a slower, propeller-driven aircraft, so the plan was for the latter to take off first so that both would arrive in Houston more or less at the same time. However, as with the mission itself, things did not go exactly as planned. It is ironic that NASA could calculate within seconds how long it took the crew to orbit the earth but had a major problem providing an estimated time of arrival at the Ellington air field, a few kilometres from the Johnson Space Center (JSC). "We could not pin down a precise time when the planes from Kennedy would be landing," said Wally Cherwinski of the NRC, who was orchestrating events with the Canadian media at Ellington. CBC-TV was getting particularly fretful; they wanted to cover the arrival as a live special but they were running up against formidable competition — "Hockey Night in Canada."

On the way to Houston, the two planes ran into bad weather. Those waiting at Ellington were told the arrival would be delayed another hour and this "blew the TV schedule all to pieces," Cherwinski said. Moreover, the slower plane, on which Garneau was travelling, was overtaken by the faster, which landed at Ellington about half an hour earlier. Greetings from family and NASA officials were accomplished and then everyone stood around waiting for the second plane to arrive. That's when the worst of the thunderstorm hit Ellington. Cherwinski describes the scene: "Something like ten minutes before that plane was supposed to land, the skies opened up and it was absolutely torrential. The Canadian media people stood there and waited anyway and they were absolutely drenched. The camera people, the reporters — soaked, drowned rats." There was uncertainty whether Garneau's plane could even land; it was finally decided the plane could come in, but that the welcoming activities would take place in a hangar rather than out on the tarmac. Cherwinski continued, "Now all this little gaggle of wet media people had to walk a quarter of a mile into a hangar." This meant that all logistics for Garneau's first encounter with the media had to be scrapped. It had been intended that Garneau would go over to a rope barrier set up on the tarmac and speak briefly with the media people, giving each a little nugget of a quote with which to flesh out their stories. Inside the hangar, there was "no rope barrier, no security, no nothing," Cherwinski said.

As soon as the plane door opened, he propelled Garneau's two children, each clutching a carnation and a drawing saying "I love you," off toward their father, realizing that if they hesitated they would surely be lost. He was right. "The kids got there just in time. As soon as the kids got to him, the Canadian media people stampeded. The poor security guy was saying, 'No, no, get back! You can't do it!' He was run over. Marc was pinned against the airplane with this little semi-circle of reporters sticking mikes in his face, shooting film and stills, asking questions." The NASA security people were fretting, but Cherwinski could see there was no way to pry the press off Garneau. "It was non-threatening, but he just couldn't go anywhere. So he stood there good-naturedly answering questions. They had him pinned for less than ten minutes and all of a sudden they dispersed." Now preoccupied with filing their stories, they thundered off en masse to the phones, giving Cherwinski the opportunity he'd been waiting for to bustle Garneau into the van that would take him to JSC. Watching this chaotic scene, Cherwinski was struck by the fact that Garneau "was the same level-headed Marc we had come to know. He was obviously elated; you could tell he was riding an emotional high, an adrenalin high. He was physically tired, but he was still so up that he could continue. He was genuinely touched by the number of people who'd come out to greet him and how *wet* they were. He was really moved by that."

Cherwinski also observed that Garneau's children were "kind of scared by all this" and they clung to their father. They'd been waiting for nearly two hours, worried about their father's safety because of the thunderstorm, and they were tense, tired and — no surprise — wet.

Cherwinski's colleague, Estelle Dorais, who was working on arrangements for the press conference at JSC, found the children still hanging on to their father like bedraggled limpets when Garneau arrived at JSC. "So here's Marc talking to the Minister [Communications Minister Marcel Masse] and he still has one kid on each leg," Dorais recalled. In the "cattle area," the JSC news conference room, Karl Doetsch read messages from Prime Minister Brian Mulroney and Science Minister Tom Siddon and then Garneau was plunged into the first of a long series of post-flight news conferences. Garneau described his experience as "an incredible odyssey" and "the voyage of a lifetime." He said that it was "something that will indelibly mark me for the rest of my life," adding that he cherished most being given the honor of representing Canada. Jesse Moore, head of the shuttle program, described Garneau as a dedicated crew member who did "outstanding" work. Garneau was rattled only once, when he was asked if he'd been homesick. "No!" he responded emphatically, evidently misunderstanding the question to be about space motion sickness. Realizing his mistake, he recovered with a sheepish laugh: "Oh, homesick. Oh yeah, every day." Later, however, he amended this answer, admitting that "I was so wrapped with the experience of space that I really wasn't thinking about anything I was missing."

Finally Garneau was allowed to fall into the welcoming arms of his family and they left JSC for a quiet evening alone. Dinner was chicken and a cold beer and Garneau was "zonked out" and in bed by 11 p.m. The next day, down-to-earth reality descended on Canada's first man in space — he went grocery shopping with his children and later helped them put together a plastic model of the shuttle.

After two weeks of scientific debriefing in Houston and a ten-day holiday in the Bahamas with his wife, Garneau was ready to face the Canadian people and press. And they were waiting for him. During the post-flight press conference at JSC, he'd said he was looking forward to "fading into the background" and helping with preparations for the next two flights, but there was not much hope that this would be allowed to happen any time soon. The urge to dissect the experience, and its impact on Garneau, began almost immediately; he was asked, for example, if flying in space made him feel closer to God. About 120 miles closer, he quipped, then added more seriously that "I don't think it changed me in any significant way in terms of my faith. I've been a practicing Christian for a long time and continue to do so."

As he began his round of public appearances and news conferences, Garneau made no bones about the fact that he was a PR man for the space program, pointing out with a grin that there was a certain self-serving aspect to his efforts: "I want to go up again." He had known from the time he was chosen as an astronaut that communicating his experiences to the public and the press was part of his job; indeed, an ability to do just that was one of the strongest criteria used in selecting Canada's six astronauts. "I think my hardest job is to talk to as many Canadians as I can, and to do a good job of informing them about my experience, about the way I think things are going to develop in the future, for mankind in space. Not just for Canada, but for everybody. It's a very challenging job to do it properly." He observed that the hoopla on his return to Canada was reminiscent of the attention paid to the first U.S. astronauts 20 years ago and his own reaction to all the attention was rather mixed: on one occasion, he described himself as a ham who gets a kick out of speaking to an interested audience, but not long afterwards said that he was "fairly shy, so it is a bit of a learning experience for me to be in the public eye … and to have microphones and cameras in front of me all the time." If this was so, he had learned his lessons well and quickly. Even before his flight, the press had described him as "the perfect celebrity, photogenic and cool."

Tanned and relaxed from his holiday, and barely off the plane from the Bahamas, Garneau, wearing military dress uniform, was plunged into his first post-flight news conference on Canadian soil at the National Press Building in Ottawa on October 30, 1984. In his opening remarks, he observed that just one year earlier he had been only an astronaut candidate and described the intervening time as a "sometimes difficult though happy year." The difficulties had not been his alone, he acknowledged, thanking his wife "for what she's had to put up with during the last year."

During the question period, the subject of space motion sickness inevitably was broached, even though the NRC had told the press not to ask Garneau if he'd been sick in space. American astronauts are extremely touchy about the matter and NASA refuses to divulge individual incidents on the grounds that this invades medical privacy; the NRC and the Canadian scientific investigators had adopted a similar approach, indicating before the mission that they would not reveal the details of Garneau's medical condition during the mission. But Garneau himself took a somewhat more indulgent view, once he had come to terms with the fact that he tended to be rather susceptible to motion sickness. He didn't like it, but it was a matter of personal physiology that he could not change. Moreover, part of his job was to study motion sickness and so he tended to deal with the subject more as a scientific rather than a personal matter and talked quite openly about it. In any event, he'd inadvertently let the cat out of the bag in Houston with his reaction to the homesickness question and so when it was raised in Ottawa, he responded: "I thought everyone knew the answer to that one. No, I didn't get sick and I was unsuccessful in making myself sick. And to tell you the truth, I don't know why it turned out that way because if I had to bet, I would have bet on myself being sick up there. It's a very much more complicated thing than anybody appears to admit."

The next day, Garneau's time was chopped up into 15-minute segments as he was farmed out for one-on-one interviews with the national media. A large contingent was in Ottawa to talk to him in person but there was also a series of cross-country phone interviews. Garneau did his level best to accommodate everyone, kept on track by a harried but efficient Estelle Dorais, who had to ruthlessly squelch attempts by nearly every interviewer to hang on to Garneau for more than the allotted 15 minutes. By mid-morning, Garneau was already justifiably frazzled by a day that had begun with an early morning TV talk show and would not end until nearly 6 p.m.

Garneau's most popular prop was a video film of life aboard the shuttle, which he narrated for the first time during the press conference. He characterized it as "a home movie that we took inside the orbiter. Not every hair is in place, but it's us." He noted that everyone on board had to help prepare meals and he pulled KP duty about half a dozen times during the mission. "It's not gourmet cooking," Garneau said — the job consists mostly of taking prepackaged containers from the lockers and adding water to freeze-dried foods.

There was the usual fascination with the shuttle's zero-gravity toilet, which had been the source of problems on several missions. When Garneau punned that "it's a job to learn that, but we had an opportunity to practice on the ground" the audience laughed, and he added: "I can see this is the part that really interests you."

At one point in the narration, he momentarily startled his audience by declaring that "there were really 14 of us." What followed was a sequence in which each crew member descended through a hatch from the upper to the lower deck, floated past and then disappeared off-camera. Nothing too surprising there — except that when the number got to seven, they just kept coming. It was a bit of a practical joke by the crew — they had each scooted back up to the flight deck through a second hatch and come down for a second fly-by. It was one of the most amusing sequences in the film and it demonstrated that space shuttle crews are not all business all the time, even in the midst of a demanding mission. As Garneau observed, "I had a ball."

36

Garneau narrated the film again that night before an audience of 1600 at his first public appearance in Hull. Given that he'd only had one chance to review the film before these first presentations, he turned in a remarkably polished performance. But he had plenty of opportunity to practice his speaking style during a rigorous month of public appearances. On November 9, he and Jacquie were introduced in Parliament to a standing ovation. On November 14, he and backup Bob Thirsk started a three-week cross-country publicity tour that took him to the ten provincial capitals, starting in Quebec City where Garneau received an honorary doctorate at Laval University and was toasted by Premier René Lévesque. Then it was on to Edmonton where he served as the Grand Marshall in the Grey Cup parade and dropped the puck in an Oilers' hockey game. After two days in Victoria, he headed east again to Regina where he met some of the students who had helped with the SIR-B soil moisture study. (One 11-year-old rated him better than pop star Michael Jackson but a shade below Prince.) Continuing their leap-frogging of the country, Garneau and Thirsk spent about two days each in Winnipeg, St. John's, Halifax, Charlottetown, Fredericton, finally ending up in Toronto for five days at the beginning of December. They were joined there for two days by Commander Bob Crippen, who told his Canadian audiences that Garneau "did a superb job and all of you should be very proud of him. I would be pleased to fly with Marc or any other Canadian astronaut." Crippen narrated the mission film with Garneau, while Bob Thirsk did the same with a film of the astronauts' pre-flight training program. Giving this presentation nearly two dozen times in less than three weeks had clearly taxed their ability to manufacture new superlatives, but they had honed their delivery to perfection, tossing off one-liners with the timing of stand-up comedians. Showing film of them spinning through the air in zero-gravity aboard a NASA training aircraft, Thirsk joked: "We were learning to breakdance."

The Toronto trip, which ended in early December, marked the end of the first phase of the Marc and Bob show. Further publicity trips were scheduled for other major cities in the new year, but for now they were able to head home for a Christmas with their families. Swept along by events, they'd had little time for reflection. But an anniversary celebration held in Toronto on December 3 focussed their attention on the fact that, in just one short year, Garneau had been chosen as an astronaut, had trained for and completed a space shuttle mission and had completed a cross-country publicity tour. If he had decided to take his holidays in July, 1983, none of it would have happened.

NOTES

1. The shuttle's computers consist of four identically programmed main computers, known as the primary redundant set, and one independently programmed backup. This ensures that a computer will be available if there is a generic software problem with the four main computers. Any one of the five computers can control the shuttle, but for critical aspects of the flight, a multi-computer operation is typically required. Each of the four main computers controls certain aspects of the flight. The others "listen in" and, about 300 to 400 times a second, they compare notes to ensure they agree on the commands being sent out; this is called "voting." The computers must all remain synchronized; if one falls out of step, it is peremptorily thrown out by the others. Moreover, it is programmed to recognize that it has disagreed with the others and that they've voted it "failed," whereupon it obligingly votes itself failed rather than insisting it's right and the others are wrong. This voting procedure allows for a major failure in one computer without affecting the others. The backup listens in on a "party line" and issues dummy commands, so it's up and running if it has to take over in flight; however, the shuttle is never launched unless all five computers are operating properly.

2. Garneau was the second non-American to fly in the U.S. space program — after West Germany's Ulf Merbold, who flew on the shuttle/Spacelab 1 mission in 1983. However, the Soviets have flown astronauts from ten non-Soviet nations: Czechoslovakia, Poland, East Germany, Bulgaria, Hungary, Vietnam, Cuba, India, France and Mongolia. By early 1986, scientists from France, West Germany, Holland, Switzerland and Mexico had flown, as had a Saudi Arabian prince.

3. Objects in orbit are in fact still under the influence of earth's gravity, so the term *microgravity* is often used instead.

4. Before the mission, Garneau asked his children: "What am I going to see when I look down on the ground?" A literal-minded Simone responded: "Well, of course you're going to see the floor."
   "No, no, looking out the window," Garneau said.
   "You're going to see aliens," Simone decided.
   "What's an alien?"
   "Big horns. Big ears and a tiny mouth. And one eye," said Simone, sounding as though she knew.

5. There was speculation that NASA, uneasily remembering the nearly fatal accident on the Apollo 13 mission, adopted this peculiar numbering system for shuttle flights in part to avoid a mission named STS-13. The "4" stands for the year, 1984. The "1" stands for the Kennedy Space Center launch site, to distinguish it from a new one being built in California, which would be "2." The "G" stands for the seventh flight of the year. It sounded logical enough, but it rapidly confused everyone. For one thing, the year referred not to the calendar year but to NASA's fiscal year, which runs from October to September. In any event, the system was almost immediately rendered inaccurate by launch delays and the cancellation of an entire mission. Since it was scheduled for an October 5 launch, 41-G should, in reality, have been re-named 51-A (the first flight of Fiscal 1985), but by that time, everyone was used to calling it 41-G and another change might well have provoked a mutiny." They got tired of changing it," said one NASA official.

6. The radar signals can penetrate dry surface layers of sand to reveal geological formations and evidence of previous human habitation. The radar studied such things as crops in the U.S. and Australia, deforestation in Brazil and acid rain damage in Germany. There were to be four Canadian projects using SIR-B: a study of meteorite craters in Ontario and Quebec rock formations in the Canadian shield, iceberg flow off Newfoundland and Labrador and soil conditions in Saskatchewan, where a severe drought had severely damaged crops. The Saskatchewan experiment had one unique aspect — a "ground truth" project involving 1000 Saskatchewan school children, who collected soil samples near their homes and packed them in plastic bags to be sent to a laboratory for tests that would determine whether SIR-B soil moisture measurements from space were accurate. However, when problems developed with the radar during the mission, the original list of 60 sites had to be pared to 11 and all but the Saskatchewan project among the Canadian sites were eliminated.

7. Sullivan, who became the first American woman to do a space walk, missed being the first woman ever by just two months; Soviet cosmonaut Svetlana Savitskaya walked in space in July, 1984. As Sally Ride had when she became the first American woman in space, Sullivan received a disproportionate amount of media attention for her pioneering effort and, for the Canadian media, there was some added "local colour" — Sullivan had received her PhD from Dalhousie University in Halifax, Nova Scotia, the only Canadian university to educate a U.S. astronaut. Sullivan's background in geology and oceanography and her familiarity with Canada proved to be of great assistance to Garneau when he was trying to identify Canadian landmarks from space — a task that is not as easy as it sounds.

8. Canadians were involved in another technical aspect of the mission, unrelated to Garneau's work. A Toronto computer company, UX Software Inc., provided computer software for a microcomputer used by Mission Control engineers to manage payload operations. The computer system generated thousands of commands and instructions sent up to the personal computers on the shuttle that were used to operate several very complex experiment payloads. It was also used to acquire, process and file the data received from these experiments. The system performed well, although serious problems were encountered in transmitting data to the ground.

9. It wasn't only the crew whose schedules were thrown out of whack by the problems. Dozens of researchers were stationed on ships, in aircraft, on farmland and in deserts and jungles to measure the strength of the SIR-B radar signal. One investigator, who was interested in whether the radar could penetrate jungle canopy well enough to find standing water where mosquitos breed, carried a receiver into a remote area of Bangladesh. When the problems caused cancellation of the initial radar pass overhead, he hiked out to a telephone and called Mission Control; they told him to go back into the jungle and wait for the next attempt.

10. Garneau's own son had some definite ideas about food in space. The following exchange, which occurred during a family barbecue, was captured by the TV cameras:

Garneau: "What am I going to do up there? Am I just going to sit around all day?

Yves: "No, you're going to eat."

Jacquie: "What happens to the food on the plate?"

Yves: "They nail it."

Jacquie: "Nail it onto the plate?"

Yves: "Yeah."
Jacquie: "No, they don't."
Yves: "It's a wood plate."

11. The ground rules issued by NASA for the in-flight press conference contained a new wrinkle in deference to the Canadians: "Questions asked in French must be prefaced with a statement in English that the question will be asked in French." One U.S. reporter was quoted in a Canadian paper as saying: "Jeez, next thing you know, they'll be asking questions in Albanian."

12. Most of the Canadian journalists covering this mission were not science or space writers; many had never covered a space mission before and their rather naive questions provided considerable amusement for the veterans. In many ways, the situation with the Canadian media was a 20-year throw-back to the crazy days chronicled in *The Right Stuff*. Many of the stories contained the kind of breathless hyperbole and scientific license not seen in space coverage for many years. For example: "Garneau may be helping pave the intergalactic path to Mars" and "Spoken like a true Right Stuff hero of space" and "So how come he [Garneau] faces vaulting past the stars with the cool confidence of a career astronaut?"

13. When told of this mix-up, one NASA woman engineer remarked sardonically: "They all look alike, right?"

CHAPTER TWO

Canada's
First
Astronauts

On July 14, 1983,
a unique help-wanted ad
appeared in Canadian newspapers.
Its message was simple enough,
but nevertheless
mind-boggling to many Canadians.
It was an invitation
from the National Research Council of Canada
for "Canadian men and women
to fly as astronauts
on future space shuttle
missions."

Of course, aspirants needed more than just an adventurous spirit to qualify: the listed requirements included having university degrees and experience in engineering or in physiology. Candidates also had to meet rather stringent medical requirements. In addition, practical flying experience and a knowledge of both English and French, though not essential, would be "an asset." (Estelle Dorais joked that, "I guess you have to know Texan, too," since astronauts have to talk to Mission Control in Houston.) According to the job description, the successful candidates would become employees of the NRC for up to three years; help develop two sets of experiments to be performed aboard the U.S. space shuttle; help inform the Canadian public about the manned space program and Canadian space activities; and, finally, the clincher: "if selected for flight, carry out and assess one of the experiments" — in short, become the first Canadian to fly in space. The salary would be "commensurate with experience," between about CDN$40,000 and $55,000.

One of the people who saw it was Marc Garneau, who happened upon it while perusing the newspaper on his backyard sun deck one summer day. "It was just fate," he said. "I saw a career ad for Canadian astronauts in the paper. If I had taken my holiday in July, I never would have applied." Jacquie admitted she "never really took it seriously in the beginning. When Marc saw the ad in the paper and decided to apply, I said: 'Well, it looks interesting but I can't imagine you as an astronaut.' "

Garneau could, however — and he was far from the only person who pictured himself or herself in the role. The ad tapped some hitherto unsuspected vein of space lust in the Canadian people; when the August 8 deadline rolled around — a two-month extension of the original June deadline — nearly 4400 people, ranging in age from six to 73, had, more or less seriously, applied for the job. NRC officials, who had been gearing up to handle about 1000 applications, were dumbfounded. "No one expected anything like this," Dorais said.

The newspapers leapt on the story. The Red Deer *Advocate* told its readers, slightly inaccurately: "Wanted: Six Canadians to take off. Must be willing to see the world in a unique way. No experience necessary." And the Toronto *Star*, choosing to focus on the motion sickness experiments, was among the first — but by no means the last — to get mileage out of the throwing-up-for-your-country theme: "A good old-fashioned strong stomach is the last thing you need to be the first Canadian in space…You might get points if your stomach flutters at the thought of a spin on a ferris wheel or if your gorge rises in an elevator … It's upchucking in a scientific cause." The headline writers had even more of a field day. The *Star* story was headlined: "A Canadian in Space, eh? Makes you sick." Other offerings included: "Want to see the world? Apply here"; "Help wanted: Must commute"; and "Take off, eh?"

The news stories were, of course, rife with allusions to *The Right Stuff,* particularly since the movie based on the Tom Wolfe book had just opened in Canadian theatres. This was in many ways an unfortunate coincidence. Wolfe had written with eloquent and memorable insight on the psyche and the role of the astronaut, but his work, which was about the selection of the first seven U.S. astronauts from the ranks of military test pilots and their flights in the Mercury program in the early 1960s, was not really relevant to the Canadian situation as the NRC embarked on its astronaut hunt. Simply put, the right stuff ain't what it used to be. More correctly, the right stuff in Canada in the 1980s is not the same thing as the right stuff in the United States in the early 1960s. Back then, no one was sure exactly what, if anything, astronauts were supposed to do. Indeed, at first space program officials did not plan to have them fly the spacecraft at all; astronauts were going to be, in the memorable phrase of veteran test pilot Chuck Yeager, "Spam in a can." To illustrate the point that no one quite knew what qualifications were needed, one of the more lunatic scenes in the movie *The Right Stuff* depicts a group of political types pondering the potential recruitment of high-wire artists (good balance), human cannonballs (able to withstand acceleration), high-platform divers (able to cope with splashdown) and race car drivers (good with machinery — and "they have their own helmets"). Although the scene was played for laughs, there had in fact been a serious debate about what types of people would be appropriate astronaut-candidates; suggestions included people with submarine, arctic, mountain-climbing, deep-diving or parachute jumping experience. University degrees and research experience in the sciences, engineering or medicine were also to be considered qualifications for a position that was originally designated (but never again referred to) as "*research* astronaut-candidate." However, in late 1958, President Dwight Eisenhower ended the debate by insisting on the selection of military test pilots, in part because they already had security clearances. It was a decision not entirely popular with space program officials of the day, although NASA was rather relieved not to have to cope with the consequences of an open invitation.

The preoccupation of test pilots is with "flying the bird," and they went into space for much the same reason that other people climb mountains — because it's there, because it pushes human beings and machines to their limits, because, as Wolfe put it, "A man should have the ability to go up in a hurtling piece of machinery and put his hide on the line and then have the moxie, the reflexes, the experience, the coolness to pull it back in the last yawning moment — and then go up again *the next day,* and the next day, and every next day, even if the series should prove infinite — and, ultimately, in its best expression, do so in a cause that means something to thousands, to a people, a nation, to humanity, to God." This was a quality much needed in the early days; at the time the original seven astronauts were chosen, rockets were regularly blowing up on the launch pad or running out of control.[1] But the space program has changed dramatically. It is no longer merely a because-it's-there challenge, an invitation to grandstand gestures. While no one is ever likely to build a laboratory or a factory at the summit of Everest, space is rapidly becoming a place in which to live and work and get things done. Increasingly, the forces driving the space program are commercial, industrial and military in nature; we are, in short, entering an era more of space exploitation than exploration — equivalent, in many ways, to the early colonization of the New World.

In this utilitarian push into space, one of the greatest articles of faith, at least among the powers-that-be in the American and Soviet space programs, is that human beings are needed up there — that they can do things that cannot be accomplished using only unmanned robots or satellites and that an on-the-site application of human brainpower and ad hoc problem-solving can make the difference between success and multi-million-dollar failure. It is therefore worth the millions of dollars it costs to supply the life-support system required to keep human beings alive and functioning in space. It is even worth the inevitable loss of life. This is an argument that has always had its critics, particularly among scientists who have seen other, unmanned space science programs wither and die in the face of the seemingly endless capacity of the manned program to gobble up funds. Yet it is a premise that is not only firmly entrenched in the U.S. and Soviet programs, but one that has, in recent years, clearly gained ground around the world, as other nations eagerly accepted the opportunity to piggyback on the American or Soviet programs to send their people into space. Now Canada was about to join their ranks.

It was, in many ways, a logical step for Canada's small but respectable space program — a program that had managed to survive after the 1959 cancellation of the Avro Arrow decimated the country's cadre of skilled aerospace engineers. Most of them left to join the nascent U.S. space program and many later played pivotal roles in the manned space projects — Mercury, Gemini, Apollo and the space shuttle.

Technologically, the Canadian program took a different, less spectacular direction, focussing on the development of communications satellites and on the use of rockets and unmanned satellites to support programs in space science — for example, studies of the earth's upper atmosphere and remote sensing of the earth's resources.

In the late 1950s, the Defence Research Board and Canadian industry developed the Black Brant rocket probes designed to carry instruments for studying the upper atmosphere. A rocket-launching facility, established by the U.S. Army at Churchill, Manitoba, and taken over in 1966 by the National Research Council of Canada, was used for many years to launch sounding rockets. Periodically, there was talk of upgrading it to a satellite-launching facility but these plans never came to anything, as Canada continued to buy launch services from NASA. A balloon-launching facility had also been established at Gimli, Manitoba, but in 1984, to the consternation of many Canadian space scientists, the rocket and balloon program became an early victim of the Mulroney government's cost-cutting sweep.

In September, 1962, with the launch of Alouette 1, Canada became the third nation in the world to put a satellite in orbit. Designed to monitor the earth's ionosphere, the electrically charged layer in the upper atmosphere that affects long-distance radio transmissions, it survived long past its one-year design lifetime, providing scientists with data for more than a decade. The ISIS (International Satellite for Ionospheric Studies) satellites followed in the late 1960s and early 1970s.

In the 1970s, Canada's use of space systems expanded rapidly, often in close collaboration with the United States, which continued to provide launch services for all Canadian satellites. In 1972, when the U.S. put up the first remote-sensing satellite, the Earth Resources Technology Satellite (ERTS), Canada was the first country outside the U.S. to build a ground receiving station to receive the resource data directly — a move that enabled Canadian industry to carve out a respectable niche in a field that rapidly became economically vital to many nations. Since then, Canadian companies have become world leaders in developing the ground technology and services required to receive and process remote-sensing data, developing a thriving export market. Resource monitoring was an application of obvious immediate benefit to a large resource-rich country like Canada, whose economy remains critically dependent on the exploitation of those natural resources. By the mid-70s, many Canadian environmental research and management programs were making extensive use of data from the remote-sensing satellites, now called Landsat, for a variety of programs, including forest management, crop fore-casting, ice monitoring and mineral exploration. Until the mid-1980s, Canada had concentrated its technological energies on the ground segment of the remote-sensing field, but in late 1984, the federal govern-ment gave Spar Aerospace Limited of Toronto a CDN$14.4-million contract to start design and development work on Radarsat, an advanced all-weather remote-sensing satellite.

Communications was another obvious area of application for a large, sparsely populated country with many remote regions — so obvious, in fact, that Canada became the first country in the world to put its own domestic communications satellite, Anik A-1, into orbit in 1972. This satellite, one of three used simultaneously to provide Canada-wide, 24-hour service, was followed by three other series of satellites, Anik B, Anik C and Anik D. In the 1970s, there had been a fierce national debate over whether Canadian industry should build the early Anik satellites. The federal government ultimately decided to contract out their construction to more experienced American firms — the Canadian content in Anik A was about 13 per cent — but today, Canadian industry plays a larger role in building Canadian communications satellites. Anik D, launched in 1982, contained 52 per cent Canadian content and, that same year, Spar landed a contract to build the first two Latin American communications satellites for Brazil. Canadian communications satellites are among the most powerful and technologically advanced in the world. The Anik C satellites, for example, are a new generation of satellites capable of direct broadcasting to very small receiving dishes. (Canadian government and industry researchers have also been working on the development of the ground technology to receive such signals.) The Anik C technology was tested in the mid-1970s in a joint Canadian-U.S. project that resulted in the launch of a CDN$60-million experimental communications technology satellite called Hermes in1976. Anik C-3 was one of the first two satellites to be launched from the space shuttle on its first commercial flight in November, 1982. Canada's domestic satellites are owned and operated by Telesat Canada, established in 1969. Another agency, Teleglobe Canada, is responsible for Canada's involvement with the international communications satellite system; its use of the INTELSAT network made the 1976 Montreal Olympics the most widely watched event in history. In the 1980s, Canada embarked on the development of a CDN$300-million mobile satellite, known as M-Sat, to provide improved mobile communications services to ships, aircraft, vehicles and compact portable terminals, particularly in remote areas of Canada.

But the Canadian space technology perhaps best known to Canadians is the Canadarm, the shuttle's remote manipulator arm, which continued to perform nearly flawlessly after its inaugural run on the second shuttle flight in November, 1981. It has proved to be a versatile tool, not only in tasks it was designed to do (moving payloads into and out of the cargo bay), but in a number of tasks that had not even been contemplated when it was designed, such as knocking ice off a vent or shaking loose frozen solar panels on a satellite. The arm was identified by NASA very early in the shuttle's design process as a vital component and it said something for the revival of Canada's aerospace industry, and the state of collaboration between the two countries, that its development was entrusted to Canada — though not without some objections from American industry. A deal was struck between the NRC and NASA in 1975 and the arm was designed and built by a Canadian industry team headed by Spar Aerospace, at a cost of about CDN$100-million (an estimated $4.50 per Canadian). The first arm was paid for by Canada and donated to NASA in 1981, but the U.S. space agency subsequently gave Spar a CDN$75-million contract to build at least three more arms. (See Chapter 6.)

The collaboration between Canada and the United States in space has not been confined solely to government and industry projects. Through the years, individual Canadian scientists had also played an important role in the American program. For example, one of the most prominent was David Strangway — formerly a professor of geology and physics at the University of Toronto and later president of the University of British Columbia — who worked for NASA full-time between 1970 and 1973 at the height of the Apollo lunar program. He was chief of NASA's geophysics and physics branches, acting chief of planetary and earth sciences and director of lunar sciences. From 1967, he was also the scientist in charge of the rock samples returned to earth by the Apollo astronauts (a position he retained into the 1980s, after he had returned to the U of T) and, in 1969, arranged for a large collection of the lunar rock samples to be moved to Canada for continuing study.

Another case of long-standing collaboration involved Ken Money, Doug Watt and another McGill University physiologist, Geoffrey Melvill Jones, head of McGill's Aviation Medical Research Unit, who worked with U.S. space scientists for many years doing research on motion sickness and other aspects of the body's physiological adaptation to zero gravity. (See Chapter 5.)

Between 1972 and 1983/84, annual Canadian government spending on space programs rose from about CDN$30-million to $131.2-million (compared with $460-million in 1983 for France, $630-million for Japan and $7.2-billion for the United States). By 1985/86, the annual budget had risen to $158-million (and was projected to increase to $180-million by 1990/91). Virtually all of these programs were the responsibility of six government departments or agencies — the Department of Communications; Energy, Mines and Resources; the National Research Council; Industry, Trade and Commerce; the Department of National Defence; and the Department of the Environment. The NRC assumed responsibility for project management of the Canadarm project, the Canadian astronaut program and later the Canadian space station program. Canada did not initially establish a NASA-style overall space agency. Major debates were waged, off and on, within the Canadian space community for more than 20 years about whether Canada needed such an agency, but the territorial imperatives of individual departments, and their reluctance to part with the substantial portions of their budgets that are dedicated to space projects,[2] always managed to defeat efforts to centralize the management of Canada's space program. However, in 1969, a co-ordinating agency, the Interdepartmental Committee on Space, was set up, with representation from about a dozen government departments and agencies, and in late 1986 the government announced its intention to set up a central space agency.

Canada has the interesting distinction of being the only country in the world whose national space industry sells more than its government spends on space. Through the 1960s and 1970s, the Canadian industry grew at a rate of more than 50 per cent annually and, by the early 1980s, it was grossing nearly CDN$500-million a year (about 70 per cent derived from exports) and employing more than 3000 people.

The success of the Canadarm — and Canada's financial contribution to the development of the shuttle transportation system — played no small part in bringing about the invitation from NASA to fly Canadians aboard the shuttle. But, as with everything else in the space program, the situation was complex and there was more to the invitation than the repayment of an un-written debt. International participation was an important component of NASA's long-term strategy of political and financial survival in the money-tight 1980s and an important stepping stone to the space station era of the 1990s. (See Chapter 7.)

For 25 years, NASA had been working toward the goal of having human beings living and working in space on a long-term basis and the space station was the logical culmination of an effort that started in the late 1950s and early 1960s with the Mercury and Gemini programs. The first order of business was to develop the basic technologies needed to operate and survive in space and, equally important, to test the potential — and the limitations — of the human body. The space environment offered many challenges and unknowns: extremes of heat and cold, radiation, micro-meteoroids, an almost complete vacuum and, of course, zero gravity. Flying a one-man spacecraft, then known as a "capsule", the Mercury astronauts explored the bare essentials of survival — proving that it was possible to eat, sleep and work in space.

It would have been logical to progress steadily from there to the development of a permanent facility in near-earth orbit, not only for earth-oriented research and development and commercial activities, but as a way-station for more far-flung adventures to the moon, Mars and even beyond. However, politics got in the way of technological and scientific logic. In 1961, with only the first Mercury suborbital flight completed, President John F. Kennedy committed the United States to "achieving the goal, before this decade is out, of landing a man on the moon and returning him safely to earth." It was an extraordinarily ambitious mandate, and all the more surprising because the manned space program, which had been suffering a series of humiliating setbacks (such as rockets exploding on the launch pad), had been virtually on the verge of extinction when Kennedy gave it this new lease on life. Kennedy had stated that "no single space project in this period will be *more impressive to mankind* [my italics] or more important for the long-range exploration of space," but it was clear he was personally more interested in the former payoff than the latter. Irritated in about equal measure by the continuing American failures and the spectacular Soviet successes, Kennedy was motivated almost solely by Cold War politics. In a single fateful week in April, 1961, Yuri Gagarin became the first man in space and the United States suffered political humiliation at the Bay of Pigs — and Kennedy suddenly saw the quest for the moon as just the grand gesture of technological one-upsmanship he needed to recoup American prestige. In a memorandum sent to vice-president Lyndon Johnson, who had responsibility for the space program, he asked: "Do we have a chance of beating the Soviets by putting a laboratory in space or by a trip around the moon or by a rocket to go to the moon and back with a man? Is there any other space program which promises dramatic results in which we could win?" (In his book *John F. Kennedy: President*, Hugh Sidey quotes Kennedy as saying: "If somebody can just tell me how to catch up. Let's find somebody — anybody. I don't care if it's the janitor over there if he knows how...There's nothing more important.") And so the two-man Gemini missions in 1965 and 1966 tested the procedures needed for the assault on the moon — for example, rendezvous and docking between two spacecraft and extravehicular activity. In July, 1969, with five months to spare, Apollo 11 landed on the moon and, among other things, provided Kennedy posthumously with the technological coup he sought over the Soviets.

As the most visible and spectacular of the space programs, the manned program always took the brunt of such political priority-setting and it always had a curiously paradoxical image. On the one hand, by its very nature, it attracted more attention from the general public and the media than the less glamorous but often more scientifically oriented unmanned space programs.[3] On the other hand, the manned program often came under attack from space scientists for being nothing but an expensive extravaganza, a grandstand play for public attention — in short, a PR front. Its critics argued then — and still do today — that you get much more science for your dollar out of unmanned programs. There is a certain validity to these claims. However, it's also true that unmanned projects generally could not, in themselves, command the kind of public and political support that the manned program did, especially at the beginning. No matter how little some space scientists like it, the fact remains that the manned program, with its high profile, is what keeps space exploration on the front pages and on the nightly news broadcasts. Politicians like to be seen with astronauts.

This means, however, that the manned program has to continue earning its keep by providing ever-greater thrills for a public and press that belongs to the TV generation used to instant gratification — a generation able to become easily and quickly bored with the impossible. The first landing on the moon managed to generate a sense of wonder but, for most people, this barely outlasted the mission itself; by the time of the last lunar walk in 1972, the attitude of the public seemed to be: when you've seen one person walk on the moon, you've seen them all.

Even as human beings were walking on the moon, NASA was returning to the concept of a permanent human presence in near-earth orbit. In the late 1960s and early 1970s, just months after the first lunar landing, the agency proposed development of both the space shuttle and a manned space station. The Skylab missions in 1973 and 1974, during which three crews of astronauts lived in a converted rocket booster for 28, 59 and 84 days, provided rudimentary experience with space station concepts. The studies done on those missions, particularly the medical and physiological experiments, answered some of the questions about long-term living in space, but raised many more. However, NASA was not able immediately to pursue the Skylab initiative to its logical conclusion — a permanent manned station in low earth orbit — even though it wanted to. At the time, its political masters weren't buying that big a package. John Lovestone, a U.S. space policy analyst, said that President Richard Nixon "liked men in space, liked the astronauts as heroes, liked the national symbolism, but he and his advisers thought that the political payoffs from space had pretty well been exhausted. The Congress was opposed to any new space initiative and public opinion clearly had gone in a different direction. All [NASA] could get support for was this shuttle concept ... It was a kind of minimal decision [that would] have some short term positive political effects without costing too much."

Accepting this reality, NASA concentrated its energies and most of its funds on the development of a reusable transportation system intended to reduce the cost of putting large payloads and large numbers of people into space. Development costs for the shuttle were originally projected to be about US$5.5-billion, but this increased to about US$10-billion[4] as the program almost immediately encountered a series of frustrating technical problems and delays — perhaps not surprisingly for such a revolutionary technology. Ultimately, there was a six-year hiatus in manned space flights before the first shuttle left the launch pad in April, 1981. After that, however, it chalked up a series of remarkable successes. After four orbital flight tests, the shuttle was declared available for business, and the shuttle Columbia accomplished the first "operational" flight in November, 1982. NASA planned a fleet of four shuttles. The second, Challenger, flew for the first time in December, 1983, and, the third, Discovery, flew in August, 1984, after a two-month delay caused by a computer abort just four seconds before launch in June. A fourth orbiter, Atlantis, flew for the first time in October, 1985, on a secret mission for the U.S. Air Force. NASA had been aiming ultimately for a "turn-around" time of two to three weeks but throughout 1984 and 1985 recurring weather and technical problems were making this goal frustratingly elusive. Launches were occurring about two months apart on average and even longer delays continued to plague the program. Nineteen eighty-five ended with a record seven postponements of the flight immediately before the Challenger accident and it was apparent that pressure to get the launch schedule back on track contributed significantly to the tragedy.

Throughout the shuttle program, especially during the increasingly expensive delays that marked its early years, NASA found itself having to defend the reusable approach to space exploitation. In particular, questions were raised about whether and when the shuttle's development costs would be recovered through commercial contracts. As the shuttle's first launch date was pushed further and further into the future, and the confidence of a nervous business community wavered, NASA's projections of the commercial demand for space transportation came under fire, which threatened not only the shuttle itself but the longer-term goal of establishing a permanent space station. Thus, for NASA, international collaboration and financial support became pivotal elements in its campaign to ensure the program's long-term survival — the reasoning being that the program's political masters would not only welcome the assistance with the budget but would find it more difficult to kill a program to which other countries had made a major commitment.

Of course, there had to be something in it for those other

countries — and one of the big plusses, NASA reasoned, was the opportunity for national prestige associated with having their own astronauts fly aboard the shuttle. By 1981, with two European astronauts already making their way through the system, NASA began putting out informal feelers to Canada and, in September, 1982, Lt. Gen. James Abrahamson, then NASA associate administrator, publicly issued a formal invitation at a ceremony in Ottawa celebrating the 20th anniversary of the launching of Alouette I.[5]

The NRC was delegated to study the offer. It, in turn, canvassed the Canadian space research community and invited submissions suggesting research that could be performed on the shuttle by a Canadian, finally narrowing the field down to the two sets of experiments related to space physiology and development of the space vision system. The physiology experiments were suggested by Money and Watt. The two scientists had originally submitted separate proposals for a series of experiments that were basically a continuation of the work they'd been doing with NASA for many years. Their proposals were not identical, but were similar enough that they were urged to submit a joint proposal. "We've been working together for years anyway, so we were very happy to do that," Money said. They both assumed that one of them would be chosen to do the experiments in space and Money recalls that their major concern was which one would be the prime and which the backup. He and Watt attended a conference in Colorado at the time and Money joked, "We decided to see who could push the other off a cliff. We were encouraging each other not to be so cowardly when we were skiing." So it came as a bit of a shock to both of them when they were told the proposal had been accepted but that the NRC was going to hold a wide-open astronaut competition and they would have to compete with others for the right to perform their own experiments in space. Though Money was not very pleased with this development, he felt that an open competition was the fair way of making the selection. Watt, however, looked at the situation differently. He took the position that the NRC was not supposed to be looking for astronauts per se, but rather scientific specialists who were qualified by years of research in their fields to perform the experiments in space. During the selection process, he was outspoken on this point, telling the press that only he or Money was qualified to do the physiology experiments properly. "It just makes sense to send someone who knows

The crew of Mission 41-G eats breakfast at 3 a.m. in the crew quarters at the Kennedy Space Center before leaving to board the shuttle Challenger. From left: David Leestma, Marc Garneau, Kathy Sullivan, Bob Crippen (mission commander), Sally Ride, Jon McBride, Paul Scully-Power. The traditional cake decorated with the image of the mission patch is in the centre of the table. Garneau said the two veterans, Crippen and Ride, appeared "more mellow" than the rookies. The crew is dressed in civilian clothes rather than their flight suits because, as Garneau said, "you don't want to get jam on it before you leave." He ate only dry toast and, mindful of a two-hour wait in the spacecraft before launch, drank only a single cup of coffee.
NASA

The 41-G crew on Challenger's flight deck. The seven-member crew was the largest to fly a shuttle mission up to that time. Top from left: Paul Scully-Power, Bob Crippen, Marc Garneau. Bottom from left: Jon McBride, Sally Ride, Kathy Sullivan, David Leestma. Faces take on a bloated appearance in space because fluids shift to the upper body in zero-gravity. Astronauts call this the "puffy face" syndrome.
NASA

The launch of 41-G, October 5, 1984. Challenger lifts off the pad at the Kennedy Space Center on a plume of brilliant yellow-white smoke that transforms the pre-dawn darkness into daylight. As the countdown clock reaches T+21 seconds, the spacecraft enters the low-lying clouds suffusing them with a warm golden glow as it vanishes from view.
LYDIA DOTTO

After an eight-day mission, Challenger returns to the Kennedy Space Center landing strip. A bit wobbly as he tries to regain his one-gravity legs, Garneau, second from the top, descends the steps from the crew compartment. After a week in zero gravity, Garneau felt very heavy during re-entry and said he experienced faintness when he got up from his seat. Astronauts returning from space are susceptible to blacking out as gravity pulls blood to the lower part of the body; they wear a pressure garment under their flight suits to counteract this effect.
NASA

Marc Garneau, sitting in the mid-deck of the Challenger, reads a flight book while sipping on a drink. Enclosed containers must be used in zero gravity to prevent liquids from floating around. Behind Garneau's left elbow is a small computer attached to a locker door with Velcro.
NASA

Canada's first astronauts were chosen during a six-month cross-country hunt in which nearly 4400 people, ranging in age from six to 73, applied for the job. Top from left: Ken Money, a physiologist with the Defence and Civil Institute of Environmental Medicine; Roberta Bondar, a Hamilton doctor and medical researcher; Bjarni Tryggvason, a researcher with the National Research Council. Bottom from left: Bob Thirsk, a Montreal doctor; Steve MacLean, a postdoctoral student at Stanford University; and Marc Garneau, an engineer and Canadian naval officer.
NRC

Marc Garneau floats upside down in the KC-135, NASA's zero gravity training plane, which is used to familiarize astronauts with the sensation of zero gravity, to study their susceptibility to motion sickness and to train them for tasks in space. "I didn't do triple flips," said Garneau, who is susceptible to motion sickness.
NASA

Bob Thirsk, floating free in the KC-135, clutches the hands of the space suit used by astronauts to perform EVAs ("extravehicular activity") outside the shuttle. NASA astronauts use the KC-135 to practice getting into and out of the suit, which weighs more than 135 kg in earth's gravity. Thirsk got a thrill out of skimming along a few inches off the walls and floor of the KC-135 "like Superman, you know."
NASA

Ken Money (centre right, in beige flight suit) is swamped by reporters, photographers and cameramen as he prepares to start tests on the other astronauts in the Precision Angular Mover (PAM), a machine he invented to induce symptoms of motion sickness. Subjects are strapped into the enclosed capsule and tumbled backwards 20 times a minute for up to 10 minutes. The tests were part of a Canadian experiment to understand the cause of motion sickness in space.
DCIEM/ KIMBERLY DEAN

NASA's zero gravity training plane, officially known as the KC-135 but called the "Vomit Comet" by astronauts because of its tendency to induce motion sickness. The plane performs steep climbs and dives, flying a roller coaster pattern that provides about 25 seconds of zero gravity as it goes over the top. A typical flight involves about 40 to 50 of these "parabolas" and is virtually the only way to experience real zero gravity on earth.
NASA

Marc Garneau and Bob Thirsk flank U.S. payload specialist Paul Scully-Power during a KC-135 training flight.
NASA

Bob Thirsk assists Marc Garneau and Paul Scully-Power during a session in the space shuttle trainer at the Johnson Space Center, Houston. The crew spends many hours practicing the mission in trainers and simulators. Payload specialists like Garneau and Scully-Power receive about 120 hours of mission-related training, including a realistic three-day simulation in which the entire crew and the Mission Control flight controllers take part.
NASA

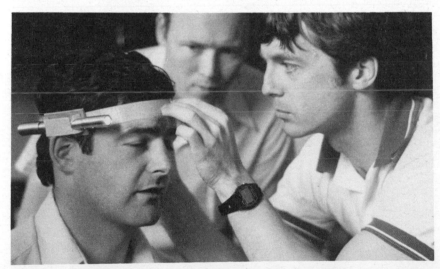

During a training session at McGill University, Bob Thirsk assists Marc Garneau in preparation for one of the physiology tests he will perform aboard the shuttle. Principal investigator Doug Watt is in the background. The test was designed to determine the effect of zero gravity on the vestibulo-ocular reflex, a reflex that helps you to continue looking at something even when you move your head.
NRC

A blindfolded Marc Garneau is spun in the coriolis chair. Moving the head up and down while the chair is rotating induces motion sickness in most people within a matter of minutes.
NRC

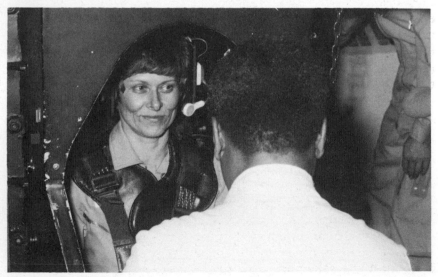

Roberta Bondar prepares for a run in the PAM.

exactly what the experiment is about."[6]

What NASA had offered to send was a "payload specialist." This was the newest of three categories of astronauts — one that NASA actually doesn't even refer to as astronauts. That designation belongs to the first two categories — pilot-astronauts and mission specialists. Pilot-astronauts are the test-pilot types, the direct inheritors of the Right Stuff legacy. They need at least 1000 hours' flying time in high-performance jets and their main function remains "flying the bird" (or, frequently these days, managing the computers that fly the bird). They are responsible for getting the space shuttle into and out of orbit, for maneuvring in space, managing flight systems and landing the vehicle. Mission specialists are scientists and engineers who do not fly the spacecraft. They are concerned with the technical and scientific goals of shuttle missions. They monitor the scientific experiments on board the shuttle and are responsible for operating the Canadarm, for extravehicular activity (EVAs), and for other activities related to payload support, such as launching satellites.

Pilots and mission specialists are NASA employees, career astronauts who train for many different missions; initially, only American citizens could belong to these categories. Later, NASA permitted a European astronaut to train as a mission specialist, but for the most part, non-U.S. astronauts are payload specialists who, according to NASA's definition, are scientists or technically qualified persons with special skills to perform specific experiments or operations on the shuttle. A payload specialist is employed by a shuttle customer — whether a country or a private company — that has paid to fly a shuttle payload requiring special expertise and he or she will not necessarily fly more than once. In October, 1982, NASA eased certain restrictions on payload specialists, in order to permit "more people to go into space, easily and safely, in order to enhance the scientific, commercial and national security objectives there." This relaxation in policy made it possible for Canada to consider selecting someone to carry out scientific experiments aboard the shuttle.

Watt took the view that what the NRC was really trying to do was choose career astronauts, or what he referred to as "pseudo-mission specialists." It was a charge that NRC officials did not trouble to deny very strenuously since it was, in fact, pretty much what they had in mind and they were unapologetic about it. The NRC and the selection committees were perfectly aware that NASA was offering to fly only payload specialists to support specific Canadian shuttle experiments. However, the U.S. space agency left the selection of Canada's space team entirely up to the Canadian authorities — with the stipulation that it would always retain the final say on whether any particular individual could fly with a shuttle crew — and, except to ensure the successful candidates could meet NASA's medical requirements, the selection committee had a free hand in establishing its own selection criteria.

From the beginning, the NRC had certain objectives of its own in mind — specifically the hope that Canada's involvement in the manned space program would not be a one-shot (or, more accurately, a two-shot) affair. The NRC, in its approach to selecting the six payload specialists, clearly signalled its interest in laying the foundation for a continuing astronaut program that would permit Canada to respond to future opportunities, such as, for example, the chance to fly people aboard the U.S./ international space station in the 1990s. Even before the six were selected, Garry Lindberg, then director of the NRC's National Aeronautical Establishment, said in a speech at York University, Toronto, that "Canada may be looking to select astronauts to dwell on the space station for a number of months to carry out a unique Canadian experiment." As the selection process drew to a close, Clive Willis, director of NRC's public relations and information services and an influential member of the selection committee, commented: "We are not picking six people to go out and do experiments alone; we are picking an astronaut corps." And, although the government had not, at the time, made any commitment to extend the astronaut program beyond the two shuttle experiments, Doetsch added that soon there would be "six candidates who are going to be working very hard ... to make sure it goes beyond that." He did not rule out the hope that Canadian astronauts might one day be able to function as mission specialists with responsibility for operating the Canadarm.

The search began. It took six months and the work fell to two separate committees and a selection panel composed of representatives of the NRC, the Ministry of State for Science and Technology and the departments of National Defence, Communications, and Energy, Mines and Resources, each of which was responsible for numerous space-related programs. The screening committee was composed of chairperson Madeleine

56

Hinchey, then Secretary-General of the NRC; Lorne Kuehn, director of science and technology (human performance) for the Department of National Defence; Ray Marchand of the Interdepartmental Committee on Space; and Doetsch and Willis.

The big question in the minds of those who would be astronauts was: What kind of person did they want? Who, exactly, were they looking for? Help-wanted ads notwithstanding, being an astronaut had not yet become just another job and, despite the changes since the early days of the space program, it was not true that the "right stuff," in the classic Tom Wolfe sense, was no longer needed, or that the new breed of astronauts would not be motivated strongly by the same sense of challenge that drove the earlier generation. Ultimately, they still had to be willing to put their "hides on the line," to sit on top of that giant firecracker and fly off in "a hurtling piece of machinery." However, while it's safe to say the selection team was not out scouting for high-wire artists or human cannonballs, neither was it looking for military test pilots. They were, in fact, looking for scientists. But if that was all, it would have been possible — and certainly a lot faster and easier — simply to handpick half a dozen suitable candidates from among those in the scientific community who were already doing research in the relevant fields. They decided instead on a cross-country dragnet, in part because it was thought this would ultimately deliver what one spokesman described as "a higher quality product."

There was more to it than that, however. The NRC was not blind to the fact that a nationwide talent hunt would generate a tremendous amount of publicity and create great public awareness of the space program. A high public profile — of the right sort, of course — is crucial to the political success of very expensive space programs, particularly ones that do not offer immediate tangible economic return. NASA has learned this lesson well — sometimes the hard way — and it is a lesson the NRC took to heart from the beginning.

Canada being what it is, there was another delicate political matter that was addressed by the cross-country dragnet: how to ensure not only the fact but the appearance of equal opportunity for people in different geographic regions, for francophones and anglophones, and for men and women. Publicly, the committee insisted that these factors did not play a role in the selection process other than the openly stated condition that the team as a whole had to have a bilingual capability (that is, at least one member would be fluently bilingual). Willis said the committee decided they could not defend the application of any of the other factors as criteria for selection: "We looked at this very frankly and decided fundamentally that we could not win on that one. We are going to pick the best six we can pick."

Six out of 4400. How does a country go about making such a choice? What is it we look for in an astronaut? Scientific and technical skills were only the starting point. It was immediately obvious that there would be far more than six people among the applicants who would more than meet any narrow definition of the scientific qualifications. But the committee wanted not only scientists who could do the experiments but also researchers who could contribute to the development of those experiments. They wanted people who were fast learners, who not only could do the required work in their own disciplines, but also could master many aspects of other scientific and technical disciplines related to the space program. They also had to be articulate representatives of the space program, able to explain their work not only to other scientists but also to politicians, the public and media. And finally there were the intangibles to be considered: personality traits, the ability to work closely with and get along with others and the psychological stamina to cope simultaneously with a demanding work schedule, a sudden and major upheaval in their professional and personal lives and the need to adjust to being almost constantly in the public limelight. All of this was deemed necessary because, whether they liked it or not, Canada's first astronauts would become national figures and instant celebrities whose role, quite aside from the work they would do aboard the space shuttle, would be, as Willis described it, to represent Canada to the world and Canadians to themselves. With these requirements in mind the committee started to sift through the mountain of applications.

The applications had come from word processor operators, fire fighters, computer experts, doctors, divers, engineers, clerks, teachers and scientists of all kinds. Not surprisingly, many applicants were also pilots — professional or amateur — even though the Canadian payload specialist wouldn't get anywhere near the shuttle's controls. Many, too, had harbored dreams of being an astronaut for years and had been thwarted by the fact that this exclusive club had for so long been open only to American and Soviet citizens.

The NRC did not, at this stage, release the names of candidates to the press, but it didn't take the media long to ferret out local applicants and soon the news reports were full of glowing favorite-son or -daughter stories about the hopefuls. It was interesting to see what the applicants thought counted in this most unusual competition. An Ottawa fireman said: "I have no fear that I would perform under stress." Similar sentiments were expressed by a Montreal medical technician who had made more than 300 high altitude parachute jumps: "I think I have the right stuff for work under stressful situations given my experience in high altitude skydiving." A Manitoba chiropractor and former naval officer said: "I've had to function while seasick." An Ontario doctor, who was also both a pilot and a diver, said he had experience "in human experiments in altered environments, such as high altitudes and underwater." He described the shuttle as "the ultimate laboratory." A British Columbia doctor said that applying for the astronaut program was one of those things he had to do, even though he believed that NASA's offer was made only for political and economic reasons and that the Canadian astronaut would be little more than a "puppet" filling a PR role.

One of the more endearing applications came from Katie Mertes of Sault Ste. Marie, Ontario, then eight years old. For her, the Right Stuff included not only getting excellent marks in school, but "doing experiments and projects ... I like to learn about the planets and stars and about bugs ... I have raised a frog from a tadpole ... I have saved three birds from cats." But the prize for the most unusual application went to Deborah Knight-Nikifortchuk, an advertising copywriter from Newmarket, Ontario, who said she was already practicing to "begin every sentence with the phrase 'Come in, Houston'" and submitted her application in the form of a five-page poem, which read in part:

> I never altered in my plan
> To travel in a metal can
> To stand upon the alien ground
> Of worlds we haven't even found...
>
> Now interspace craft are so small
> That astronauts must not be tall.
> They'd need bigger suits and seats
> And have you seen what a grown man eats?!
> Oh, no. The perfect candidate
> Must be small in height and light of weight.

I'm barely pushing five foot three
So there's no better choice than me!
My boss has promised it's okay
To take time off without my pay
'Cause he thinks I'm already gone
Far from the earth we're standing on.

Although he was snowed under by the load of applications, NRC personnel chief Ray Dolan, who had the responsibility for processing the paper, made an effort to respond personally to some of the most innovative applicants rather than sending a standard form letter. Some of the children received personal responses because "you don't just write them off and forget them." He also wrote Knight-Nikifortchuk to tell her that her application "stands apart from all others not only for its entertainment value but also because ... it seems to accurately capture the feelings of so many other applicants as well." (When Dolan asked permission to release the poem to the press, Knight-Nikifortchuk said she had no objections. "I knew I would never in a million years be chosen for the program but thought that I might be able to brighten up someone's day." Irrepressible — and optimistic — to the end, though, she added a P.S.: "If, in a last minute decision, my application is reconsidered, I can be reached at...")

Dolan, who hadn't anticipated the sheer volume of applications, admitted he was "flabbergasted with the number." He was even more surprised by how few were outright crank applications; in his letter to Knight-Nikifortchuk, he commented that "one could reasonably expect that a fair percentage of the applicants would be glib and insincere. This, surprisingly, was not at all the case ... the one common element noted time and time again ... was the sincere desire expressed by all applicants to be a Canadian astronaut."

There were four rounds of elimination, starting in July and ending with the selection of the six in December. The first two rounds were strictly a paper exercise designed to eliminate those who had not sent enough information, were too young, or clearly did not meet even the minimum professional and educational requirements. By the end of August, the list had been pared to about 1800 people, who were asked to send further documentation concerning education and work experience and detailed information on their medical background and physical fitness.

About 1600 responded. The medical standards, established to "assure that candidates are *physically and temperamentally* [my italics] fit for the performance of space crew duties," outlined minimum and maximum height requirements (152 to 193 cm), blood pressure maximum (140 over 90) and visual and auditory acuity limits. It indicated that "defects and diseases" would be considered disqualifying if they: prevented the performance of duties requiring physical exertion, dexterity, sensory acuity and the ability to speak clearly; interfered with the wearing of special equipment (such as pressure suits and helmets); reduced tolerance for rapid changes in atmospheric pressure, acceleration or weightlessness; required frequent or regular medical treatment or medication; or if they were likely to become disabling with time. The medical form asked applicants to indicate whether they'd ever had any of about 70 medical or physical disorders, including heart trouble, gallstones, arthritis, sleepwalking, amnesia, bedwetting, VD, stuttering, dizziness or fainting spells, asthma and depression or "excessive worry." It even asked whether the applicant had ever attempted suicide. (Filling out this list was optional; a statement from the applicant's personal physician stating that he or she was not aware of any disqualifying disorders could be substituted.) The form also asked about car, air or sea sickness. Ken Money, who had been deliberately making himself motion sick for years, indicated his susceptibility was average and his experience had occurred mostly in the course of doing his research. Marc Garneau indicated that he had experienced motion sickness in his early days at sea, but had overcome it; however, he admitted later that he had been concerned about what this would do to his chances of being selected. Although all of this medical information was supplied by the applicant, the form indicated that applicants selected for final screening would have to undergo a thorough medical with special tests. At this stage, applicants among the 1800 began to be eliminated on medical grounds. Dolan said that the doctors recommended dividing the applicants into three groups: "Those for whom they anticipate no problems whatsoever, those for whom there may be a problem, and those who they suggested they could not pass." With so many highly qualified people to choose from, it didn't take much in the way of a medical or physical problem to prompt a thumbs down decision on an applicant.

Only 68 made the second cut. This was one of the more difficult stages in the selection process because the 68 were chosen — and many more were eliminated — from among 1600 applicants on the basis of a paper review only and "there was some risk in making a mistake interpreting all of that," Dolan remembers. "You want to be sure to the best of your ability that those 68 are in fact top-notch candidates. You've already rejected some people who may be equally good or even better, and we ran the risk of including in those 68 some real clinkers because they were sight unseen." The 68 were interviewed by the first committee, the screening committee, in six cities during October and November, 1983; by this time, the field had been narrowed to those with degrees and work experience in the relevant scientific and technical fields.

The media in the cities that could lay claim to a candidate who had made it this far — whether by birth or by residence — had a field day. (Others had to content themselves with "down-in-the-dumps" and "better-luck-next-time" stories about eliminated candidates.) Misapprehensions about the nature of the Canadian program persisted; one headline, for example, said that NASA had narrowed the field of applicants. And the editorial writers started getting into the act, taking their usual license with scientific and technical details in their attempt to be cute: "Their bags are packed with tubes of sirloin substitute and jars of evaporated coffee, their maps of Europe have been replaced by charts of the cosmos ... In a land filled with Star Wars movies, Pac Man and Space Invader games, it was only a matter of time before the adventurous among us opted for escapism as a way of life."

For many of the hopefuls, this was their first real exposure to the realities of dealing with the media and most underestimated the demand. Bondar said she was "deluged without warning" with calls from newspapers and TV and radio stations. She was in the middle of seeing patients in Hamilton when a Toronto newspaper called to say they were sending a reporter and photographer in 20 minutes. She did not object to speaking with the media — although she wondered why they were "wasting a lot of their time and money" on candidates who might not be among the final six — but she did find it time-consuming and disruptive because she hadn't been able to plan for it. And she was concerned about the reaction of her patients, though she quickly discovered they were pleased to have a celebrity for a doctor. "I haven't had one no-show since this was announced. Clinics tend to get longer and longer," she laughed, adding that she seemed to be seeing a lot of conspicuously healthy patients. She was particularly touched by the gift of one patient — a ceramic seagull with one wingtip pointing to the heavens and her name and "good luck" written on the base.

By November, 1983, the short list was down to 19 finalists from all across Canada. This group included three francophones. Slightly more than 11 per cent of the original 4400 entries were from women,[7] but Bondar was the only one to make the cut to 19. The sexual politics of the 1980s being what it is, this aroused immediate speculation that she would be chosen simply because she was a woman. Bondar herself was annoyed by such reasoning because it implied that, if she did get in, she would be a token woman, not considered as good as the others who made it. "No one likes to be referred to as a token about anything in life." Asked what role she thought being a woman would play in being selected, she shot back: "None, and it should play none. I feel equal with the other people." She added that she did not feel she was being treated differently from the other candidates by the interviewers.

It appears that this was genuinely the case; one insider who was privy to the committee's deliberations said that chairperson Hinchey, the only woman on the committee, stated at the outset that she would not support any suggestion that tokenism should play a role in the selection process. Willis noted that the committee felt that such an approach would not be doing the cause of women in space any favor. "If there's a woman, there will be a woman in there because she's among the best." Certainly there's little doubt that Bondar qualified on merit alone, but the committee was glad to be able to choose a woman with a clear conscience, or, as Doetsch put it, "without forcing the system."

As the only woman to make the group of 19, Bondar inevitably received a great deal of media coverage. The fact remained that, although the Right Stuff was no longer exclusively male (Wolfe had actually described it as "nothing less than manhood itself"), women astronauts still had novelty value. At the time the Canadian astronauts were being selected in late 1983, only Sally Ride among the small contingent of American women astronauts had flown a shuttle mission two years before — the first woman to go into space since the Soviet cosmonaut Valentina Tereshkova had flown two decades earlier. Bondar had rather mixed feelings about the inevitable attention she received as the only Canadian woman astronaut. She was content to speak to women's groups and to act as a professional role model. "A hundred years from now, people will be shaking their heads and saying, 'What was it all about?' For now, it's important and if I can fill this role for Canadians, then so be it." However, she could not suppress a sense of irritation with what she regarded as "gossip" about her personal life in the media.

The 19 finalists were invited to Ottawa in mid-November for a week of further interviews and intensive medical tests (which, Money noted, included being "stabbed with needles 21 times in two days"). Bondar was given one test the others were not — a pregnancy test. She revealed this in one press interview because she was being "badgered" about any tests the men had undergone that she hadn't or vice versa. But she said that, as a doctor, she wasn't bothered by having to take the test or by the revelation that she had.

At this stage, all of the candidates were extremely well qualified on strictly technical and scientific grounds, but there were the other factors to be considered. Canada's first astronauts would be expected to be enthusiastic promoters of the space program and the interview committee was intent on carefully evaluating the communications skills of the 19. Most of them seemed to accept this public relations role willingly, at least in principle — after all, people who weren't enthusiastic supporters of the space program would hardly have applied to be astronauts — but few of them were really prepared for the reality of this role and the demands it would place on them. As Bondar observed at the time, "The hype this week has been more than I think any of us bargained for or could understand prior to coming to Ottawa."

Each of the 19 candidates was required to give a 12-minute oral presentation on one of four philosophical themes — "The Role of Heroes," "Space: The New Frontier?," "Man [sic] or Machine" and "The Role of Science and Technology in Society Today." Some found this the most unnerving part of the process, knowing that their performance in these speeches would be a key element in the committee's evaluation. Many of them found the committee members pleasant but virtually unreadable. "One doesn't know how one does," Bondar commented shortly after her session. "They're going to smile at you even if they don't think you're going to make it. They want to let you leave feeling good, and they do a good job of that so you don't really have any indication of how well you've done." A year later, Steve MacLean, while narrating a film about the astronaut selection process and training program, described the committee as the "hardest audience" he'd ever faced — "twelve stonefaced interviewers in front of us who were programmed not to react to us." Little wonder, then, that Bondar likened the 19 to army buddies sharing the trenches together. The group did develop a strong camaraderie despite the essentially competitive nature of the exercise. One night, several of the 19 went off to see *The Right Stuff* together and, one morning at breakfast toward the end of the week, they ran around collecting autographs from each other in a chaotic scene that was, in Bondar's words, like "the final day at camp." "The week was really great," agreed Steve MacLean as it was drawing to a close. Still, it *was* a competition among highly competitive people and there was the inescapable fact that only six would be chosen. Virtually everyone was making up a private list of who would be chosen — lists that some candidates acknowledged tended to consist of self-plus-five. (As one put it, if you didn't put yourself on the list, "you don't want the job bad enough to deserve it.")

At the end of the week, the 19 were sent away to chew their nails for several weeks, awaiting the promised call in early December. The interview committee submitted its recommendations to the selection panel of the Interdepartmental Committee on Space, which held a meeting between 9 and 11 a.m. on Saturday, December 3, to make the final choices.

It fell to Ray Dolan to make the calls. He had alerted the 19 to be waiting at home between 6 and 7 p.m. on Saturday, so he went into his office that afternoon and organized his list. The 13 unsuccessful candidates would be called first, then the six who had been selected. "It took very little time," Dolan remembers, adding dryly: "Everyone was in fact waiting for their call." With those who were not selected, Dolan did not beat around the bush; he told them they were unsuccessful, thanked them for their involvement and wished them luck. Their reactions ranged from "a real downer and surprise ... to expressions of gratitude for being involved. None of them, I got the impression, thought so much of themselves that they were an automatic in. They knew what they were up against; I think they were all awed to some extent by the quality of the competition." They all knew that, for most of them, the news would be bad.

Dolan enjoyed the next six calls a great deal more. He has a mischievious sense of humor and affected nonchalance and an extraordinary interest in the weather that was rather aggravating to the recipients, who were by now in the terminal stages of nervous tension. Two of the calls were local; the others went out to Texas, California, Dundas, Ontario, and Montreal.

Bob Thirsk, then an MD at Montreal's Queen Elizabeth Hospital, had been thinking about the call all week. He found that he was preparing himself psychologically only for dealing with a "yes," even though he acknowledged to himself that he could be turned down. "I would acknowledge that it could happen, but I didn't prepare myself to deal with the disappointment I would feel afterwards. I was preparing myself only for a yes. I don't know why. It's strange." On Saturday, he was nervous all day but "trying not to show it." During the day, he forced himself to leave his apartment, going Christmas shopping with his girlfriend, Brenda, and when he got back, he started lifting weights, which is his way of coping with stress. When the call came at 7:10 p.m., he and Brenda just stared at each other for a moment, letting the phone ring; then he answered and he and Dolan danced through a little Bob-and-Ray routine of inconsequential chat about Montreal's weather. "Ray!" Thirsk finally exclaimed in exasperation when he'd had as much of the suspense as he could take; in response, Dolan asked him if he'd like another trip to Ottawa. Thirsk broke out in a big smile and gave Brenda a thumbs-up sign. "She got a little bit emotional," he commented later. And he didn't? Well, yes, he admitted rather sheepishly, "I guess I was very exuberant. [Ray] had to give me time to calm down."

After he hung up, Thirsk announced they were going to celebrate by having dinner in one of Montreal's most exclusive restaurants. It was an indulgence they'd discussed before and rejected as too expensive, but Thirsk was not to be dissuaded, particularly since he had an engagement ring for Brenda in his pocket. He proposed that evening and they were married in early January, but had to forego a honeymoon because he had to move to Ottawa almost immediately to take up his astronaut duties. (They didn't actually manage to have their honeymoon for nearly a year because of Thirsk's subsequent selection as Garneau's backup and the demands of training for flight 41-G.)[8]

In Steve MacLean's neck of the woods, the weather had actually been rather interesting. He was living in California at the time, attending Stanford University. The night before Dolan's call was due, a severe winter storm in the Santa Cruz mountains pulled down the phone lines, "so when I woke up in the morning, I was quite concerned they wouldn't be able to reach me." Fortunately, the phone was still working, but a tree had fallen over the downed line and he was worried the phones might go out at any time. When the call came at 4 p.m., California time, he was outside chopping wood, helping out neighbors whose house had been clipped by a tree, and he was rather breathless from running inside. Dolan pulled much the same routine as he had with Thirsk. As MacLean remembers it, the conversation went something like this:

"Hi, Steve. How are you?"

"Oh, I'm fine, Ray. How are you?"

"Oh, pretty good, Steve. The weather is fine up here. How's the weather down in California?"

"Well, Ray, the weather is just fine down here." (This was not strictly true, of course, but MacLean wasn't about to get into an involved discussion about wind storms, felled trees and downed power lines.)

When this had gone on for a minute or so, MacLean finally blurted: "Ray, why are you phoning me?"

"Well, Steve, do you have your bags packed for Ottawa?"

When he got off the phone, MacLean, who was a champion gymnast, felt the need to express his reaction physically: right then and there, he did a backflip. Later, remembering the conversation with amusement, he realized that Dolan's very manner should have tipped him off. "He wouldn't do that number with someone who didn't make it. He would have been very sincere and serious if he had been saying no."

For Roberta Bondar, Canada's first woman astronaut, Dolan's call was perhaps the best birthday present of her life. In fact, it arrived in the middle of her 38th birthday celebration with her parents and friends at her home in Dundas, Ontario. (The party had been moved up a day, just in case she had to leave for Ottawa.) Sitting amid the party hubbub anticipating the call, she admitted that, although she'd been able to sleep, the tension had taken a toll on her appetite and she'd be glad when the waiting was over, whichever way the decision went. Bondar took the call herself at 6:45 p.m. and let out a great whoop of assent when Dolan asked her if she was "ready to travel again."

Marc Garneau let his wife answer the phone when it rang at his Ottawa home at 7 p.m. He knew how astronauts were supposed to act: "I asked her to answer it so it would look like I was keeping my cool."

Dolan wasn't really buying it: "That's exactly what I said to him — who are you trying to fool? He started to chuckle."

Garneau admitted later that he had been rendered a bit of a "nervous wreck" by the waiting. "I found it very difficult to concentrate on my work back at the office. I was on the verge of a dream coming true. I was so psyched up, I knew it was going to be a tremendous disappointment if I didn't make it." He said that he tried to prepare himself for the letdown, telling himself that he'd given it a good go, that he'd made it to the 19, that it was an interesting experience and good fun, that he still had a challenging career in the Navy and that his wife would probably relax for the first time in months. None of this rationalizing was doing any good by the time December 3 rolled around.

After going through the familiar song-and-dance with Dolan for a few minutes, Garneau, like the others, was warned not to talk to the press, but he hadn't been off the phone 15 minutes before he had a call from *Maclean's* magazine. He tried not to spill the beans, but he admitted he was "not the picture of disappointment. I was so elated that I probably gave it away without actually saying anything." (He later commented that he did not tell his children before the public announcement was made because "they're not terribly reliable about keeping secrets.")

Bjarni Tryggvason, a researcher with the National Research Council who also lived in Ottawa, received his call at his apartment around 7 p.m. "My knees were shaking, but I was really trying to be cool. He [Dolan] says, 'Why don't you quit trying to be so damn cool? You made it, you know.' " A quiet-spoken, self-confident type given to understatement, Tryggvason allowed that he was "pretty excited" at being selected. "This has been a dream for a long, long time ... one that I never thought I would see come true," he said, adding that when he first applied, "it was like buying a lottery ticket" because no one knew what the NRC was looking for.

Ken Money was the most predictable choice of the six, given his long association with the space program and his scientific qualifications in the field of space physiology. In fact, he was at the Johnson Space Center in Houston, supporting one of the shuttle missions, when he received his call at his hotel on Saturday night. He was sleeping at the time, since he was working 10 p.m. to 9 a.m. shifts in Mission Control. "Night and day was so confused for me at that time." A press conference was scheduled in Ottawa on Monday morning to introduce the six, but he could not leave Houston. At 8 a.m. that morning, while he was sitting at a computer console in Mission Control, he received a congratulatory phone call from then science minister Donald Johnston. "I took it on one of those nifty NASA headsets," he recalled with a laugh. He also remembered that he had been watching a computer display of the shuttle's ground track as it orbited the earth and, during the call, it coincidentally passed over Ottawa.

Money was, of course, delighted to have been chosen, but his elation was punctured when he walked into Mission Control and encountered Doug Watt, who was taking the alternate shift supporting the shuttle mission.

"Congratulations to us," he said to Watt.

"No, congratulations to you," Watt responded. Watt had been sitting at a computer console in one of the science support rooms in Mission Control when he received the call from Dolan and so he had little opportunity at the time to ponder the news. "It was a very busy time; I had to get back on the console."

Money remarked later that he was "really deflated" by the fact that Watt had not been selected. "It took all the joy out of it for me. He and I had always planned to do this together." Watt, however, reflected later that "it was probably the right decision." If both he and Money had been members of the astronaut corps, "there is no way we would have put the [life sciences] experiment together. It's more than a full-time job, an enormous responsibility."

Assembling the other five astronauts in Ottawa for the press conference on Monday morning posed some challenges for Dolan because the NRC was determined to keep the information from leaking to the press ahead of time. "There was a battle of wits all the way," he acknowledged. From the time the 68 had been identified, the media had been calling candidates regularly and they knew the decision was imminent, so Dolan asked each of the

19 not to discuss his call with reporters. "I asked them not even to indicate whether they were in or out. For the six that was particularly important; I even suggested that they might consider not being home." Their travel arrangements also created complications. The NRC wanted them in Ottawa by Monday morning; in order to ensure that they could make it in time, flight reservations had been made well in advance for all 19. Those for the 13 unsuccessful candidates were later cancelled. Dolan said they didn't take any precautions against the media calling the airlines, but a peculiar reverse problem did occur: before the final decision was made, Air Canada called at least two of the candidates to confirm the flight reservations. Ken Money was one — his wife took the message in Toronto and conveyed it to him in Houston — so Dolan's call on Saturday night did not come as a surprise. "I assumed it was in the bag," Money remembered. When Dolan told Money the good news, he was startled when Money responded: "Oh, that's great. In fact, I already knew." One of the unsuccessful candidates also received a call from Air Canada and had leapt to the same erroneous conclusion, and was doubly disappointed by Dolan's call. Dolan was upset too, "because we were dealing up front with them all the way along. It was unfortunate, in whatever cases it may have happened, that they went on a high, then came barrelling down."

By this point, the cat and mouse game with the media had intensified. The six were to be unveiled on Monday, December 5, by the minister, and the NRC, acutely sensitive to the political winds, was anxious that Johnston not be upstaged by any premature disclosures. But the press knew that the decision was being made on the weekend and that a press conference was scheduled for Monday — and they'd been keeping close tabs on many of the candidates — so the NRC decided to employ some evasive maneuvres to thwart any reporters who might have staked out the Ottawa airport. Dolan told Bondar and MacLean to fly to Montreal where they joined up with Thirsk to be driven to Ottawa. Tryggvason and Garneau, of course, were already in Ottawa and Dolan asked them to come to his office to meet with the others. "Garneau arrived first, in uniform, and a little bit ill at ease, but I simply had him sit and wait." Dolan also asked him to guess the names of the other five; he got four right. When Tryggvason walked in, Dolan asked him the same question and he also got four out of five right.

On Monday, December 5, 1983, the NRC, with a certain amount of self-congratulatory hoopla, unwrapped its first team of astronauts as if they were a Christmas gift to the nation. Their credentials were impressive even in statistical form: among them, they counted a total of 16 university scientific degrees, including five PhDs and two MDs. Three were accomplished pilots; one was a graduate of the military's advanced flying school. Two had been Olympic-class athletes. All were personable, articulate and for the most part outgoing and friendly. The profiles they presented to the country at the time of their selection looked like this:

Steve MacLean: Ottawa-born MacLean was the youngest of the six; he turned 29 less than two weeks after his selection. (Bondar often calls him "the kid".) He received an undergraduate degree in physics (1977) and a PhD in astrophysics (1983) from York University in Toronto and was, at the time of his selection, a postdoctoral student at Stanford University, doing research on lasers under Nobel Prize-winner Arthur Schawlow — research that would be applicable to the Canadian shuttle experiments contemplated on the space vision system for the Canadarm. MacLean had heard about the search for Canadian astronauts from a friend who called him after reading about it in the press.

MacLean's recreational interests include hiking — in March, 1983, he hiked to the base of Everest — and canoeing, tennis and flying. He also listed gymnastics, but this was far more than just a hobby. He started very late for the sport — he was in Grade 11 before he began training seriously. On one occasion, he competed with one foot in a cast — and had to do the routine several times because he kept tying for first with another competitor. He went on to become a member of the Canadian national gymnastics team for three years and was Canadian university champion in 1976. His goal of reaching the Olympics eluded him, however; he didn't make Canada's three-man team in 1976 and the combination of a bad shoulder and the Olympic boycott put him out of contention in 1980. The experience was frustrating for him, since he had been training four to six hours a day for eight to ten years with this goal in mind, but it says something about MacLean's psychological approach to challenge that he uncompromisingly refuses to make any excuses for not making it to the Olympics. "If you don't make a team, like an Olympic team, it's because you're not good enough," he said. "You have to accept that. You can't go through the rest of your life saying 'Well, I would have if...'" Making the astronaut team was not quite the same thing, he said, because absolute talent wasn't the only requirement; you also had to be the kind of person with the kind of background that was wanted at the time. "You just had to be yourself and hope that that was what they wanted."

Still, making the astronaut team seemed to be a more than adequate substitute for the lost Olympic dream, at least in a psychological sense. MacLean certainly felt he worked as hard to achieve this new goal: "I felt that same enthusiasm, trying to make this team of six, that I felt trying to make the Olympic team. I never got the feeling of what it's like to actually make the Olympic team. When I made the astronaut corps, it felt really good." But it had all happened so quickly that he had little chance at the time to reflect on the fact that a childhood fantasy, long ago rejected as impossible, had come true. He remembers that he was about five years old when he first became aware of the American space program and that, even at that age, he realized that his chances of ever participating were slim because only Americans qualified. From the still-new perspective of his position as one of Canada's first six astronauts, he commented: "It's a fantasy, but you don't think it'll ever come true..."

Bob Thirsk: Thirsk, 30 when he was chosen, was born in New Westminster, B.C., and spent most of his youth in the West. At the time of his selection, he was chief resident in family medicine at Queen Elizabeth Hospital in Montreal. He had detoured into medicine, on his way to a research career in biomedical engineering, after receiving an undergraduate engineering degree from the University of Calgary in 1976 and a masters in mechanical engineering at the Massachusetts Institute of Technology in 1978. He said that he has always been fascinated by the human body as a "marvellous piece of engineering." By 1983, he had received his MD from McGill University and the one-year residency was by way of completing the requirements to become a full-fledged doctor. His discovery of the Canadian astronaut program involved some serendipity; so busy that he hadn't seen a newspaper in weeks, he happened to glance through a paper in the staff lounge one day when he saw a front-page story on the program. This rewrote the script for his life, a script that had originally included "working in a small town with a teaching position in a university and maybe a ... medical practice. I'd rather stay in the astronaut program the rest of my life. If they want me for the next 20 years, I'll stay."

Thirsk has a particular interest in cardiovascular problems associated with space flight because "with my engineering background, I love the pipes and pumps."

Bjarni Tryggvason: Born in Reykjavik, Iceland, Tryggvason moved to Canada with his family when he was eight and became a Canadian citizen seven years later. He grew up in B.C. and received an undergraduate degree in engineering physics from the University of British Columbia in 1972. When he was selected for the astronaut program, he was working as a researcher in aerodynamics at the National Research Council in Ottawa and was also a part-time lecturer at the University of Ottawa. His work at the NRC focussed on the effects of extreme winds on buildings and other large structures, and one of his major projects was an aerodynamic investigation of the wind forces on the Ocean Ranger offshore oil platform after it sank off the coast of Newfoundland in 1981. (He also did wind tunnel tests on Canadian ski jumpers.) While working at the NRC, Tryggvason was also taking a PhD in engineering at the University of Western Ontario, specializing in applied mathematics and aerodynamics.

Tryggvason's recreational interests included karate, skiing and jogging but he has a great passion for flying. He has not only a private pilot's license, but airline transport and instructor's ratings as well. He had thought about becoming an airline pilot, but the intellectual lure of scientific research proved stronger. "When I went to university it was with the idea that that was going to help me get on with Air Canada. When I got through university, I didn't even bother applying to the airline because I liked what I was doing." After he was selected as an astronaut, Tryggvason was asked if he would rather be a pilot-astronaut than a payload specialist. "It would be great to fly the shuttle, but if I had to choose between training as a shuttle pilot and spend 10 or 15 years doing that, or continue on working in the research environment, I'd go with the research. There are more challenges there." But then he admitted, "I'd like to do both. I've always been involved in a whole lot of things at once." Despite the demands of the astronaut job, Tryggvason steadfastly refuses to abandon his flying; in fact, he channelled his energies into instructing the three members of the team (Bob Thirsk, Steve MacLean and Marc Garneau) who did not already have pilot's licenses.

Marc Garneau: Garneau, the only francophone of the group, was born in Quebec City to a French-Canadian father and an English-Canadian mother and he grew up fluently bilingual. Garneau received an undergraduate degree in engineering physics from the Royal Military College in Kingston, Ontario, in 1970. He entered the Canadian Forces planning to make a career as a naval officer. In 1970 he took a leave of absence to obtain his PhD in electrical engineering at the Imperial College of Science and Technology in London, England (1973). While in London, he met and married Jacqueline and then returned to Canada to take up his military duties in Halifax. Garneau's work focussed on shipboard combat systems, including weapons, command and control systems such as radar, sonar, communications and electronic warfare equipment, computers and display systems. He was in charge of the first missile firing trials for Canada's newest warship and later was an instructor in naval weapons systems in the Canadian Forces Fleet School in Halifax. He developed a simulator for training on weapons systems and an aircraft-towed target system for scoring naval gunnery accuracy. At the time of his selection as an astronaut, he had attained the rank of Commander and was based in Ottawa, responsible for approving the designs of all naval communications and electronic warfare equipment and systems. He was seconded to the NRC for the astronaut program but remained in the Canadian Forces until after his first mission.

Garneau's hobbies include jogging, swimming, squash, scuba diving, wine-making and car mechanics and he twice sailed across the Atlantic in a 59-foot yawl with 12 other crewmen — an exercise in getting along with others in close quarters that he found useful while preparing for his shuttle mission.

Ken Money: Money, a Toronto native, was the oldest of the six — he turned 49 a month after being selected — and the one whose previous career was most directly related to his new job as an astronaut. He obtained two undergraduate degrees and a PhD (1961) in physiology from the University of Toronto. That year, he joined the Defence and Civil Institute of Environmental Medicine in Toronto, a research unit of the federal Department of National Defence, where for the next two decades he specialized in research on vestibular (inner ear) physiology. In particular, he investigated problems of motion sickness and disorientation in pilots and astronauts. He contributed to the development of an aircraft instrument called the Malcolm Horizon, which provides orientation information to a pilot's peripheral vision. Starting in 1962, Money collaborated with NASA scientists doing space motion sickness studies and was one of the scientific investigators responsible for the vestibular experiments conducted by astronauts aboard Spacelab missions in 1983 and 1985.[9] He is also a senior researcher at St. Michael's Hospital in Toronto and an associate professor of medicine (physiology) at the University of Toronto.

His long association with the space program put Money in a position to fly aboard the shuttle long before he was selected as a Canadian astronaut, but, ironically, his being a Canadian caused him to lose the opportunity. Money's application to the astronaut program was unique, in one respect; he and Watt proposed to do their own experiments before the astronaut program was even officially launched.

Money is the most accomplished pilot of the six astronauts; he graduated with RCAF Pilot's Wings from the military's advanced flying school in Manitoba in 1957 and had logged about 4000 hours at the time he was selected for the astronaut program. He can fly both jets and helicopters and for many years flew search-and-rescue missions with the Canadian Forces Air Reserve — an activity that provided a grim real-life counterpoint to his academic research since, in many cases, he was searching for pilots who had suffered the worst consequences of disorientation in the air.

Money is also a skilled athlete. He represented Canada as a high jumper at the 1956 Olympics and at the 1958 Commonwealth Games and he is a championship badminton player.

Roberta Bondar: Bondar first heard about the Canadian astronaut program on the radio and the application was on its way almost immediately. Her dream of becoming an astronaut went back to her teenage years in her home town of Sault Ste. Marie, Ontario, when she first heard about NASA's selection program from an aunt who worked for the space agency and would send her posters and mission crests. As a youngster, she made rocket and spacecraft models and plastered her bedroom walls with space posters. She knew she would lack the qualifications then required for the U.S. astronaut program — 1000 hours of jet flying experience (NASA took only test pilots in those days) — and she also wanted to remain a Canadian, so she put the dream on hold at the time and pursued her medical and scientific career instead. But the dream was never entirely abandoned; after becoming an astronaut, she said: "I never watched a NASA launch without wanting to be on board, so when I read the advertisement for Canadian astronauts, it called out loud and clear: 'Roberta Bondar, where are you?' "

Both Bondar and her sister Barbara are academic overachievers — the legacy of parents who actively nurtured their daughters' curiosity about the world. Bondar is the most "degreed" of the astronauts, with an undergraduate degree in zoology/agriculture from Guelph University (1968), a master's degree in experimental pathology from the University of Western Ontario (1971), a PhD in neurobiology from the University of Toronto in 1974 and an MD from McMaster University in 1977. In 1981, she became a member of the Royal College of Physicians and Surgeons of Canada. At the time of her selection as an astronaut, she was an assistant professor of neurology and director of the Multiple Sclerosis clinic at McMaster Medical Centre in Hamilton, doing both clinical work and research. Her research, which focussed on the body's nervous system and inner ear balancing system, especially as it related to the functioning of the eye, had direct application to the Space Adaptation Syndrome Experiment planned for the Canadian shuttle flight.

Bondar was one of the three astronauts who was already a pilot when she was chosen. She got her license in 1968 at the age of 23, and, over the years, was active in several flying organizations, including the Canadian Owners and Pilots Association, the Canadian Society of Aviation Medicine, the Flying Physicians Association and the Flying Ninety-Nines International Women Pilots Association. Her interest in flying extended to her career: she had considered obtaining an advanced degree in aviation medicine. Her other hobbies included canoeing, swimming, fishing, cross-country skiing and target shooting with rifles and handguns.

Initially, the astronauts were on a two-year contract and their responsibilities were limited to carrying out the experiments then scheduled for two shuttle missions. In its approach to selecting the six, the NRC had clearly signalled its intention to lay the foundation for a continuing astronaut program that would enable Canada to respond to future opportunities in space, not only on the shuttle but on the space station. The astronauts, however, had more immediate concerns — trying to cope simultaneously with a gruelling work schedule, a major reorientation of their lives and the need to meet the demands of celebrity. Intellectually, they accepted that their lives had, to a certain extent, become public property. Accepting the idea and coping with the reality are two different things, however; except for Money, none of them had ever before been the target of so much media and public attention.

It rapidly became clear that Canadians felt possessive about these six. In some fundamental sense, they are us. They were viewed as part of the face that Canada presents to the world, symbols of the fact that Canada can play in the big league in space. Rightly or wrongly, their accomplishments would be taken as a measure of Canada's scientific and technological success. There was an important element of national pride involved, because space is one of the comparatively few fields in which Canada has a tradition of scientific and technological success and innovation. In this one field, at least, we felt we had rightful entry to the ranks of the elite — and this is exactly what having our own astronauts represented to us.

NOTES

1. In the movie *The Right Stuff,* a test pilot comments to Chuck Yeager that the astronauts are "just doing what monkeys have done." Yeager pins him with a stare and says: "Monkeys! Do you think a monkey knows he's sitting on top of a rocket that might explode? These astronaut boys, they know that, see? I'll tell you something, it takes a special kind of man to volunteer for a suicide mission, especially when it's on TV."

2. For example, in 1984/85, remote sensing accounted for 32 per cent and communications accounted for 24 per cent of the total Canadian space budget.

3. One possible exception was the Viking mission to Mars — and a large part of its public appeal was the fact that it was designed to search for life on the red planet.

4. By the mid-1980s, the total NASA infrastructure represented a 25-year investment by the U.S. taxpayer that exceeded US$200-billion.

5. In April, 1985, it was revealed that, as early as August, 1979, NASA had sent a letter to John Chapman, former chairman of the government's Interdepartmental Committee on Space, inviting Canadian participation in the astronaut program. However, Chapman died in September and the letter was never acted on.

6. Two years later, Watt had changed his mind about this, saying that he had been naive about the kind of research that was feasible in space. He came around to the view that astronauts did have suitable skills to perform the kinds of experiments possible in space. This is further discussed in Chapter 5.

7. The Sudbury *Star* made the following utterly baffling observation: "Many women are among the applicants for this trip into space but the sorting process has not yet determined if they are all mothers with children at home for the school holidays."

8. The Thirsks went sailing in the Bahamas after the October mission, but "it was still hurricane season at that time," Bob remembered with some chagrin. "When that week was over, Brenda said: 'You owe me another week.' " They signed up for a show tour in London, England. "That went a little bit better."

9. Spacelab is a pressurized module for doing scientific experiments that fits into the cargo bay of the shuttle. It was built by the European Space Agency. Further discussion of Spacelab missions is contained in Chapters 5 and 8.

CHAPTER THREE

Getting Ready to Fly

Early
in 1984,
the astronauts pulled up
the stakes of their former lives
and began settling into
their new routine at the
National Research Council in the
eastern outskirts of Ottawa.
Their office was a modest place,
almost ostentatiously anonymous.
Housed in a squat, nondescript building,
known only as M-60,
it was located in a small room
tucked under a staircase in the back.
It was almost impossible to find; there was no obvious main
entrance to the building and the most direct access was through a
locked staff door at the back. For several months, there was
nothing to identify the office except for the astronaut program
decal pasted on the door's window. As if the six were newly
acquired pieces of high-tech equipment, their work place was
identified on the phone as the "space technology office."

The astronauts shared three tiny offices with face-to-face desks:
Thirsk and MacLean, Money and Tryggvason, Bondar and
Garneau — one medical and one engineering astronaut per team.
Over the coffee machine in the corner was a payment checklist —
even Canada's first six astronauts had to buy their own coffee. It
all seemed like a calculated attempt to keep the hoopla that
dominated their lives away from this room. On home ground, at
least, they were getting down to serious business.

However, even they were unprepared for how fast the business did get very serious indeed. Before they'd had a chance to get fully settled into their new offices, the pattern and the pace of their lives again changed dramatically. In late January, they were called to a meeting in which NRC president Larkin Kerwin informed them that NASA had invited Canada to fly on a shuttle mission in October, 1984, a full year earlier than originally planned. He told them the government had accepted. The astronauts were excited by the news, not so much because the first flight had been moved up — that was a mixed blessing — but because it was an extra flight, another chance for one of them to realize their shared ambition of flying a space mission. It could not help but feed their optimism, evident from the outset, that each of the six would ultimately get his or her chance to fly. "The program has barely begun and already it's expanded," said MacLean exuberantly.

NRC officials had received the invitation more or less out of the blue from senior NASA officials about a week earlier. Not surprisingly, "we didn't give a response immediately because it was such an important decision," said Karl Doetsch, the head of the Canadian astronaut program. "At that time, we didn't even have all our astronauts on board. This was before they were even sitting in their offices learning to be astronauts." Up to that point, his thinking had been firmly fixed on the goal of flying two missions, one in late 1985 and another in early 1986. One mission, dedicated to physiology experiments, was to be flown by one of the three "life sciences" astronauts; the other, to develop the Canadarm's space vision system, was to be flown by one of the three "engineering" astronauts. The offer of a new flight a year early changed all of this and, with typical understatement, Doetsch admits that his first reaction to the idea "was not one of unbridled enthusiasm." As the man who would ultimately be responsible for making it all come together, his first question to himself was: "Can we cope?" It was unquestionably a challenge. U.S. astronauts train for years for a mission and, while the Canadian astronaut would not be trained as extensively, Doetsch had been banking on having 18 months to get the neophyte team ready. Now he would have less than half that time.

Thirsk remembers initially feeling quite fearful. "I was quivering as I was talking to people on the phone. I thought, 'How can we get our act together by October?'"

It wasn't just a question of training the Canadian astronaut from a standing start. There was the matter of preparing a suitable group of scientific experiments — and the equipment necessary to perform them — in time. A flight in October meant delivering equipment to NASA by about August — no trivial task, since everything destined for a shuttle locker, no matter how seemingly simple, had to meet stringent safety and flight-readiness criteria. Doetsch said they had to rely on equipment that already existed or needed only very small modifications. It was decided that a mix of life sciences and engineering tasks would be performed, rather than dedicating the flight to one or the other. Doetsch said they did not want to exclude half the astronauts from qualifying for the flight by virtue of selecting only one set of experiments. In the end, several space science experiments unrelated to the two major experiments were also included in the flight plan. This was intended to increase the perceived scientific value of the mission and take up any slack in the life sciences and SVS experiments that might result from an inability to get equipment ready in time.

The NRC was determined that the mission would not be flown strictly for the PR visibility it offered. If they could not be ready in time or if nothing scientifically worthwhile could be accomplished, "I think we would have given very serious consideration to not going," Doetsch said. Asked whether the astronaut program would nevertheless have benefitted from the publicity, even if little of scientific value would have been accomplished, he said: "You have to ask yourself, 'Is that such a big benefit or not?' " There might be an initial sense of national euphoria about sending a Canadian astronaut into space but, afterwards, he said, there would be questions: " 'What happened on the flight? What did you do?' And if the astronaut says, 'Well, actually, I just had a good view,' I think that would create cynicism, both in the media and amongst the public, which would have a very distinct downside in terms of publicity."

It's not clear that Doetsch's concern on this score was well-founded. Although, in his subsequent cross-country tours, Garneau did discuss his scientific activities aboard the shuttle, his audiences tended to be much more curious about what it was like to eat, sleep and go to the bathroom in space. The media emphasized mostly the quirky, the anecdotal and the personal aspects of the mission. By the time the detailed results of Garneau's shuttle experiments were released at a scientific conference seven months after the flight, the media had lost interest in the mission. Although the scientific findings did receive some attention in science-oriented magazines, they were not widely reported in the general press. In fact, despite their lack of interest in the scientific aspects of the flight, the media continued to disparage it as more a PR exercise than a true scientific mission. For example, one newspaper article six months after the mission stated: "It is quietly acknowledged in Canada's scientific community that the ten experiments Garneau conducted ... were useful but not weighty. Despite the way they are hyped ... few serious observers expect them to push back the frontiers of human knowledge." This demonstrates an ignorance of the nature of scientific research, which is a long drawn-out process, not a series of sudden "breakthroughs." Garneau's scientific work on 41-G was always considered by the scientists associated with the mission to be just a few more steps along the way; none of them was expecting daily cries of "Eureka!" over the air-to-ground loop.

Still, the mission's reputation as a PR exercise was not entirely undeserved. It was clear from the outset that, whatever else the mission accomplished, it would serve as a public showcase for Canada's fledgling astronaut program. It was clear also that, on NASA's part, the offer to Canada was motivated to a significant extent by political factors. The invitation to Canada was virtually coincident with an announcement by President Ronald Reagan that the U.S. would build a permanently manned space station. NASA was already actively trying to marshal international support and co-operative funding for the multi-billion dollar project. (See Chapter 7.) It was, in effect, Canada's turn in the pecking order, because its contribution to the shuttle, in the form of the Canadarm, was second only to the European contribution of Spacelab. A European payload specialist — West German scientist Ulf Merbold — had already flown and a French scientist was scheduled for a flight in early 1985; so, it was suddenly reasoned, Canada should be sandwiched in between if at all possible.

Canadian officials, always cautious when international political sensitivities are involved, were predictably reluctant to speculate on NASA's motives. Pressed on this point, Doetsch noted, correctly, that NASA's scheduling for shuttle flights always involved an extremely complex choreography of manpower, orbiters and customers. Not only were there foreign shuttle customers, such as Canada and Europe, to be considered, but American commercial interests were also clamoring for space aboard the shuttle.

For about a week after receiving NASA's invitation, Canadian space program officials, both in the NRC and in other government departments, operating through the Interdepartmental Committee on Space, debated whether something scientifically useful could be accomplished on the flight. The conclusion was to go for it and Canada was added to the manifest for Mission 51-A (sometimes referred to as 51, eh?), scheduled for launch on October 24, 1984. The astronauts were not consulted about this decision, but Doetsch wasn't seriously worried that they might revolt. "Our major concern wasn't the willingness of the astronauts," he said. "It was more a question of whether they could get everything together in time." Not surprisingly, similar thoughts were occurring to the astronauts. Garneau, for example, remembers thinking: "October. That's *this* year." At the time, perhaps luckily, none of them fully appreciated just how much work was required to prepare themselves and the experiments for the flight. With the perspective gained after completing his mission, Garneau commented with magnificent understatement: "You don't just grab a bunch of hardware and put it in your briefcase and then walk on board."

It fell to Karl Doetsch, as head of the Canadian astronaut program, to revise the training program to suit the new circumstances and to select the first Canadian to fly in space. The NRC's objective was to announce the prime and backup crew members by mid-March. Since it was already mid-February, Doetsch would have less than a month to observe the team at work and it was clear that the choice would have to be based primarily on the knowledge of the six gained during the initial selection process.

In fact, the first real training sessions did not get underway until early March, when the six travelled first to Doug Watt's lab at McGill University in Montreal and then to Ken Money's lab at the Defence and Civil Institute of Environmental Medicine (DCIEM) in Toronto. This marked the start of their research into the various physiological adaptations of the human body to zero gravity. These early exercises began the process of determining their individual susceptibility to motion sickness, taught them how to recognize and record the signs and symptoms of the malady in themselves and others and laid the groundwork for the physiology experiments that would be performed on the shuttle.

At McGill, they rode a prototype of the "space sled," a device invented by Watt that moves back and forth along a track and is designed to test the effects of motion on the body's balancing system in the inner ear. The sled is intended to be flown aboard the shuttle — accompanied, it is hoped, in at least one case by a Canadian astronaut. However, it had not gone through all of NASA's flight-readiness checks and would not be available in time for the October flight.

In Toronto, the astronauts found not one but two diabolical spinning machines that Money had been using for years to induce motion sickness in himself and other test subjects. The lab containing these devices is located in a deep and narrow two-storey room at DCIEM. The entrance, at the top of the room, opens onto a platform from which a catwalk extends along two walls near the roof, overlooking the room below. A narrow ladder-like staircase that hugs a third wall descends from the platform, providing access to the lower level, which is almost completely filled with the two machines and their related control and monitoring equipment. The first device is known as the Precision Angular Mover or PAM; it is an enclosed capsule into which the subject is strapped and then tumbled backward, heels over head, twenty times a minute for up to ten minutes or until symptoms of motion sickness appear. Although the body is being tumbled backwards, most people experience a subjective sensation of being on a ferris wheel and there is a stomach-churning final flourish — a sensation of rapidly flipping upside down, then right side up — when the machine is brought to a halt. The average person lasts about four minutes in the PAM before feeling nauseated. Subjects are asked to count backwards out loud, so the scientists outside can be sure they're all right, and they are also monitored by a camera mounted inside the PAM that projects an image onto a video screen outside.

The second device, known as the coriolis chair, can be even more provocative for people susceptible to motion sickness. It consists of a chair attached to the end of a beam, which is rotated at 30 rpm. While sitting in the chair, often blindfolded, subjects are asked to move their heads up and down. Moving the head up usually causes a sensation of climbing and turning in one direction while moving it down causes a sensation of diving and turning in the other direction. For a short — very short — period of time, it is exhilarating, but it provokes symptoms of motion sickness in nearly everyone in a matter of minutes.

On March 8, 1984, five of the six astronauts faced the PAM for the first time. Ken Money was the only one to be spared; he had invented the machine and had already spent many hours being tumbled and spun in the course of doing his own research. He was present in the lab more as a scientific investigator, helping to run the tests, than as a subject. The others all felt some trepidation. Getting motion sickness goes against all the unwritten tenets of the Right Stuff code and U.S. astronauts are particularly sensitive on the subject because they view anything that even smacks of a medical problem as "career-limiting." The fact that susceptibility to motion sickness is a matter of basic personal physiology over which an individual has little control doesn't make any difference to them; they don't want to talk about it.[1] Motion sickness is psychologically frustrating for such people, because it threatens the fundamental Right Stuff tenet that all situations can and should be brought under control through the judicious application of intelligence, skill, talent and willpower.This attitude is understandable, since their jobs entail precision piloting of the shuttle, performing EVAs, and operating hundreds of millions of dollars worth of high-tech equipment — all of which can be adversely affected by motion sickness.

The Canadian astronauts were in a rather different situation, however. Not only did they not have the same degree of responsibility for the success of a shuttle mission, but studying motion sickness itself was, after all, one of their major objectives. Certainly, within the Canadian program, greater scientific objectivity was brought to the whole subject; in fact, as the astronauts prepared for their PAM runs, Doetsch assured them that these tests would have no bearing on the choice of the first one to fly in space.

Despite these assurances, it was only natural that the astronauts wanted to acquit themselves well in the PAM. Once, early in their training, they got into a spirited debate over whether controlling motion sickness was a matter of motivation and willpower. Garneau, for one, wasn't buying the theory that susceptibility could be explained away as a lack of willpower. As a naval officer, he had known many highly motivated sailors who experienced severe motion sickness; he had experienced it himself at sea. Perhaps it was partly this perspective that made him unusual among astronauts in his willingness to discuss openly his own experiences in the space program. As he progressed in his training, he also seemed able to bring more scientific objectivity to the matter, perhaps because it had not been "career-limiting" — he had, after all, been chosen for a mission. But, facing the PAM for the first time, he gave evidence of some understandable anxiety when he remarked to Money, only half-jokingly, that "I hope you want at least one person who's normal."

An unexpected complication cropped up as the PAM tests were about to begin in the early afternoon. The media had heard about the training session and, immediately after lunch, there had been a brief but largely unsuccessful attempt to appease them with a simple "photo opportunity" in the conference room at DCIEM. The reporters were told the actual PAM tests were off limits, but they were having none of it, demanding access to the lab so they could get some real action shots. They literally overran the lab, taking the astronauts by surprise as they swarmed over the balconies and down the stairs. The lab was soon awash with scribbling reporters and TV camera crews lugging equipment, all talking at once, jostling for position in the tight quarters and trying to elbow others out. Someone hit the nozzle of a tank hanging on the wall and the hissing noise of escaping oxygen briefly startled everyone in the room. It was all very reminiscent of a scene in the movie *The Right Stuff*, in which reporters swarm over fences to get at astronauts and their families. Referring to that scene, one journalist who was watching the mêlée in the lab muttered ruefully: "I tell people things like that don't happen in real life." A bemused Karl Doetsch just shook his head.

This was not the first time the Canadian astronauts had been subjected to pack journalism, but it was the first time it had happened without any advance warning and in such an uncontrolled fashion. They had barely begun to adjust to having cameras and microphones poked in their noses at every turn and they visibly shrank back from the tidal wave that engulfed them. The fact that the room was not suitable for such a mob scene made everyone nervous; it was far too small and full of moving machinery that made the situation potentially dangerous.

The five who were to be tumbled in the PAM were not particularly happy about having their first potential encounter with motion sickness in the line of duty captured by TV cameras. At NASA, such a scene would be unthinkable — a blatant violation of the medical privacy of the astronauts, which is protected by law. Caught off guard, NRC officials agreed to allow the press to stay for the run of one astronaut in the PAM and then they had to go. The five then pondered who would go first; with a philosophical shrug, Steve MacLean stepped forward. When he emerged ten minutes later, he was sweating slightly and said he felt "a bit high," but he'd obviously weathered the run very well. Money remarked that it was unusual for anyone to last the full ten minutes.

The room was then cleared of the media. The astronauts became a little less tense and even began to joke with each other, but there was still a palpable unease in the room as they awaited their turn in the PAM. This seemed to be the result of uncertainty more than anything else, for once the PAM became a known quantity, each astronaut visibly relaxed. At one point, MacLean sat down beside Bondar, who was still waiting, and rubbed her cheek, saying: "It isn't so bad." When they opened the hatch on Thirsk, he smiled and mimicked tail gunner motions at Bondar and Tryggvason, who were facing him.

During her run, Bondar had some difficulty with the backward counting. At one point, losing track of the number, she muttered "shit" and picked up the count, unaware that a film crew making a movie for CBC was recording her run. She later requested that the expletive be edited from the show. This was not done because she was worried about her image, she said. "We've all said some swear words one time or another." She objected more because she had not been aware that her PAM run was being filmed.

Garneau was the last to enter the PAM and he did call a halt before the full ten minutes were up. Initially, he felt upset over this and "for a very short time, I thought, this is going to can it for me." But, in the end, he accepted the fact that he was physiologically susceptible and there was nothing he could do about it. He'd tried his best, "but this thing is stronger than me and that's all there is to it." He admitted that, at the time, he was "secretly glad that the press wasn't there" but after a while, this no longer bothered him because he felt he had in his own mind overcome any stigma attached to the situation.

None of the five threw up during the PAM tests — "They're all tigers," Money laughed — but, as expected, they all experienced the more moderate symptoms of motion sickness, such as sweating, dizziness, stomach awareness or skin pallor. This was the first of many sessions in the PAM, during which the astronauts would learn to recognize and assess the symptoms of motion sickness in themselves and others.

On their second training day at DCIEM, the astronauts were treated to another dubious pleasure — a "run" in the high altitude chamber, an air-tight compartment that simulates the decrease in atmospheric pressure with altitude. These chambers are generally used to train military jet pilots to cope with life-threatening physiological hazards that can occur at high altitudes if an aircraft loses pressurization. In an unpressurized plane without oxygen, a pilot's time of useful consciousness drops rapidly with altitude; it is one to two minutes at 30,000 feet and only 15 to 20 seconds at 40,000 feet. Astronauts are required to take the chamber tests because their training involves flights in high-flying aircraft and the KC-135, NASA's zero-gravity training plane. Most non-U.S. payload specialists do their chamber work at the Johnson Space Center, but Money had long ago obtained NASA approval for the DCIEM facility and thus the Canadian astronauts could satisfy their high-altitude training requirements at home.

Before going into the chamber, the astronauts were briefed on the proper use of oxygen masks and the signs and symptoms of hypoxia (insufficient oxygen). The range of possible symptoms is very large — including headache, fatigue, nausea, tingling or numbness, dizziness, apprehension, hot or cold flashes, euphoria, tunnel vision and blurred vision — but each person usually and characteristically experiences only a few. The purpose of the chamber test was to enable the astronauts to identify and recognize their own unique symptoms. In one test, they were taken off the oxygen masks at the equivalent of 25,000 feet and asked to draw a series of simple figures on a piece of paper. As soon as they started to experience symptoms of hypoxia — accompanied by a deterioration in their ability to draw the figures — they were to go back on oxygen. Afterwards, they were asked to identify their symptoms and told to remember them, because this would be their consistent reaction to hypoxia in the future.

The most dramatic moment in the chamber occurred during a simulation of explosive decompression (a very sudden loss of pressurization), a test designed to teach the astronauts the proper oxygen mask procedure in such a situation. In a pressurized aircraft, the atmospheric pressure on the body is maintained at a level close to that on the ground. If pressurization is lost, the body is rapidly exposed to the lower pressure that exists at whatever altitude the plane is flying; the higher the altitude, the greater the change in pressure and the more urgent the need for emergency oxygen. During the chamber run, the drop from ground-level pressure to 10,000-foot-level pressure occurred in just half a second; it was accompanied by a loud thumping noise and a noticeable drop in temperature, and the chamber was instantly enveloped in fog, resulting from the condensation of moisture in the air. Although everyone had been briefed on what to expect, they still jumped involuntarily when it happened.[2]

During these early days in their training program, the astronauts developed a very strong sense of camaraderie and mutual preservation. At times they gave the impression of having drawn their wagons in a circle. They were not unfriendly to outsiders, but their interactions with the outside world were increasingly guarded. This wariness was most in evidence when dealing with the media and least so when they were surrounded at public appearances by the inevitable hordes of children seeking autographs and bombarding them with non-stop and often very knowledgeable questions.

From the moment they were chosen as astronauts, the six were overwhelmed by a rapidly accelerating demand for public appearances and interviews. Informing the public about the space program was a responsibility they took seriously, but the sheer volume of requests quickly outstripped their ability to accommodate the demand. Some of them also were concerned that their families and friends were being swept up in the media dragnet. This was a period of adjustment for all the families. The NRC had told the astronauts that their public responsibilities did not extend to their spouses, children and friends and many preferred to stay out of the limelight. Thirsk said his wife Brenda often travelled with him on his public speaking engagements to lend moral support, but had "zero involvement with the media, at her own request." Money advised both his wife and daughter "not to be bothered because they can't benefit from it and they might get hurt by it. But they'll make their own decisions; so far, they've decided to stay out of it." He admitted, however, that if he was chosen for a shuttle flight, they probably wouldn't have much choice. This was the case with Garneau's family; after he was selected for his mission, the NRC public affairs people told him it was becoming impossible to fend off press demands for access to his wife and children. "Eventually, they'll break down the door," he was told. Accepting the inevitable, he tried to prepare his wife by easing her onto the interview treadmill gently. He was glad, however, that "my weekends and evenings at home are very normal. I am very glad that nobody's making a fuss in the neighborhood where I live and that my wife and I can still live a normal life. I live in a neighborhood where people know me and respect my privacy and treat me the way they treated me a year ago." Asked how his children's friends reacted to his new celebrity, he commented: "They don't come in and stare at me."

Bondar also found it difficult to shield her family, friends and professional colleagues because of the unique media interest in her as a role model for women. Her parents, she said, were not used to dealing with the media and were often asked questions that made them uncomfortable — questions, for example, about her personal life or about her feelings. She also found it difficult to deal with requests that came through the unofficial channel of her parents, rather than through the approved route of the NRC's public affairs office. People would call her mother to ask if she could get "Bobbie" to make an appearance. "My mother would ... be spending money on long-distance phone calls telling me what these people wanted. And I'd say, 'Mother, they'll have to go the appropriate route.' My mother's caught in the middle, but now she's dealing with it."

Inevitably, their celebrity status left the astronauts open to quirky demonstrations of attention. MacLean, one of the two astronauts who were then bachelors, received a few marriage proposals. Bondar said they were getting letters suggesting everything from unusual motion sickness cures ("a drop of vinegar in the ear") to sex experiments in space. She also had some early problems with "peculiar" phone calls, not exactly crank calls but disturbing nonetheless — "calls from people I don't know, wanting to know where I live so they can write me a card, or wanting to know if I knew so-and-so and could they come over and talk to me." The calls were not overtly threatening but she found them an invasion of her privacy and, after being selected for the astronaut corps, she decided to get an unlisted number.

It is not surprising that the astronauts sometimes felt the need to distance themselves from the unceasing demands of this world and, during these early days, they seemed to feel they could find a special kind of emotional support only among themselves, because no one else they knew had experienced what they were experiencing. (At this stage, they had little day-to-day contact with the U.S. astronauts.) Asked whether they sometimes felt they had a large world to fend off, Garneau reflected: "People naturally tend to form strong bonds when they're united by a common purpose and an unusual job. We sort of seek comfort and refuge amongst ourselves."

Early in their tenure a plan was hatched among the three non-flying astronauts — Garneau, MacLean and Thirsk — to get their pilot's licenses. Tryggvason, who continued to make time for flying despite the demands of his astronaut duties, agreed to be the instructor. Before long, the four had purchased a Cessna 172 and formed their own small flying club; Bondar, who was already a licensed pilot, later also bought a share of the plane. In part, this appeared to be another way of cementing the bonds within the group, but there was more to it than that — it seemed to be partly a matter of image as well. Even though the job of the Canadian astronauts did not call for piloting skills per se, there still seemed to be a sense that it was *de rigueur* to be a pilot, even if only of a Cessna 172 — that it some how made one more truly a member of this rather exclusive club to which they now belonged. Tryggvason suggested that the interest in flying was basically a manifestation of a personality trait characteristic of people who become astronauts — a desire to test themselves in demanding circumstances.

In the spring of 1984, with snow still on the ground, they took to the air — only to be overrun almost immediately by the demands of preparing for the October mission. In fact, none of the three even soloed until more than a year later and Garneau may well have been the first pilot-trainee anywhere to enter space shuttle flight time in his log book before his first solo in a Cessna 172.

As the March deadline for the announcement of the first astronaut to fly approached, each of the six weighed the personal pros and cons of taking the first flight as opposed to opting for one of the later ones. Doetsch had told them that being selected to fly the first mission would not reduce anyone's chances for a subsequent flight. He had also said that a request *not* to be considered for the first flight wouldn't prejudice eligibility for a later mission.

However, although the astronauts had come into the program believing they would be working primarily on either the physiology or engineering experiments, none of them was about to ask to be left out of contention for the October flight, even though it would not be dedicated exclusively to either set of experiments, as had originally been planned. It had the virtually irresistible attraction of being the proverbial "bird in the hand." There were no guarantees who would be chosen for the two later flights, or whether there would be any subsequent flights, so, predictably, no one was prepared to run the risk of not flying at all.

The six knew that the regular weekly staff meeting scheduled for the afternoon of March 13, 1984, wouldn't be an ordinary meeting. Doetsch had told them he would announce the names of the prime and backup crew members chosen for the October flight; however, surmising that little work would get done *after* he made his announcement, he informed them when they walked into the small conference room in the astronaut office that they would first attend to business as usual. They were able to turn their attention to the issues at hand for the next hour, although not entirely undistractedly. "I don't know how many people paid attention to what was going on during the meeting. It was hard," said Garneau, who found the waiting this time just as nerve-wracking as it had been when he'd been in the original competition to get into the astronaut program.

Finally, the moment arrived. With little preamble or embellishment — "I won't beat around the bush on this one" — Doetsch told them that Garneau had been selected, with Thirsk as backup. A round of handshakes and the breaking out of champagne followed in rapid succession and then the six were given a briefing by Wally Cherwinski of the NRC's public affairs office on the type of questions they could expect during the press conference the next day — "Is this the culmination of a personal dream? Is it something you were looking forward to doing for Canada? What does it mean to the Canadian astronaut program?" Cherwinski did not tell the astronauts what their answers should be, but they were given a written summary of potential questions and possible responses. The fact that this briefing so accurately anticipated the next day's queries said much about the predictability of the media.[3]

Garneau decided to break the news to his wife in person rather than phoning her. Jacquie, who said she'd spent much of the afternoon "wandering around in circles," not entirely sure what she was feeling, rushed out the door when she heard his car pull up in the driveway. He teased her for a moment, saying that he hadn't made it, then cheerfully announced: "I did it, I'm going."

"Her face dropped — she went into shock," Garneau said later. "It's a very big emotional adjustment to make. It complicates life and there's an element of worry. So the two of us were really quite silent for a while. Then the conversation resumed and she sort of sighed a few times and started to focus on the reality of the situation."

"I can't pretend that I'm not a little anxious," Jacquie remarked at the time. "I think there isn't a wife in the world who wouldn't be a bit anxious with her husband going off into space, but I try not to think of that side of it. You've got to think positive, otherwise it's just too mind-boggling."

That night, the six astronauts went out for a lavish meal together and presented the bill to Garneau, starting a tradition they hoped would eventually be repeated for each of them. They picked one of Ottawa's more expensive restaurants, but in the end tried to have mercy on Garneau's wallet when they saw the prices. As MacLean said, "Most of us just had the entrée." This was one of Garneau's duties for which Thirsk was not required to provide backup. "There are going to be six flights," MacLean said confidently. "Bob will get his turn." In many ways, the dinner served to reinforce the cohesiveness of the team at a time when two of their number had been singled out for special duties and would soon, to some extent, be following a different path. It was a reaffirmation that they were "still a group … still working for the same thing," Bondar said.

Money said that he believed social interaction was particularly important at this pivotal stage. "We knew that after the announcement, we would have certain adjustments to make in our own minds and that we should get together and be actively social — become comfortable with the new situation. There will be subtle changes in our relationships."

Garneau's selection was announced to the Canadian media the next day, March 14, by then science minister Donald Johnston during a press conference at the National Press Building in downtown Ottawa. In fluent English and French, Garneau told the assembled media that he was thrilled, excited and "deeply honored" to be chosen as the first Canadian to fly in space. It was "a dream come true" and he felt like "the luckiest person in Canada today." The mission would be "an incredible challenge," but he was looking forward to the fun of being in weightlessness and seeing the earth from space. He also defended the scientific usefulness of the mission, saying that his mission was not a token gesture from NASA. "I could understand that [feeling] if a Canadian was only going up there to push a button every two or three days. That definitely isn't the case."

Garneau was asked about his family's reaction. His kids, he said, didn't know much about the space program yet, but they knew the shuttle is launched from Florida and this seemed to them like a good chance to get to Disney World. As for his wife, he admitted he hadn't yet entirely convinced her about his safety, but said: "She's as happy as I am that I've been chosen and she is behind me 100 per cent." The matter of safety seemed to be very much on everyone's mind; Garneau's comment that a shuttle flight would be less hazardous than a flight on a commercial airliner was prominently featured in the news stories and headlines the next day.

It was clear that Garneau had fulfilled the image of a national hero more than adequately as far as the national media were concerned.[4] The news reports contained glowing references to his personal style; *Maclean's* magazine, for example, described him as "articulate and charming, with a gentle self-mocking humor in both official languages."

Bob Thirsk was also on stage during the press conference, playing the bridesmaid-like role that is the fate of backup astronauts. It is always a little difficult; honesty compels an admission of some disappointment, but, at the same time, there is an unwritten rule that astronauts must adhere in public to their own variant of the Three Musketeers code. It is one of the paradoxes of the astronaut game that people selected in part for the commitment to excellence and achievement that comes from personal ambition are nevertheless expected to be — and to *appear* to be — self-effacing team players. Thirsk fulfilled the requirement gracefully and, in the process, managed to provide some unique imagery on the role of the backup. His reaction, he said, "was similar to the feeling when you go to a movie and it's an exciting movie but you have to leave ten minutes before the end." Later, Thirsk did express some concern about the impact of his demanding training schedule on the first year of his marriage, but he said his wife of two months was very supportive.

The media were on the alert for evidence of crushing disappointment on the part of the rest of the team, but they were left to remark on the absence of it. One report described the four "passed-over" astronauts as looking "more like overjoyed relatives than jealous co-workers ... The six seem to radiate an energy that rubs off on everything they do." MacLean told one reporter: "The excitement overrides any disappointment. We're already a team; we complement each other perfectly." This was not just window-dressing for the press; nor was it at all inconsistent with their personal ambition to fly in space. A certain disappointment at not being chosen was natural, but they knew that the long-term survival of the astronaut program — and the hope for more Canadian flights beyond the three already committed — rested to a great extent on the success of the first mission. That, in turn, called for solid teamwork. "I'd like to be the first one up there [but] I want more than anything to see the whole thing work," Tryggvason said. "I think it's far more important that this whole astronaut program is a success. That has to come first." MacLean, who said he had always been "impressed with the guys on the ground who put it all together and made it work," expressed similar sentiments. "You want the best for the space program and that's not necessarily the best for the individual." For Money, it was the third opportunity gone, but he said it was in some ways the "easiest failure to take of the three — partly because there's still another chance and because the selection was done in a reasonable, rational, fair way and I had a part in it. The other ones seemed to be so out of my control."

Why Garneau was chosen over the others was not revealed by the NRC. As usual, Doetsch kept his own counsel, steadfastly refusing to be drawn into a discussion of the subject by speculation about the role played by non-professional factors, particularly bilingualism. The policy from the outset had been that the astronaut corps as a whole would have facility in both official languages, but individual bilingualism was "not mandatory," Doetsch said. "But it's an ability that can be used so we don't ignore it either. It's one of the things that we put into the mix." Still, Garneau's effortless bilingualism, unique among the six, was clearly an asset, both for practical and symbolic reasons — there were, after all, going to be a lot of speaking engagements in Quebec. Several of the others started taking French lessons soon after joining the astronaut corps.

At the press conference, Garneau admitted that his situation "hasn't quite sunk in yet" and for a while during the early days of his training, he often felt like it was all a dream. "Sometimes I feel a physical sensation akin to lightheadedness," he remarked at the time. "I think someone who wins millions of dollars must have that same sort of feeling — how could this really have happened to me?" He also found himself being more careful — driving with greater than normal caution, for example — because he wanted to ensure that nothing "silly or trivial" would prevent him from going on the mission.

With time so short, Garneau was plunged immediately into the most demanding work schedule of his life. The training program had two parallel components — preparing Garneau for the mission and getting the equipment he needed for his experiments through NASA's labyrinthine approval process. The latter job fell to Bruce Aikenhead, program manager of the Canadian astronaut office, who was responsible for ensuring that the equipment met NASA's safety requirements, that it would fit in the mid-deck locker allotted to it and that it was delivered to NASA on time. These were not trivial problems. NASA's safety standards for anything that goes aboard the shuttle are extremely stringent — for example, even paints and dyes must be approved to ensure they will not release toxic gases into the closed environmental system of the shuttle. It takes a long time and many NASA reviews to get new equipment accepted as "space-ready," so the Canadian experiments for the most part had to employ materials that had already passed muster. Locker space in the mid-deck is at a premium and the Canadian equipment — amounting to more than 30 items, including some delicate scientific instruments — had to be crammed into a container not much larger than the proverbial breadbox *and* packaged in a way that would keep it safe through the launch and the return to earth. Finally, everything had to be delivered to the Johnson Space Center by August, so it could be approved and sent to the Kennedy Space Center to be stowed in the crew compartment before Challenger was rolled out to the launch pad.

Meanwhile, there was the matter of Garneau's training. Garneau was one of the first foreign payload specialists to go through the NASA mill and the first to attempt the task of getting "space-ready" in about seven months. Only one non-American payload specialist had flown before Garneau — West German Ulf

Merbold. When Merbold flew aboard the STS-9/Spacelab 1 mission in November, 1983, he had been in the shuttle program for nearly five years and had spent nearly two years on mission-related training at NASA.[5] But many more payload specialists were coming down the line, not only from other countries, but also from private industry in the United States, so by the time Garneau appeared on the scene, NASA was already trying to come to grips with the problem of streamlining payload specialist training. Garneau became a test case.

During the early part of his training, Garneau concentrated on his own experiments and had relatively little contact with NASA. During the first six months, there were a few visits to NASA centres, but most of the work was done in Toronto, Montreal and Ottawa with the principal investigators in charge of the scientific experiments Garneau would do aboard the shuttle. Initially, all six of the astronauts trained together. They all continued to experience the joys of riding the PAM and the coriolis chair at DCIEM, and there were many other tests as well, including one in which they were lowered into a water tank blindfolded and strapped down to get used to the sensation of moving their arms in zero gravity.

Relentless in his pursuit of new motion sickness tests, Money had the team lurching about wearing special eyeglasses. One set had very thick lenses that, when used in combination with custom-designed contact lenses, made everything appear 40 per cent larger than normal. The test involved wearing the glasses while walking a figure-eight pattern and bobbing the head up and down at various times. The second set were reversing prism glasses that made everything appear upside down. "This is what happens when you work an astronaut too hard," Bob Thirsk would quip while showing a film of them bobbing their heads up and down and bumping into walls while wearing the glasses. The image never failed to draw a big laugh from audiences, but the tests did have a serious purpose — Money hoped they might be useful in forecasting individual susceptibility to motion sickness in space.

Training for other aspects of the Space Adaptation Syndrome Experiment was done in the McGill University lab of principal investigator Doug Watt. There the astronauts practiced and refined the procedures for the various SASSE tests — vestibular-ocular reflex, sensory function in limbs, awareness of the position of external objects and proprioceptive illusions. (See Chapter 5.) It was also important to test the devices that were to be used in space. Sometimes very subtle things could skew the scientific results. For example, several of the astronauts felt that uneven numbering on the cloth strips used in two of the experiments caused their eyes to be drawn to the larger numbers. The problem was corrected by ensuring that uniform numbers were marked on the cloth strips that would go into Garneau's space shuttle equipment locker. Most of the equipment for the SASSE experiments was simple — a pen-sized flashlight, a headband, two cloth strips with numbers on them, a blindfold, a ridged metal cube, a small mirror, a tape recorder and the checklist — but it all had to meet NASA's safety standards.

All of the astronauts participated in this training and during the early stages there were spirited discussions on a wide range of scientific topics related to the experiments — such as how the eye tracks objects, what effect free fall has on the vestibular system, whether different types of head movements have different effects on motion sickness and so on. The ambience was very different from that during the first training session in Toronto. For one thing, there were no media around. For another, there were no large, spinning machines, although Watt's lab was dominated by a rack and harness device used for suspending subjects a few inches from the ground and dropping them. With the astronauts sitting in a circle on plastic chairs or a counter top in one corner of the small lab, the scene resembled an academic seminar more than an astronaut training session. The circumstances were perhaps the most purely research-oriented they'd been in since becoming astronauts and they seemed to relish the opportunity to get down to scientific brass tacks. "They're all basically university type people and it was a nice chance to get back into the university environment and ... knock around some ideas," Watt said. He said the extra mission was "a real godsend — scientifically, a marvellous opportunity" because Garneau could perform some useful preliminary experiments that would enable Watt to further refine the more formal space adaptation experiments scheduled for the later flight. It was also an opportunity to explore some fascinating but unexpected results from the Spacelab 1 mission, which had flown the previous December. (Both Watt and Money had been involved as scientific investigators on the physiology experiments done on that mission.) Watt still believed that a physiology expert should be flying the mission but he was impressed with Garneau's dedication to learning the ropes and said after the mission that Garneau had done a superb job.

All six astronauts were initially involved in the tests, but with a tight deadline bearing down on them, the work in Watt's lab rapidly focussed on honing Garneau's (and Thirsk's) expertise. They went through the experimental procedures — known as *protocols* — time and time again; the scientific validity of the experiments depended on Garneau's knowing and meticulously following the protocols during his mission and it was particularly important that he perform the tests properly early in the flight, when he might be suffering from motion sickness.

The SASSE tests appeared, on the surface, to be very simple and even a bit strange — for example, the test that required Garneau to press his bare toe to a ridged metal cube often drew quizzical reactions — but they were carefully designed to test some rather complex and subtle aspects of the human body's nervous system and its ability to adjust to zero gravity. Garneau said the experiments were necessarily kept simple because of the limited time for training and the cramped quarters aboard the shuttle, but he accorded them the highest praise a scientist gives to experimental procedures — they were "elegant."

With his long experience in the space program, Watt was one of the most knowledgeable Canadian scientists when it came to preparing for a space mission; in fact, he and Money were uniquely qualified in Canada to prepare astronauts to do experiments aboard the space shuttle. So, as the work on the SASSE experiments progressed, Watt knew better than most just how much had to be done before October. One of his major responsibilities was to ensure that the protocols were realistic, given the time and space constraints aboard the shuttle and, of course, the zero-gravity factor. His previous experience working with astronauts on space missions and testing them on the KC-135 helped him anticipate potential problems. During one test in the McGill lab, Garneau needed both hands for a task and dropped his notepad and pencil on the floor. It was a perfectly natural move — on earth — and no one even noticed. No one except Watt.

"They've floated off," he pointed out laconically.

Garneau and Thirsk also had similar training sessions with the other principal investigators, both to gain an understanding of their experiments and to learn to use the equipment needed to collect data. Much of this data collection involved photography; Garneau would be using a 35mm camera with special filters to take pictures of the orbiter's reddish glow, the earth's atmospheric glow at night and the southern aurora. He would also photograph small strips of advanced composite materials that would be placed on the Canadarm to test the degrading effects of the space environment. For the preliminary tests of the space vision system, he had to learn to use the shuttle's closed circuit TV cameras in order to film targets (black dots) placed on a satellite released from the shuttle's cargo bay. Finally, Garneau also had to learn to take measurements with the sun photometer, an instrument used for atmospheric and pollution studies, and to record data on a small portable computer.

The short time available before the flight precluded putting SVS hardware aboard the shuttle, but it was necessary to provide Garneau with targets to photograph outside the shuttle so he could record the data to be relayed to the ground-based SVS unit in Houston. NASA vetoed the idea of putting a special targetted payload in the shuttle cargo bay, but offered instead to allow the four 15-centimetre black painted circles to be placed on the solar panels of the Earth Radiation Budget Satellite (ERBS), which was to be deployed during the mission. As part of his responsibilities for the mission, Steve MacLean worked on the development of the targets and acted as liaison with the ERBS project managers and, when the time came, pasted the black circles onto the satellite's solar panels himself.

As Garneau and Thirsk rehearsed the experiment protocols time and time again, the scientific investigators and the other astronauts worked with them to fine-tune the checklists, the step-by-step set of procedures that Garneau would take aboard the shuttle. Like everything else on a space mission, the checklists had to be as streamlined and compact as possible, yet still very detailed. Developing a workable checklist can take many trial runs of the protocols, said Bjarni Tryggvason, who had responsibility for putting together the final lists for all the experiments. It's critical that no steps are left out, that everything is in the right order and that enough time has been allotted for the performance of each task. Tryggvason said that the timing can be difficult to pin down accurately beforehand, because it tends to take longer to do things in zero gravity than it does on earth. Garneau was expected to have complete checklists for all his experiments in hand by the time he and Thirsk left for the Johnson Space Center in August. NASA would then print the flight versions of the lists on special fire-resistant paper before allowing them on the shuttle.

While all of this was going on, the astronauts were also carrying a heavy reading and study load. In preparation for their public appearances, they were expected to become familiar with all past, present and projected Canadian space activities. They also branched out from their own scientific specialties, attending lectures and seminars on a wide range of space-related topics, including astronomy, space mechanics, communications satellites, earth physics and space medicine. During a visit to the Toronto plant of Spar Aerospace, they had an opportunity to try the computer simulator used to train American astronauts to operate the Canadarm. Although operating the arm was not at that time a job open to Canadian astronauts, it was important for them to have a thorough understanding of it; the SVS experiment, in particular, would require one of the Canadian astronauts to work closely with a NASA mission specialist operating the arm on a shuttle mission.

At the same time, the astronauts continued their demanding schedule of public appearances, although Garneau and Thirsk were increasingly relieved of their PR responsibilities and the other four picked up the slack. Throughout the early spring, they crossed the country, not only telling people about the astronaut program and the shuttle experiments, but trying to inspire them with visions of the future — life aboard the space station, bases on the moon, voyages to Mars. For Garneau, one of the most memorable of these events occurred at the Ontario Place Cinesphere theatre in Toronto in early May. The occasion was a special showing of the first film from space taken with the 70mm IMAX camera invented by Toronto-based Imax Systems Corp. The large format system produces a film frame ten times larger than a normal 35mm camera; the resulting images, which are shown on giant screens six storeys high, are breathtakingly colorful and clear. With the co-operation of NASA and funding from the Smithsonian Institution and Lockheed Corp., IMAX was producing a film about the shuttle called *The Dream Is Alive*. The company had received permission to put cameras on board three shuttle flights in 1984 and was training the crews of those flights as amateur cinematographers.

The footage shown in early May, which had been shot by the crew of mission 41-C only a month before, was unedited and without a sound track. Showing film in raw form was not common practice, said IMAX president Graeme Ferguson, but the images were so spectacular that they could not resist sharing them immediately. Many astronauts who have seen IMAX films say they are the next best thing to being there. For most of the nearly 800 people invited to the special screening, the images were as close to "being there" as they'll ever come. But for Garneau, the pictures were an awesome preview of a reality that would overtake him less than six months hence. Even so, the demands of his experiments were never far from his mind; while he was absorbing the emotional impact of the film, the analytical part of his mind was assessing the lighting conditions in space so critical to the space vision system experiment.

Given the extremely tight deadline for the first Canadian mission, the question of integrating Garneau and Thirsk into the NASA training system became a matter of concern almost immediately. They would not have the luxury of several years of preparation and training, as the European payload specialists had enjoyed, so it was a whole new ball game, for the Canadians and for NASA. Initially, NASA planned to have the Canadian astronauts take up full-time residence at the Johnson Space Center four months before flight, but Doetsch and the Canadian scientific investigators resisted this. They would have little enough time to train the astronauts to do the scientific experiments as it was. A compromise was struck that would later establish the pattern for payload specialist training: Garneau and Thirsk were allowed to do a lot of the reading and studying required by NASA in Canada. Soon the Canadian astronauts were poring over NASA's technical workbooks on space shuttle systems and listening to videotaped lectures on safety requirements at the Kennedy Space Center launch site. These tapes, which contained information about such things as fire-fighting, electric shock, toxic propellants and evacuation of the shuttle, were intended to prepare them for more intensive training at the launch site later on. They also completed some of NASA's medical requirements in Canada, including CPR and first aid training and being checked out in the high altitude chamber. "This allowed us the flexibility to keep them involved in our own experiments," Doetsch said.

The job of delivering the right bodies to the right place at the right time fell to Bernard Poirier, who was in charge of co-ordination and logistics for the Canadian astronaut program office. In early 1984, this was not the world's easiest job. Throughout the spring and summer, he was grappling with schedules that were constantly changing, not only because of the need to pull the Canadian scientific experiments together in an extremely tight time frame, but, even more importantly, because of a highly fluid situation at NASA. Shuttle flights and crews were repeatedly being juggled and changed — one mission was cancelled outright — and in the middle of this, NASA was trying to decide itself how to cope with training a new payload specialist who had less than eight months to prepare for his flight.

During the early part of the training program, the Canadian astronauts made periodic trips to JSC and KSC. The first, in April, was more of a familiarization visit than a true training trip, but all six of the Canadian astronauts toured the training facilities for the first time — Mission Control, the shuttle simulators, and the one-gravity trainer, a full-size mockup of the shuttle crew compartment used for "dress rehearsals" of the mission. They were also able to watch U.S. astronauts training for the Solar Max mission, the first rescue and repair of a disabled satellite in space. (See Chapter 6.) Bob Crippen was the commander of that mission, and meeting him for the first time was a highlight of the trip for the Canadian astronauts. (No one knew then that Crippen would end up being Garneau's commander.) At KSC, the Canadian astronauts were able to observe behind-the-scenes preparations for a shuttle mission and to visit the giant Vehicle Assembly Building and the launch pad. This visit was particularly instructive because KSC was bustling with preparations for an imminent launch. Except for Money, none of the Canadian astronauts had other than a normal layman's knowledge of how NASA worked, so this visit represented an important first step in integrating them into the NASA system, according to Doetsch. "The time spent there with the hardware reduced very significantly the time needed to be spent on books," he said. Garneau concurred: "To me, that week probably was worth more than 20 weeks of classroom study."

These early trips also enabled them to accomplish some important preliminaries of fitting into NASA's system. Garneau and Thirsk received special badges permitting them to come and go with relative freedom throughout the campus-like Johnson Space Center. Security has been increased at JSC in recent years, primarily because of the increasing involvement of the military in the shuttle program, and access to many facilities, particularly Mission Control and the shuttle mission simulators, is limited. Even badged payload specialists required escorts to some highly restricted facilities. Badging involved the inevitable paperwork, including, in the case of foreign nationals, a letter from their embassy confirming that they were in fact who they purported to be and that they were not a security risk.

During these early visits, Garneau and Thirsk were also fitted for clothing. They selected their in-flight wardrobe (flight suit, pants, shorts, T-shirts, etc.) and were fitted for their G-suits, the pressure garment used to protect against possible faintness or blacking out during re-entry. They were also measured for helmets, which must be custom-fitted so that the padding will provide a secure air-tight seal. They were also zipped inside a ball made of the same material as the space suits, which would be used to transport astronauts from a disabled shuttle to another craft in case of an emergency. (Each shuttle carries space suits for only two astronauts, who would be able to carry the other crew members in the rescue balls from one vehicle to another.) Garneau and Thirsk each sat quietly inside the rescue ball for about 15 minutes while their heart rate was monitored. This was a test for claustrophobia or a panic reaction to enclosed spaces. "They just want to make sure you don't get uptight," said Thirsk. Sitting in a cross-legged yoga position inside the ball, he found he was drifting toward sleep. "Your mind starts to wander. They don't tell you how long you're going to be in there and you're getting bored right away because you just have the walls of the rescue sphere to look at."

The two also received NASA physicals and a two-hour psychiatric examination by a NASA doctor who had been evaluating pilots and astronauts for more than two decades. NASA payload specialist co-ordinator Lynn Collins said the objective of this examination is crew compatibility. "He is basically looking to see if you are not too introverted, if you're capable of working as part of a team and how you're likely to react under stress," Garneau said. "They want to know what kind of a person you are." He was asked about his background and then presented with a series of "what if" scenarios and asked how he would react. Garneau said there were some questions that did give him pause. "He asks you questions like: 'Tell me, how do you like the furniture in your house?' And you're sitting there thinking, if I answer this, he'll think I'm this type…"

During their early visits to JSC, Garneau and Thirsk also met some of the NASA astronauts, including those with whom they'd be working. Initially, they were introduced to astronaut Daniel Brandenstein, who was then scheduled to be the commander of Garneau's mission. However, throughout the middle of 1984, the shuttle mission schedule was in such a state of flux that crew assignments kept changing and ultimately Garneau was reassigned to a crew led by Bob Crippen. Lynn Collins said that, before things settled down that summer, Brandenstein had been introduced to payload specialists for four different missions and she began to tease him about being her "generic crew commander."

As summer approached, Garneau was working at a killing pace, driven by his own perfectionism and a rather vivid image in his mind of how difficult he would find it to explain failure to the scientific investigators. "I don't want to blow anything," he said at the time. "I want to make sure I take in all the requirements for each and every experiment so that when I come back I can look the principal investigator straight in the eyes and say, 'I did what you wanted me to do,' and avoid the embarrassment of saying, 'Oops, I forgot to press this button or, I'm sorry, I wasn't able to do this.' " Based on his previous experience with motion sickness at sea, he believed he would be able to do his work aboard the shuttle even if he didn't feel well, but he wanted to minimize any potential obstacles by getting the protocols down pat. He was also inescapably aware of the fact that any failure on the part of the first Canadian to fly in space would be highly visible. "I felt this enormous pressure," he admitted. "Canada is looking at me and what if I don't rise to the expectations?"

His situation was not made any easier by a dramatic change in plans in early June. NASA had been struggling for some time with complex scheduling problems and, in the aftermath of some serious reshuffling of crews and payloads, Garneau suddenly found himself assigned to a different shuttle flight with a new crew and a different orbiter — Challenger instead of Discovery.[6] This had been happening frequently and Doetsch commented that "during one of our visits down there, we had some words of wisdom given to us: 'Don't fall in love with your orbiter and don't fall in love with your crew.' "

One of the most significant aspects of this change was that the new flight, 41-G, was slated for an early October launch, lopping three weeks off Garneau's already hard-pressed training schedule. He took it in stride, although he admitted at the time that the mission now so dominated his life that "I don't go much more than an hour without thinking of it, no matter what I'm doing."

A week later, NASA announced the addition of Paul Scully-Power to the mission as a payload specialist, giving 41-G the largest crew up to that time. This, too, would have an impact on Garneau's work because the shuttle's crew compartment is not the roomiest place in which to conduct scientific experiments even under the best of circumstances. "The first reaction was to gulp, because we'd heard these tales about how difficult it would be to accommodate six people," Doetsch admitted. But he said that NASA assured him that this would not curtail Garneau's plans. Actually, Scully-Power turned out to be a godsend; his willingness — unique among the crew — to help Garneau with the SASSE experiments and to serve as a guinea pig himself contributed substantially to the success of that effort.

The change of mission inevitably had a number of other important ramifications for the Canadian experiments. Orchestrating the often conflicting demands that scientific experiments and payloads place on the shuttle's systems and its crew involves a series of complex tradeoffs at the best of times and switching missions at virtually the last minute is guaranteed to give everyone involved headaches. "Shoe-horning into that obviously caused a lot of thinking on both sides," Doetsch said. Some things had to go. Doetsch had been working on an idea of putting a small payload in the shuttle cargo bay to carry the targets for the SVS experiment, but it was uncertain whether this could be managed even for a late October mission. The move to the earlier flight — one with very different payloads in the cargo bay — put an end to this possibility. "There wasn't room for our own little payload and in fact there wasn't the time either to fully develop it and integrate it with NASA," Doetsch said. But luckily the ERBS satellite was an alternative.

The presence of another payload, the SIR-B antenna, also had an impact on planning for the Canadian experiments. The SIR-B experiment called for the shuttle cargo bay to be pointed toward the earth for a good part of the mission, but this was, for example, incompatible with the orbiter attitude needed for the Canadian OGLOW experiment. The operation of the SIR-B antenna would also affect the use of the Canadarm, which, in turn, could affect the Canadian SVS and ACOMEX experiments.

The changes weren't all troublesome, however; there were some significant plusses. The early October mission would fly a "high-inclination" (57°) orbit, which would give Garneau a much better vantage point for his photography over Canada. In particular, it would greatly improve the prospects for photographing the aurora. In the end, Doetsch was satisfied with the tradeoffs: "We've had good support from NASA and through discussions and compromises on both sides, I think we've got a good package together." But life did not get easier for Garneau or any of the other members of the team. For example, the scientific investigators immediately came under the gun to accelerate development of the procedures for Garneau's training and to get their hardware ready for an earlier delivery to NASA. The other four astronauts were also necessarily carrying heavy loads in helping Garneau prepare for the mission and Doetsch said this provided "an excellent training opportunity for each of our payload specialists to become intimately involved in some aspect of getting ready for the flight. It's been an eye-opener."

The maiden voyage of the shuttle Discovery was scheduled for the end of June and the Canadian astronauts began campaigning for a visit to the Kennedy Space Center to witness the launch of mission 41-D. Except for Money, none of them had ever seen one live. On the evening of June 24, the night before the scheduled launch, MacLean, Tryggvason, Garneau and Thirsk found themselves sitting in the grass almost within touching distance of the shuttle, watching a support structure being rolled away from Discovery. They had joined a sunset pilgrimage of press and photographers to the base of the shuttle and they were surrounded by people snapping pictures of the sun going down behind a vehicle brilliantly aglow in the crossfire of powerful spotlights. There is a calm, waiting quality to this scene; a few kilometres away, at the NASA control complex and in the press room, the air fairly crackles with high voltage night-before energy, but out at the pad itself the emotional tone is unexpectedly serene.

The same could not be said for launch day, particularly not for this first launch of Discovery. The first launch attempt, on June 25, was scrubbed less than half an hour before liftoff because of a problem with a backup computer. The second attempt came a day later and it turned out to be one of the more dramatic things that has happened in a place that has seen more than its share of high drama over the years. The countdown got as far as the last ten seconds, when even the most hardened space shuttle watchers still feel their pulses quicken a little. Everything was proceeding normally as the clock reached T-6.6 seconds, when the on-board computers, now controlling the countdown, gave the "go" signal for the first of the shuttle's three main engines to fire. One-tenth of a second later, just as the computers commanded the second engine to start firing, they noticed that the first had not started and commanded the second to stop. The cutoff was almost instantaneous; the third engine didn't even get the start command. The computers had started and stopped the whole thing in just two-tenths of a second, although the clock continued to run until just four seconds before launch. The second engine, which fired briefly, emitted a plume of smoke and, after the shutdown, hydrogen-fuelled fires broke out near the base of the launch pad.

This was the closest call for a shuttle launch up to that time[7] and it was the first time a countdown had been stopped after a main engine had fired. Observers in the viewing stands held their collective breath, instinctively anticipating disaster. In the KSC firing room, more drama was being enacted: there was immediate concern that a buildup of pressure in the shuttle's propellant tanks could lead to an explosion and controllers briefly considered ordering an emergency evacuation of the crew.[8] Also, in the first minute after the shutdown, the controllers were momentarily startled by an indication on a computer console that one of the engines had not shut down, an extremely dangerous situation. In a few minutes, however, it became apparent that the computers had done their job and "safed" the shuttle almost immediately and the crew was told to wait for a normal exit, which occurred about 40 minutes later. It was later determined that the problem had been caused by a faulty valve in one of the main engines.

The Canadian astronauts were variously described in the press as glum, dismayed, disbelieving and strained, but these descriptions of their reaction do not entirely jibe with their own recollections. They were concerned for the safety of the crew, of course, but otherwise they reacted as scientists and engineers typically do — they were intrigued by how the system worked and, unlike many lay people, reassured by this dramatic demonstration of the shuttle's ability to cope with trouble.[9] "It was good to see an abort because you get a feeling for how that system works," said Steve MacLean. "It was all so calm, cool and collected." Tryggvason said it inspired confidence in the NASA system to see how much control they had over the launch even so late in countdown. "I'm amazed they can shut it down so fast."

Garneau's reaction to the abort contained the added perspective of a man entitled to speculate on how he would personally deal with such an eventuality. Then half-way through his own training, he had already given much thought to what might be going through the mind of a person sitting inside the shuttle as the engines start to fire. In those last few seconds of the countdown, it would be natural to assume that you're really on your way. "I have a feeling you do have your own internal countdown ... your own final committing of yourself to leave the earth for a while." But the cliffhanger abort was a graphic demonstration that "you haven't left the ground until you've left the ground," he said. "It must have been a big disappointment to get down to four seconds prior to launch, and to actually feel and hear the engines starting up — at that point, they must have committed themselves in their own minds to the mission — and to suddenly have to stop."

Like everyone else at the launch site, the astronauts were anxious to follow what was going on in the first few minutes after the abort, but they found it difficult to concentrate on the NASA commentary coming over the KSC public address system. At the request of the media, they were sitting in the press stands, rather than in the VIP stands where they had been the day before, and so they faced a barrage of TV cameras and mikes and the usual horde of reporters intent on recording every nuance of their reaction, every twitch of their eyelids. Garneau was amused by press reports that he had stood up in a surfeit of excitement when his main motivation had been to see over the TV cameras trained on him.

The astronauts found it difficult simply to experience the event because they were being asked every few minutes how they felt.

What they felt, mostly, was that they were expected to perform to specs. "You really felt like you had to do a job for these people," said Thirsk. "Every ten seconds, you could feel … someone turning around to look at you to see if your face is lighting up, or showing extreme disappointment. They would ask for your emotions all the time." The others had similar reactions. "It was not a pure, undistracted experience," Garneau said. MacLean concurred: "You never got a chance to reflect about the whole thing at all because you were supposed to be feeling something. It's somehow contrived. You can't relax."

The astronauts were understandably disappointed that two scrubs in as many days temporarily put an end to their quest to see a shuttle launch. When NASA announced that the turn-around would take at least two weeks (in fact, it ultimately stretched to two months), the four were forced to return to Ottawa. Eventually, five of the astronauts did see a launch. The exception was Steve MacLean, who still had not managed to do so by the time he was selected for the second Canadian shuttle mission. Unless he succeeded in getting to KSC for a launch during his training, he faced the possibly unique prospect of experiencing a launch before seeing one.

By the summer of 1984, Garneau and Thirsk, though still working hard on the Canadian experiments, were beginning to shift increasingly to NASA's training requirements. In early July they finally got an opportunity for a much-anticipated experience — a ride aboard the KC-135, NASA's zero-gravity training plane. All six of the Canadian astronauts had hoped to get on the flight but, unfortunately, the plane had been down for repairs for several months and there was such a large backlog of people waiting for flights that anyone not actually working on a mission had to be put on hold.

The force of gravity is not easily escaped on earth; the KC-135 provides one of the few ways of doing so and then only in brief episodes of less than half a minute. This is achieved by putting the plane through a mad roller-coaster ride — climbing 2500 metres, pitching over and then going into a 45° nose-down dive of 2500 metres. Going over the top, you get about 25 seconds of zero gravity; during the dive and the climb, you are pressed flat on the floor by gravity forces twice those normally experienced on the ground. During a normal two-to three-hour run, the plane will go through some 40 to 50 of these climb-and-dive maneuvres, known as parabolas, providing about half an hour of zero gravity in half-minute stretches. The KC-135 is dubbed "The Weightless Wonder" but those who fall victim to its penchant for causing motion sickness refer to it, less affectionately, as "The Vomit Comet." The plane is about the size of a Boeing 727, with all but about 20 seats removed to make room for equipment. People on board are strapped into the seats for landing and takeoff, but otherwise are free to float around the cabin, which is heavily padded to minimize bruised knees and elbows. One of the purposes of the flight is to learn how to move in zero gravity. Neophytes usually have to learn the hard way that the trick is to move hardly at all. "It's not like swimming," warns Bob Williams, manager of NASA's Reduced Gravity Test Program, picking up on a common fault. "You don't kick your feet; it won't do a bit of good and you'll probably just kick someone." Instead you push off gently with a finger and try to aim yourself in the direction you want to go. (You can forget about changing your mind — or your destination — in mid-flight.) Thirsk said he learned very quickly that if he pushed off with as much force as you do in one gravity (1-G), "you're going to go slamming into the next wall. By the end of the flight, you just make finger movements."

Many first-timers on the KC-135 cannot resist the temptation to indulge in some acrobatics — bouncing off the walls, floating free through the middle of the cabin or doing somersaults off the roof. Many first timers pay a price for this. Thirsk said he got a big thrill skimming along a few inches off the walls and the floor — "like Superman, you know" — but then suddenly he got sick. On the SASSE "feeling bad" scale, he went from zero to 20 in no time flat. In a few minutes, however, he felt fine again and happily went back to his acrobatics. Garneau played it a bit more cautiously. "I floated around upside down, feet on the ceiling. I didn't do triple flips."[10] He too experienced some motion sickness, but not enough to ruin the experience which, he said, "had all the novelty I was looking foward to."

NOTES

1. This is one reason why Canada was told that no other members of Garneau's crew would serve as test subjects for the SASSE experiments and that the assistance they could give Garneau in performing his tests would be minimal. Garneau was therefore very appreciative when the other payload specialist, Paul Scully-Power, voluntarily offered his time and assistance.
2. During the briefing, a cameraman who was going into the chamber to film the test listened to the explanation and apprehensively murmured to the person sitting next to him: "Are they going to do that to us?" He visibly blanched when told that they were.
3. From time to time, there was sniping in the press about this coaching of the astronauts, but any problems reporters had with "rehearsed" answers could easily have been solved by an avoidance of utterly predictable questions. The astronauts denied that they were being told what they could or could not say and initially seemed to welcome some guidance on what questions to expect. "When we first started, I was somewhat concerned that the press was going to know more than I knew about what was going on because I had just got the job," said MacLean. "I was very relieved when I realized that they didn't. I figured they had been following space much more seriously."
4. Not everyone reacted to the event with ponderous solemnity. The Frantics, a Toronto-based comedy group, wrote an article in which they remarked: "The depths of space might seem inhospitable to other nationalities, but we are a breed of people used to the desolation of Sudbury, the cold of Edmonton, the loneliness of Inuvik and the sterile white metal of the Eaton Centre. The space shuttle will seem like a home away from home." They added: "The astronauts must learn to work in a vacuum, but if the Liberal Cabinet can do it, so can a Canadian astronaut."
5. Merbold and two other European scientists — Dutch physicist Wubbo Ockels and Swiss astronomer and pilot Claude Nicollier — had been selected as payload specialists by the European Space Agency in December, 1977, and began scientific training in mid-1978. Nicollier later became a NASA mission specialist.
6. Even NASA mission planners had trouble keeping up with the changes; a note tacked to the wall in one beleaguered office said that the launch date "will be determined by lottery."
7. The countdown on the first shuttle mission had been stopped by the computers at T-30 seconds.
8. In an emergency, the astronauts leave the shuttle cockpit, climb into two large wire baskets located at the top of the launch tower and slide down a wire to a bunker where an armored vehicle waits to carry them rapidly away from the launch pad.
9. People outside the space program tend to regard an event like this as a failure of the system, whereas those involved in the program see it as an important success. Henry Hartsfield, commander of the mission, pointed out that "the system did exactly what it is designed to do and I am very pleased that it did. If there are engine problems, you want to know about them on the ground and not in the air."
10. In a classic case of 1-G chauvinism, the Toronto *Star* published a picture of the upside-down Garneau upside down — that is, he appeared in the picture to be right side up when in fact he had his feet on the roof of the plane.

CHAPTER FOUR

Life Among the Astronauts

In
early August,
just two months before the flight,
Garneau and Thirsk
moved to Houston
to train with the U.S. crew for the duration.
They were given office space
in one wing of Building 32,
located on the outer fringes of JSC,
which had been designated
the payload specialists' domain.
The office was far removed
from the hub of astronaut activity
and was as typically sterile as most transient
quarters, in sharp contrast to the vital,
lived-in look of the third floor of Building 4, where the offices of
most of the astronauts and many of the flight operations engineers
were located.[1] NASA officials said the location of the payload
specialists was dictated mostly by a lack of space in Building 4.
In fact, the corps of NASA's own career astronauts had already
outgrown these quarters and many of the newer members were
located in another building, but they were not located with the
payload specialists. Lynn Collins, payload specialist co-ordinator,
said that the payload specialists had a much quieter work
environment where they were, but their apparently deliberate
isolation from the other astronauts nevertheless left a strong, and
probably correct, impression that they were not really perceived
within NASA as part of the gang. This seemed to echo the

perceptions of the European payload specialists, some of whom said they'd found it difficult to gain acceptance within the NASA operation, even after training with the U.S. astronauts for several years. "In many ways, NASA is a closed group," remarked Swiss astronomer and pilot Claude Nicollier. (Recognizing the importance of crew bonding, NASA later changed the rules for payload specialists: once they were assigned to a crew, they were moved to Building 4 where they could maintain close contact with their NASA colleagues.)

The ambience that Garneau and Thirsk found on their arrival at JSC was influenced by the fact that some U.S. astronauts, especially those who had never flown, were quietly resentful of the newcomers who were taking up still-scarce slots in shuttle crews. This attitude is not surprising. Many NASA astronauts had persevered in the program for years without being assigned to a flight; the record was then held by nuclear physicist Don Lind, a mission specialist who had been doggedly hanging in for almost two decades without flying. (He finally flew in April, 1985, 19 years to the month after he was chosen as an astronaut.) Just when the pace of shuttle launches was finally beginning to pick up, and larger crews were being selected, foreign payload specialists who had been involved in the space program for relatively short periods of time — Garneau, for example, had been a payload specialist for less than a year — were leapfrogging to the front of the line and being assigned to missions. The U.S. astronauts were aware that this was part of NASA's strategy to enhance the future security of the space program by promoting international co-operation and funding, but this could not dispel their irritation at being bumped from the queue. (After the Challenger accident, there was renewed sentiment that only NASA's astronauts should fly shuttle missions.)

Acceptance of foreign payload specialists among the NASA astronauts was a highly individual thing, said Watt. Garneau was fairly well accepted but nevertheless he "was in a very difficult situation and he performed extraordinarily well." Garneau said there were some U.S. astronauts who "would pretend not to know who you were when you walked down the hall. They didn't warm to you." He and Thirsk were aware of these undercurrents and could not help but feel somewhat isolated at the beginning of their training. Garneau accepted this philosophically. "I understand that the crew members probably look at me as a bit of an outsider. They are, in their own minds, professionals who are making a career of being astronauts, while people like Bob and myself are passing through. In any group, you go through rites of initiation. I haven't been around long enough." This did not seem to unduly concern the self-possessed Garneau, who said he didn't feel "a compelling need to belong to the group of American astronauts." Throughout the two months they were at JSC, contact with the U.S. crew was confined largely to business and, since everyone was so preoccupied with their individual and collective responsibilities for the mission, there was very little time or opportunity for a lot of socializing. "I squeeze in jogging at noon with Marc and that's about it," Thirsk said.

However, Garneau was concerned about getting to know his fellow crew members, because they would have to live together in extremely cramped quarters. It was like going on a very demanding camping trip with people you'd never met before. Garneau remembers the first time he saw the mid-deck. "I said, 'My goodness, seven of us are going to live in here for eight days?' I hadn't met these people at this time and I was thinking of them as strangers. I thought, 'This is going to be tough.' But during the two months as I got to know them and became more familiar with the compartment, I felt more and more comfortable."

Garneau and Thirsk were particularly pleased when Crippen extended a rare invitation for them to use the astronauts' gym. The gym is a bolthole, a haven zealously protected from the outside world. "It's the one place where the astronauts are by themselves, away from anything else. Nobody gets in," Garneau said. "To get that sort of reception is certainly very nice, and more than we would have expected, considering we've only just joined." Kathy Sullivan lent them some squash equipment and in no time, Garneau was being beaten by her on the courts. This type of interaction was good, he said, because it went beyond "just shaking hands in the passageway."

In the end, Garneau and Thirsk proved to be very able ambassadors for the Canadian program. They worked very hard to become good team players, knowing that it was almost as important for them to perform well in training as it was for Garneau to do so during the mission itself. Even before they arrived in Houston, they knew they were considered a test case. The payload specialist program was still very new and NASA was just beginning to come to grips with the problem of developing a long-term plan for training such people on a regular basis and for accommodating late additions to shuttle crews. With the projected increase in foreign, corporate and even civilian payload specialists that would be coming through JSC in the following years, and a need for increasing flexibility in crew and orbiter schedules, NASA was aiming at a minimum-time, assembly-line approach to their training of payload specialists. Garneau said: "Bob and I are the guinea pigs, not only for the Canadian experiment in manned space, but for NASA as well. They're trying to figure out whether two months is enough. They've got to get a routine and I have a feeling that if this experiment works out, this is going to be the format." The "experiment" was the concept of sending the NASA workbooks and tapes months ahead of time and bringing the payload specialists down for on-site training only during the last two months before launch instead of four to six months ahead of time, as NASA had originally planned.

Although NASA had abandoned the practice of training backups for each crew member, the managers of Canada's program were insistent that Thirsk train in tandem with Garneau. NASA's no-backup approach was predicated on the fact that it had a large enough contingent of experienced astronauts that someone else could step in if necessary. This was not true of the embryonic Canadian program and Thirsk's involvement was viewed as an essential form of insurance that would enable the mission to proceed even if something happened to Garneau. But there was more to it than that: Thirsk also played a vital role in ensuring Garneau's readiness for the mission, particularly given the short training time available. He not only provided another set of eyes, ears and hands and another brain to absorb information, he also provided moral support and comradeship in the pressure cooker atmosphere in which Garneau was working.[2] "Bob and I work very well together," Garneau said as the training program neared completion. "We complement each other and he's very supportive. He provides very good feedback."

"Bob was a big factor in helping Marc be ready," Doetsch said. In fact, their experience so successfully demonstrated the importance of the backup astronaut that "all the other countries are following the same procedures," he added.

For his part, Thirsk was not overly concerned that he was putting in an incredible amount of work without the likelihood of flying the mission. The training itself was a high, something that "very few people will ever have the opportunity to do. A year ago, I never would have thought that I would have even gotten close to NASA except on a tourist basis, and now I'm down here, interacting with the crew, going through training. For me, that's satisfaction enough." And, as one of the youngest of the Canadian astronauts, he could afford to wait. "I have the patience to wait for whenever my flight's going to come."

The move to Houston marked the first really obvious division of labor among the six Canadian astronauts, but Garneau and Thirsk said this did not mean the team had drifted apart. There had undoubtedly been "a branching off" but the two in Houston remained in frequent contact with the others, who were intimately involved in various aspects of the mission and made several visits to JSC. "I think the team spirit will certainly transcend each of the missions," Garneau said. "It's going to be the typical process for the future."

With only two months to go, Garneau and Thirsk were thrown into a merry-go-round of technical briefings and training exercises as soon as they arrived at JSC. Their work day started at about 8 a.m. and went until 6 p.m. and the evenings were usually taken up with reading and studying the myriad NASA workbooks that went along with the classroom instructions and training sessions. Payload specialists are first given an overview of the shuttle program and then one of NASA's training co-ordinators briefs them on what to expect. Payload specialists receive nearly 120 hours of basic mission-related training, but they put in an estimated four to five hours of study for each of those 120 hours. NASA tries to occupy only about half their time with this training, even at this late stage, since they usually are still preparing for their own experiments. Garneau pointed out that, as a new payload specialist, he had to fit into a training operation in which several shuttle crews were preparing for missions, all at different stages of their training.

Much of the training during the last two months is devoted to simulations of the mission, starting with "stand alone" or "single-system" training and culminating in integrated simulations of the whole mission involving the entire crew and the flight controllers. By the time the final month rolls around, the NASA astronauts are spending 40 hours or more a week in the simulators. "The payload specialists don't need to be with them the whole time, but they are with them a large portion of the time," said Kathie Abotteen, one of NASA's training managers.

There are several kinds of simulators, which are used for different aspects of training. Some of the most important are:

• *The shuttle mission simulators:* These are two highly realistic computer-driven versions of the shuttle's flight deck. Similar to the flight simulators used to train commercial airline pilots, these devices are used by the pilot astronauts to practice flying the shuttle and to sharpen their skills in handling failures at critical times. A sophisticated visual system projects realistic images through the space shuttle windows — for example, the payload bay and the earth, moon and stars in space or the landing site and runway during the return to earth. One of these simulators is mounted on hydraulic lifts, which permits simulations of the actual motions of the shuttle, and it can be swivelled to a vertical position to simulate liftoff. It is used to train the pilot-astronauts for launch, ascent into orbit and landing, and particularly for emergency aborts shortly after launch. The other "fixed-base" simulator, which does not move, is used for simulations of flying tasks in space (e.g., maneuvring to grapple a satellite with the Canadarm) and for other on-orbit activities.

• *The orbiter 1-G trainer:* This representation of the interior of the shuttle crew compartment (flight deck and mid-deck) is used to train the crew for most of their non-flying tasks, such as preparing for EVA, operating cameras and the closed-circuit TV, practicing scientific experiments, operating the waste management system, food preparation and general housekeeping. It is also used for practicing getting into and out of the shuttle under normal and emergency conditions.

• *Orbiter engineering mockup:* This is similar to the 1-G trainer, except that it includes a full-scale mockup of the payload bay. It has several uses, including crew training, especially for activities involving interaction with the payload bay (e.g., video and still photography of cargo in the bay).

• *The weightless environment training facility (WETF):* This is a large water tank used to simulate some aspects of zero gravity. Astronauts use the facility to practice EVA techniques.

• *The manipulator development facility:* This is a simulator used by the astronauts to develop and practice techniques of handling payloads with the Canadarm. The effect of zero gravity is simulated by using lightweight inflatable "payloads" filled with helium or by using a special 1-G arm supported on an air-bearing floor. (A computer simulator of the arm and its control station at Spar Aerospace in Toronto is also used as a training facility by U.S. astronauts.)

NASA also uses several "single-system" training facilities for very specific tasks. The most notorious of these is the mockup of the waste collection system — the shuttle's infamous and frequently troublesome zero-gravity toilet. NASA's training is nothing if not thorough; after explaining the operation of the toilet to newcomers, the instructors "leave them there to figure it out and practice," said Abotteen. This is what one NASA training instructor refers to as "potty training."

As they began training, Garneau and Thirsk and the other neophyte payload specialist, Paul Scully-Power, concentrated primarily on safety and "habitability" training, mostly in the 1-G trainer or in single-system trainers. This was done independently of the rest of the crew, who had long since been through the basics. "We try to get all of their single-system training out of the way early so they feel comfortable working with the crew," Abotteen said. The objective is to ensure that the payload specialists know enough about the spacecraft systems to be safe and efficient members of the crew; much of the training involved just learning where things were located on the shuttle (and, even more important, where they were *supposed* to be located). "I learn just enough about the shuttle not to be dangerous," Garneau said. The training thus included medical, emergency and survival operations, the use of the communications system, how to take samples of the crew compartment's atmosphere, how to change the scrubber device that absorbs carbon dioxide in the cabin and how to use the zero-gravity toilet. Payload specialists are also familiarized with the exercise equipment (a zero-gravity treadmill) and various devices for either aiding mobility or restraining themselves in zero gravity (e.g., adhesive straps on the floor to anchor their feet).

Housekeeping in zero-G is not a trivial matter, so Garneau had to be trained how to do such things as stowing and unstowing sleeping bags, packing and unpacking lockers, managing trash, taking care of personal clothing and cleaning the crew compartment. Since all crew members are required to take turns getting the meals, these lessons also included how to prepare the food and clean up afterwards; how to operate the small oven; to reconstitute freeze-dried or dehydrated food packages with hot water; and to pack and unpack the food containers, trays and utensils from the mid-deck lockers. This test gave Garneau the opportunity to try out some of the food he'd be eating aboard the shuttle and he discovered what many other astronauts had already learned: shuttle cuisine falls somewhat short of being *haute*. The food is, however, a considerable improvement over the liquid and mush rations that sustained astronauts in the early days of the space program and there is a more varied menu to choose from. Thus one of Garneau's early tasks was to meet with the NASA nutritionists to select a meal plan for his week in space.[3]

Garneau and Thirsk also received instructions on how to operate the wide variety of still and movie cameras carried aboard the shuttle. Photography plays an important role in every mission and all crew members are expected to know how to use this equipment. Garneau had a particular need to learn how to operate the closed-circuit TV system, since he would be using it to collect data for the space vision system experiment.

Neatness and proper procedure is vital on board a crowded shuttle, so virtually all of the shuttle's habitability systems and procedures are described on a series of checklists and cue cards called the Flight Data File. Even the most seemingly mundane things are detailed; astronauts don't just sleep — they go through procedures called "pre-sleep," "sleep" and "post-sleep." Garneau had to learn how to read the FDF and where to locate information on any systems he might have to use in flight.

"Our main intent in training is to provide an environment where they can experience *everything* here before they go, to actually go through the motions of doing it," Abotteen said. "We think it's important for them to actually be in an orbiter where everything is placed where it should be." She added that, since motion sickness in space can be a problem during the first day or so of a mission, "it's important for them to practice what they're going to be doing up there so that even if they're not a hundred per cent, they'll still be able to do it."

The flow of information was not only in one direction. Early in the training program, Garneau and Thirsk briefed Commander Crippen in detail about the Canadian experiments. Although Garneau was expected to conduct his research on a "non-interference" basis, he was nevertheless competing for space in the mid-deck for the SASSE experiments and a place at various windows in the upper flight deck for his photographic tasks. The latter in particular required some co-ordination with other crew members. Some of the space science experiments (the sun photometer and the OGLOW experiments, for example) required the shuttle to be maneuvred into an appropriate position. There was also a requirement for Garneau to co-ordinate with Sally Ride while she was operating the Canadarm, since part of his duties included photographing the strips of composite materials attached to the arm and taking closed-circuit TV recordings of the targets on the ERBS satellite for the space vision system experiment. Except for Paul Scully-Power, none of the other members of the 41-G crew would be directly involved in the life sciences experiments, but Crippen wanted to know how Garneau would be using the mid-deck for these tests. Garneau and Thirsk showed Crippen the SASSE equipment and described where the subject would be sitting and where the numbered strips would be taped to the lockers and so forth.

"Where there was co-ordination and interaction with the crew members, or there were particular requirements put on the orbiter itself, Crip wanted to know exactly what was involved," Garneau said. "There are certain times in the mission when Crip wouldn't want anyone up in the flight deck and there are certain times … when he doesn't want anyone down in the mid-deck. One of the reasons we had this meeting was to verify that the times we chose for each of our individual experiments were OK with him." Thirsk said that Crippen was very good about telling them explicitly what they could and could not realistically do. He found Crippen, whom he described as one of his heroes, very approachable and "a supreme diplomat" who made the two Canadians feel that they were making a valuable contribution to the mission, even though Garneau had been added to the crew virtually at the last minute.

Garneau and Thirsk also participated in meetings to review the "crew activity plan" and the mission rules,[4] again to ensure that there would be no unexpected conflicts among crew members and their activities — or at least none resulting from a pre-flight lack of communication. During the mission itself, of course, a variety of unexpected problems caused a massive juggling of the crew activity plan and much of the detailed advance planning went out the window. This is one reason why certain personality traits —

121

notably adaptability and unflappability — are most prized in astronauts.[5]

Early in their NASA training program, Garneau and Thirsk also took a quick trip to the Kennedy Space Center for a "walk down" of the launch pad. This is a combined technical briefing and familiarization tour given to payload specialists before they are badged for access to the launch pad area and is mainly intended to ensure they understand the safety requirements while training at KSC. At the time of their visit, Challenger was already sitting on the launch pad and they were able to climb aboard the spacecraft to familiarize themselves with the layout of the vehicle. Although the training facilities at JSC include an accurate mockup of the shuttle crew compartment, it may not replicate the crew compartment on any given shuttle down to the tiniest detail, Garneau pointed out. "You want to make sure that you know what the real article looks like."

By mid-August, Garneau and Thirsk started training with the full NASA crew in the simulators at JSC. A great deal of attention was focussed on the beginning and the end of the mission — the ascent into orbit and the "deorbit" and return to earth; this was intended to enable them to practice their assigned tasks during these phases of the mission. The simulators got pretty crowded with the seven prime crew members plus Thirsk and a clutch of NASA instructors and photographers as well — particularly in earth's gravity. Lacking the luxury of zero gravity, "they're all just elbow to elbow on the floor," Abotteen said. "All the crews feel zero-G helps the situation."

The first part of the exercise involved pre-launch tasks, such as donning flight suits, climbing into the simulator, putting on the LEH (launch and entry helmet) and hooking up communications and oxygen lines. As a payload specialist sitting in the lower deck, Garneau had little to do during the ascent and re-entry portions of the flight, but it was important for him to know what was going on. Crippen provided a running commentary of the events during the ascent and, when they had achieved "orbit," instructed the crew to prepare the crew compartment for their first day of work in space. Mostly this involved stowing the removable chairs (all but the two on the flight deck used by the commander and pilot) and unneeded personal gear, such as helmets and boots, and then unstowing equipment required for the first day's operations. After participating in these general housekeeping duties, Garneau was coming to the conclusion that, cozy as it was, the crew compartment could be quite comfortable "providing you keep it tidy. That's going to be quite a demanding requirement ... It's very easy to make a mess."

The "deorbit prep" involved the reverse operation: stowing all equipment away safely, putting the chairs back in place and donning flight suits, boots and helmet for the return to earth. Garneau also learned how to put on his G-suit, an inflatable pressure garment that squeezes the legs and lower torso to prevent blood from rushing to the lower part of the body. If too much blood drains from the head during re-entry into earth's gravity, it could cause dizziness or even blackouts. After landing, the crew must complete a number of tasks before anyone can get out of the shuttle. Under normal circumstances, Garneau, as a payload specialist, would have few post-landing responsibilities except to unbuckle himself and stay out of the way until it was time to leave the spacecraft. However, the entire crew did practice quick escapes — for example, learning to evacuate through the top windows and rappel down the sides in about two minutes in case of emergencies such as a post-landing fire. They also practiced procedures for an emergency landing in water; these included opening the hatch, swinging out on a handlebar and dropping into the "water." "We also throw out the lifeboat and they show us the cookies and the shark repellent," Garneau said. (The probability that the shuttle and crew could survive a water ditching is considered very low. In calm waters with no cargo in the payload bay, survival might be possible. In rough conditions, the vehicle would likely break up and the force of deceleration as it hit the water would probably cause any cargo in the bay to break loose and slam through the crew compartment. This is why pilot-astronauts do not consider a water ditching shortly after launch to be survivable.)

As September approached, Garneau and Thirsk participated in increasingly elaborate simulations of the mission involving the full crew, NASA's training instructors and eventually the flight controllers in Mission Control. "If you were listening to the [communications] loops, you'd think it was a real flight," Abotteen said.

Garneau added that the simulations are "not just for the benefit of the astronauts. These are integrated sims; you're with the people over in Mission Control and it's really for everybody to get their act together."

Some of these simulations, intended primarily for the flight crew, allowed Commander Crippen and pilot McBride to practice flying skills during ascent and landing and in orbit. Malfunctions figured prominently in these exercises. Garneau observed one run in the moveable shuttle mission simulator that involved a post-launch emergency abort to a landing site across the Atlantic Ocean. "It's a very busy time for those guys," Garneau said. "I just sat as the passenger in the back and watched it because Crip said, 'Why don't you come along for the ride?' "

Other simulations enabled the entire crew to practice much of the mission in "real time" so they could gauge the timing of their activities and minimize interference with each other's work. These exercises culminated in a three-day real-time simulation involving the crew and the flight controllers. The astronauts were allowed to go home to sleep, but for the rest of the time, they lived and worked in the simulators, just as they would in space.

"Even though you do not have the weightlessness, you finally have a good visual idea of what you're going to do," Garneau said. "And that's when you also meld closely with the rest of the crew." He said that the first day of the mission was rehearsed in particular detail because it would be "a very busy day all around. It's also the most demanding day, all of us getting used to that strange atmosphere ... and being perhaps a little bit tired because of over-excitement."

One of Garneau's priorities on the first day was to obtain video recordings of the release of the ERBS satellite, which would constitute a large portion of the data needed for the SVS experiment. This required him to be up on the flight deck, along with Crippen and McBride, who would be controlling shuttle maneuvres, with Ride, who would be operating the Canadarm, and with other crew members who would be busy with photography tasks of their own. "It's going to be a real crush," he observed. "I hope it's not quite like the Keystone Kops." Since many critical activities would be controlled from the flight deck — flying the shuttle, handling large payloads with the Canadarm, supervising EVAs — it was vital for reasons of both safety and efficiency that Garneau know exactly what he was supposed to do and where he was supposed to be while in the upper deck.

In mid-September, the crew went to the Kennedy Space Center to participate in a simulation, called the Terminal Countdown Test, aboard Challenger on the launch pad. The exercise, which took several hours, took them through pre-launch procedures right up to the moment when the solid rocket boosters were supposed to fire. At KSC, they also practiced emergency procedures on the launch pad. This exercise included familiarization with the launch tower escape system, a basket device that slides along a wire to the ground, where an armored vehicle is located to carry the crew away from the site. This system would be used in situations where there's a danger of fire or explosion of the shuttle while it's on the pad. "A lot of people figure it's a fairly academic exercise," said Garneau. "If you have to evacuate, chances are you're not going to make it off. My feeling is that it is still worthwhile."

The crew practiced evacuating the crew compartment and jumping into the baskets, but they did not actually ride the baskets to the ground (there seems to be some question whether this is because of the potential danger involved or because it would be too much trouble to keep hauling the baskets up if all the astronaut crews were riding them down.) After descending in the launch tower elevators, the crew then got into the tank and drove it around. (All members of the crew are expected to be able to drive the tank, so both Garneau and Thirsk received instruction on this.)

Greg Hayes, then manager of personnel at JSC, noted that a major criterion for being selected as an astronaut is the ability to "function well under stress and as a team" and to adapt to rapidly changing circumstances. These qualities are tested time and again during gruelling sessions in the simulators, where just about anything can, and usually does, go wrong. Although everyone hopes a real shuttle mission will unfold largely "as written" in the flight plan, the "sims" are rarely a piece of cake. The training instructors work in teams consisting of people who are expert in different aspects of the shuttle's systems, and they are particularly adept in using their computer consoles to throw in "off-nominal" occurrences. Since these malfunctions can be more or less serious, depending on the timing and whether other malfunctions occur at the same time, there are myriad creative opportunities to play "what if" games with the flight crew. In fact, the instructors work very hard to put the astronauts through a wringer, operating on the philosophy that it is always better to encounter trouble in the simulators before it catches up with you in real life. "You never have a 'nominal' mission," Garneau said of the sims.

Training manager Kathie Abotteen said: "We try and anticipate everything that could possibly go wrong, even down to two-fault tolerance — if this goes wrong *and* this goes wrong, what do you do?" A major objective of this intensive training is to enable the crew to act instinctively, decisively — and correctly — when something goes wrong, she said. Of course, not every glitch and gremlin encountered in the simulators actually shows up in real life, but, on more than one occasion, malfunctions that have occurred in space had been previously simulated and solved on the ground, so the crew often knows immediately what to do and "don't spend two days talking about it."

The astronauts spend long hours perfecting emergency techniques they may never be called upon to use in space and there's little in the way of trouble they can't handle, given half a chance. However, no amount of training can prepare them for a sudden, utterly catastrophic failure that gives neither the crew nor anyone else time to respond. The explosion of Challenger's fuel tank during the launch of Mission 51-L was just such a failure and it was all the more devastating and poignant for those who are aware of the incredible effort that the astronauts and training crews put into preparing for emergencies.

While Garneau and Thirsk were concentrating on training, the flight equipment for the Canada experiments was being prepared at an equally intense pace. Bruce Aikenhead, program manager of the Canadian astronaut office, had the responsibility of keeping hardware development on track and shepherding it through the NASA checkpoints. "Because of the urgency, we did get a great deal of assistance from NASA," he said. The space agency accelerated the process for reviewing the equipment — accomplishing in a week what would normally take more than a month — and on one occasion, they sent a safety engineer to Ottawa to expedite matters.

By early August, the equipment was delivered to JSC for its final safety review and locker fit check.[6] "We literally set the record for packing the most stuff in a locker," said Aikenhead. The final delivery of the flight hardware was accomplished by late August, in time for a review of all the mid-deck lockers by the flight crew, and it was installed aboard Challenger in mid-September. The installation of the materials for the ACOMEX experiment ran into last-minute problems. As a result of the change in flights, it appeared that the plates to which the samples would be attached would not be ready in time. However, the principal investigator, Dave Zimcik of the federal Department of

Communications, and his colleagues worked feverishly to devise a simpler method of installation — wrapping strips of material around the Canadarm — which worked very well.

Like everyone else involved in that first mission, Aikenhead felt as though he'd been running at sprint speed over a marathon course. "It was pretty hectic. I felt a bit burnt out by the end of it."

In early September, NASA held the traditional T-30-day press briefing and "photo opportunity" with the crew of 41-G. This rather stagey affair was the closest the Canadian media came to Garneau while he was at JSC. The NRC's determination to sequester the two Canadian astronauts during the final two months of their training had been greeted with loud complaints of press management. One major problem was that the media wanted to be in on the simulator runs and other training sessions, something that NASA does not permit. "Our philosophy is that the training process is so damned critical we want no distractions at all," said one NASA spokesman. In fact, some of the facilities in which Garneau trained — notably the shuttle mission simulators — are strictly off-limits to outsiders under any circumstances, let alone during training runs.[7] The media had to be content with the rather predictable ritual that astronaut press conferences have become. The only unusual, and the most lighthearted, moment occurred at the end of the conference. It stemmed, surprisingly, from a question posed by Craig Covault of the normally staid and highly technical aerospace journal, *Aviation Week and Space Technology,* who pointed out that the crew consisted of "three U.S. Navy officers, one Canadian Navy officer, one professional oceanographer and Kathy Sullivan [who] has an oceanography degree, I believe, right?"

"That's right," Sullivan responded.

"And I bet [Sally] Ride's been swimming at least once a month," Covault quipped.

"I was wondering how you were going to get me in this crew," Ride observed mildly.

"Would it be accurate to characterize ... that this crew is all wet," Covault persisted, tongue in cheek.

"I won't touch that one," Commander Crippen said.

"Sounds like these questions are deteriorating fast," interjected the NASA public affairs officer, bringing the briefing to a close.

By the time Mission 41-G had become history, both NASA and Canadian space program managers and scientific investigators were more than pleased, not only with Garneau's performance in space but with the success he and Thirsk had made of the training program within the constraints of an unprecedentedly tight deadline. NASA payload specialist co-ordinator Lynn Collins said their experience helped NASA to establish guidelines for payload specialists. Doug Watt concurred: "The Canadian flight has become the standard for how a payload specialist flight should be flown." He was very pleased with Garneau's diligence regarding the SASSE experiments. "It's not easy to turn an engineer into a life scientist overnight. It's a tribute to Marc that all this has been done in under eight months." Garneau had fulfilled his promise to himself that he would be able to look the scientific investigators in the eye and tell them he'd done his job.

"NASA now believes they don't need quite as much time to get people ready to fly as had been envisaged," Doetsch said. "They also recognize that they do have to accommodate people on much shorter notice than their routine had been." He also pointed out that, while NASA imposes a virtual news blackout on crews in training, they had to make some allowances for the interest of the foreign media in their own payload specialists.

In the year following Garneau's mission, a wide variety of payload specialists flew shuttle missions. They included privately employed engineers (Charles Walker, Loren Acton), politicians (U.S. Senator Jake Garn and Florida Congressman William Nelson) and half a dozen foreign payload specialists from Europe, Mexico and Saudi Arabia. Representing the last was Prince Sultan Salman Al-Saud, acting director of the Saudi Arabian Television Commercial Department, and also a commercial pilot, who was along mostly as an observer. In July, 1985, NASA chose teacher Christa McAuliffe as the first participant in its new citizen-observer program and later that year also began the process of selecting a journalist to fly aboard the shuttle sometime in 1986. Those plans were, of course, put on indefinite hold after the Challenger explosion in which McAuliffe was killed; in fact, the accident raised questions about the whole concept of the observer program and whether NASA had been overzealous in its pursuit of PR brownie points by taking "ordinary" citizens into space too soon. Even before the Challenger accident, however, many of those professionally involved in the space program were becoming irritated by the allocation of valuable space aboard the shuttle to non-astronauts, particularly to non-scientists. NASA may have been trying to prove that ordinary people could fly in space, but it was clear that not everyone who flew in space wanted to be considered ordinary.

There is a great disparity in the responsibilities and training load of the NASA pilot-astronauts and mission specialists and those of others who fly on the shuttle. Just how taxing this load can be became apparent in late 1985 when John Fabian, a seven-year NASA veteran with two shuttle flights under his belt, suddenly resigned in the middle of training for his third mission. He cited the pressures of his workaholic lifestyle on his family life: "I came home one night and told my wife, 'I put the job first for 24 years and I'm not doing it anymore.'" What worried NASA was that Fabian's resignation capped a 16-month period in which no fewer than eight of their most experienced astronauts left the program, compared with a previous average of about one resignation a year. Joe Allen, another who resigned, said his wife kept asking him: "Joe, when are you going to get a real job?" James Beggs, who was then NASA administrator, said: "We've now begun to lose the guys we've educated and trained to do the most difficult things we do, like spacewalks." Then, in a comment that perhaps unconsciously revealed part of the problem — that NASA sometimes tends to treat astronauts as biological machines — he described those who had resigned as men "who still have a lot of tread left on them."

Scientists and engineers who fly as payload specialists don't train as extensively for space operations per se, and they typically fly far fewer missions than career astronauts, but they generally invest as much or more time preparing for their space experiments, and the work they do on the shuttle is helping to lay the scientific and economic foundation for permanent human habitation of space during the next two decades. It is understandably difficult for people such as this to take very seriously civilian observers who, for the most part, were little more than sightseers taken along for political or PR reasons and who received only a very basic indoctrination — just enough to teach them how not to endanger the mission or get in the way of others doing real work.[8]

The Europeans were openly critical of the observer program. Hans-Ulrich Steimle of DFVLR, the German aerospace research establishment, who served as manager of the Spacelab D1 mission,[9] complained that the U.S. space agency had become involved in running "a travel office for visiting dignitaries. This is counterproductive when you want to perform a serious science mission." NASA's insistence on designating all non-NASA crew members as payload specialists was also irksome to the European scientists who had flown on the shuttle. Ulf Merbold, the first European to fly on a shuttle/Spacelab mission, said: "There has to be a difference between some senator or Arab prince and the qualified scientists who fly aboard the shuttle." Europe urged NASA to establish a new category of science-astronaut to distinguish those with research credentials from other types of payload specialists NASA was flying. The three Europeans who flew the D1 mission were referred to as scientist-astronauts by European space officials, but NASA continued to call them payload specialists. Garneau said he had no objection to sharing the payload specialist designation with non-scientists.

For two to three months following Mission 41-G, Garneau was preoccupied with nationwide publicity tours. In contrast to the year before, he and his wife could rarely appear in public without his being recognized and asked for autographs. "My wife has days when she doesn't mind it and other days when she really prefers it wouldn't be that way." He said he too wanted to "get back to being a very private person" and admitted to mixed emotions when an evening out is interrupted by people asking for autographs. "I never blame young people because there's that enthusiasm. Sometimes, with older people, perhaps they should know a little bit better." But, he said, lack of privacy is "part of the price you pay and I realize that."

The other Canadian astronauts, especially Thirsk, rotated duty, accompanying Garneau on major trips in addition to making their own appearances. Requests for appearances by the astronauts continued unabated; by the beginning of 1986, Garneau had made more than 230 appearances. Thirsk was second with nearly 120, followed by Bondar with more than 65. The other three clocked in at about 55 to 60 appearances each.

The press continued to comment disapprovingly on the way in which the astronauts were being used for political purposes. One incident that provoked the most disparagement was a command performance Garneau made at the gala in Quebec City in honor of the first "Shamrock Summit" between Prime Minister Brian Mulroney and U.S. President Ronald Reagan. "There was a desire at very senior levels for Marc to participate and we're certainly not going to say no to a situation like that," Doetsch said at the time.

The problem was the script: Garneau, wearing a flight suit and baseball cap, appeared on the stage in a puff of smoke, dutifully spoke his line — "Take me to your leaders" — and disappeared down a trap door in another puff of smoke. It was, said the Ottawa *Citizen*, "a journey to the very boundaries of bad taste." It certainly was not a scenario the astronauts particularly cared for; they were too diplomatic to say as much, but the event clearly made them uncomfortable.

Speaking about his PR duties more generally, however, Garneau said: "Let's not underestimate the fact that Canadians are very interested in [the space program]. A lot of people accuse me of being a front man [but] I'm not stupid and I wouldn't work in this organization if I thought I was being manipulated. I think I stayed true to myself; I managed to keep my sense of perspective. I don't think I've conned anybody; I think I've informed people, along with all of the other [astronauts], and the media's helped in that respect. I think, in a way, we've bootstrapped the country into an awareness of what we've done in space."

As spring approached, the PR duties reverted to normal and the astronauts could turn their attention once again to their scientific duties. They were by this time pursuing education on a much broader front than had been anticipated when they joined the program. In late 1985, they took a special geology course at Carleton University, designed to teach them to interpret features on earth from space. In particular, it was intended to "help them recognize specific geological features they want to photograph," said Carleton geology professor Al Donaldson, who organized the course. The need for this kind of training was prompted by the difficulties Garneau experienced during his mission in identifying specific regions of the Canadian prairies in order to take measurements for one of his space science experiments. Later, similar courses in astronomy and oceanography were organized. The team also received additional instruction in photography.

131

With Mission 41-G under their belts, the Canadian astronauts increasingly turned their attention to the two subsequent missions and more long-term projects (although there was still no guarantee from their political masters that the astronaut program would be continued beyond the original three missions).[10] The division of labor between the three medical astronauts, Money, Bondar and Thirsk, and the three engineering astronauts, Garneau, Tryggvason and MacLean, became more pronounced as each group started to concentrate on the detailed requirements for the upcoming dedicated SVS and SAS missions. (Before the Challenger accident, it appeared that the two missions might occur in 1987 only two months apart.)

Tryggvason, Garneau and MacLean spent much of their time working on development of the SVS system. Their tasks included working out the details of the experiments MacLean would perform in space, overseeing the design of the small payload that would carry the targets, writing an SVS operator's manual, developing a computer program and videotapes that would be used to create a ground-based training simulator, and developing a computerized data base needed to generate the graphic display that would be provided to the astronaut operating the SVS-equipped Canadarm. (See Chapter 6.) Money, Bondar and Thirsk, meanwhile, continued to work with Doug Watt and other Canadian scientists developing a series of space physiology experiments they then hoped would fly on a shuttle/Spacelab mission in May, 1987. In addition, Money and Watt continued their motion sickness and other physiology experiments with U.S. and European astronauts on the Spacelab-D1 mission in November, 1985. (See Chapter 5.)

Throughout 1985, however, the Canadian astronauts were increasingly branching out from their individual fields of expertise and the narrow confines of the two sets of experiments for which they had originally been chosen. "People in our office have knowledge about the [shuttle]," Thirsk said. "We have mission experience behind us now and we're acquainted with the NASA way of doing things." He said that the NASA astronauts had already demonstrated their adaptability in doing scientific and technical tasks outside the fields in which they had been formally educated; for example, the mission specialists who do the EVAs, operate the Canadarm and conduct a wide range of scientific experiments include astrophysicists, medical doctors, engineers, physiologists, biochemists and geologists. Garneau demonstrated a similar adaptability on his mission. "I think all of us are able to carry out operations in space outside our area of expertise," Thirsk said. "We're only now starting to get into this diversification." Aikenhead said that the decision to have Garneau perform a wide range of scientific experiments on his mission was a wise one because it helped the astronaut program to mature quickly into "an organization that's prepared to do useful work on behalf of Canadian scientists."

Some of the astronauts participated in the NRC's studies on Canada's contribution to the U.S. space station project, which was then under consideration by the federal government. Garneau, for example, began attending meetings as a Canadian representative on an international working group studying issues related to the operation and management of the space station. (See Chapter 7.) Meanwhile, Bondar headed a life sciences committee that began to examine future possibilities for Canada in doing basic and clinical life sciences research and perhaps even operational medicine in space. One of their tasks was to evaluate a potential Canadian contribution to the development of a medical and health maintenance facility — essentially a mini-hospital — on the space station. (See Chapter 5.)

Thirsk worked with the designers of Radarsat, an advanced remote-sensing satellite, which may become the first satellite designed to be serviced and repaired by astronauts in space.[11] This move was prompted by the successful retrieval and repair of several disabled satellites by shuttle astronauts in 1984 and by projections that servicing and repair would double the satellite's lifetime and increase its net value by CDN$500-million. Thirsk concentrated on the aspects of the satellite's design that would affect astronaut operations — for example, the placement of handrails, warning placards and panels; the avoidance of sharp edges and corners; and the design of tools and work stations.

In fact, most of the Canadian astronauts were now thinking seriously of the possibility of training to perform EVAs themselves. In late 1985, Garneau and Thirsk, both qualified scuba divers, received approval to take a course at JSC that would qualify them to work in the large water tank that NASA uses to train astronauts for EVA. Although there were no definite plans at that point to train the Canadian astronauts for EVA, this was seen as an investment in the future. The idea was "to build up some expertise," said Garneau. "To have that qualification and to maintain it gives Canada a little more flexibility if there's a requirement later on to get involved [in EVA]." However, the Challenger accident occurred before the two had a chance to start the course, which, like many other aspects of their work, was put on hold until things got back to normal.

Thirsk, who was also a member of the life sciences committee, worked on a proposal to improve the anti-gravity suit worn by astronauts during the shuttle's return to earth to prevent blood from rushing to the lower part of the body in 1-G. When he was a biomedical engineering student at MIT, Thirsk worked on a device intended to reduce blood clotting in the legs of cardiac patients and he believed that the techniques developed for that purpose might be adapted for use in the space program. (See Chapter 5.)

Tryggvason and MacLean developed computer programs and a videotape film to be used for training in a simulator of the SVS system that was being set up in Ottawa. Meanwhile, Garneau prepared an SVS operator's manual and checklists for the mission. (See Chapter 6.) Tryggvason also worked on a proposal for a Canadian Space Carrier, an unmanned carrier for materials processing experiments that could be deployed and retrieved by the shuttle and left in space for days or months at a time. (See Chapter 8.)

By late 1985, Doetsch's attention was turning toward the selection of the prime and backup astronauts for the second mission, the date of which had already slipped into 1987. One reason for the delay was that, even before Garneau's mission, it had been decided that the space vision system mission would be flown before the space adaptation syndrome mission; scheduling the second Canadian flight was thus dependent on the time needed to develop and flight-qualify the SVS hardware, a long and complex process. The NRC was also still negotiating with NASA the possibility of putting a targetted payload in the cargo bay to be deployed by the Canadarm while the SVS system tracked its motions. In addition, the NRC had been out canvassing the scientific community for other projects that might be flown on the next mission, since this strategy had produced good results on Garneau's mission, even though it had initially been inspired more than anything else by the lack of time to mount either the

SVS or SAS experiments properly. "I think we'll actually be better off in terms of the [experiment] package that we fly if we keep to the [longer] time frame," Doetsch said. "I don't think anybody would have been ready for the middle of 1985 anyway."

Doug Watt said the life sciences experiments could probably have been ready to fly by late 1985, before the Challenger accident. He was not happy with the decision that the SVS flight must go first, which "clearly blocked our experiment." In his view, this smacked of outright favoritism for the NRC-sponsored project; the fact that the NRC was managing the program and sponsoring one of the projects created a "serious conflict of interest situation," he said.

Doetsch contended that there were sound reasons for wanting to develop the new SVS technology as rapidly as possible. "Its use, its marketability, would be enhanced by an early develop- ment and for that reason we were pushing pretty hard to get that fellow onboard." In particular, he was anxious to bolster the case Canada was making to build the servicing facility on the U.S./international space station. Life sciences experiments in space, on the other hand, would continue to be done for a long time, he said. "The urgency of flying [the SAS experiment] early really isn't as great." Watt was unpersuaded that flying the SAS experiment first would affect the demonstration of Canada's remote manipulator technology. In the end, however, the point was moot: the Challenger accident intervened to ground both experiments indefinitely and Canada reached agreement with NASA on its plan to build a space station servicing facility long before the SVS system was demonstrated in space.

By early December, 1985, the NRC was ready to announce that Steve MacLean had been chosen for the second Canadian shuttle flight. During a press conference in Ottawa on December 10, just four days before MacLean's 31st birthday, the new science minister, Frank Oberle, announced that MacLean would be a member of the crew of Mission 71-F, then scheduled for March, 1987. A hiatus of about 2 1/2 years would have separated the first and second flights of Canadian astronauts — a much longer period than originally anticipated. In part, the delay was caused by the complexities of fitting into a shuttle launch schedule that had continued to slip throughout 1985 because of problems on the launch pad, including incidents in which the shuttle's on- board computers stopped the countdown just seconds before launch. After the Challenger explosion, of course, MacLean's launch date was put on indefinite hold.[12]

MacLean's major task on his mission will be to test the CDN$4-million space vision system. (See Chapter 6.) In addition, he will perform five other scientific experiments, including further research on two experiments done on Garneau's flight. One of the experiments, designed to study the effect of the space environment in degrading plastics and composite materials, has a special significance for MacLean: it gives him a chance to work with his father, Paul McLean,[13] a researcher with the NRC, who is a member of the scientific team investigating the phenomenon. The senior McLean was pleased by his son's selection to fly the mission, although he said he had initially prompted Steve to think twice about leaving the academic world for the life of an astronaut. MacLean's mother admitted to some apprehension; even though she'd had two years to get used to the idea of her son flying in space, "it still scares me a little at times," she said at the time of her son's selection.

At the press conference, MacLean described his reaction to the fulfillment of a dream that, as a young boy, he had thought would never be permitted to a Canadian. "I guess you didn't notice that I floated into the room," he remarked to the assembled reporters. "Inside, you really feel like jumping up and down and saying, 'Wow, it's my turn.'" MacLean joked that there was one perk he was looking forward to. He commented that every time he and Garneau travelled together, Garneau was besieged by autograph hunters "and if I didn't carry his bags we would be there for an hour before we got out of the airport. I am really looking forward to Marc carrying my bags."

However, despite his pleasure at being chosen, MacLean admitted to some mixed feelings because he was aware that the colleagues with whom he had been working so closely for two years must feel some disappointment. "All of us will feel much better when all of us have flown."

The one who was undoubtedly the most disappointed was Tryggvason, who was selected as the backup astronaut for the mission. At that point, he was facing the prospect of not getting a mission at all, since the third mission, which would focus on the life sciences experiments, would go to Money, Bondar or Thirsk.[14] Although the astronauts were optimistic that the Canadian astronaut program would be continued, there was still no guarantee of shuttle missions beyond the original three. "The feelings of back-up astronauts are certainly mixed," Tryggvason acknowledged in response to a reporter's question. "It would feel much better to be the prime." At the same time, he said, preparing for the mission would be "very much a team effort. Even as back-up, I still feel very proud and very lucky."

There was more to this than simply a faithful adherence to the astronauts' Three Musketeers code. The preoccupation of the media in seeking evidence of crushing disappointment among astronauts not selected to fly a mission reflected a lack of appreciation of just how much of a team effort is involved in preparing for a flight — and just how much it is *perceived* as such by the astronauts. Long before he was selected, MacLean himself had commented that he had always greatly admired the flight controllers and other support teams on the ground. He added that the excitement of being "on the inside ... tuned into the whole organization" overrides any sense of personal disappointment.

An issue that has dogged the Canadian astronaut program since its inception — the application of criteria other than strictly scientific ones to the selection of astronauts — arose again at the press conference. It was prompted by a comment by NRC president Larkin Kerwin, who said that all six were highly qualified for any mission "and therefore the choice is made on the secondary aspects." This was followed almost immediately by an observation on the team's bilingual abilities: "All six of the astronauts have a bilingual capability. I speak with them myself regularly in French." The implication was that bilingualism had been a major factor in the selection. Tryggvason, however, did not speak French and he rightfully acknowledged as much when he was later cornered by a reporter.

Doetsch reiterated the position he has always taken on the subject — that, although bilingual capability was one of the factors considered, it was not the sort of thing that "tipped the scales." He said the policy established when the astronauts were originally chosen — that the group as a whole must have bilingual capability — was still in effect.

In any event, MacLean did not consider himself to be fluently bilingual, although he had taken French lessons and had given some speeches in French in Quebec. "I had never spoken French in front of a crowd before," he said. "They laughed at my jokes so I figure they understood me. It was quite demanding to do that because I don't have full command of the language yet. I have to work very hard at it." Doetsch said MacLean would continue taking French lessons to become more comfortable with the language because "we feel it still causes him too much stress." For his part, MacLean believed the whole issue was largely a manufactured one — that the media were "trying to get a story that wasn't there."

Following the tradition started with Garneau's mission, the six astronauts went out together for dinner after they were told of MacLean's selection. MacLean was, of course, presented with the bill. The team had lost its inhibitions since the first celebratory dinner. "They were not gentle with me," MacLean commented wryly. "It wasn't *quite* a four digit check."

Less than two months after MacLean was selected for his flight, and an approximately equal amount of time before the NRC planned to announce the selection of the astronaut for the third Canadian mission, the Challenger accident intervened, immediately affecting the near-term future of everyone in the Canadian astronaut office. Few of the astronauts were in their Ottawa offices at the time of the accident. Garneau, for example, was at the Johnson Space Center, attending a meeting related to the upcoming Canadian mission. The meeting broke for coffee just as Challenger was to be launched and someone turned on the TV set in the conference room. Garneau recalled that, as they watched Challenger streaking across the sky after a seemingly normal liftoff, the mood in the room was one of "Oh, well, another successful launch." They were almost on the verge of returning to their meeting when the mind-stunning image of the explosion flashed onto the screen. Unlike many lay people who witnessed the tragedy, this group was not even momentarily confused by the idea that what they were seeing might be the expected separation of the solid rocket boosters, which normally occurs about two minutes after launch. "I knew that the two minutes hadn't gone by," Garneau said. "Whenever I've watched a launch, my eyes have always been on the exhaust of the [solid rocket boosters] because I know that is the critical phase. You're helpless, totally helpless. Those are the two minutes when you are in the hands of God." Everyone else around him also knew this, but nevertheless, an air of disbelief permeated the room.

Everyone went quiet and "nobody wanted to face anybody," Garneau said. "We didn't want to make eye contact. That would sort of be like saying, 'We both did see that explosion, didn't we?' And then some people started to cry."

Back in Ottawa, Steve MacLean was making the five-minute walk to his home to watch the launch on TV. He was interested in the mission because he knew some of the crew members professionally; he had met pilot Dick Scobee while observing astronaut training sessions at JSC and had worked with Ron McNair, who had been a "capcom" during Garneau's mission. MacLean arrived too late to catch live coverage of the liftoff, but when he turned the TV set on, the image that filled the screen was one of the many replays of the explosion. Like everyone else, he couldn't believe what he was seeing, even though he knew the risks involved better than most people. "We have a good perspective of what the risks are," he reflected later. "Every astronaut has known that, before the solids separate, there's very little chance. Before the first two minutes, they all knew that you were helpless. But actually to see it happen was hard … it was hard."

MacLean remembers identifying not only with the crew but also with their families, not only because he was "in the business" but also because he had been selected for a flight. One of his first thoughts was for the parents of the crew members. "I can remember thinking what my parents might feel if it had been me." Later, he went back to the NRC and spent the rest of the afternoon watching TV coverage of the accident with others in the space program office. "Nobody wanted to leave," he said. "There was going to be a long break in the coverage and so there was no point in watching TV anymore. The TV went off and everybody sort of sat there. We didn't move for what seemed the longest time to me."

Later that evening, MacLean went to see his parents. He expected his mother to try to discourage him from flying, but "she has a very realistic approach to this. She said that she accepted these possibilities two years ago. It doesn't make it any easier, but she knows she can't change the way I think."

Like MacLean, Tryggvason had gone home for lunch; his wife had a lunch engagement and he was babysitting their small son. He didn't have the TV on, but his wife phoned to tell him she'd heard about the Challenger accident on the radio. He too was unbelieving: "My immediate reaction was very similar to the kind of shock that I felt when Kennedy was shot." The shock was not just because of the loss of the crew, but also because it was "a real blow to what everybody views as a program taking us into the future. I think that is why there was such a uniform reaction. The number of people lost was not a large number compared to the crash of the DC-8 in Newfoundland, and yet the reaction was totally different, because everybody was so supportive of this program. It was a program about the future and all of a sudden it got clobbered." However, he did not believe, even in the worst moments, that the accident would bring the Canadian astronaut program to a halt. Tryggvason went back to his office for part of the afternoon, but later returned home to watch the unfolding story on TV.

Thirsk was attending a French-language class when he heard the news about the explosion. "We had a coffee break and all of a sudden one of the professors came racing into our little coffee room where there's a color TV set. The only thing he said was, 'Bad news.' It was about the time when all these assassinations were going on so I thought, 'Oh boy, it's probably an assassination.' He turned on the TV set. Before the image even came on the screen, I thought: 'Tuesday ... Tuesday ... shuttle. God, don't let it be the shuttle.' Everybody was sort of quiet; they really felt for me." The others in the class, aware of his involvement in the space program, began to ask him questions, so he gave them an impromptu mini-lecture — in French — about the space shuttle before they went back to work on their lessons. "When I was writing on the board, my lines were wavy and there was a waver in my voice," Thirsk said. He knew Judy Resnik from the Radarsat meetings and Hughes Aircraft engineer Greg Jarvis "because we worked out of the same payload specialist office. I think amongst the six of us, we got to know all of them, socially or professionally, except the school teacher."

Ken Money walked into the astronaut office about ten minutes after the accident occurred and, when one of the secretaries told him that the shuttle had blown up, his first thought was that she must be mistaken. Turning on the radio quickly disabused him of this idea. A few minutes later, Bondar walked into the office. She was, she said, "bouncing with enthusiasm" because she'd just come from a meeting in which funding for one of the space physiology experiments had been approved. "Ken had his radio on and he says, 'The shuttle blew up.' If Ken said it, I didn't have to ask twice. And then the next thing, the phones are ringing off the hook."

Money said that Doetsch "called over and said that he didn't want us talking to the press about it until we knew what really happened." Money and Bondar were the only two astronauts in the office at the time, but Bondar soon decided to beat a retreat; she went home to watch the TV coverage. Some reporters did get through on Money's direct office line and when he told them he wasn't supposed to comment, they persisted with questions like: "Well, how do you feel about it? We want to know your feelings."

MacLean didn't think the Canadians could contribute anything useful at that time, since they didn't know any better than anyone else what had happened. But, as the next Canadian slated to fly a shuttle mission, he was inevitably besieged with questions about the impact of the accident on his flight and the future of the Canadian astronaut program. "I didn't care about that stuff that day," he remembered. "Your reaction is much more on a personal level."

This was also true for Bondar, who found her reactions colored by the fact that she comes from a very close-knit family and that her father had died suddenly a few months before. She found it hard to watch the funeral service for the astronauts because "I could feel for the families. I knew what it was like when I lost my father, who had just turned 70, who had lived an exceptionally good life. And then you think of these young people who had years of life to give." She admitted that the accident had shaken her, even though she'd known what the risks were. "I think that if I were a married person with a young family, that might make me think about the risks again. I think we all must have taken some time in wondering, do I really want to put my family through this if something happens to me? It would be pretty unusual if it did not cross our minds." But, like the others, she was not swayed in her commitment to the astronaut program.

At a news conference a few days after the accident, MacLean said that it is "a natural evolutionary process for us to go into space. I still feel very much a part of that commitment and I still am very anxious to fly." Garneau said: "We loved them, we were proud of them and we felt that what they were doing was important for mankind."

After the initial shock wore off, the Canadian astronauts began to assess the impact of the tragedy on their own careers. They knew their missions were on indefinite hold until NASA could put its house in order. In the first few months after the accident, there was no telling when the shuttle would start flying again, much less when the Canadian flights might be rescheduled. This climate of uncertainty about the future was compounded by changes occurring closer to home — for example, in late March, the NRC's space-related programs were reorganized into a new space division and the Canadian astronaut program was transferred to space research operations, a new section headed by Roy VanKoughnett, previously associate director of the NRC's Canada Centre for Space Science. The other new section was the space projects office, headed by Doetsch, which would be responsible for development of the Mobile Servicing Centre, the CDN$800-million contribution to the U.S./international space station, which the federal government had approved in mid-March. (See Chapter 7.) Moving the astronaut office into closer association with the part of the program that focussed on the "users" of space systems was a logical change. The astronauts were increasingly working with the university and industry scientists and technical experts who would be preparing experiments and projects for the shuttle and, eventually, the space station. But they also continued to be involved in the development of space technology and would undoubtedly play an important role in Canada's space station project as well.

The space station announcement, coming in the aftermath of the Challenger explosion, was especially welcome news to the astronauts. Not only did it presage a vital Canadian space program to the turn of the century, it carried a clear implication, if not yet an explicit commitment, that the astronaut program would be continued. The fate of the program had not been officially announced — this was to be part of the government's much-delayed long-term space plan — but the astronauts had good reason to be optimistic. When science minister Frank Oberle announced the space station project in March, 1986, he said that one of the things Canada expected to get in return for its contribution was the right to put Canadian astronauts aboard the station "on a continuing basis." In an interview shortly afterwards, the minister unequivocally stated that the astronaut program would continue. "There will definitely be Canadians associated with most if not all of the space station activities."

Earning a place for Canadians aboard the station has been one of Doetsch's admitted objectives since the inception of the Canadian astronaut program. "We hope there is room for the Canadian astronauts," he frequently remarked. "We see them or their successors as being an integral part of the space station in the future." NASA officials appeared to be amenable to the idea; Robert Freitag, then director of policy and plans in NASA's space station office, said that if Canada builds and operates the servicing facility, this would "absolutely" open up permanent operations-related jobs on the space station for Canadian astronauts.

For their part, the astronauts had always expressed optimism about the continuation of the program, although they tried to refrain from wallowing in guessing games about the future. "Sometimes it's not good to speculate too far ahead," Bondar said. As their work load increased and expanded, they found it increasingly incomprehensible that the program would be abandoned after just three flights. Still, as 1985 drew to a close, the signs had not seemed good: the long-awaited announcement of the government's space plan, which was to reveal the fate of the astronaut program, kept being put off; rumors abounded that the Canadian space station program might fall victim to the government's war on the national debt and, in January, 1986, everything seemed about to grind to a halt because of the Challenger explosion. "It was pretty sombre here after the accident," MacLean said. "But I don't think I ever thought that anything would stop. Everybody knew that we would continue to fly, that we would continue to have a program. In fact, even during the explosion, I remember saying, 'Well, I still want to fly.'"

By the spring of 1986, the long-term picture was definitely looking up. Canada's commitment to building the space station servicing centre was publicly announced and the astronauts were buoyed by Oberle's hints about the continuation of the program — a copy of his words was prominently displayed on the bulletin board in their office. Even the delay in the shuttle program could not squelch their optimism that, ultimately, there would be space flights for all of them; in fact, they were already beginning to think in terms of qualifying to perform EVAs. "The astronaut program really has to continue so you don't have to have a brand new start in ten years time, to start learning how to use [the space station]," Tryggvason said.

"Our long-term future is really looking good because we are into the space station in such a big way," said Money. "It's just our short-term future that's the pits."

The delay caused by the Challenger accident had a different impact on the three SVS astronauts than on the three life sciences astronauts, and not only because the SVS mission had already been announced. It was clear that MacLean's mission would not be going in March, 1987, but it was hoped that he could fly within the first year after shuttle launches resumed. In order to ensure that Canada could take advantage of an early opportunity if it presented itself, the schedule for development of the flight hardware was not relaxed; the contractors were told to proceed as if they still had a March, 1987, flight date to meet. "We're going to stick very much to that schedule," said Bruce Aikenhead. "We could say, there's no rush now, let's put everything on hold, but I think that would be unwise. We've got a couple of contractors that are going flat out to try and meet that schedule and then that contract can be closed. I think that's a more economical way of doing things than just having their team drift along." Once ready, the hardware could if necessary be moth-balled until the shuttle started flying again. Aikenhead said the system could then be ready to fly with about six months' notice, most of which would be required for astronaut training and installation of the system aboard the shuttle.

The SVS hardware consists of two major components: a computerized display and control system that must be installed on the shuttle's flight deck and the Canadian target assembly (CTA), the small payload carrying the targets, which must go into the cargo bay. Both elements are essential to the experiment, so it would be necessary to find a shuttle flight that could accommodate both. Aikenhead said they tried to maximize the chances of getting an early mission by making the CTA small enough to fit along the side of the cargo bay. A larger payload that would take up substantial room in the bay could cause even further delays; the CTA is a secondary payload compared with high-priority military and commercial payloads.

The three SVS astronauts were also proceeding as if the flight was still scheduled for early 1987. MacLean and Tryggvason continued their training program with the principal investigators for the Canadian experiments — teams of scientists located from

British Columbia to Nova Scotia and including some U.S. researchers as well. The major unknown was when the two would do the NASA-related training at JSC and KSC. It was expected that they would move to JSC on a full-time basis about three months before the flight; the longer training time was necessary because the SVS experiment called for MacLean to work more closely with the NASA crew than Garneau had. However, by mid-1986, with a projected hiatus in shuttle flights until 1988, there was no telling when the move to Houston would occur. Maintaining the pace of the program in Canada would keep the momentum and the morale up for the time being; it was too soon to consider what should be done if the delay in resumption of shuttle flights extended beyond two years.

The three life sciences astronauts were potentially facing even greater delay and uncertainty. NRC had been negotiating for some time for a place aboard a flight that would carry the European-built Spacelab. Spacelab had been flying infrequently and available slots for payload specialists were at a premium; in fact, even before the Challenger explosion, Money had been pessimistic about getting a Spacelab flight before the 1990s. However, just before the accident, it looked as though a Canadian could be accommodated on the International Microgravity Laboratory (IML), a Spacelab flight then scheduled for May, 1987.

The close proximity of this mission to MacLean's flight was a major reason for the marked split in training activities between the two groups of astronauts that occurred in late 1985 and early 1986 before the shuttle accident intervened to change everything. One consequence of this division of labor was that the choice of the crew member for the SVS flight was essentially restricted to the three engineering astronauts. The crew member for the space physiology flight would be chosen from among the three life sciences astronauts. The choice was close to having been made at the time of the shuttle accident but this too was put on hold. Later, it fell to VanKoughnett to make the selection.

Getting on board the IML mission was particularly important for one of Doug Watt's physiology experiments. Watt had developed a "space sled," a device used to accelerate the astronaut along a track to test the adaptation of the inner ear and the central nervous system to weightlessness. (See Chapter 5.) NASA would not carry the sled in the mid-deck; doing so would require removal of the treadmill used for exercise in space, which was strongly opposed by the U.S. astronauts. Spacelab, on the other hand, had plenty of room for the device. However, flying on a Spacelab mission did have some important ramifications for the training of the Canadian astronaut selected: he or she would be expected to become part of the Spacelab research team and participate in the non-Canadian experiments that would be done on board.

In the aftermath of the Challenger accident, amid projections of a one- to two-year delay in resumption of regular shuttle flights, the Canadian astronauts were dismayed by predictions that the IML mission might not fly until as late as 1990 or that it might be cancelled altogether and its experiments farmed out to non-spacelab shuttle flights. This would have an effect on the space sled experiment. In the fall of 1986, NASA announced that the mission would be scheduled for 1990, but it was still uncertain whether the Canadian astronaut would be part of the team.

No one was more interested in the fate of this mission than Ken Money, who, at 51, was more than ever aware that time was running out on him. "I could get eliminated now just by being delayed. My big worry is that I'm getting too damn old; you can't count on a pass in the medicals over 50." Facing the prospect that his fourth and last chance for a space flight might well be slipping away, Money admitted that he was beginning to feel a little "picked on" by the fates.

For Bob Thirsk, the delay raised questions in his own mind about what he wanted to do with his career. It was not that he wanted to leave the astronaut corps — "I'd never leave the astronaut program, never" — but he was chafing because of the suspension of shuttle flights and the consequent interruption in the training program. In part, his reaction may have been prompted by his unique experience of having gone through the "high" of training intensively for a shuttle mission without actually having flown one. "They say, we can keep you busy, but I did not join this program to take on a desk job," he said. "I'm 32 years old; this is the time of life when I'm most aggressive, most competitive. I need something to do; I need a challenge." He had already made plans to resume clinical medicine on a part-time basis, but he also believed that it might be possible to make profitable use of the delay in the shuttle program by starting to think about mission specialist training for the Canadian astronauts. In the near term, however, their problem was when they would fly again as payload specialists. The presidential commission investigating the Challenger accident did not explicitly recommend that non-NASA astronauts be prohibited from flying on the shuttle when flights resumed. However, NASA officials and astronauts testifying before Congress in May, 1986, suggested NASA might reassess its policy of flying payload specialists from industry and foreign countries (and the citizen-in-space program) and would likely not fly such people until confidence in the shuttle program could be restored. There was little doubt that NASA would fly only its own astronauts at first. NASA spokesperson Barbara Selby said that payload specialists are "not going to fly early, but I doubt if they'll be kept off. We don't expect to suspend them."

Doug Watt expressed concern that the U.S. astronauts would try to keep payload specialists off the shuttle. Some astronauts, he said, "would like to keep payload specialists off permanently, but I don't think they could ever do that." He predicted, however, that they "will have to be forced" to accept payload specialists as crew members again.

Roy VanKoughnett, head of the Canadian astronaut program, said in mid-1986 that they still hoped Steve MacLean would get a flight within the first year after shuttle flights resumed. "NASA has indicated this is a possibility and there even might be less of a delay," said VanKoughnett. "There's a commitment — a very strong one — to support that flight." However, he acknowledged that NASA had many other commitments as well and said it was impossible to guess when MacLean would fly "until we see something in the form of a manifest from them, some kind of schedule." Even if NASA resumed launching by early 1988, as administrator James Fletcher was then predicting, this could well push the Canadian mission into 1989. In the fall of 1986, NASA announced a list of projected shuttle missions and VanKoughnett said there appeared to be about four possible flight opportunities for the MacLean mission in 1989.

VanKoughnett said the Canadian program had not been informed of any policy change at NASA regarding flying foreign payload specialists and "our sense is that NASA's commitment to international collaboration seems to be unchanged." He added that the crew member for the life sciences mission would probably be selected by the fall of 1986, even if the situation with the IML mission was not clarified; this was in part an attempt to reduce some of the uncertainties facing the Canadian astronauts.

NOTES

1. In defiance of regulations, the walls in Building 4 were plastered with cartoons and jokes and acerbic comments. For example: "All of this stuff is so confusing to me — I just hate to send it to an engineer." Or: "From now on, it's all disapproved."

2. JSC was like a pressure cooker in a literal as well as a figurative sense. Within a week of their arrival, Garneau and Thirsk had acquired the damp, frazzled look that afflicts most northerners subjected to the oppressive heat and humidity of Houston in mid-August.

3. The food Garneau selected was loaded aboard the shuttle several weeks before the mission. Thirsk would later comment, when discussing his willingness to step in at the last minute if Garneau were unable to fly the mission, that he would be more than happy to eat whatever Garneau had chosen.

4. The mission rules are really a series of commandments about what to do if things go wrong. These range from relatively minor malfunctions to serious failures that would dictate an early termination of the mission and an immediate return to earth. Although many rules apply to any mission, each flight also has rules that apply to the payloads and activities unique to that flight.

5. These are qualities equally prized among the flight controllers, the training teams and the people responsible for preparing the crew activity plan (CAP), all of whom have to have the flexibility to respond to everything from a minor change in the astronauts' sleep schedule to a back-to-the-drawing-board overhaul of the plans, including (in the case of Mission 41-G) the last-minute addition of two payload specialists and a change of flight crew and orbiter. Life is never dull in the CAP office.

6. No item in the equipment lockers, no matter how seemingly innocuous, escaped the NASA safety engineers. Garneau received a note concerning a pair of ordinary white nylon gloves worn to protect camera filters: if he preferred them to the surgeon's gloves he had already tried, they would have to be sent for testing to ensure they didn't "outgas" toxic chemicals.

7. In large part, this was because of the increasing involvement of the Department of Defense in the actual operation of shuttle missions. Military personnel were training as shuttle flight controllers and an astronaut crew was preparing for a secret military flight (Mission 51-J in October, 1985). The military presence at JSC was expected to decrease, however, when the shuttle control centre and launch site that the Air Force was building at Vandenberg Air Force Base in California was ready in 1986. The new launch facility was not used before shuttle flights were suspended after the Challenger accident.

8. Christa McAuliffe, who proposed to conduct two classes for school children from space, might have been able to turn this perception around; in the wake of her death, it became apparent that her infectious enthusiasm, adventuresome spirit and commitment to the space program had managed to touch a responsive chord in many children.

9. During the mission, Steimle clearly demonstrated that science comes before politics in his books — he cancelled a televised exchange between the three European Spacelab astronauts and German chancellor Helmut Kohl because the European ground control team was preoccupied with troubleshooting several technical problems that had beset the mission. "I felt that the

mission science was more important than a VIP broadcast," the uncompromising — and unrepentant — Steimle said later.

10. Even with Mission 41-G out of the way, their schedule did not let up very much. One result was that, by early 1986, none of Tryggvason's pilot-trainees — MacLean, Garneau or Thirsk — had yet received their licenses, although they all soloed in the summer of 1985. "They've been slowed down somewhat. They don't have their priorities right," joked Tryggvason, to whom there is little that is more important than flying. By mid-1986, MacLean and Garneau had their licenses.

11. This project lost out in a battle with the space station project for major federal funding and, in mid-1986, its fate was uncertain. See Chapter 7.

12. During the press conference, which occurred less than two months before the Challenger explosion, NRC president Larkin Kerwin made a comment that reflected the widely held public faith in NASA's attention to safety, which would be sorely tried in the aftermath of the tragedy. "Because of the intense preoccupation with the security of the human passengers, any small glitch has to be ironed out, solved, before flights are allowed," he said.

13. The senior McLean spells his name differently than his son because the "a" in "Mac" was mistakenly left out on his birth registration. His children were registered as MacLean.

14. Although previously Doetsch had repeatedly emphasized that all six astronauts would be eligible for all three missions, he admitted at this point that, because of the different demands being placed on the astronauts by the two major sets of experiments, the group had for all intents and purposes split into an SVS team and a SAS team, as had originally been planned.

CHAPTER FIVE

The Human Body in Space

For
billions of years,
life on earth has evolved
in an environment
that has in many ways
changed dramatically,
but there is one respect
in which it has not changed:
the force of gravity on earth
has varied hardly at all over the millennia.
Now, in a span of time
that does not even qualify
as a blink of the eye,
evolutionarily speaking,
the human body is being expected to adapt to life in zero gravity. After the turn of the century, many people will be spending months at a time living in space, aboard permanently manned stations in earth orbit. This new breed of space worker will include not only professional astronauts, but scientists, doctors, engineers, construction workers, technical experts, managers, journalists, artists, entertainers and many others — people whose physical and mental condition, age, medical background and physiological susceptibility to zero-G will vary widely.

Although the body has proved to be a remarkably adaptable biological machine, it will remain very much a product of the earthly environment for a long time to come. How well will it cope with an environment it has never encountered in its entire evolutionary history? To date, it *appears* to have coped surprisingly well. In the early days of the space program, before humans had experienced zero-G, there were fears about its physiological effects that, in retrospect, seem exaggerated and even funny — for example, that astronauts would not be able to swallow, or that their eyes would bug out. This is why dogs and monkeys were sent into space first. When the first human flights occurred with no apparent damage, opinion swung the other way — zero gravity was, it seemed, a piece of cake. Twenty-five years of research has shown that reality is, as usual, somewhere between these extremes — and certainly far more subtle than anyone guessed in those early days. Scientists are learning that zero-G does exact a physiological cost — potentially quite a serious one — and the future of humans in space will depend to a great extent on how much they can learn about this cost and what they can do to counteract it.

Gaining an understanding of the effects of zero gravity on human physiology has been difficult for many reasons. It is impossible to simulate adequately the long-term space environment on earth. Most U.S. space missions have been of relatively short duration and so packed with work that astronauts have generally been left with little time for extensive physiology testing. In any event, most astronauts, particularly the test-pilot and engineering types that have dominated the program, don't like participating in physiology experiments because of their concern that anything smacking of a medical problem could affect their chances for future flights. Only three long-duration missions have been conducted in the U.S. space program; the three Skylab missions in the mid-1970s lasted approximately one, two and three months respectively. In contrast, Soviet cosmonauts have spent much longer periods continuously in zero-G aboard the Salyut space station — they hold the record at 237 days. However, Western scientists have received relatively little information about the medical results of these missions.

Nevertheless, much has been discovered about the problems that long-term living in space creates for the human body. The most common and serious medical and physiological effects associated with zero gravity include:
- space motion sickness
- disorientation and alterations in the awareness of body position

- muscle deconditioning
- shifting of bodily fluids
- loss of fluid volume
- loss of red blood cell mass
- cardiac effects
- loss of bone calcium

These effects can be expected in the course of living a "normal" day-to-day life in space. In addition, with the expected increase in EVAs and heavy-duty construction and repair work on the space station, there will be an increase in occupational hazards and injuries — burns, electric shocks, exposure to toxic substances, lacerations, concussions, penetrating wounds, and increased exposure to higher levels of radiation. A variety of moderate to serious medical emergencies are bound to occur and deaths are inevitable.

The challenge facing space doctors is two-fold: how to keep people healthy on a day-to-day basis and how to diagnose, treat and/or prevent acute and potentially life-threatening conditions. People *will* die in space — there is no avoiding that fact — but NASA hopes to minimize the number of serious medical emergencies, and the cost of dealing with them, by putting a health maintenance facility on the space station. The exorbitant cost of sending the "ambulance" has been a major incentive for the development of this mini-hospital in space. A shuttle rescue flight (what NASA euphemistically calls "emergency resupply") could take as long as two to three weeks to arrive[1] and would cost between US$125- and $175-million per flight. NASA has estimated that, without an in-flight medical facility, a space station with a crew of 12 and a lifetime of 20 years would require more than one emergency shuttle flight a year, or approximately 21 such flights over its lifetime. Even at a "bargain basement" cost of US$100-million per flight, the total bill would exceed US$2-billion, said James Logan, chief of medical operations at the Johnson Space Center. In contrast, the station's medical facility is expected to cost about US$40-million, less than half of 1 per cent of the total cost of the station.

He said it would have several purposes: to maintain crew health and safety, prevent "excessive" mortality, prevent early termination of a mission for medical reasons, prevent unnecessary rescue missions, and increase the probability of success of a rescue mission by stabilizing and keeping patients alive until the shuttle can arrive. In deciding what medical conditions can and should be treated in space, a form of triage has necessarily been adopted. Class I conditions fall into the "no big deal" category, Logan said. They result in only mild symptoms, have a minimal effect on work performance and can be treated with off-the-shelf medication. A mild case of motion sickness or a cold would fall into this category. Class III conditions are at the opposite end of the scale. They are immediately fatal or acutely life-threatening — such as major body burns, penetrating head wounds and complicated heart attacks. "These are not survivable in the space station," Logan said. The only equipment planned for these contingencies is a body bag in which to store the body for return to earth. (Logan pointed out that since a death might occur while an astronaut is working outside the station, the body bag must be big enough to accommodate the bulky EVA suit as well.)

The Class II conditions are the ones that the doctors are most concerned with because they have the greatest potential impact on the mission. Included in this category are conditions with moderate to severe symptoms that could become life-threatening if not attended to — such as chest or head trauma, abscesses, kidney stones, appendicitis, perforated ulcers, air embolism or mild heart attacks. Individually, none of these ailments has a high probability of happening, but Logan said that the "cumulative probability is high that somebody is going to get very ill. The problem is, you don't know what they're going to get ill with." The probability of medical emergencies will be increased by the fact that space station crews will include older people and people whose physical condition and medical histories will generally not be as good as those of the traditional test-pilot career astronauts. "If we don't have an in-flight medical capability, we'll have to go back to the Right Stuff mentality in the selection program," Logan said.[2]

He said it is important to have an in-flight capability to diagnose ailments and to treat, or at least stabilize, a patient's condition to prevent death before a rescue flight arrives. NASA is not anxious to be confronted with a situation in which an astronaut dies slowly over a period of one to two weeks because of a lack of medical help aboard the station, especially when feasible on-the-spot treatment could make the difference between life and death.

The medical facility is expected to be set up on the station as soon as crews are left aboard without a shuttle attached.[3] The total weight of equipment allowed is about 540 kg and the total volume allotted to the entire facility is about nine cubic metres — which has been variously described as the size of "two telephone booths back to back" or "two intermediate-sized caskets." This facility is expected to accommodate one person as an in-patient for 28 days or four to five people as outpatients.

Conditions requiring minor surgery and/or anesthesia — suturing cuts, draining abscesses, setting fractures — could be treated on board the station. "Cuts and lacerations can certainly occur and they'll be sewed up," said Philip Johnson, a doctor with the medical sciences divison of the Johnson Space Center. Although fractures are expected to be less common than on earth, the medical officer will be able to apply a cast; Johnson said it wouldn't have to be much of a cast, because the patient won't be putting any weight on the limb in zero gravity. He also said that zero gravity is ideal for burn treatment "because you can float. We just tie you in the middle of the cabin and let you swing there and you're not pressing on your burns. You're probably better off there than you are on the ground." (However, massive body burns would be difficult to treat in space because of the requirement for large transfusions of liquids.)

The capability for general surgery will not exist in the early years of the station — for example, an appendectomy could not be performed, so someone suffering from appendicitis would have to be maintained with ice packs until a rescue craft arrives. Space doctors consider the ability to do surgery in space a high priority for the future, but it does pose some interesting problems. A method must be found to keep blood and other bodily fluids from floating around and body organs from floating up.

The ability to treat dental problems — toothache, abscesses, tooth fractures and chips and soft tissue lesions — will also be important and tooth extraction may be necessary. The Skylab crews were taught to do extraction and Johnson said that this will likely be the most common form of surgery on the space station. Here again, zero gravity poses some problems: for example, blood and saliva might float freely rather than settling to the floor of the mouth. On the other hand, weightlessness offers some advantages: the person being operated on can easily be positioned "heels over head," providing the person doing the dental work with a much improved viewing angle and access to the mouth.

Designing medical and surgical equipment for use in zero-G has proved a considerable challenge to medical engineers. A surgeon requires foot restraints at the operating table and a method of keeping instruments from floating away. NASA has designed a small surgical table with a magnetized shelf to hold instruments; all the surgeon has to do is give the instrument a small push and, as it floats over the shelf, the magnet snaps it down. Developing a zero-gravity intravenous system was also a challenge. On earth, IV bags are simply hung on a stand and the solution is pulled down by gravity. In space, IV solution does not drain out of the bag and even if it is pumped out, air remaining in the bag would not rise to the top and must be prevented from entering the patient's veins. NASA has developed a zero-G intravenous system that straps around the patient's waist and overcomes these problems. There is also a major problem in storing IV solution on the station — a large volume would be required and it has a short shelf life, so it would have to be replenished frequently. NASA is investigating the possibility of recycling water, using special filters to purify it to the level required for use in IV solution. Among other things, this might mean recycling and purifying waste water containing urine, which Bondar said could present some problems. For example, if a crew member is taking penicillin, it would be excreted in urine and could not be filtered out; the reclaimed water, introduced in IV solution into another patient, might result in a reaction to penicillin. "We'd like to have clean water to make IV solutions," she said. One possibility is recycling water from electrical fuel cells, as is done on the shuttle; but again the volume required poses a problem. "For things like burns, where you're losing a lot of fluids, it requires litres and litres," said Bondar.

Another major medical requirement on the station will be to control infections and the spread of disease. It will be difficult to maintain sterile conditions in space, particularly since bacteria will float freely in zero gravity and won't settle down. This is one reason doctors are trying to develop non-invasive techniques for treating and diagnosing patients.[4] "As soon as you open the skin, you have a wound that's exposed to all the bacteria and bugs that are floating around," said Bondar. "You cannot sterilize the area properly. The blood's drifting around." Moreover, some preliminary biological studies done on shuttle/Spacelab missions suggest that the risk of infection may be higher in zero gravity. Studies done on the shuttle indicate that the response of the body's immune cells to invading cells (antigens) is almost non-existent in zero gravity; other studies suggest that bacteria multiply more rapidly and are more resistant to antibiotics in zero-G. Although these studies were done only with cell cultures, and it is difficult to know whether the same results will occur within the human body, the combination of these two factors does give cause for concern about the ability to stem the spread of infection and disease on the space station.

To aid in the diagnosis and control of various ailments, the medical facility will have a small lab, capable of handling standard microbiological and biochemical testing, including analyzing blood, urine, feces and other biological samples. EKG and EEG equipment, a ventilator and a cardiac "crash cart" will also be included, as well as an imaging system, although neither X-ray nor ultrasound machines may be suitable because they are too heavy, use too much power and require too much operator skill. Bondar said X-ray machines also involve the use of toxic liquids, which could cause serious problems in zero gravity. "The liquids will fly around, so you can't use the wet film technique that we have down here on earth. There are many, many constraints. We may be looking at laser technology, reusable films — that is just being worked on right now."

Logan said that NASA plans to develop a computer system that will integrate the information from all the medical devices to create a medical data base for the station. To support the telemedicine operation, this information could also be accessed by ground-based doctors. He said that this kind of total integration of medical devices and information has never been done before; there is no industrial standard on earth that enables the various medical devices to "talk" to each other. He expected this development to have a spin-off benefit on earth.

One of the most important items of medical equipment on the station will be an airlock that can double as a pressure chamber, to be used in the treatment of astronauts suffering from decompression sickness. This malady, which commonly afflicts divers who surface too quickly from a deep dive, occurs when nitrogen dissolved in the body at higher atmospheric pressures bubbles out of blood and tissues as the pressure outside the body decreases. In its most common form, known as the "bends," the bubbles lodge in the joints, causing severe pain. Other forms of decompression sickness, resulting in a variety of severe symptoms and even death, can occur if bubbles accumulate in the lungs and chest or in the brain, spinal cord or nervous system.

In space, decompression sickness is a potential hazard of EVA. In the EVA suit, the astronaut breathes pure oxygen pressurized to about 4 psi (pounds per square inch). The suit is too soft to accommodate a higher internal pressure, which would cause the joints to seize up or leak and would also further degrade the performance of the thick EVA gloves, which already hamper the astronauts' manual dexterity.

The environment inside the suit is very different from that of the space shuttle crew compartment, and the expected environment of the space station, both of which mimic conditions on earth. On the station, the crew will breathe air (80 per cent nitrogen/20 per cent oxygen) pressurized to 14.7 psi — the pressure that the atmosphere exerts at sea level on earth. The presence of the inert gas nitrogen in the crew cabin greatly reduces the danger of fire and permits greater leeway in the choice of materials for use on the station. (A pure oxygen atmosphere was used in the Apollo spacecraft and was a major contributing factor to the intense flash fire that killed three astronauts during a pre-flight test on the launch pad in 1967.) However, since astronauts on the shuttle or the station breathe a nitrogen-oxygen atmosphere, nitrogen is dissolved in their blood and tissues as they prepare to go from the higher-pressure shuttle or space station environment to the lower-pressure environment of the EVA suit. This creates the potential for decompression sickness.

To avoid trouble, shuttle astronauts flush nitrogen from their bloodstream by "pre-breathing" pure oxygen while hanging on the walls of the airlock inside their suits for three to four hours before leaving the shuttle. Even with such precautions the risk of decompression sickness remains. This has prompted space station planners to design the EVA airlock as a pressure chamber capable of supporting two people in a pure oxygen atmosphere at up to 25 psi, which is standard treatment for the bends. Canada has considerable research experience in the use of pressure chambers to support deep diving operations and Bondar said this is one potential area of involvement for Canada in the space station medical program — perhaps in the development of hardware for monitoring patients in the chamber. Canadian payload specialists might also play a role in testing such equipment.

In the future, NASA would like to eliminate the time-consuming pre-breathing requirement, for efficiency and safety reasons. In the space station era, EVAs will occur far more frequently, possibly on a daily basis, and quick, efficient turn-around will be important. In addition, there is the possibility that astronauts may have to leave the station quickly on emergency or rescue missions. One possible way of eliminating pre-breathing, favored by some space station designers, would be to reduce the atmospheric pressure and use a higher percentage of oxygen inside the station. However, this option was strongly and successfully opposed by NASA's task force on the scientific uses of the space station; life scientists objected on the grounds that if the station did not have an earth-like atmospheric pressure and composition, all the physiological data gathered on earth would be useless as a baseline against which to compare human adaptation to space.

Another potential solution is to use a more rigid space suit that could operate well at a higher internal pressure. NASA is considering the development of more rigid space station-based EVA suits. One innovative design that NASA has looked at is a new underwater diving suit developed by Vancouver diver and engineer Phil Nuytten, president of Can-Dive Services Limited. The suit is called the Newtsuit and has what Nuytten describes as a "Darth Vader" look because of its dark color, which results from the use of a new material — a lightweight carbon-fibre composite that is several times stronger than steel. Unlike the cumbersome armored diving suits of the past, the Newtsuit permits the diver great mobility and flexibility underwater. Its most important feature is the unique design of its rotary joints (which Nuytten has patented), which permits them to function without seizing up at underwater pressures of up to 350 psi. This breakthrough will allow divers to work at depths of more than 300 metres, but it could also be used by astronauts working 400 kilometres above the earth's surface. Nuytten says the suit's joints could be adapted for use in space simply by reversing the joints to withstand greater internal, rather than external, pressures.

NASA is also concerned about maintaining the purity of the recycled atmosphere aboard the station. The health effects of impurities could include nausea, eye and respiratory tract irritation, mental impairment, and long-term damage to organs such as the liver and kidneys. The space station will likely have a variety of alarm systems to alert the crew to the presence of dangerous levels of toxic contaminants. Nevertheless, NASA will likely continue to prohibit the use of certain materials, such as plastics, insulation materials and paints that can "outgas" harmful substances into the cabin air. Charles Harlan, head of quality assurance at the Johnson Space Center, said things will likely never reach the stage where someone can "go to the store and buy any product and take it [into space]. Some of them — even with a more sophisticated atmospheric revitalization system — will still represent a hazard."

Another hazard that space dwellers face is the possible loss of pressurization in a living module caused by penetration by micrometeoroids or space debris. NASA estimates that the space station will be penetrated at least once in its 20-year lifetime. There will be four habitable modules, however, and they will be designed so that each can be sealed off from the others, in order to provide a safe haven for the crew in the event that pressurization is lost in one module.

Space station crew members will be exposed to increased levels of radiation because the station, at an altitude of about 460 kilometres, will receive more radiation than the earth's surface does. However, like the earth, it will still be protected from the worst of this radiation by the earth's magnetic field, which traps charged particles streaming through space in two sets of semi-circular belts, called the Van Allen belts after their discoverer. For the most part, these belts are far above the station's altitude: the higher belt is located between about 13,000 km and 19,000 km above the earth and the lower belt is located between about 1600 km and 5000 km. However, in one location over the South Atlantic, the inner belt dips quite low and this would be a source of radiation affecting the space station. Other sources of radiation — such as cosmic rays and radiation produced by solar flares[5] — would also largely be deflected by the magnetic field; however, it is possible that extraordinarily intense solar flares, though very rare, could at times bathe the station in very high levels of radiation. A research paper published in *Science* magazine in 1982 said that major solar flares can "start suddenly and can deliver in a few hours a disabling or even lethal dose of radiation. The largest doses can be two to three times the level lethal to man."

Because the semi-circular radiation belts dip down to the earth at the poles, the radiation risks would be very much greater for missions in high-inclination or polar orbits than for those in orbits closer to the equator. (High inclination orbits are needed for any missions requiring flight over high-latitude areas of the earth — for example, remote-sensing or military surveillance missions.) Up to the time of the Challenger accident, most shuttle flights were in low-inclination orbits, but military polar missions originating from a new launch site at Vandenberg, California, were planned.[6] Manned missions in geosynchronous orbit, at an altitude of about 36,000 km, would also experience higher radiation levels, but such missions are not planned at present. In all cases, astronauts doing EVAs outside the spacecraft would be more vulnerable and NASA is considering increasing the radiation shielding on the EVA suits that will be based on the space station. The *Science* paper suggested that there is a need for improved short-term forecasting of solar flares, but it pointed out that the processes on the sun that produce the flares are very complex and there appear to be some fundamental limits to how accurate the forecasts could be.

One NASA study has estimated that, under normal conditions, the amount of radiation that a person would receive in an average 90-day tour of duty on the station would exceed the occupational limits set for radiation workers in the United States. Although this amount of radiation would have a negligible immediate health impact, it could increase the person's lifetime risk of contracting cancer. It is estimated that, statistically, this amount of radiation would cause about 15 cancer deaths among 10,000 crew members exposed — less than 1% of the approximately 1600 people in every 10,000 who would normally be expected to die of cancer anyway. The NASA study calculated that each 90-day tour of duty would reduce an astronaut's life expectancy by an average of about 15 days, which is less than the expected reduction in life expectancy associated with some risky jobs on earth — construction and mining, for example.

Since being an astronaut has been considered a high-risk job anyway, the upper limit on the amount of radiation they could be exposed to over their entire careers has, in the past, been set higher than the limits set for workers on earth. This may change on the space station, where career limits may be reduced to about the same level as terrestrial industrial limits. This might also cause

160

restrictions on the number of repeat tours of duty individuals would be allowed to serve. An attempt might be made to reduce crew exposure by increasing radiation shielding on the station. This could impose a considerable weight and cost penalty if special shielding is used; however, extra shielding could be provided by careful placement of materials already on the station — e.g., water stores, wastes and equipment. The study suggests that special measures might be taken to protect certain parts of the body that are particularly radiation-sensitive (the lens of the eye, for example) and that astronauts who plan to have children after returning to earth might wear a lower abdominal shield (referred to as a "lead-loaded girdle").

The space station will have a medical officer on board — preferably a doctor, but at least someone trained as a paramedic. Nevertheless, a great deal of consultation with medical experts on the ground will still be necessary. This is already done with shuttle missions; Logan said that "long-distance house calls" were discontinued for a time but were "re-instituted because of the frequency of illness on the orbiter."

"The space station is really the ultimate in remote medicine," said Roberta Bondar, who is head of a life sciences working group looking into possible Canadian contributions to the space station medical facility. She has a long-standing interest in telemedicine and points out that Canada already has considerable experience in the use of voice and/or video systems to link specialists in large urban medical facilities with doctors or nurses in remote locations, such as Northern communities and offshore oil rigs. She gave an example in which an oil rig worker with an eye infection was first evaluated by a specialist on shore and was then treated on the rig, saving the CDN$2000 it would have cost to transport him to an on-shore hospital. Although the station, at an altitude of about 460 km, will not technically be as far away as, say, an Arctic community is from Toronto, obviously "the distance between us and [the station] is going to be insurmountable for quick rescue."

Bondar said that Canada plans to propose to NASA that the telemedicine units developed for the space station be tested in this country. "We'd like to be able to take this unit and put it out on an oil rig, for example, or put it up in a northern nursing station and see how we can use it in a real remote sense." She said such trials would prove useful in testing the system "on a 24-hour-a-day basis in a situation where there are no doctors. We want to be able to test whether the education we're giving people is adequate ... whether or not there are things we hadn't thought of in terms of day-to-day routine use of it. Canada has so much experience in telemedicine and we have people [who are] very, very knowledgeable." She added that the experience gained by participating in the space telemedicine program will produce spin-off benefits that will improve remote medicine in Canada.

Dealing with medical emergencies is only one part of the space doctors' job, however — one they hope will not dominate their activities. Equally important items on their agenda are preventative medicine, long-term maintenance of health in zero gravity, and gaining a better basic understanding of the effects of extended periods of weightlessness on human physiology. In many ways, these are more of a challenge than dealing with the emergencies: not only do they involve far more subtle factors, but, in the long run, they also will have a greater impact on the successful human colonization of space.

Space motion sickness is the effect that has attracted the most public attention to date. This is perhaps understandable — many earth-bound sufferers of motion sickness can commiserate with the astronauts. Motion sickness is, in fact, the most serious medical problem encountered on short-duration missions because it can reduce productivity for several days. It typically occurs only during the first few days and it has afflicted at least half the people who have flown in space.[7] The fact that it occurred at all came as a bit of a surprise, since most of the people who flew in space, especially in the early days, were experienced test pilots who could flip a jet into a 360-degree roll without batting an eyelash. The astronauts can take medication in space if they need it, but this is not always completely effective. At present, there is no way to predict ahead of time who will experience space motion sickness; it does not seem to be correlated with susceptibility to earth-bound variations, such as sea sickness, car sickness or even air sickness.[8] Nor have scientists come up with any tests they can do on the ground that will reliably predict who will succumb in space.

Ken Money and Doug Watt have been doing research in this field for more than 20 years. (In 1986, Money received an award from the Canadian Society of Aviation Medicine for his contributions to this field of research.) They have done experiments with U.S., European and Canadian astronauts in an effort to understand the underlying mechanism of space motion sickness, in the hope of helping not only astronauts but also people who suffer from motion sickness on earth.[9] They are also studying various forms of disorientation in space. Their research is aimed at gaining a better basic understanding of the functioning of the vestibular system — the motion-sensing and balancing system in the inner ear. This is a biological system that has evolved in a 1-G environment and scientists want to understand what happens to it when the gravitational factor is removed in space. They are also trying to understand what happens to the body's balancing system when a person returns to earth after an extended stay in zero-G; returning astronauts typically experience temporary difficulty in standing, walking, turning corners and in getting their feet to move in the direction they want them to.

This research is intended not only to give scientists insight into the physiological effects of zero gravity, but also to help them study the role that gravity plays in the normal functioning of the vestibular system on earth — something that could not be done before because there was no way of eliminating gravity as a factor. New clinical methods for studying the function of the inner ear that could never be tested on earth can now be tested in space. This research will be discussed in more detail later.

Some of the serious medium-term and long-term physiological effects of weightlessness on the human body are:

• *Shifting of bodily fluids and the loss of fluid volume:* Almost immediately on encountering zero-G, blood and other fluids become more evenly distributed throughout the entire body, rather than being pulled to the lower part of the body by gravity. One effect of this is that there is more fluid in the upper body than normal and the face takes on a bloated appearance. The legs, in contrast, appear thinner. The astronauts have given a highly technical name to this syndrome: "puffy faces and bird legs." The body's sensors that regulate blood volume interpret this shifting of fluid as an actual increase in the amount of blood; to counteract this seeming increase, the body rapidly loses about two litres of water in the urine, resulting in an average reduction of about four to nine per cent of blood plasma. (The plasma is the fluid portion of the blood.) This loss levels out within the first two weeks in space and ultimately reverts to normal back on earth.

However, the reduced blood volume does cause problems immediately after the return to earth. Gravity once again pulls the blood into the lower part of the body and, because the volume has been reduced, blood may drain from the head, making the astronaut susceptible to lightheadedness and blackouts. Shuttle astronauts drink one to two litres of water and take salt tablets to aid water retention before re-entry, and many of them also inflate a pressure garment around their lower torso and legs to prevent the blood from rushing to their legs.

The existing pressure suit is made up of three bladders, one each around the lower leg, the thigh and the lower abdomen, which are inflated with air to push blood to the upper part of the body. According to Bob Thirsk, this method can cause restrictions in the flow of blood. He is working on the design of a new type of pressure suit that he believes may be more effective in protecting astronauts against the possibility of blackouts on return to earth.

"A better way to apply pressure is in a graded fashion, so that the pressure near the ankle is higher and gradually drops off as you get up to the level of the abdominal bladder; or to segment these bladders into many segments and apply [pressure] in a wavelike fashion, so the cuff near the ankle would inflate first, then the next cuff and the next cuff. That method would get more blood out of the veins in the lower leg and it would do it faster."

A modified suit is being designed with segmented bladders and a pressure control unit that will supply the correct amount of pressure to each bladder and time the sequence of their inflation. Thirsk said his modified design is intended more for longer missions than for short shuttle flights. Although returning shuttle astronauts sometimes do feel symptoms of lightheadedness, the current suit for the most part "does the trick," Thirsk said. "I'm thinking about long-duration flights, where the cardiovascular deconditioning effects are a lot more severe."

Thirsk plans to do some tests of the system on the third (life sciences) mission of a Canadian astronaut. The suit will not be flown on the shuttle; Thirsk said it is necessary first to give NASA some evidence that it would be more effective than the existing suit. Instead, he will test astronauts within an hour after their return to earth by monitoring blood pressure near the forehead (a measure of the blood flow entering the head) while they are wearing the current pressure suit, then the modified one and then neither. They will have to lie down between the tests so the results of each test won't alter those of the next.

The Canadian astronaut on that flight, along with at least one other crew member, will also do some tests designed to help Thirsk decide how much pressure should be applied to the segmented air bladders to retain comfort but ensure effectiveness. The in-flight tests involve using a pressure cuff placed around the leg to force blood from the veins, and then measuring the resulting changes in the volume of the leg, which will be due mostly to blood moving out of the veins. Similar tests will be done before and after the flight for comparison purposes.

• *Red blood cell loss:* Astronauts lose between about 5 and 20 per cent of their red blood cell mass in space. This is believed to be another consequence of the loss of fluid; when the blood plasma volume is reduced, the body senses a higher concentration of red cells in the plasma and reduces production of the cells, which occurs in the bone marrow. More recently, it has been suggested that the loss may be caused by an increased rate of removal of red blood cells from the body. Red cell loss is below the amount that would cause observable symptoms and it too levels off after a time and returns to pre-flight levels on earth.

• *Heart and circulatory effects:* Cardiac effects have been observed in astronauts. For example, some have experienced irregular heartbeat, particularly during EVA, which is thought to be caused by the loss of electrolytes such as potassium and sodium from the body. Another major effect is an increase in blood pressure in the upper part of the body and an increase in the volume of the chest area, caused by the shifting of fluids. There is concern that the pressure of the blood going into the heart (central venous blood pressure) may be increased, which would in turn increase the risk of heart failure among astronauts on long-duration missions. Bob Thirsk has proposed an experiment for Steve MacLean's flight to determine whether central venous pressure is elevated early in a space flight (measurements taken of Spacelab astronauts after they'd been in space for a day did not show an increase in pressure). As soon as possible after reaching orbit, MacLean will do a simple test involving the use of a blood pressure cuff and a stethoscope (both of which are carried in the shuttle medical kit) to provide an indirect measure of any increase in central venous blood pressure. Thirsk also plans to study whether sitting in the shuttle waiting for launch increases venous pressure. Astronauts typically sit for several hours before launch with their backs to the ground and their feet up — a position that shifts fluid to the chest region. "I don't know if it replicates the same effect that you get in zero-G, but it's an important question to answer," Thirsk said.

• *Muscle deconditioning:* Most of the muscles in the human body are designed to counteract the effects of gravity on earth. In space, they simply don't have enough work to do. The legs, in fact, are hardly used at all, other than to anchor astronauts in foot restraints when they need stability for two-handed chores; otherwise, most movement in zero gravity is accomplished by using the hands and arms. In this environment, the muscles start to atrophy rapidly, particularly in the lower body. Even astronauts who have been in space only a week are often wobbly on their feet when they return to earth, although they are usually back to normal within a few hours. Astronauts who have spent a month or more in space have experienced greater difficulties. For example, the members of the first Skylab crew, who spent a month in space, had to be supported by members of the ground medical team; one crew member, doctor Joe Kerwin, was visibly sagging as he walked from the spacecraft and he had to keep his pressure garment inflated for some seven hours after his return to earth. Soviet cosmonauts who have spent six to eight months in space have been carried from their spacecraft in reclining chairs and reportedly are often not able to stand for days after their return to earth. When cosmonaut Valery Ryumin, who spent 175 days in space, was presented with a bouquet of flowers on his return, the Soviet space doctors immediately confiscated it, saying it would tire him as much as holding "an enormous sheaf of wheat."[10] To offset the worst of these effects, the cosmonauts on the 1984 Salyut mission that lasted a record 237 days exercised about 2 1/2 hours a day. One crew member, cardiologist Oleg Atkov, has told Western scientists that he walked with his wife the evening of the day he returned to earth.

It appears, then, that a great deal of exercise will be required on long-duration missions to maintain even a semblance of the muscle tone needed to cope with earth's gravity and this may pose some problems. Bondar points out that, on earth, "it's very difficult to get someone to exercise three times a week for 20 minutes." The fact that astronauts are highly motivated, disciplined and goal-oriented people doesn't mean they'll always stick to a demanding exercise program, says Ken Hranchuk, an Ottawa psychologist working with the NRC. Astronauts are busy people and reasons to postpone exercising are not hard to find on a space mission. Money said that one crew of Spacelab astronauts, who returned to earth with muscles that were "remarkably wasted," found that it was too much effort to set up the exercise equipment and, in addition, "they were very busy; they wanted to get a lot of work done and basically they just didn't exercise."

Hranchuk has proposed the development of a special training program designed to encourage astronauts to comply with exercise requirements in space. He believes that one of the best ways of encouraging someone to stick with an exercise program is by providing frequent feedback on the physiological effects of the exercise — monitoring changes in heart rate or respiratory capacity, for example. This monitoring must be largely self-administered, rather than imposed by someone else, because people generally don't respond very well to demands in these circumstances, he said. "Forced compliance is not the best way." Hranchuk also hopes to teach the astronauts how to predict and deal with episodes of backsliding or relapse that often occur after the initial burst of enthusiasm; however, if the feedback technique is successful, "relapse may not even occur."

• *Bone calcium loss:* In zero gravity, astronauts experience a small but steady loss of calcium from their bones, particularly the weight-bearing bones of the legs and feet. U.S. astronauts have lost an average of about 7 per cent of the calcium in their heel bones. (Most of their missions were only 7 to 10 days, but the three Skylab missions lasted one, two and three months respectively.) Although so far this has not been enough to produce clinical symptoms, the scientific evidence indicates that the longer the mission, the more calcium is lost and this phenomenon does not appear to level off in space as others do. This makes calcium loss potentially the most serious health problem limiting long-term human activities in zero gravity and some space doctors have indicated that artificial gravity may be necessary for very-long-duration missions (such as a two-year manned mission to Mars) or for permanent colonies in space.

Calcium loss has two serious effects — it makes the bones more fragile and susceptible to fracture, and it could lead to an increase in the incidence of kidney stones in space. In astronauts, the amount of calcium in the bones does not rebound to pre-flight levels as quickly as with some of the other physiological effects; more than a decade after the Skylab missions, the heel bones of some Skylab astronauts had not returned to pre-flight calcium levels. Bondar says that if bone calcium loss proves irreversible, "we'll have a bunch of astronauts who will be at workmen's compensation with pathological bone fractures." Bondar said that doctors would be delighted to find a countermeasure for calcium loss, not only for astronauts but for bed-ridden patients and post-menopausal women on earth, who suffer similar problems.

Doctors have been searching for a method of preventing calcium loss in space but, so far, neither exercise nor diet seem to have had much effect, at least in the U.S. program. Noting that it has been suggested that as much as 12 hours of exercise a day might be required to counteract calcium loss, Money said that "the amount of time required for the desirable effects of exercise might be more than you can give it." (He commented that the amount of treadmill exercise done during shuttle missions is "really just a bit of voodoo as far as the effect on muscle and bone is concerned. In eight days, it doesn't do anything.")

Comparatively little is known about the success of the diet/exercise regime practiced by the Soviet cosmonauts, which has not been reported in the scientific literature. However, according to informal reports, calcium loss in cosmonauts has been retarded by a combination of drugs, diet, calcium supplements and 2 1/2 hours of exercise every day that included hard impact of the feet on a surface. This may just work the legs hard enough to have a beneficial effect, Thirsk speculated. "If you do impact work, you get several Gs [several times the force of gravity on earth]. That's what the bones need. Maybe we should start looking at that too."

• *Back pain:* During the first few days in space, many astronauts experience severe back pain, especially while asleep. It can be relieved only by pressing the back against a solid surface. This problem has not been studied by space doctors; in fact, only recently have they discovered how widespread it is among shuttle crew members. "Apparently it's extremely common," said Money. "I had heard of it but I didn't know how general it was until Marc got back. He said he was surprised that, when the first sleeping period arrived, somebody got out Tylenol and said,

'Anyone want Tylenol for sleeping?'" When Garneau queried this, he was told, "Oh, it's for the back pain."

Money said that astronauts typically sleep for about 45 minutes before being awakened by the pain. "You then find yourself a corner to push against. You put a force on it and that immediately relieves the pain. Then you can go back to sleep for another 45 minutes." This interruption of sleep by back pain occurs only for the first three or four "nights" (i.e., sleep periods) in space.

Although the exact cause of this pain is not known, it is believed to be related in some way to the stretching of the spine that occurs in zero gravity and causes astronauts to "grow" as much as 6.5 cm. A small increase occurs during the first two or three days, but most of this "growth" occurs from days six to nine. A research team headed by principal investigator Peter Wing, medical director of the back pain clinic at Shaughnessy Hospital in Vancouver, suggests that the greatest increase in height, which occurs toward the end of the first week in space, is caused by the increased spacing between the discs. They have hypothesized that the resulting changes in the pressure on the discs and the spacing between them cause painful tension in the spine and in the ligaments, nerves and muscles associated with it.

To test this theory, they are planning experiments for two shuttle missions on which Canadian astronauts will fly. On his flight, Steve MacLean will be asked to keep a daily record of back pain symptoms, including marking the location and type of pain experienced on a drawing of the human body. This will be the first time that the pain will be scientifically documented. Wing said it is necessary to train someone to report this pain objectively because most astronauts simply won't do it on their own; "astronauts are not known for complaining about pain and discomfort," he said.

A subsequent and more elaborate back pain test will be done on the life sciences mission that will follow MacLean's mission. In addition to keeping the daily pain record, the payload specialist will also set up two cameras to take stereo pictures of his or her back in space. (This technique, which produces a three-dimensional image of the back, is similar to the method used by surveyors to produce surface contour maps.) Before flight, the payload specialist will have a vertical line drawn in indelible ink down the back with crossing horizontal lines at four locations from near the base of the neck to the tailbone. He or she will also undergo a pre-flight back examination, including X-rays and stereo photographs.

During the mission, daily photographs will be taken of the payload specialist's back markings.[11] The priority is to obtain as much data as possible on the later days of the mission, the period of most rapid growth. Another set of photos, along with a second set of X-rays, will be taken during an examination as soon possible after the flight. It is hoped that comparison of the in-flight data with those taken on the ground will allow doctors to correlate the occurrence of back pain with changes in the spine (particularly in the distance between the discs) caused by zero gravity. "We also hope to find out whether the spinal cord and the attached nerves are being stretched enough to affect their function," Wing said.

• *Taste and smell in space:* In the past, astronauts have reported that their sense of taste seems to be altered in space; typically they find foods sweeter and less spicy than they do on earth. Intrigued by this phenomenon, which had not been formally studied by scientists, Roberta Bondar developed a taste and smell test for Garneau to do on Mission 41-G. The experiment was aimed at gaining a better basic understanding of the effect of zero gravity on the central nervous system; measuring taste was simply a mechanism for isolating the sensory function of a facial nerve, one of three major nerves in the head that convey taste sensations. However, since the experiment was referred to as a "taste test" in the press releases, it was generally misconstrued as just that and was treated by the media as an experiment to improve the cuisine in space.

The equipment provided for the tests included numbered vials containing weak solutions of sucrose, citric acid, urea and sodium chloride, plus distilled water, all identical in appearance. During the mission, Garneau used Q-tips to apply the solutions to various locations on each side of his tongue and he recorded whether the taste was sweet, sour, bitter, salty or whether he thought the sample was distilled water. One objective was to measure Garneau's recognition thresholds — the lowest concentrations at which he could identify each taste. Garneau's sense of smell was also tested by having him close his eyes and smell the contents of four bottles, identical in appearance, containing spearmint, lemon, vanilla extract or distilled water. No alterations of his normal sense of taste or smell were detected by this test. This experiment will be repeated on MacLean's flight.

• *Other physiological effects:* Astronauts generally eat less than an optimal amount of food in space and often return to earth with a weight loss. They also drink less and can be quite dehydrated after the mission.

It has also been found that their capacity for exercise is reduced in space and that their exercise tolerance in space is reduced. It has been discovered that EVA requires a great deal more in energy than expected and astronauts get tired much more quickly while working in space than they do on earth. A certain amount of energy is expended counteracting the effects of zero gravity; for example, in space the arms have a natural tendency to float up, and keeping them down while wearing the bulky EVA suit requires a lot of energy. Working with the hands is also taxing because manual dexterity is hampered by the thick EVA gloves, which do not lend themselves well to some of the fine manipulation tasks the astronauts have been required to perform. During an EVA, astronaut Sherwood Spring reported that his hands were tired and his fingers were getting numb.

A team of researchers at the University of Calgary, headed by principal investigator Howard Parsons of the department of medicine, are planning an experiment for the third (life sciences) Canadian astronaut flight to measure human energy expenditure in zero gravity. Understanding the effect of the space environment on the ability of humans to work productively will be increasingly important during the space station era, when many more people will be living and working in space for extended periods of time. The test will be done in three steps: the astronaut will first drink a special kind of water, then he or she will perform a series of exercises and then collect a urine sample. The water is "doubly labelled" — that is, both the oxygen and hydrogen are different forms (isotopes) from those found in normal water. Therefore the amount remaining in the urine can be analyzed. This will provide an indirect measure of the amount of carbon dioxide the astronaut produces while doing the exercises. (A human being exhales carbon dioxide in every breath and the amount exhaled is an indication of how much energy is being expended.) The astronaut will also do the test on earth for comparison purposes.

Since the experiment is simple and needs almost no equipment, it was not difficult to obtain approval to put it on the flight. "The requirements are simple, though the science is complicated," said Jane Thirsk, a doctoral candidate working on the project.

Most of the space physiology research done by Canadian scientists over the past 20 years has focussed on the vestibular system — the balance and motion-sensing system in the inner ear — and the role it plays in telling us the position of our bodies and limbs, in maintaining upright posture and in helping us cope with the types and ranges of motion to which the body is subjected. The vestibular system consists of two organs: the semicircular canals, which sense angular (rotational) motion, and the otoliths, which sense linear (straight-line) motion and the pull of gravity. Scientists anticipated that the semicircular canals would perform normally in space, but that the function of the otoliths might be significantly altered by the absence of gravity.

On Mission 41-G, Marc Garneau performed a set of vestibular experiments. U.S. Navy oceanographer Paul Scully-Power, the other payload specialist on the flight, assisted him by acting as both a subject and a record-taker. The same tests were run on these two subjects before the flight, to establish their normal ("baseline") responses, and afterwards, to determine whether any of the changes that occurred in flight persisted on the ground and, if so, for how long.

These tests were designed to test the behavior of the vestibular system (and, more generally, the human nervous system) in space. They were also intended to investigate the functioning of the proprioceptive sense — the ability to sense the position of the body and its limbs — and the ability to sense body position in relation to the outside world. It has been known for some time that astronauts often have a poor perception of where their bodies are and how they are oriented. After returning from his mission, Garneau remarked: "You have a very, very poor perception of where you are. Keep your eyes closed for five minutes and there's absolutely no way you know where you are. You just don't have any clues to tell you that you're upside down or right side up. If you try to point at something with your hand, and you're floating freely, you may think you know where something is that you looked at before you closed your eyes. Chances are you'll be completely out."

One of the most striking and curious things about being in zero gravity is that many astronauts report having a strong sense of up and down, even though, technically, there is no up and down in space as we know it on earth. Skylab astronaut Joe Kerwin reported that there's a tendency in zero-G to feel that "up" is where your head is and "down" is where your feet are — regardless of the orientation of the outside world. He reported that when floating in a tunnel in Skylab, he experienced a fear of falling if he went feet first; however, going head first through the tunnel produced no sensation of falling. In another instance, an astronaut turned himself with his feet toward the spacecraft ceiling so he could watch the earth go by "right side up." When he looked back into the spacecraft, everything seemed upside down to him. He could not, just by an act of will, perceive himself to be upside down and everything else right side up.

There has also been some indication that astronauts returning from space may become hypersensitive to G-forces and that this might cause some disorientation. For example, shuttle pilot Ken Mattingly reported feeling vertigo as he was coming around the turn just before landing — a maneuvre that produces increased G-forces on the body.

These subjective reports have tantalized scientists with their implication that the body's nervous and sensory systems react in complex and poorly understood ways to the unique zero-gravity environment. The Canadian physiology experiments on Mission 41-G were part of a large number of experiments designed to investigate various aspects of these puzzling phenomena. They included:

• *Survey of sensory function in limbs:* Astronauts have reported changes in their sense of their own bodies; for example, they sometimes feel "pins and needles" in the skin and often find it difficult to tell exactly where their arms and legs are in zero-G in the dark and when their eyes are closed or when their muscles are relaxed.[12] On a Gemini mission in the 1960s, an astronaut reported being startled when he awoke to see the luminous dials of five wristwatches floating before his eyes. His reaction was to reach out and touch the image — which floated away from him as fast as he was reaching for it. It took him a while to realize that the five wristwatches were in fact on his wrists and those of his partner; their arms had floated up to eye level in their sleep but the astronauts could not "feel" where their arms were. On a Spacelab mission, an astronaut reported being startled as he was falling asleep by something touching his left hand; when he opened his eyes, he discovered it was his right hand.

In another case, Spacelab astronauts who were "dropped" a short distance to the spacecraft floor (they were actually pulled down by elastic cords) found they were consistently landing with their legs too far forward and tumbling over backward — an effect that persisted for a few days back on earth. Yet, before the flight, Doug Watt said, they were "like cats — not so much as a single stumble." He suggested that this might be due in part to faulty proprioception rather than faulty vestibular function; in other words, the problem may not have been a failure to balance correctly after the drop, but rather an inability to sense the position of the feet correctly before the drop. If this was the case, Watt said, "they were in a mechanically impossible situation when they landed" — their feet were simply in the wrong place and there was nothing the balancing system could do to prevent the tumble.

On Mission 41-G, Garneau and Scully-Power did an experiment to test whether sensory function in limbs is altered in space. The first part of the test measured the tactile sense in the finger and toe. Several times during the mission, Garneau had Scully-Power press a ridged cube against his index finger and his big toe; progressively finer sets of ridges were used to determine whether he could distinguish the direction of the ridges. A second part of the test, designed to test the proprioceptive sense, involved having Garneau and Scully-Power move each other's fingers, toes, and elbow and knee joints and ask the other to estimate the extent of movement or the angle of bend. These tests were conducted with eyes closed.

The results indicated that finger and toe tactile senses do not appear to change in space. However, the proprioceptive sense in relaxed limbs appears to be significantly degraded. Watt reported a significant number of errors in estimating knee-bend and elbow-bend angles. "The subjects reinforced this finding by commenting that they had little feel for the position of their limbs ... The poor awareness of limb position was considered sufficiently dramatic by [Garneau] to be described as one of the most striking phenomena of the entire trip." Later, Garneau commented: "I didn't know where my arms were. After a while, you learn where they're going to end up ... but you don't feel them there. It's quite an interesting sensation." He added that, when he woke up in the morning, "I had absolutely no idea before I opened my eyes where I was going to be and what position I was going to be in."

What causes the loss in sensory function is not fully

understood, but Watt speculated it might have something to do with disuse of the limbs (particularly the legs) in space, or perhaps the body's sensory system is less active when it does not encounter the loads normally placed on it by gravity. Money said that experiments with Spacelab astronauts suggest that, in zero gravity, the muscles may not be sending the same messages to the brain that they do on earth. He found that when astronauts tensed their muscles or moved their limbs in space, they had a better, though still degraded, sense of where the limbs were. "It tends to support the idea that muscle receptors are involved," Money said. "Without gravity pulling on [the muscles] and without the muscles resisting the effect of gravity, the relaxation is so perfect that you don't get much information from muscles." In space, relaxed limbs naturally adopt a certain position — the arms, for example, float upward and outward and hang at about mid-chest level. It is impossible for muscles to relax in the same way on earth, since they are still being pulled by gravity.

• *Awareness of the position of external objects:* This experiment was designed to test a phenomenon reported previously by astronauts — a loss of orientation in zero gravity in the absence of visual cues. The phenomenon was first reported during one of the Skylab missions, when astronaut Owen Garriott said that when he awoke in the morning, he could not locate the light switch on the wall of his sleeping compartment. This was puzzling because the compartment was only about as big as a broom closet and, on earth, most people don't have any trouble reaching out and flipping on a nearby light switch in the dark. Garriott's inability to perform so simple a task obviously irked his astronaut's soul. "It was very annoying because I was so incapable of reaching the spot I wanted in the darkness," he commented after the mission. "In two months, I never learned to locate that light switch. On the ground, you can reach anything with your eyes shut; in zero-G, it's an entirely different phenomenon. You don't miss things by a little, you miss them by a major amount."

Money did some tests with astronauts on a Spacelab mission and found that blindfolded astronauts who were not tightly tethered made large errors when trying to point at targets. On his mission, Garneau did an experiment to evaluate how fast disorientation occurs following the loss of visual cues, and whether it becomes more or less pronounced during the course of the mission. During the test, which has been described as a zero-gravity version of pin-the-tail-on-the-donkey, Garneau first looked at a cross made of two one-metre cloth strips attached to the front of the mid-deck lockers. The arms of the cross were marked "up," "down," "right" and "left" and had numbers written on them, from zero at the centre to 20 at each end. Garneau memorized the position of the target and was then blindfolded. He then tried to point at the centre of the cross with a small flashlight while Scully-Power recorded his accuracy. Then Garneau pointed at each target again, this time opening his eyes when he felt he was pointing correctly and noting whether the target and his arm were where he thought they would be. Later, Garneau and Scully-Power switched positions and Scully-Power also performed the tests.

Although both were able to point very accurately during tests on the ground before the flight, they had very poor pointing accuracy in-flight. One improved during the flight, but the other did not. The performance of both Garneau and Scully-Power returned to pre-flight accuracy almost immediately after returning to earth. In his report, Watt said that the results suggest that, in space, a person's "impression of the world is not simply shifted, rather it is compressed and distorted." It seems that the presence of 1-G is necessary to form an overall accurate image of the outside world, not just the location of external objects. The poor performance of the task may also have been partly due to poor proprioception, he said; one subject remarked that he was never really sure where his arm was pointing.

• *Proprioceptive illusions:* During ground tests after a shuttle mission in 1983, astronauts reported a strange illusion when they hopped up and down. Even with their eyes open, they felt that the floor was moving up and down, not themselves. It is believed this illusion may occur because it takes time for the body to re-adapt to earth's gravity. On flight 41-G, Garneau and Scully-Power studied this phenomenon in space for the first time. They performed a series of movements including deep kneebends with feet restrained; armbends (flexing and extending the arm while grasping a handhold); moving their eyes back and forth with the head fixed; and rubbing a hand or bare foot back and forth under a fixed, solid surface. They reported in each case whether they felt their bodies, the world around them, or both, were moving.

Garneau experienced illusions while doing arm and kneebends

in space; in all the other cases, no illusions were reported. After the mission, he commented that, when he pulled himself toward the wall, he had a very strong sensation that it was rushing at him. "It was something I certainly felt quite convinced about." Doug Watt, reporting on the experiment later, said: "Surprisingly, he did not experience the reverse illusion of the wall moving away during arm extension, and this led to the paradoxical situation of the wall periodically moving towards him, never retreating, but never getting closer." In space, this illusion occurred only when Garneau had his eyes closed. During tests within the first two hours after he returned to earth, he experienced the illusion both with eyes closed and open, though less intensely in the latter case. "The perception of wall movement never changed during the flight, but disappeared rapidly within 24 hours of landing," Watt noted. "Despite the fact that he could feel the wall moving, [he] could never see it move."

The second illusion occurred while doing deep kneebends, but only after landing. "It consisted of a perception that the floor was behaving like a trampoline under [his] feet, moving down as he moved up and vice versa," Watt reported. It occurred both with eyes closed and open, but again less intensely with eyes open. The illusion was very strong during the first 20 minutes after landing and did not disappear when Garneau grasped the back of a chair; however it too was gone within 24 hours. "Once again, [he] could never see the world moving, only feel it with his legs."

Watt said that it is still not known why these illusions occur or why they affect only some astronauts; further research is needed. Nor is there an explanation why the illusion of floor movement occurred only after flight, while the illusion of wall movement occurred both in and after flight; Watt speculated this might have something to do with "the differing demands placed on arms and on legs by gravity."

• *Vestibulo-ocular reflex:* This reflex helps us to continue looking at something in spite of movements of the head. For example, it allows you to fix your eyes on an object directly in front of you while moving your head from side to side, without taking your eyes off the object. It was thought that in space this reflex might be less effective and might cause visual images on the eye's retina to "slip," resulting in motion sickness. If this were true, corrective lenses worn during the first few days of flight might help to reduce motion sickness.

The VOR reflex was measured in two ways. First, Garneau and Scully-Power were asked to look at a fixed point and shake their heads (back and forth and up and down), slowly at first, then increasingly rapidly. They were to report any sensation that the world was moving; in both cases, they reported no more than the amount of movement normally experienced on earth under similar conditions.

Garneau and Scully-Power also did a second, more elaborate test. Each sat in front of the cloth cross with the light pointer strapped to his head and the beam pointed at the zero cross-point. Each focussed his eyes on the same spot, then covered them with a piece of paper and made a rapid head movement while trying to maintain his gaze on the zero. He then removed the paper to see whether his eyes were still looking at the zero or had wandered. The position of the flashlight beam along the horizontal or vertical grid was recorded to indicate how far his head had moved. The results again indicated that the VOR reflex operates normally in zero gravity. This was somewhat surprising because scientists had observed evidence of a change during tests in the KC-135 zero-gravity training plane; however, they speculated this might be explained by the fact that, in the KC-135, the brief zero-gravity episodes are interspersed with periods of 2-G (twice the force of gravity on earth). They also speculated that, if the VOR reflex is initially abnormal in space, it might adjust within the first minute or so, too soon to have been detected by these in-flight experiments. On his mission, Steve MacLean will carry in his flight suit pocket a small card with a series of lines on it. The instant zero gravity is encountered after the shuttle's main engines shut down, he will hold the card in front of his eyes and shake his head left and right to test whether or not his VOR reflex is normal during the first minutes of the flight.

• *Space motion sickness:* Scientists studying space motion sickness have several major objectives. They are trying to develop a method of predicting which astronauts will become sick in space and to develop pre-flight procedures that could reduce or eliminate their susceptibility. They are also trying to develop techniques and countermeasures (such as drugs or biofeedback[13]) that can be used to ameliorate or eliminate motion-sickness symptoms during flight. To do this, they have to document scientifically the occurrence of motion sickness in space and gain a better fundamental understanding of exactly what it is, what makes it better or worse, and how it relates to motion sickness on earth. It is believed that motion sickness is caused by the "sensory conflict" that results when your eyes are telling your brain and nervous system that your body is doing one thing while your vestibular sensors are telling them something else.[14]

One curious aspect of space motion sickness is that the sensation of being "upside down" with respect to one's surroundings is strong, despite the absence of a true gravitational "down," and this seems to provoke sudden queasiness in many astronauts. Spacelab crew members reportedly avoided working "upside down" whenever possible and disliked moving through the tunnel connecting the shuttle with Spacelab because it had no defined ceiling or floor. One astronaut who had to sleep upside down "like a bat hanging from a ceiling" said he found waking up to an inverted world very disconcerting.

Garneau's tests on Mission 41-G, which consisted mainly of observing and documenting his own motion-sickness status, were part of a continuing, long-term research effort to solve some of the mysteries of this phenomenon. In a variety of pre-flight tests, he was found to be more susceptible than average to motion sickness on earth. In space, Watt noted, he was "decidedly *less* susceptible than average, experiencing only occasional trifling symptoms and only during the first day and a half." On the sixth day of the mission, he did a series of nodding head movements in a deliberate attempt to provoke motion sickness, but he experienced only minor symptoms. Tests done three days after the flight indicated that his susceptibility to motion sickness on earth was the same as it had been before the mission.

The fact that Garneau did not get sick in space, despite pre-flight indications of susceptibility, is consistent with findings on a previous Spacelab mission. In that case, the crew member who was most susceptible on earth proved to be least susceptible in space, while the one showing least susceptibility in the pre-flight tests was the most susceptible in space. Some people are immune both on earth and in space, but otherwise, the evidence seems to suggest a negative correlation between motion sickness on earth and in space. (Based on this evidence, Money made a bet with one of the other Canadian astronauts that Garneau would not get sick in space. "I won ten bucks," he said.)

Garneau was surprised that he did not get sick spontaneously, and even more surprised that he could not make himself sick when he tried to do so. Money was less surprised because the head-nodding exercise was done near the end of the mission, when even people who get sick during the first few days have adapted to zero gravity and become "just as immune as the next person."

The fact that Garneau's susceptibility to motion sickness did not temporarily disappear after the flight was surprising, however. Other astronauts had demonstrated an immunity to all forms of motion sickness for about three or four days after they got back, Money said. All of this simply proves how difficult it is to generalize or to develop ground-based tests that might be useful in predicting who will get sick in space when only about half a dozen subjects have been tested and when there is a wide variation between subjects and in the day-to-day responses of any given individual.

Experiments continue, however. When asked if he's running out of ideas for tests that might predict space motion sickness, Money responded with a grin: "Not really. There are lots of ways to get people sick."

Motion sickness is a major medical problem on short-duration flights because it can reduce an astronaut's productivity for several days.[15] It also poses serious risks for astronauts performing EVAs because vomiting in the space suit would be life-threatening. (In November, 1982, during the fifth flight of the space shuttle, a space walk to test the shuttle EVA suits for the first time had to be postponed because astronaut William Lenoir was suffering from nausea and vomiting.) Motion sickness is expected to be a less serious problem during the space-station era, because having astronauts under the weather for a few days will have less impact on a 90-day mission; however, Money pointed out that having people sick while crews are being exchanged could cause difficulties. "If you send off a crew with eight people to the space station and they are all sick, you still have a problem even though they're going for 90 days."

Watt summarized the major findings from the 41-G physiology experiments as follows:
- the VOR reflex continues to be effective in space;
- the ability to distinguish between self-generated and externally generated movement of the limbs is reduced in some individuals and this continues for up to a day after returning to earth;
- the sense of touch in the arms and legs remains normal in space;

- the sense of body and limb position (proprioception) is degraded in space, resulting in a poor awareness of the position of relaxed limbs; contracting the muscles improves this sense somewhat;
- in the absence of vision, the image of the outside world becomes distorted;
- predicting an astronaut's susceptibility to space motion sickness remains difficult;
- the senses of taste and smell appear to be normal in space.

While Money and Watt worked on the Canadian life sciences experiments, they also conducted a series of similar experiments with European and U.S. payload specialists on three Spacelab missions. These included studies on motion sickness and awareness of body position and Watt also ran an experiment called the "hop and drop" test,[16] intended to shed light on the role gravity plays in the ability to hop, walk and run on earth. It involved "dropping" astronauts from a handlebar device a short distance to the floor of the spacecraft. (Since there is no gravity, the subjects were actually pulled down to the floor by elastic cords.) The astronauts' legs were wired with electrodes that measured electrical activity in the muscles; this was another way of testing the functioning of the vestibular system by measuring leg movement and muscle activity.

Watt's subjects included an astronomer, a physicist, a jet instructor pilot, a naval commander, an oceanographer and once, "by accident," a vestibular physiologist. During this period, he changed his view of the type of person most suitable to do these life sciences experiments in space. At the time the Canadian astronauts were being chosen, he expressed a strong opinion that "the person has to be a researcher first of all ... an expert in a specific area of science. The reason you need a real expert is because science is not always predictable. You start doing an experiment and half way through you get a result which you don't expect, and you've got to react appropriately." With the perspective that came from coping with the limitations of doing life sciences experiments on the shuttle, Watt said: "I had an incredibly naive view of what was going to be possible. It is not possible to do conventional laboratory experiments in space." The constraints include an experimentor (the payload specialist) who is about equivalent to a "good post-doctoral student" and who will likely be suffering from motion sickness; about half the time to do the experiment that would normally be devoted to it on earth; a high-stress environment; and pressure to succeed on the first try because you may not get another chance. This is not the way scientists usually work, Watt said; if something doesn't work the first time, they go back and try again and then try new things out just to see what happens. "That's usually not going to work in space," he said. Describing one of his own experiments, he said: "Fifteen years of development all come down to three 22-minute test sessions in space. You have to ensure a very high probability of success on the first attempt. Get it in, get it out and get it right."

In view of these realities, Watt concluded that the best type of person to do the experiments in space is a "fast thinker who doesn't fold under pressure" and someone who can function well within the time and operational constraints of a typical shuttle mission. People chosen primarily for their research backgrounds often "didn't work very well because they would insist on thinking too much. They would lose sight of the real goal — to do the experiments in a given amount of time."

Still, the physiologists need subjects who are willing and able to understand the scientific underpinnings of the experiments. The researchers are sometimes irritated by NASA's attitude that you can just slap a few electrodes on any available non-astronaut body — for example, a senator who's along basically for PR reasons.

For their part, astronauts — even scientifically oriented payload specialists — are not always enamored of the doctors and physiologists who drop them and spin them and generally do everything possible to make them sick and disoriented.

The work on Spacelab not only provided Money and Watt with more subjects on which to collect physiological data, it helped them to stay abreast of research developments in this field in other parts of the world. Money said this would ensure that the subsequent Canadian experiments "will be entirely up to date and we won't be ignorant of something that somebody else has done or is planning to do."

By early 1986, Watt, Money, Bondar and Thirsk were well along in their planning for Canadian life sciences experiments on future shuttle missions. Although Steve MacLean's flight would be devoted primarily to testing the SVS system, some life sciences experiments were planned for the mission, including the daily back pain recordings, a repeat of the taste test, and the new VOR test. All have the advantage of requiring very little mid-deck locker space.

The third flight of a Canadian astronaut will be devoted almost entirely to life sciences experiments and the planning for this mission was well underway when the Challenger accident happened. By late 1986, NASA was projecting the IML flight would occur in 1990, but it was still uncertain whether the Canadian astronaut would be on it.

The planned experiments included the second back pain assessment test, the energy expenditure experiment, the blood flow measurements for Bob Thirsk's pressure suit tests, and more than half a dozen physiology experiments, including repeats of some of the tests done on 41-G.

Two new types of experiments are also planned for the mission:

• *Space sled experiment (H-reflex test):* Watt has developed a "mini-sled," a small chair-like device mounted on a track, which accelerates a subject in a straight line.[17] The subject, blindfolded and wearing ear plugs, will be seated on the sled and moved to and fro in different directions while small electric shocks are applied to the back of the knee. These shocks, which can be sensed but are not painful, are the electrical equivalent of a tap on the knee and produce a reaction similar to the knee-jerk reaction; in this case, it affects the ankle area and is called the H-reflex. This is a way of stimulating electrical activity in the muscles and the spinal cord; since there are powerful connections between the vestibular system and the spinal cord, this experiment provides another means of testing the effect of zero gravity on vestibular function and the human nervous system.

• *Visual stimulator experiment:* On earth, a person can some-times get a false impression of self-motion. For example, if you're sitting on a train that's not moving and a train on the next track pulls away, you can experience a sensation that the train you're on is moving. This is called "linearvection." A similar phenomenon, known as circularvection, can occur with rotating motion. On earth, if you look at a rotating circular disc, you will soon begin to think that you are rotating in the opposite direction. This illusion is called "visually induced roll." It is believed that gravity acting on the vestibular system limits the sensation of roll on earth; the gravity-sensing otolith organ in the inner ear "tells" the brain that the body is not rolling, despite evidence to the contrary provided by the eyes.

To gain a better understanding of the role gravity plays in this illusion, tests were done on a Spacelab mission, in which astronauts looked into a rotating dome that had polka dots inside. In space, all subjects experienced some increase in visually induced roll, some more dramatically than others. A variation of this test, using a rotating umbrella, is planned for the Canadian life sciences mission.

Comparatively little attention has been paid to the psychological stresses of space flight. It has been suggested that such studies have suffered from benign neglect, but active hostility would more closely characterize the Right Stuff attitude to the fields of research that are known as "psychoastronautics" or "socio-astronautics." This type of research will, however, become increasingly important as human beings move into space to live and work on a permanent basis. Space station crews will be made up of diverse groups of people from many different countries and cultures, who may not train together extensively or know each other as well as current shuttle crews do. They will be living and working together for months at a time in a closed, remote and hazardous environment. They will be under considerable pressure to turn in maximum performance and will often be called on to do dangerous work. At the same time, they may suffer from boredom, insomnia, restlessness, isolation and loneliness, and a sense of confinement. (It will be a little difficult to stomp out and slam the door in the space station.)

According to B. J. Bluth, a NASA psychologist, the Soviets have paid far more attention to the psychological stresses of space flight than the U.S. program has. In a paper on the Soviet program, Bluth said they do extensive social and psychological testing before and after their flights, several of which have set records for long-duration missions. She quotes Georgy Beregovoi, a former cosmonaut and head of cosmonaut crew training, as saying: "Most men die psychologically before they die physically. They are not prepared." To ensure that the crews are prepared, Bluth says, they undergo rigorous testing, including having to perform demanding tasks while parachute jumping and undergoing no-fooling survival treks into wild, remote regions of the Soviet Union. This type of training permitted at least one Soyuz crew to survive for several days after making a harrowing landing at night far from the designated pick-up point where the recovery crew was waiting for them.

Some of the psychological training is less threatening, however. One crew was sent off on a month-long car trip before their three-week Salyut mission.

In flight, cosmonauts on long-duration missions aboard the Salyut space station are provided with amenities and surprises, such as favorite foods, letters from home, videotapes and, in one case, a much-missed guitar. Two-way communication with family, friends and colleagues is permitted; one cosmonaut carried on a running chess game with a friend back on earth. For all this, there has been evidence of hostility among crew members on the longest missions; in 1984, a Soviet newspaper made a rare admission that one of the cosmonauts then aboard the Salyut 7 space station had suddenly become irritable and troublesome — a personality change attributed to taking large doses of sleeping pills. "He began expressing in a very strong way his complaints about the organization of work on board ... and his dissatisfaction with the difficult living conditions."

One unique contribution that zero gravity apparently makes to these psychological problems relates to the "puffy face" syndrome that results from the shifting of bodily fluids. This so alters the appearance of the face — one cosmonaut said he literally did not recognize himself in the mirror — that it may affect interpersonal communications. "Since much communication is visual and physical, this condition distorts the facial gestures, leading to confusion about the intent and significance of the messages," Bluth notes.

NASA officials tend to dismiss the scientific underpinnings of all this; one said: "They talk about music and entertainment as something which a scientist can determine. We just ask the astronauts what they want to listen to and play their favorite music."

Nevertheless, more serious attention will have to be paid to the sociological and psychological aspects of space flight in the future. NASA may want to treat astronauts as biological machines, but, self-disciplined as they are, they are also only human. As we start to colonize space on a permanent basis, we are certain to carry with us all the usual human foibles, failings and emotional baggage.

Roberta Bondar likes to show two slides from Marc Garneau's mission. "We tend to think that astronauts are indestructible — that they are like Superman," she comments, showing the first picture of Garneau floating as he works on the shuttle. Then she shows a second picture of Garneau peering owlishly through horn-rimmed glasses. "But we have to remember they are like Clark Kent."

NOTES

1. This applies in the case of a permanently manned station that is visited periodically by shuttle flights bringing supplies and exchanging crews, but which is otherwise on its own. In a "man-tended" operation, the shuttle would remain attached to the station for a period of time; the crew would work on the station, but would leave with the shuttle. In the latter case, the crew could return to earth in a matter of hours if there was a medical emergency. This is exactly what happened during a Soviet mission, which had to be hastily terminated when one cosmonaut on the Salyut station became seriously ill.

2. Bondar commented that, traditionally, astronauts have never been as concerned about health in space as the doctors have. The health facility is not at the top of their list of priorities and they would probably prefer that the space taken up by the medical equipment be used instead to support the presence of an additional crew member.

3. Initially, NASA had hoped that the station could be permanently manned by 1994, but delays resulting from the Challenger accident and severe financial problems may force NASA to opt for a man-tended operation first.

4. A Toronto doctor, Joseph Fisher of Wellesley Hospital, is involved with NASA in a project to develop a non-invasive system for measuring blood flow in space; a prototype is being built to undergo a series of ground-based tests with animals and humans to determine if it works on sick patients.

5. Cosmic rays are highly energetic charged particles that stream through space. Solar flares are huge storms on the sun that eject large amounts of charged particles that sweep through the solar system.

6. A large solar flare occurred during the first shuttle flight in April, 1981. The highly energetic particles that bombarded the earth's atmosphere an hour later could have been lethal to astronauts doing an EVA in polar orbit at the time. However, astronauts John Young and Bob Crippen were not endangered because they were in a low-altitude, low-inclination orbit that was adequately protected by earth's magnetic field and they did not go outside the spacecraft.

7. Officially, about 40 per cent of space crews have reported being sick, but the number of people actually affected may be much higher — they just aren't admitting it. "Who's going to tell on them?" says Ken Money. "Crew members are very tightly knit together and you're not going to rat on your buddy if he doesn't want to admit he was sick."

8. No one has checked for a positive correlation with camel sickness, which afflicted Lawrence of Arabia.

9. The phenomenon is not well understood on earth. For example, scientists don't know why people vary so widely in their susceptibility, or why some people get sick in cars, but not in planes, while others get air sick but not sea sick. And it's a mystery why infants can't be made motion sick until they learn to walk. Finally, of course, there are the infuriating types who are utterly immune and who regularly endanger life and limb by enraging sufferers with the lofty observation that "it's all in your head." It is — but not in the patronizing way they usually mean it.

10. Radio Moscow once reported that cosmonauts who had returned from a 96-day mission were having trouble lifting a cup of tea or turning a radio dial and were "trying to 'swim' out of their beds in the morning instead of getting up in the normal way."

11. The payload specialist will be required to adopt various positions for these photographs — for example, curled up forward, bent over backward and flexing the leg in various ways. To teach the payload specialist how to adopt and maintain these postures in zero gravity, practice sessions underwater and in the KC-135 zero gravity training plane are anticipated.

12. This has implications for work productivity in space. For example, if astronauts cannot tell the position of their hands by feel alone, they will be hampered in doing work that involves putting their hands inside or under equipment that blocks their vision.

13. Patricia Cowings, a scientist at the Ames Research Center in California, suggested more than 10 years ago that biofeedback might help control space motion sickness. Her theory was initially rejected by physiologists but the technique has been shown to be very effective in ground-based tests.

14. Money had found in earlier experiments that the brain seems to use information from the vestibular system as one of the ways of sensing poison. When the brain received false information in the vestibular system, it concludes that poisons have been ingested and it initiates vomiting (to get rid of the poison) and nausea (to prevent eating the poison again). Motions that cause motion sickness generate false information in the vestibular system and cause similar recactions.

15. It appears that squirrel monkeys have the same problem. One of two flown on a Spacelab mission in November, 1985, was confused and listless during the first few days of the flight. Astronaut Bill Thornton reported that the monkey was huddled in a corner of his cage with his head between his paws and was unable to operate his food dispenser. Finally, Thornton resorted to hand-feeding banana-flavored food pellets to the monkey. This pulled it out of its lethargy. "Our feeding crisis is over," Thornton reported to Mission Control. "I would not have believed the effect of a caring human hand on an animal. I could not feed him fast enough once he got the first couple down." The other monkey was frisky throughout the flight.

16. The astronauts had special T-shirts made up. The front said: H O P and the back said: D R O P.

17. This device was specially designed to fit in the shuttle mid-deck if the exercise treadmill is taken out, but the U.S. astronauts refused to give up the treadmill. Money said: "To my mind, leaving out the treadmill on an eight-day mission is not a big problem. It's a recreational device. It has been shown that the amount of time you can spend on it doesn't influence fitness." However, the astronauts were unwilling to sacrifice it — and they don't much care for life sciences experiments anyway — so this meant that the sled experiment could only be accommodated on a Spacelab mission.

CHAPTER SIX

The Canadarm

The mood was celebratory,
the beer and shrimp were plentiful —
and if the grins
were a trifle smug,
well, the T-shirts
the space engineers
were sporting said it all:
"It's hard to be humble
when you've worked on RMS."
There was ample cause
for celebration.

The astronauts aboard the space shuttle Challenger, working closely with flight controllers and teams of engineers on the ground, had pulled off a major coup — the first rescue and repair of a disabled satellite — overcoming obstacles and setbacks that had threatened to turn the salvage mission into a well-publicized debacle. The Canadian-built remote manipulator system (RMS) had played a key role in the mission, later described in *Aviation Week and Space Technology* as "one of the most crucial for the shuttle in all its history." Engineers with Spar Aerospace of Toronto, who were providing technical support in one of the "back rooms" at Mission Control, were understandably elated that the Canadian-built arm had performed flawlessly to help pull NASA's bacon out of the fire.

The major goal of Mission 41-C, in April, 1984, was to retrieve and repair a solar observation satellite known as Solar Max. Launched in February, 1980, Solar Max had operated for only nine months before fuses in its steering system blew, rendering the satellite useless because ground controllers could no longer point it properly. Fortunately, Solar Max had been designed with some foresight: many of its systems were contained in replaceable modules and it had a device, known as a grapple fixture, which the remote manipulator arm could grab — though the arm hadn't even been built when Solar Max was manufactured.

Part of NASA's motivation in attempting the salvage was economic: the US$50-million rescue effort would revive a satellite worth US$235-million. But there was far more to the rescue bid than the immediate dollars-and-cents return. NASA had long touted satellite retrieval and repair as a major justification not only for the shuttle program but for the human presence in space. A failure on the first attempt would have been a major political and PR disaster that could have seriously undermined the effort NASA had been making to persuade manufacturers to design future satellites with refurbishment in mind. *Aviation Week and Space Technology* said that "a successful flight would be a visually spectacular demonstration of the capabilities of the shuttle as a work platform that could stimulate and accelerate more Defense and commercial confidence in similar undertakings, such as retrieval and refueling of reconnaissance satellites." Alternatively, a failure would "make Defense and commercial users much more reluctant to consider new space operating concepts possible only with the space shuttle." The mission was also crucial for Canada, not only because of the pivotal role played by the Canadarm, but because of Canada's interest in providing a repair and servicing facility for the space station. "In much the same way that the offshore industry has its own repair companies, we are looking at the space equivalent as a niche for Canada," said Karl Doetsch.

In the end, the mission turned out to be a three-day cliffhanger worthy of a prime-time soap opera. Written as fiction, the script would have been beyond belief.

The trouble for the shuttle crew, which had dubbed itself the Ace Satellite Repair Company, started early on the morning of Sunday, April 8. Commander Bob Crippen, flying a record third mission, had maneuvred Challenger, nose perpendicular to the earth, to within 60 metres of Solar Max. The white and gold satellite, glowing brilliantly in the harsh lighting of space, was slowly rotating at about one degree per second around its vertical axis. Astronauts George Nelson and James van Hoften, who were to perform the retrieval and repair operation, donned their bulky white EVA suits and emerged into the shuttle's cargo bay, where Nelson strapped himself into the manned maneuvring unit (MMU), the jet-powered backpack that enables astronauts to fly untethered away from the shuttle. Nelson also carried a simple device, called the TPAD, which had a set of jaws designed to clamp onto a large pin protruding from the side of Solar Max, known as a trunnion pin. Once attached, he would use the MMU jets to slow the satellite's rotation. This would be the first major operational test of the MMU, which had been flown for the first time only two months previously.

The idea was that Solar Max, once stabilized, would then be grappled by the Canadarm, operated from inside the shuttle by astronaut Terry Hart, who would pull the satellite into the cargo bay and berth it in a "flight support station" so that Nelson and van Hoften could operate on its innards. Later, Hart would use the arm to put Solar Max back out into space with a new lease on life. Anyway, that's what was supposed to happen.

Shortly after 10 a.m. EST on Sunday, Nelson set off toward his quarry. For a while, everything went "as written." After a ten-minute flight from the shuttle, he approached the two-tonne Solar Max with understandable caution — its solar panels were rotating at about his head level so, to avoid decapitation, he moved between them toward the body of the satellite and matched his own rotation rate to the satellite's rotation rate by using the small jets on the MMU. Having done this without a hitch, he moved forward to push the TPAD against the trunnion pin. The device was a simple one, almost foolproof, and as Nelson homed in on the pin, everyone confidently awaited the announcement of success. "We've practiced the maneuvres for hundreds of hours. We're very confident of success," a NASA spokesman had crowed before the mission.

"The jaws did not fire," Nelson announced, to the stunned disbelief of ground controllers. "I had a good dock, too. Now I did it again and it didn't fire again." Nelson backed away to check the TPAD jaws; they seemed to be operating properly so he tried docking again. The result was worse than failure — by this time, his bumping against the satellite had increased its rotation in all three axes and it was threatening to tumble out of control. Crippen warned Nelson: "Watch out for the solar array there."

Crippen became concerned that any plan to grab Solar Max with the Canadarm could be jeopardized by the increased rotation rate of the satellite. "We've really got to stop that," he told

Nelson, suggesting an unorthodox and unpracticed technique: "Is there any way you think you can do it with your hands — if you can grab hold of it?" Nelson tried gently grasping one of the solar panels with both hands, but he did not improve the situation. In fact, for a while, it appeared he had actually aggravated it. By this time, the factors conspiring against success were starting to accumulate at a rapid rate. Nelson was facing another problem — the fuel remaining in the MMU was fast approaching the level at which mission rules required him to return to the shuttle.[1] This in itself would not have precluded a second attempt — there was a second fully fuelled MMU in the cargo bay — but the shuttle was also running low on fuel in its forward reaction control system (RCS), the small thrusters needed for operating in proximity to Solar Max.[2] Misson rules required that, if Nelson were to fly off with the MMU again, there had to be enough fuel left in the forward RCS for the shuttle to go and collect him if his backpack should fail. There wasn't — and that put an end to any hope for another astronaut trip to Solar Max.

With options disappearing fast, and uncertain whether he'd get another chance, Crippen decided to try a grab with the Canadarm, even though Solar Max was now tumbling in all three axes. Jim Middleton, who was head of Spar's technical support team in Mission Control, said that the rotation rates could only be estimated, but when NASA sought an opinion, the Spar team said they believed the loads were tolerable. "They asked. We said go," Middleton remembers. "We had no qualms about him going ahead and trying to catch it."

As Challenger moved out of voice contact with the ground, Crippen maneuvred to within 12 metres of the wobbling satellite and then flew around it while Terry Hart made four attempts to grapple it — an effort that has been likened to "steering an elephant around to pick up a penny." In one instance, the satellite was in complete darkness and had to be illuminated by floodlights from the shuttle cargo bay. While all this hotdogging was going on, Nelson and van Hoften were still outside in the bay, preparing to re-enter the airlock.

With voice contact lost, the flight controllers could follow the action only by watching the telemetry — computer numbers from the shuttle streaming out on their monitors. This was an exciting and nerve-wracking period for the Spar team. "We could see him going at it on the data," said Middleton, who was well into a 12-

hour shift in Mission Control by this time. "I was praying to God that Terry could get it; I could see him jerking the arm around a lot. The flight director was calling: 'What's he doing, What's he doing?' And all Reeves [the NASA controller responsible for the RMS] could say was that he was manipulating the arm." Middleton was looking for a couple of signals — one that indicated Hart had pulled the trigger on the Canadarm, and a "capture" signal that would mean the payload was securely in hand. Neither came before the shuttle passed out of range of the satellite that was relaying the telemetry to the ground, so everyone on the ground was left hanging for about ten minutes. When voice contact with Challenger was re-established, Crippen's report was disappointing: "Close, but no cigar." In fact, it appeared that the exhaust from the shuttle's jets had worsened the tumbling. Solar Max was rotating much faster than had been estimated[3] and Crippen had been worried that the satellite's solar panels might hit the shuttle. "You're not going to risk it all," Middleton observed. "You're going to give it your best shot, but you're going to go away if you can't do it."

The rescue bid that had seemed so straightforward had fallen apart in barely an hour. Solar Max had always been considered an "unco-operative target" but this was ridiculous. "The general feeling is that things don't look too good," admitted one ground controller gloomily. "We're going to need a lot of luck." Everyone retreated to consider the problem, but the situation continued to deteriorate rapidly and the mood in Mission Control became increasingly glum. By now the satellite was rotating more rapidly than ever around all three axes and the prospects for grabbing it with the arm were looking bleak unless the rotation rates could be slowed. Ironically, the arm could probably have captured Solar Max when the shuttle had first arrived on the scene.

Controllers trying to stabilize the satellite from the ground were now in a desperate race against time; the on-board batteries that controlled the position of the satellite were no longer being charged because the wobbling was preventing the solar panels from picking up enough solar energy. The solar cells were facing the sun for only about a quarter of the time and were also subject to a half-hour eclipse of the sun by the earth once every orbit. Within about six hours all control over Solar Max would be lost.

To make matters worse, Crippen had been forced to use about 15 per cent of the precious remaining fuel in the forward RCS thrusters during the abortive grapple attempt and it was beginning to look doubtful that there was enough fuel left for one last pass at Solar Max, even if it could be stabilized enough for the arm to grab it. When the ground suggested sending Nelson back out with van Hoften in the other MMU as backup in case an astronaut rescue was needed, Crippen nixed the idea, saying he didn't want "three things flying around" outside the shuttle.[4] With the rescue beginning to look all but lost, the day was being dubbed "Black Sunday." *Aviation Week and Space Technology* described it as "ebb tide for shuttle credibility."

Nevertheless, the ground controllers doggedly labored on. "We're not quitters," they said. Engineers at NASA's Goddard Space Flight Center in Maryland worked feverishly to save Solar Max. First, they shut down almost all the spacecraft systems to preserve power. For the next three hours, they tried unsuccessfully to stabilize the satellite using one of the attitude control systems aboard the spacecraft; finally, they decided that they had to send a new computer program up to Solar Max before this system would do the job. At this time, information received from Solar Max indicated that its rotation rates were now far too high for the manipulator arm to handle.

Loading the computer program took another 2 1/2 hours. By mid-afternoon, ground controllers were estimating that Solar Max's batteries would die around 7 p.m. that night. But by 6:30 p.m., the tumbling had been slowed enough to permit the solar panels to pick up some energy, so the estimated battery life was extended to 8 p.m. The ground team continued to command a slow-down in the satellite's rotation rates throughout the evening and the solar panels miraculously continued to soak up just enough power to keep Solar Max alive. But it was touch-and-go; by 10:30 p.m., flight controllers were expressing doubts that the satellite would make it through the next eclipse of the solar panels. They turned off a transmitter to save power and this gave them a few extra minutes, just enough, as it turned out, to get them through the eclipse. But, at 11 p.m. Sunday night, the batteries were still discharging.

Controllers were resisting the extreme option of blowing away the solar panels, a desperate measure that would slow Solar Max further and increase the chances of the arm's being able to grab it.

However, lacking solar panels, the satellite would have to be returned to earth for major repairs. They would need some battery power to trigger the explosive devices on the solar panels, but they determined they could wait until ten minutes before total battery failure to do this. The batteries were still discharging.

By 11:30 p.m., the rotation rates had slowed essentially to zero. The spacecraft was stabilized. But there were only minutes left before the battery power would run out. "We were down to the fumes," said one ground controller. For a change, luck was with Solar Max; when it stabilized, its solar panels happened to be in an ideal position to soak up the sun's energy for an uninterrupted half hour. By midnight, the satellite was up to full power again. "Some of us might believe that we had a little bit of divine intervention when we had our moment of crisis," said Frank Cepollina, Solar Max mission manager. "The fact is we also had a lot of human intervention, a lot of expertise that came to bear to pull us out."

By mid-morning on Monday, things were back to square one. Ground controllers had sent up a new program to Solar Max that put it into enough of a spin — about half a degree per second — to keep the solar panels oriented toward the sun but not too much for the Canadarm to handle. This rotation was also desirable because it would bring the grapple fixture around within reach of the arm, eliminating the possibility that Crippen might have to waste precious fuel maneuvring the shuttle into position to grapple the satellite.

The next step was up to Crippen; with fuel in the forward RCS running low, he had a very tricky flying job to do. It was going to be so tight, in fact, that ground controllers told him he could go until the fuel gauges read zero; they'd calculated that this would still leave just enough fuel to back away from Solar Max if the grapple didn't succeed. It was clear there would be only one shot at the rescue.

Crippen began his final approach at 8:40 a.m. on Tuesday morning. Eight minutes later, he was within 30 metres; he had to use a maneuvre designed to keep the plume from the shuttle's jets away from Solar Max but which consumed fuel at 12 times the normal rate. During this period, Crippen was silent, concentrating intently on his flying, but controllers could deduce much of what was going on by monitoring the telemetry from the spacecraft. At 8:52 a.m., they knew the shuttle was within striking range when they saw computer data indicating the Canadarm was on the move. At that critical point, the shuttle moved out of communications range with the ground. Now it was all up to the Canadarm and, in the mission evaluation room where the Spar team was camped out, there were a few breath-holding minutes. "People were saying, 'I hope to hell we can do this,'" said Terry Ussher, who was then director of programs for Spar's RMS Division. "And I was saying, 'I hope everything goes smoothly with the arm.' Everyone felt bullish about it. I felt positive and I kept saying, 'God, I hope all of this is well founded.' It doesn't matter how long you've worked with it — when you first switch it on..."

For his part, Middleton had his eyes glued to the big AOS (acquisition of signal) clock on the wall that marked off the six minutes until voice contact with Challenger would resume. "I was watching that clock count down. I walked around a little bit, smoked a cigarette, drank some coffee and came back down, put my earphones on and waited to hear what the call was."

He wasn't the only one itching to hear the news. As Challenger was due to come back into range, astronaut Jerry Ross, the capsule communicator in Mission Control, called: "Challenger, Houston, we're standing by." (This is NASA jargon that encompasses everything from "Good morning" to "We're all sitting on the edge of our seats down here.")

"Okay, we've got it," Crippen announced to his anxious audience. The capture, accomplished by the arm operator, Terry Hart, was "a piece of cake," he added. (This is Right Stuff jargon that encompasses everything from "It was a piece of cake" to "We just saved the ballgame up here.")

Everyone in Mission Control broke into cheers. Middleton banged his fist on the table and scribbled "We've got it!" in his log book.

Crippen's skillful flying techniques had managed to leave twice the amount of fuel in the forward RCS that ground controllers had predicted would remain at the moment of capture; his virtuoso performance cemented a reputation that was already little short of legendary around NASA.[5]

Shortly after 4 a.m. the next morning, Nelson and van Hoften donned spacesuits again and went out into the cargo bay to do the fix-it job during a 7 1/2-hour EVA. Using a specially designed wrench, van Hoften unbolted the module containing the satellite's fuses, then removed and replaced it with a new one. Employing the Canadarm for the first time as a work station, van Hoften was anchored by a foot restraint on the end of the arm, which permitted him to stand still while using both hands to work. (Without this support, an astronaut trying to unscrew a bolt would be just as likely to turn himself as he would the bolt.) About 15 minutes after the change was made, the ground began receiving data from the new module.

Van Hoften's next task was considerably more difficult and risky: he had to repair a coronograph — an instrument for observing the gasses surrounding the sun — that had failed, apparently as a result of being flooded by radiation from a solar flare. Standing on the arm, with Nelson assisting at his left — they looked like a pair of space-age surgeons — van Hoften first cut through Solar Max's insulation, then unscrewed a metal plate and cut the wires on the coronograph's electronics box. He then removed the electronics box, replaced it with a new one and connected the wires with clips. In contrast to the events of Black Sunday, the repair work went "like a charm," he reported. "Haven't had one glitch yet." In fact, the work took an hour less than scheduled. The only casualties were two screws. "One disappeared over the tail but I don't know where the other one is," Nelson said.

Later, Nelson, intent on finding out why his attempt to grapple Solar Max had failed, rode the Canadarm up to the top of Solar Max to inspect the trunnion pin. The culprit proved to be a small button-like clamp holding the insulation blanket to the satellite; it extended outward from the side of the satellite about a half a centimetre, just enough to prevent the TPAD from firing automatically to close around the pin. Ironically, the TPAD had been considered such a simple and foolproof device that Nelson was not provided with a means of firing it manually. NASA officials were feeling a bit sheepish about the whole thing. "The poor people were devastated," said Ussher, who added that anyone involved in the space program feels sympathetic when something like this happens. "Everybody feels, there, but for the grace of God, go I."

After spending a night sitting on the end of the Canadarm, Solar Max was sent on its way, alive and well, the next day, and was still operating in 1986.

At the shrimp and beer party after the mission, everyone was wearing the "hard to be humble" T-shirts that NASA had had made up. Ussher said the shirts had been printed the day before the rescue was accomplished, which, he admitted, had made him "nervous as hell."

Afterwards, NASA touted the mission as a demonstration of superb teamwork between humans and machines. It certainly was that, but the press raised questions as to whether the initial capture attempt by Nelson had even been necessary. Lt. Gen. James Abrahamson, then NASA's associate administrator for the shuttle, said NASA had not known until just two months before the mission that the arm was probably strong enough to grab Solar Max. Several NASA astronauts had done tests in Spar's Toronto computer simulator to evaluate the limits for grappling a rotating payload. (In part, these tests were done in anticipation of a future requirement to grapple tumbling payloads that have lost their attitude control systems.) The simulator runs showed that an astronaut controlling the arm could handle the rate at which Solar Max was rotating at the start of the mission (1 degree per second around one axis) but that if the payload was rotating about two or three axes — tumbling, essentially — the rotation rates that could be handled decreased rapidly. "I've run the simulation myself," Middleton said. "I know what it's like to see the payload going fast ... how scary it is."

By the time the results of these simulator tests were known, however, Nelson and van Hoften had already spent more than a year training with the MMU. NASA decided to stick with Plan A — MMU rescue with the Canadarm as backup — particularly since it anticipated that the MMU would be used frequently in future rescue missions. "It was a 51-49 call," said Abrahamson. Still, there was more than a slight suspicion that NASA was at least partly motivated by a determination to show off what humans could do. However, NASA almost outsmarted itself; to some observers, the mission showed that one of the things humans can do is make things worse. But this was not an entirely fair assessment of what happened. Plan A foundered not because Nelson failed to do his job, but because a tool failed to perform due to unforeseen circumstances. Had Nelson been given a means of overriding the automatic system, he probably could have accomplished the rescue. (If one wanted to get picky, one could say that the human error had taken place on the ground.) In any event, the mission did demonstrate the versatility of humans in getting themselves out of a jam. In the end, their ability to triumph in the face of adversity — even if it was largely of their own making — was probably more of a testimony to their value in space repair than a straightforward and seemingly easy success would have been.

On the other hand, the success of Plan B — using the Canadarm as the primary rescue tool — could not be viewed entirely as proof of the superiority of machines over humans. "Who do you think was on the other end of the arm?" growled Abrahamson, fielding media questions. "It wasn't the tooth fairy."

Still, the team of engineers from Spar were justifiably proud of the arm's flawless performance. Not only had it proved its worth as a mainstay of space rescue and repair operations, but it had, in a single mission, recovered a satellite worth more than twice the CDN$100-million invested in the arm's development. All in all, not bad for a week's work.

For the Canadians involved, the Solar Max rescue culminated more than a decade of research and development work. As early as 1969, the year NASA landed men on the moon, the U.S. space agency was trying to drum up international support for the post-Apollo program. In those heady days, visions of space stations and lunar bases danced in their heads, but by the early 1970s, financial reality had stripped those dreams down to the shuttle.

Thomas Paine, then NASA's administrator, had first invited Canada to participate in the shuttle project in 1969. Garry Lindberg of the National Research Council, who became the first RMS project manager, said there was a lot of scurrying around to evaluate Canadian research and industrial ability to do the project, but "after some initial discussions with NASA, things sort of ground to a halt." One problem, he said, stemmed from something of a misapprehension that NASA was offering a contract — that the U.S. agency was proposing to pay for space technology development in Canada. When it became clear that NASA was asking Canada to pay for the project, this caused some retrenchment and rethinking — "getting our minds around the fact that it was to be co-operative and hence we had to find something that Canada wanted to do, that would be beneficial to

Canada," Lindberg said.

It fell to engineers in the NRC and in Canadian industry to dog the problem of finding something worthwhile to do. Lindberg credited industry — notably DSMA ATCON Ltd., a Toronto engineering consulting firm, and Spar — with the perseverance that carried the idea through the "quiet period" that followed the initial flurry of interest.[6] "[They] continued thinking about it and poking at it and trying to come to grips with what to do. That took some time."

Ultimately they happened upon the remote manipulator system as something Canadian industry was capable of doing. Although NASA had identified the RMS as an important component, it had not defined the system in any great detail, concentrating as it then was on getting the shuttle itself off the ground. Since it was not a top priority for the first shuttle flight, the RMS had been temporarily relegated to the backburner. "So, in a sense, it was there for the plucking," Lindberg said. "Again, by happenstance, it fitted Canadian capabilities."

The RMS also had the advantage of having what engineers call a "clean interface" — i.e., it was a discrete item, not just another anonymous part of the vehicle's basic structure. (Choosing such a highly visible component would ultimately prove to be one of the smartest things Canada did.)

But it wasn't quite a matter of Canada's simply selecting what it wanted from a technological smorgasbord placed before it by NASA. The arm had been designated a "mission critical" item, so NASA looked the Canadian team over very carefully before agreeing to let them build it. In 1973 and 1974, NASA engineers paid several visits to Canada to make a first-hand assessment of the capabilities of the NRC and Canadian industry. "In any business dealing, when you enter an agreement, you want to have some assurances that the person who's in the agreement with you will honor the terms and conditions, so we had to provide those assurances to them," said Art Hunter of the NRC, who succeeded Lindberg as the Canadarm project manager.

NASA satisfied itself that Canada could do the job, but turning the project over to another country was not a simple matter; the U.S. space agency came under considerable pressure from the U.S. aerospace industry to award the contract in the United States.[7] Manipulator technology was rightly viewed even then as important for the future, providing, as it does, a focus for research on advanced automation and robotics. (Canada's persistent interest in space robotics was a continuing source of irritation to the U.S. industry and this dispute was revived more than a decade later when Canada proposed to build a robotic servicing facility for the U.S./international space station. See Chapter 7.)

In July, 1975, the Canadian government signed an agreement with NASA to build the arm. The deal required Canada to fund the design, development and testing of the first arm and to turn it over to NASA by 1980. In return, NASA agreed to buy three more arms at a cost of about CDN$75-million. The three additional units were to be delivered in 1982, 1983 and 1984. Privileged access to shuttle launches and a discount (then estimated at 20 to 25 per cent) on launch costs were supposed to be among the benefits of participation in the shuttle project, but, in fact, Canada never did get any particular breaks in this regard.

The NRC was assigned to manage the Canadarm project. One of its major functions, Lindberg said, was to act as an intermediary between NASA and Spar. "We had to ensure that Canada satisfied NASA's requirements and that Canada lived up to its obligations. But we had another interesting role. Since NASA wasn't paying [for the arm], in principle they could ask for anything. Now, that's being unfair to NASA, because they didn't. But they did have that latitude." There was a certain amount of faith involved on both sides, because when the agreement between NASA and Canada was signed, the technical details of the RMS had not been worked out. One important move was to ensure that Canada was represented on NASA's "change control boards," which had to consider and approve changes to the design of the various shuttle systems.

The contract to build the arm went to a consortium of Canadian companies, including Spar Aerospace as prime contractor, and DSMA ATCON, CAE Electronics and RCA as subcontractors. Spar Aerospace had been created in 1968, after a group of employees in the Special Products and Applied Research Division (SPAR) of de Havilland Aircraft of Canada broke off to form their own company when the parent company decided to sell or close down the division. One of the "special products" it took with it was the STEM (Storable Tubular Extendible Member), a telescoping metal tube that found application on many spacecraft including Alouette, Canada's first satellite, and the U.S. manned vehicles, Mercury, Gemini and Apollo. In the 1970s, Spar acquired experience in building space systems as a subcontractor to Hughes Aircraft Company, which built Canada's first to Hughes Aircraft Company, which built Canada's first Anik communications satellite — skills that ultimately enabled the company to become a prime contractor in its own right. Spar had also become a leader in the production of precision aerospace gears and transmissions. The company's expertise in these fields — and the experience it had gained in learning how to build technologies for the unforgiving space environment — were essential to the successful development of the Canadarm.

CAE Electronics of Montreal (which had started as Canadian Aviation Electronics Ltd. in 1947) had been involved in the development of aerospace and aviation systems, mostly for defence purposes, for more than 20 years when it became part of the RMS team. It had already achieved a worldwide reputation as a designer and builder of aircraft digital flight simulators — skills that it applied to the development of the simulator that was used to test the RMS system and train astronauts in its use.

In general concept, the arm is fairly simple but, like the human hand, this apparent simplicity conceals a subtle complexity. It is just over 15 metres long and capable of maneuvring payloads about the size of a bus (this is about the maximum size of the largest payload the shuttle cargo bay can carry — 18 by 4.5 metres and weighing up to 30,000 kg on earth). The arm had six joints: three in the "wrist" to permit up and down (pitch), side to side (yaw) and circular (roll) motions; two in the "shoulder" for pitch and yaw motions; and one to bend the "elbow." Each of the joints is driven by a motor small enough to fit in a human hand. The two long booms were constructed of new lightweight composite materials and contained more than 300 electrical wires. The booms were wrapped in a white and gold multi-layer insulating blanket; small electrical heaters were included to maintain minimum temperatures in the extreme cold of space.

Although the Canadarm functions like a human arm, its "hand" — known as the "end effector" — does not much resemble a human hand. It is a cylindrical device that houses three snare wires that rotate to snap around a pin protruding from the grapple fixture on the payload. (See Figure 1.) The snare wires are mounted on a retractable carriage, which is pulled back once the grab has been made to ensure that the end effector has a firm lock on the payload. In the future, special-purpose end effectors may be designed for unusual payloads.

Figure One

1

PAYLOAD GRAPPLE SHAFT INSIDE MOUTH OF END EFFECTOR.

PAYLOAD GRAPPLE

WIRES STORED

END EFFECTOR

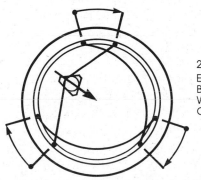

2

END EFFECTOR RING BEGINS TO ROTATE STARTING WIRES TO CLOSE ONTO PAYLOAD GRAPPLE SHAFT.

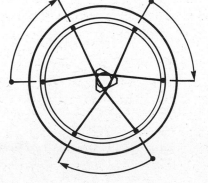

3

END EFFECTOR RING FULLY ROTATED & WIRES CLOSED ON PAYLOAD GRAPPLE, SHAFT CENTERING THE SHAFT (SNARED) & CAPTURING PAYLOAD.

SNARE OPERATION

The snare design also enabled the arm to satisfy another important requirement — that it be capable of grabbing or releasing a payload without imparting a push or other motions that might cause the payload to start tumbling. "It was a problem to come up with a device that could retrieve and grip a satellite without giving it an impulse if the grab motion failed," said one engineer who worked on the arm. "We came up with a concept to achieve that and we were proud of that."

The arm's control and display panel is located in the aft section of the shuttle flight deck. The operator stands facing the cargo bay, which is visible through the two aft windows; there are also two overhead windows for viewing activities in the region above the cockpit. Two monitors display TV images transmitted by cameras mounted on the arm's wrist and elbow, as well as several located around the cargo bay. The hand controller system, designed by CAE, includes two joystick-type controllers, which are used by the astronaut to move the arm; there are various modes of operation, both manual and automatic and the operator can also control the arm a single joint at a time.

One of the great challenges in building space technology is to develop systems that not only can survive, but also can function reliably and efficiently in the harsh space environment. Some of the major design challenges the Canadian team faced included building gears that could handle maximum shuttle payloads and that would survive for 100 missions; designing a thermal control system that would enable the arm to withstand the cold of space, but would also prevent overheating of the joints when they were in use; keeping the weight of the system as low as possible; and ensuring that the astronauts could maintain very fine control over the arm's movements.

All of the materials used in building the arm had to meet exacting standards of stiffness, weight and tolerance to extreme heat and cold. These requirements posed several challenges. For example, it was found that when the stainless steel gears were heat-treated to toughen them, they shrank a few micrometres. This was less than the thickness of a sheet of paper, but it was still enough to throw the gear tolerances off; the solution was to machine oversize gears and then heat-treat them until they shrank to the right size. Even though NASA's standards were exacting, Canada imposed even more stringent quality requirements on parts and materials, according to NRC project manager Art Hunter. "This ended up costing us more money than we needed [to spend], but it's paid off; I think the results are self-evident. It was like an insurance policy. We were very much aware that ultimately [the arm] would be highly visible and that a lot was at stake for Canada in terms of self-identity. As well, we were trying to find a niche in the international marketplace for some of our space hardware and develop a sound reputation for Canadian industry."

Two serious and interrelated technical problems that the team encountered early in the development of the arm related to weight and the question of what would happen if the arm should fail in space. "Weight was a very sensitive issue," Hunter said. Lindberg described one "upheaval" that occurred when it was discovered that Rockwell, NASA's prime contractor on the shuttle program, had not allowed enough weight for the arm in its shuttle design. Compared with the overall vehicle, the arm might seem like small potatoes, but at the time, NASA was paying something between US$20,000 and $50,000 for each half-kilogram of weight saved.[8] "[Rockwell] had a weight budget of about half of what we ended up with" (about 225 kg). At that point, it looked as though the arm would weigh in at more than twice that amount and this precipitated "quite a number of emotional meetings," Hunter said. In the end, the limit was set at about 450 kg; the joints took up about 360 kg of that, leaving less than 100 kg for the two long booms. In the end, they weighed in at about 55 kg.

The weight issue was further complicated by the question of failure modes for the arm. NASA wanted the arm to be what it referred to as "fail-operational, fail-safe." This meant that the arm should still be able to perform its duties fully with one failure; a second failure would render it non-operational, but in a way that did not endanger the vehicle or crew. It was the fail-operational mode that caused most of the trouble; if the arm was expected to continue operating normally even after the failure of a component, it meant that practically everything in it had to be redundant. "You pay a big weight penalty for that," said Hunter. Ultimately the arm was required only to be "fail safe." (Provision was also made to cut it loose from the shuttle if it couldn't be properly stowed after use; the arm must be latched down to the side of the cargobay before the bay doors can be closed for the return to earth.)

Lindberg said there were concerns about the loads and stresses the arm would be subjected to in space as a result of the shuttle's movements and this got them entangled in a bit of a chicken and egg problem with NASA and Rockwell. Simulations were needed to define the extent of these potential problems, but it wasn't really Canada's responsibility to do them. NASA and Rockwell, on the other hand, had quite a few other problems on their plates, since the shuttle was going through some difficult and expensive birth pains. According to Lindberg, there was a tendency for them to say, "'Yeah, well, OK, I guess you're right, it's our job. But we can't do it yet. We don't have the funding for it, or computer programs aren't developed yet,' or what have you. And we would say, 'But we can't do our design without it.' " In fact, he said, concerns about loads and stresses remained right up to the time the arm was launched on its first mission in November, 1981.

Another question that had to be addressed early was whether one person could, in fact, operate the arm alone. "Nobody had ever done it before," said Hunter. "Operational requirements were laid on us, [but] even the people dreaming up the requirements didn't for one minute concern themselves as to whether one person could do it. We couldn't even argue that the workload would be too great because we didn't know ourselves." The solution to this problem was found in the development of a CDN$5-million ground-based computer-controlled simulator, which was built by CAE. (Its name was inevitably reduced in aerospace shorthand to SIMFAC.) Hunter said that building a simulator had been planned from the beginning, but it took on even greater importance after the single-operator question became an issue. In fact, the simulator served not only as a design tool, but as an astronaut training facility; a steady stream of NASA mission specialists started slipping quietly into Toronto on a regular basis to go through their paces in the SIMFAC. The astronauts helped evolve the design to make the operator's tasks manageable.

The simulator mimics the RMS operator station on the shuttle's flight deck, including the control and display panels and the two hand-controllers the astronauts use to operate the arm in space. Instead of windows, there are CRT screens that display computer-graphic images of the arm and its payloads. These are dynamic images — as the astronaut manipulates the hand controllers, the line-drawing images of the arm and its payloads move in a slow-motion waltz across the screens. This facility can be used by astronauts to practice activities such as capturing and releasing satellites, berthing and unberthing payloads in the shuttle cargo bay, changing replaceable modules and performing space construction activities. The untrained operator can quickly perpetrate disasters of various sorts — mostly collisions of the arm with the cargo bay or the payload — but it usually takes an astronaut only a few hours to gain the proficiency necessary to avoid such errors. Of course, many more hours of practice are required for the type of elaborate task demanded of the RMS operator on a shuttle mission.

"The simulation facility proved to be much more valuable than people originally thought it would be," said Karl Doetsch, then RMS deputy project manager, whose major responsibility was overseeing the development of the simulator and the computer model that ran it. He said the simulator was "absolutely crucial when it came to testing and verifying any design changes that were proposed. Verification of the arm before things got into orbit was such an important element. It was the first time, really, that space hardware was being qualified by simulation."

The computer model that runs the simulator was a particular source of pride to its developers. It was dubbed "ASAD." When the press asked what this acronym meant, clearly expecting some typical example of jaw-breaking aerospace jargon, Spar officials rather sheepishly admitted that it stood for "all singing, all dancing." (A precursor program later incorporated into ASAD was known as Manual Interface and Control — MANIAC for short.) In fact, "all singing, all dancing" was a pretty good description of what the program entailed, said John Graham, then manager of R&D for the RMS Division. He explained that hundreds of equations are needed to describe the motions of a complex piece of machinery like the arm. The engineers kept adding more and more equations to "take into account more of the real characteristics of the arm ... And I guess, as the people were going through it, they'd just about covered everything. They found they had an 'all singing, all dancing' model."

Testing the arm's intended zero-gravity operation on earth represented a considerable challenge. Although the arm could lift the equivalent of a fully loaded bus in the weightlessness of space, it could not even lift its own weight in earth's gravity, much less a payload. To test its joints on the ground, DSMA designed and built a special 1-G rig, which carried the arm on air-bearing supports, miniature hovercraft-type devices that floated over a specially designed smooth floor. The rig was passive — that is, it did not control the motion of the arm, which was moved by its own joints. Although this system permitted testing in only one plane at a time, and not in three dimensions, as the arm would move in space, it could be arranged so that all of the arm's joints could be tested. At the Johnson Space Center, NASA has two RMS hardware simulators involving the use of a heavier, more powerful version of the arm, which is capable of bearing its own weight. In one, heavy payloads are supported on an air-bearing floor; in the other, astronauts use the arm to lift helium-filled mockups of large payloads, to practice maneuvring the arm in close-to situations, such as berthing a payload inside the cargo bay. It is a measure of the unique nature of the space environment that four facilities are necessary to simulate different aspects of the arm's operation, since no one alone can completely and realistically duplicate the conditions it will encounter in space.

One of the last design changes made — one that was to have far-reaching repercussions for the visibility of the project — was the decision to put the Canada wordmark and flag on the arm. Hunter said the idea was initially prompted by a *National Geographic* magazine picture of Spacelab, a laboratory module that fits in the shuttle's cargo bay, which was then being built by the European Space Agency. The letters ESA were written in big, bold letters across the module and the Canadians decided that if Europe was going to advertise its contribution to the shuttle, then Canada should do the same. "Knowing the way that large programs like this work, there is not sufficient due recognition given to the various contributors," Hunter said. Putting the Canadian symbol on the arm might sound like a simple enough thing, but nothing in the space program is ever that simple. A series of letters and phone calls were exchanged with NASA and ultimately, Hunter said, "we received a letter from NASA headquarters saying that putting on the Canada wordmark would be appropriate." There were provisos, though: approval was subject to there being no objections on technical grounds from the shuttle managers or from the astronauts, who might find the wordmark a distraction.

Encouraged, Hunter and Bruce Aikenhead, then deputy manger of he NRC's RMS program, set to work on a design and "within a matter of ten minutes ... decided on the location and the size of the wordmark. We picked the upper arm rather than the lower arm because it was less likely there would be any strong objections, yet it would be very well seen by all the cameras." (Astronauts controlling the arm would for the most part have their attention focussed on the end effector, which would be far away from the wordmark.) The Canadian proposal, which included assurances that only approved space-rated materials would be used and that the patch would not have unacceptable thermal effects, was duly sent to NASA and met with no objections on technical grounds. Fabrication of the wordmark masks cost about CDN$6000.

NASA apparently decided that it simply wouldn't do to have American television viewers see only the Canadian flag on a shuttle that had been mostly paid for by U.S. taxpayers, so it launched its own study on where in the cargo bay a U.S. flag could be placed. But putting something in the cargo bay is never a trivial matter; NASA had to do a full thermal analysis and it reportedly cost them about US$40,000 to put the flag in the bay.

Development of the arm took nearly seven years in all. It was officially signed over to NASA in February, 1981, in a formal acceptance ceremony at Spar's RMS Division laboratory, during which NRC President Larkin Kerwin christened it the Canadarm for the first time (a name that the Americans rarely use and that the Canadian media initially strongly resisted, although it later slipped unobtrusively into common usage in Canada). Alan Lovelace, then acting NASA administrator, was on hand for the festivities and he said the arm was at "the front edge of technological development. It may appear to be a simple device, but it was a very challenging engineering job." After the plaque on the wall was unveiled, and the Canadians were duly patted on the back, the arm was loaded onto a truck for the ride to the Kennedy Space Center. (It was trucked by the same driver who had hauled the treasures of King Tut around North America the year before.) At KSC, the arm was installed aboard Columbia, the first shuttle, which had made its maiden orbital flight in April. This involved setting up the display and control unit in the aft crew compartment, installing the positioning mechanism and hold-down latches that would secure the arm to the left side of the cargo bay, and, finally, settling the arm itself into its cradles. The process of integrating the arm with the shuttle proceeded without major difficulties and, by mid-July, Hunter was able to report that "the RMS is now a sub-system of the vehicle." The arm was to receive its first on-orbit workout during the secod flight of Columbia, which finally took place in November, 1981, after a couple of delays.

For a time in September, it looked as though the arm might be pulled from the flight for fear that it would be damaged by vibrations during launch. This was the legacy of an incident during the first launch of Columbia in April. During the first few milliseconds after the solid rocket boosters fired, a shock wave several times greater than expected shook the vehicle. Bob Crippen, who flew the mission with Commander John Young, later described it as a "kind of twang that starts at the back and travels up." The resulting vibrations were severe enough to damage fuel tank struts slightly and shake some of the shuttle's protective thermal tiles off. If the arm had been on that flight, it probably would have been damaged.

NASA immediately set about developing a system to absorb the shock and ultimately came up with a US$2-million water-deluge system, installed at the base of the launch pad, that sprayed more than a million litres of water into the solid rocket boosters' exhaust in the moment of launch. For several months, it was uncertain how effective this effort would be in reducing the launch vibrations. NASA's major concern, of course, was the overall structural integrity of the shuttle, but officials did give some thought to the problems of the Canadarm and talked openly of the possibility of removing it from Columbia's cargo bay, a task that would further delay the already-postponed second flight. "It's going to be a real cliffhanger," said one NRC project official at the time.

By mid-September, tests with the water system indicated that the vibrations should be reduced enough to make it safe for the arm to be launched. However, NASA officials did comment frequently that if the arm were to be so damaged by the launch that it failed to operate properly, it might have to be ejected into space. "There are things we can do to try to free the arm if it gets stuck, but we can't return with the cargo bay doors open," said George Abbey, then director of flight operations. Nevertheless, in the middle of all this, NASA confirmed its order for the three additional arms.

For their part, the Canadians who'd worked on the arm, although naturally concerned about its safety, adopted a much more upbeat tone. "We're positive it's safe to fly the arm on the second and third shuttle flights," said Ussher. "Losing the arm would be very disappointing, especially since it would happen on national television. But we're confident it won't happen."

Still, the Canadians couldn't help anticipating the approaching mission with all the pride and nervous optimism of anxious parents whose kid has the lead in the school play. After several delays, the second launch of Columbia occurred on November 12, 1981, with Commander Joe Engle and pilot Richard Truly[9] flying the first vehicle to make a second trip into space. ("I wish I could buy a used car that looks as good as this one does," Truly commented.) The water-spray system worked perfectly, reducing the shock wave by more than 75 per cent, and the arm handily survived its first trial by G-forces.

Twelve hours of the five-day mission had been set aside to run the arm through its paces, including tests of its manual and automatic modes of operation, the ease of control, the operation of the joints, positioning accuracy and so forth. A great deal of testing on the ground had indicated that the joints and the control systems were working properly but "you can do only so much assurance on the ground," Hunter said. Truly commented that "we want to see how limber it is. We want to see what its dynamics are in the weightless state." The wrist-mounted camera would also be tried out during an inspection tour of the shuttle's exterior and the all-important sequence of swinging the arm back into its cradle along the side of the cargo bay and latching it down would also be tested. However, the arm would not be used to lift a payload on this first flight; a design flaw in the end effector's wire snare system had been discovered before flight and NASA decided to postpone the grappling tests. Hunter said the problem would be corrected before the next flight.

In the end, the testing was limited to only four hours on November 13. Columbia developed problems in one of the three fuel cells that convert hydrogen and oxygen into electrical power and drinking water for the crew and the mission rules called for the termination of the flight in the minimum 54 hours, so the shuttle came home three days early. Fortunately, the arm performed almost flawlessly in the tests that were done. "As soon as it came out and it started to move, the heart pounded a little bit," Hunter admitted. "But there was, I recall, a sense of 'There's nothing more I can do; I don't have control any more. The child's left home.' "

"The arm is out and working great," Truly reported. "The movement is much smoother than it was in the sims [simulations]. There's no jerky movement whatsoever." This prompted cheers and the breaking out of cigars among the Canadians in Mission Control.

The camera on the arm's elbow was used to take some unique pictures of the shuttle — close-up shots of the crew cabin windows and the upper part of the nose, for example. Truly was unable to resist doing what thousands have done when confronted with a TV camera; as the arm's camera was trained on the aft window where he was standing at the RMS control station, he held up a sign reading "Hi, Mom!" It was another initiation of sorts for the arm — the first time it had played a role in one of the frequent pranks perpetrated by astronaut crews.

The only hitch in the testing was caused by a recalcitrant shoulder joint that refused to operate while Truly was trying to stow it. This was overcome by switching to another power system.

For the Canadians, perhaps the moment of highest drama came early on the morning of November 13. The tests of the arm had begun at about 9 a.m. EST, while Columbia was out of communications range with Houston, so it was not until about an hour later that the first TV pictures were transmitted to earth from one of the cameras inside the crew compartment, as the shuttle passed over the United States. The arm, bent down at the elbow and slightly up at the wrist, glowed brightly as it was suspended against a breathtaking backdrop of black space and the hazy blue-white of the earth floating overhead (the shuttle was "upside down," with the open cargo bay facing the earth). "It's beautiful," said engineer Wayne Houston, who was in Mission Control. "One look at the arm on TV is worth a thousand bits of analysis. We all knew it was going to work."

The patch with the Canada wordmark and the Canadian flag was not only clearly visible but, in fact, inescapable. One of the Canadian contingent was overheard to mutter: "Thank goodness Canada is spelled correctly." Hunter admitted to feeling a lump in his throat when he saw the Canadian symbol. This image, which flashed on TV screens around the world, had a dramatic impact both at home and abroad; perhaps one of its most important consequences was that it forced acknowledgement of Canada's contribution by the U.S. media, which probably would have virtually ignored the arm's genealogy had they not felt compelled to comment on the evidence before their eyes.[10] "It's not just a tool, it's a billboard," quipped CBS anchorman Dan Rather.

Hunter said he'd thought that the presence of the patch would ultimately have an impact, but at the time, he hadn't guessed just how enormous: this experience strongly shaped Canada's later strategy in seeking to build a highly visible, discrete element — the mobile servicing facility — on the U.S./international space station. Lindberg said that, though the arm was not the most high-tech thing Canada had ever built, it was perhaps the most visible and "I do think Canadians took a greater pride in that than they have in almost anything else in high tech. We're pretty bad at putting ourselves down and we don't really take pride too often in this sort of thing. I don't think many people really appreciated that it would have a continuing high exposure and be a bit of a catalyst for Canadian high-tech capabilities."

The Canadians were naturally disappointed that not all of the tests of the arm could be performed during the shortened mission, but the most important basics were done and the rest were described by Hunter as "luxury" tests. Doetsch estimated that about two-thirds of the objectives had been accomplished in about one-third of the time originally allotted for the test.

NASA officials proclaimed themselves "extremely pleased" with the arm's performance and said that some of the missed tests would be done on the third mission. James Beggs, then the administrator of NASA, sent a telex to NRC President Larkin Kerwin, saying: "On behalf of all my colleagues at NASA, I wish to extend our congratulations to you and the entire Canadian team on the excellent performance of Canadarm on the STS-2 mission. All of Canada can be justifiably proud of your outstanding achievement and of the very significant contribution that the Canadarm is making to extend the capability of the space transportation system. We look forward to continued close co-operation in use of the Canadarm and in future joint activities." He added that "we certainly recognized the impact a failure would have on Canada in terms of publicity. [We] were very conscious of the need to make sure it was done right. I guess everybody went through the checklist one more time."

The political kudos for the Canadian team started coming in almost immediately. Prime Minister Pierre Trudeau congratulated "those men and women who contributed to the success of the second mission ... whose talents were directly responsible for the design and construction of the Canadarm, which lived up to all expectations during its first test in space." In the House of Commons, a motion was passed "that this House affirm our commitment towards Canadarm as an international joint project of tremendous significance, commend the skill and dedication of those responsible for the design and construction of the space arm, and express the hope that this joint effort involving Canadian expertise will be the first of many such undertakings."

The arm flew again on the third shuttle mission, which took place in March, 1982, and received a 43-hour workout on the eight-day flight. The two-man crew consisted of commander Jack Lousma and pilot Gordon Fullerton. Several extremely important tests of the arm were scheduled, including a detailed evaluation of the arm's thermal protection against extremes of heat and cold (the arm would endure a day-long "hot soak" in intense, direct sunlight), tests of its braking abilities in a runaway or other failure situation, tests of the loaded arm's reaction to movements of the orbiter and, most important, the first use of the end effector to grab and move payloads in the cargo bay.

Unfortunately, the first grapple attempt was thwarted by a failure of the camera mounted on the arm's wrist. The camera is crucial because it provides the astronaut controlling the arm with an essential view of the grapple fixture on the target payload. "That's a bad one to lose," said Lousma, after the third unsuccessful attempt. "When I went to do the grapple test, I got no picture and I looked down and noticed the circuit breaker had popped out." The grapple test was postponed until two days later, when Fullerton lifted a payload nearly eight metres above the cargo bay using his own eyesight, a pair of binoculars and some assistance from cameras in the cargo bay and on the arm's elbow. This time the news for the Canadian ground team was very good: "It's as close to perfect as it could be," Lousma said. "If there's any surprises here, they're all pleasant. I am really impressed with that piece of machinery." Later, they grappled a second payload but did not raise it out of the bay because it was not within their line of sight and could not be seen by the elbow camera either; Mission Control told them to abandon the lifting exercise for fear of damaging the arm or the payload.

The predictable congratulatory orgy followed. Mission Control told the crew that the Canadian ground support team "sends a big thank you ... for all the care shown with the Canadarm manipulator. Your skill with the robot arm has already made this mission a resounding success." In return, the crew and NASA officials were effusive in their praise: Fullerton sent his compliments to "the people who built that arm. It couldn't have performed more exactly like they said it would in every respect. Every time there was a little doubt about how it would operate, it actually turned out to be easier or quicker or nicer or smoother. It's a fantastic piece of machinery ... Canada should be proud of the technology that produced it." A NASA flight director, Tommy Holloway, described its performance as "spectacular. The crew was jubilant over it, as were we."

The arm was tested again on the fourth shuttle flight in June, 1982, and in November was declared "ready for operational use" in an agreement signed by NASA and the NRC. The U.S. astronauts awarded members of the Spar team their "Silver Snoopy" pin. A letter from John Young, head of the NASA astronaut office, described this as their "personal award for professional excellence ... given only to those whom we regard as the very best."

The successful test flights had "given the rest of the world some assurance that Canada has the capability," Hunter said. "We've paid our dues and now we're in." The success of the arm in 1981/82 prompted then Governor General Edward Schreyer to comment that Canada should be sending more than an arm into space; he said he would like to see a Canadian astronaut fly.

During the next three years, the arm proved its operational worth many times and in many ways. On the seventh flight, in June, 1983, the arm released its first payload into space — the European free-flying satellite SPAS — and later retrieved and berthed it in the cargo bay. On the ninth mission, in November, 1983, it deployed and reberthed its first large, heavy payload — a 3400-kg test article — and in April, 1984, it deployed the 6800-kg Long Duration Exposure Facility, the largest operational payload it had handled up to that time. (LDEF was designed to expose various space construction materials and biological samples to the harsh space environment for nearly a year. See Chapter 8.) The arm was able to release the satellite without imparting a push or causing any tumbling motions. This was important because the payload had no attitude control system to correct any inappropriate motions imparted by the arm.

On Mission 41-B in February, 1984, the arm was used for the first time as an astronaut work platform. Astronaut Bruce McCandless, anchored to the end of the arm by a foot restraint, was maneuvred into the cargo bay over a mock-up device that would enable him to practice procedures for the Solar Max rescue, scheduled for the following mission. "Just remember, one false move and it's plop," McCandless commented to Ronald McNair, who was controlling the arm. Later in the mission, the arm suffered a failure in one wrist joint that prevented it from making side-to-side motions, forcing cancellation of a planned test requiring the arm to rotate a satellite. Not knowing what had gone wrong, "we decided the safest thing to do was to leave it stowed and it was not used in the test," said NASA spokesman Terry White. Shortly afterwards, Middleton said that the arm worked fine when subsequently tested on earth. "We've never been able to recreate the fault on the ground. It's some obscure, silly little thing that happened. We're taking the components apart piece by piece."

The Solar Max rescue mission, which followed 41-B, kicked off a two-year period that will go down in space history as the beginning of the era of space repair and servicing. It would include many important firsts: the first retrieval, in-flight repair and redeployment of a satellite; the first capture of a satellite to be returned to earth for repair; the first on-the-job workouts for the MMU; the first test of a system for refuelling spent satellites and — most important for Canada — demonstrations of the Canadarm's versatility as a stable work platform and as a tool for performing both planned and unplanned "fix-it" tasks. Lindberg said that space hardware built before the arm flew was often not designed to take advantage of the arm because of uncertainty about how well it would work but "I think the arm will see increasing use because it's performed so well."

Even then, Canada had its eye on an important role in space servicing. "Servicing has to be a strong justification for work in manipulators," Doetsch said. In a comment that accurately presaged Canada's later approach to its participation in the space station program, Doetsch said: "We see this [the Solar Max rescue] as one step down that path, a path that Canada obviously is looking at fairly seriously — not just building arms but the whole question of construction and servicing on orbit. The way the Solar Max repair job will help is that it is a concrete example that one can use."

The Canadarm prepares to release the Solar Max satellite. Solar Max, a sun observation satellite, was the first satellite to be retrieved and repaired in space. The arm was used to grab Solar Max after a failed rescue attempt by shuttle astronauts.
NASA

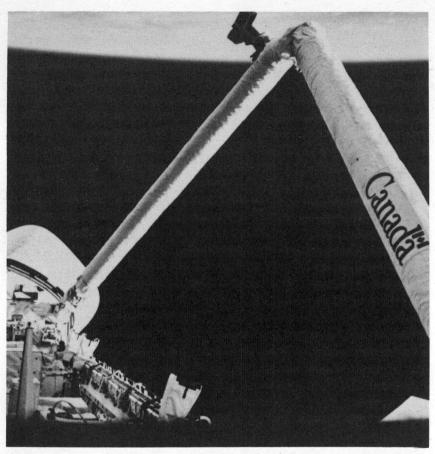

The Canadarm floats above the shuttle's cargo bay with the earth moving by in the background. The Canada wordmark on the upper part of the arm gave worldwide visibility to Canada's aerospace technology.
NASA

The Canadarm cannot bear its own weight in earth's gravity, so ground-based tests must be done using a special one-gravity rig that carries the arm on air-bearing supports, miniature hovercraft-type devices that float over a specially designed smooth floor. Shown here without its protective covering at Spar Aerospace's Remote Manipulator Systems Division in Toronto.
SPAR

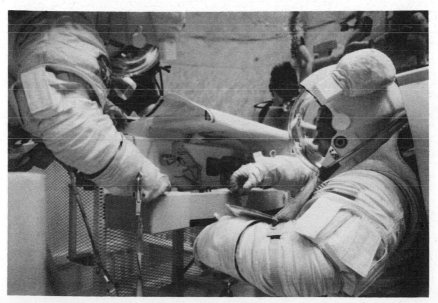

Performing EVAs is a tricky, risky business, so astronauts practice every step on the ground before the mission. Here, David Leestma (left, upside down) and Kathy Sullivan (right) train for an EVA in a large water tank at the Johnson Space Center. Neutral buoyancy in water is similar to zero gravity in many respects.
NASA

The Canadarm, with the "flyswatter" attached, reaches out to flip a lever on the Leasat satellite. This was part of an unplanned rescue to get the satellite's small rocket motor to fire, but the attempt was unsuccessful and the satellite had to be retrieved and repaired on a subsequent mission.
NASA

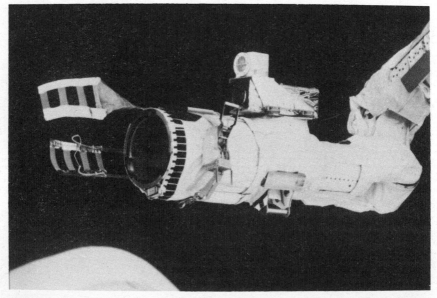

A close-up of the "flyswatter." The device was constructed from plastic document covers inside the shuttle and strapped onto the arm during an unscheduled EVA.
NASA

Astronaut Dale Gardner sets out with the "stinger" to capture the Westar IV satellite. Westar, and an identical satellite called Palapa, both failed after being launched during a previous shuttle mission; they were the first satellites to be retrieved and returned to earth for repair.
NASA

Gardner locks the stinger into the engine nozzle at the bottom of the Westar satellite and stops the satellite's rotation using the small jets on his backpack. The Canadarm was then used to move the satellite, with Gardner still attached, to the shuttle cargo bay.
NASA

Dale Gardner (left) and Joe Allen (standing on the end of the Canadarm) prepare Westar for berthing in the shuttle cargo bay.
NASA

Allen (left) balances on the edge of the cargo bay, holding Palapa while Gardner stows the stinger in the bay. Allen held the half-tonne satellite over his head for 77 minutes; although it did not weigh anything in space, it was large and unwieldy and Allen had to work hard to keep it from hitting the shuttle.
NASA

Gardner (left) and Allen take a moment to pose for pictures after their satellite rescue job is done.
NASA

Gardner holds a "For Sale" sign up to the shuttle's aft window, a joking reference to the fact that the rescued satellites will be offered for sale after being refurbished.
NASA

An artist's drawing of the U.S./international space station, showing the dual keel design and the Canadian-built Mobile Servicing Centre (MSC) being used for assembly and construction tasks. A "smart" dextrous manipulator with two small arms is shown attached to one of the larger arms.

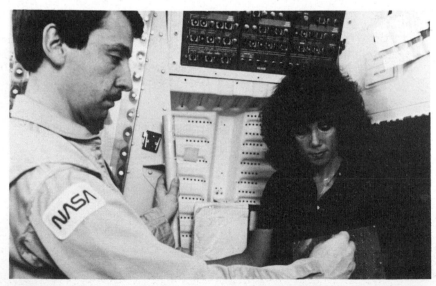

McDonnell Douglas engineer Charles Walker and NASA astronaut Judy Resnik work with samples from a McDonnell Douglas drug-processing experiment during training session at the Johnson Space Center in Houston. Walker's presence on the mission enabled him to trouble-shoot technical problems with the equipment. Resnik, who subsequently became a member of the ill-fated 51-L mission, lost her life in the Challenger explosion. NASA

The second example was provided in November, 1984, with the retrieval of two communications satellites that had gone astray when their small booster rockets shut down prematurely and failed to propel them into geosynchronous orbit, 36,000 kilometres above the earth. This job was more complex than the Solar Max rescue, not only because it was a double header but also because, unlike Solar Max, neither of the satellites had been designed with repair in mind and they lacked grapple pins for the Canadarm to grab. This forced NASA to develop special retrieval equipment and to devise an elaborate rescue plan involving a lot of hands-on work by the astronauts.

The two satellites, Westar VI, owned by Western Union, and Palapa B-2, owned by Indonesia, had been launched from the shuttle in February. Although the shuttle was not directly responsible for their failure, the confidence of the business community in its reliability for satellite deployment was nevertheless shaken. This was not entirely unjustified, since the use of the boosters had been necessary in the first place only because the shuttle could not deliver satellites directly to their high geosynchronous orbit. One insurance spokesman said that until the cause of the failures was identified and corrected, insurers' confidence in the space business as a whole would be undermined.

NASA immediately started developing a rescue plan to save the two satellites — and, not incidentally, its own reputation. Despite the fumbles during the Solar Max mission, its ultimate success in the face of formidable odds helped NASA sell the idea of another dramatic rescue bid later in the year. The satellite's new owners, the insurance companies that had paid US$180-million in claims to the original owners, gave NASA the go-ahead and US$5.5-million to do the job.

The failure of the booster rockets had been a stroke of bad luck, but the fact that they had quit within a matter of seconds was sheer good fortune because it left the satellites at a relatively low altitude. If the boosters had fired much longer, the satellites would have been well on their way to geosynchronous orbit and far beyond the shuttle's reach. Instead, the satellites were left in elliptical orbits ranging from 260 to 1125 kilometres high; these orbits could be circularized from the ground, stabilized for several months, and later lowered to an altitude of about 300 kilometres, which was within the shuttle's range of operation.

In November, 1984, the five-person crew of Mission 51-A ventured forth in the shuttle Discovery to retrieve the two satellites and return them to earth for repair. (The spent booster rockets could not be serviced or refuelled in space.) As with Solar Max, things did not go exactly as planned — flawed equipment design once again foiled Plan A — but this time, the scenario was reversed and the astronauts were forced to do the job that had been intended for the arm.

Plan A, which called for an elaborate procedure involving two free-flying astronauts and the Canadarm working in concert, was dictated by the lack of grapple pins for the arm to latch on to. First mission commander Fred Hauck parked Discovery a mere 11 metres from Palapa. The slowly rotating cylindrical satellite, covered with solar cells shining in the bright sunlight, looked a bit like one of those spinning mirrored reflectors found in déclassé disco joints. "There sure isn't any problem seeing this baby," Hauck remarked.

It was astronaut Joe Allen's first task to fly out to Palapa carrying a two-metre probe called "the stinger," which he inserted into the satellite's spent engine nozzle. (This was not as dangerous as it appeared, because the fuel inside the booster engines had been exhausted by this time.) Once securely locked on to Palapa, Allen fired the thrusters on his MMU to stop the slow rotation of the satellite. He remained attached to Palapa while the Canadarm, controlled by astronaut Anna Fisher from inside Discovery, approached at right angles and grabbed the whole package using a grapple fixture on the side of the stinger. Fisher suspended the satellite over its berth in the cargo bay, where astronaut Dale Gardner was waiting to decapitate Palapa by pulling off its dish-like antenna (necessary so the shuttle cargo bay doors could close over the satellite) and attach an A-frame structure across the top of the satellite. This A-frame carried another grapple pin for the Canadarm; once it was attached, the plan was for Fisher to use the arm to lift the satellite, release it so that the still-attached Allen could flip it over 180 degrees and then grab the A-frame and lower the satellite to be latched vertically into its berth. This complicated three-step was required because both the original capture and the berthing had to be done from the nozzle end of the satellite.

Unfortunately, the plan came apart when Gardner tried to attach the A-frame. It didn't fit. Gardner estimated it was out by less than half a centimetre, but it might as well have been a kilometre

— the A-frame couldn't be attached and thus the arm could not be used for the berthing. "I've tried everything I can think of," a frustrated Gardner finally said.

"We are proposing to go to the no A-frame procedure," Hauck told Mission Control. It was actually more like the "human being as A-frame" procedure, since it required Allen and Gardner to wrestle the satellite into the cargo bay by hand. Remembering the lessons of Solar Max, the astronauts had presciently worked out this back-up maneuvre just three weeks before the flight.

Fisher used the arm to lift Palapa and release it into Allen's hands. Allen, balancing on the edge of the cargo bay, held the half-tonne satellite over the bay for 77 minutes while Gardner attached a device needed to secure it in its berth.

"I assume you are comfortable, Joe," Gardner said at one point.

"Not ... very," responded Allen, with a long pause between the words. Then he added: "I'm doing okay." At 168 cm, Allen was not one of the giants of the astronaut corps, and he could be heard gasping as he strained to hold the 6 x 2-metre satellite. It did not weigh anything in space, of course, but it was still large and unwieldy and had to be moved carefully as he rotated it to facilitate Gardner's work in the bay below. Several times, Allen was cautioned by crew members inside to keep Palapa from hitting the side of the shuttle. Later, as he and Gardner returned to the shuttle, he said: "It was a heck of a day."

Plan B worked so well that the astronauts didn't even attempt to use the A-frame two days later when they recovered the Westar satellite. "When we found out we could turn a man into an A-frame, there really wasn't any need for the equipment," said a NASA spokesman. This time, it was Gardner who donned the MMU to collect Westar. Allen again served as the human A-frame — holding the satellite for nearly an hour and a half — but the job was much easier because his feet were anchored in a foot restraint on the end of the Canadarm.

When Gardner and Nelson had finished their repair job, they held up a "For Sale" sign to the TV camera inside the orbiter. This was a joking reference to the fact that the underwriters who had paid for the mission hoped to refurbish and sell the satellites in an effort to recoup some of the money they'd paid in claims.

The mission demonstrated that, when things do not go exactly as planned, an on-the-site application of brain power — and sometimes just plain old elbow grease — can save the day. It also showed once again that the combination of human and machine skills provides far greater flexibility than either alone in coping with the unexpected. "The two are inextricably linked," said Ron McCullough, Spar's vice-president for technology and development. The mission, he said, demonstrated the value of having "a thinking presence there and, in a contingency, a pair of hands."

The Canadarm was called on to perform miscellaneous unforeseen tasks; on Mission 41-G, for example, Sally Ride used it to gently shake a satellite to jog loose balky solar panels. "If we hadn't been able to do that, I'm afraid we would have had to bring the satellite home," she said later. On the same mission, the arm was also used to tamp down a folding antenna in the cargo bay that refused to latch properly. On Mission 41-D in September, 1984, it was used to knock ice from vents used for dumping waste water from the shuttle. Icicles up to 45 cm long had formed on the sides of the vehicle and could have damaged the shuttle's protective thermal tiles if they had broken off during re-entry. The crew considered an unscheduled EVA to knock the ice off but the arm came to the rescue.

Its most unusual impromptu performance involved the "flyswatter" rescue of a US$85-million Navy Leasat satellite attempted during Mission 51-D in April, 1985. The satellite, deployed on the second day of the mission, was the only large satellite flown on the shuttle that had no provision for electrical checkout by the astronauts before it was launched into space. Minutes after the satellite left the cargo bay, astronaut Rhea Seddon reported that its antenna had not popped up — an indication that all was not well. It was quickly deduced that the problem most likely stemmed from a failure in a six-centimetre arming lever that was supposed to have switched the satellite's electrical power on. This in turn would start an automatic timer that would, in sequence, raise the antenna, fire small thrusters to increase the satellite's spin rate and, at about 45 minutes after deployment, fire a booster motor to carry the satellite into a higher orbit.

When it became apparent that none of this was going to happen, controllers and astronauts on the ground concocted an incredible makeshift rescue plan, involving two major unplanned and unrehearsed activities — a rendezvous with the disabled satellite and a "fix-it" EVA by astronauts Jeffrey Hoffman and David Griggs.

The plan centred on the theory that the arming lever was either stuck in the off position or not fully deployed. The lever protruded from a five-centimetre slot on the satellite's side and, in its open position, it was supposed to be located at one end of the slot. Four emergency teams were set up to investigate various methods of pulling the lever and more than a dozen astronauts spent long hours in the water tank and other simulators over a three-day period, evaluating a wide variety of proposed rescue options.

There was considerable concern that the satellite's motor might suddenly come to life while the shuttle or the astronauts were working nearby. This seemed less and less likely the longer it remained dead and the motor did have a number of built-in safeguards against being prematurely armed. Nevertheless, no one really knew what had gone wrong with it and everyone was justifiably nervous about any operation that called for close proximity with the satellite.

The result of all the simulation activity on the ground was a determination that doing a rendezvous with the satellite and an emergency EVA at the same time posed risks to the crew and vehicle that were too great to accept. Plan B called for the use of the Canadarm to snare the arming lever. Since there was no way to get any new gadgets up to the crew, the snare had to be devised using materials already available aboard the shuttle and an EVA plan had to be worked out for attaching the snare to the arm's end effector.

A ground team fashioned a device from plastic document covers and metal rods used to reach shuttle circuit breakers. It was christened the "flyswatter" but it actually resembled a stubby ladder, with the rungs designed to snap as the satellite lever was pulled so that the arm would not get caught itself. (When the Canadarm was being developed, Spar engineers said that, in future, special end effectors would be developed to handle unique payloads — but this was not quite what they had in mind.) A second device employing a wire snare and dubbed the "lacrosse stick" was also designed and procedures for manufacturing the snares on board the shuttle were read up to the crew. Meanwhile, both designs were being tested back on earth. The snares were attached to a full-scale ground-based replica of the arm and a team of astronauts headed by Sally Ride spent all day and all night evaluating the effectiveness of the snares in pulling the arming lever. Another pair of astronauts went into the water tank to practice attaching the snares to the Canadarm.

Finally, at 6:30 a.m. on April 16, Griggs and Hoffman emerged into the cargo bay to perform the first unplanned spacewalk by a U.S. crew — what flight director John Cox described as a "free-form" EVA. Employing straps and a buckle normally used to hold down payloads, the astronauts tied the flyswatter and the lacrosse stick to the end effector of the arm in an arrangement that owed much to the baling-wire school of technological design — and looked it. The next step was up to Rhea Seddon, who was operating the arm. She had just six minutes to snare the lever. This was dictated by the fact that the motor would be expected to fire 45 minutes after the lever was tripped and, when that happened, the satellite had to be in a particular location to achieve its proper orbit.

Nearly two minutes into her six-minute "window" Seddon made the first swat; the flyswatter was nearly torn by a large pin and she pulled the arm back. During the next minute, Seddon solidly snared the lever twice, ripping the flyswatter as planned. Nothing happened. She then poked at the lever with the solid base of the flyswatter twice. Still nothing. Just as she was moving in for a third try, Mission Control announced: "Discovery, the window is closed — perform the separation maneuvre." The rules called for them to beat a hasty retreat "with great vigor" as soon as the window closed. A few minutes later, watching from a safe distance, the crew conveyed the disappointing news that the spacecraft remained dead, despite the successful snare attempt.

This led to the inescapable conclusion that the lever had not been the cause of the problem; instead, it appeared most likely that the failure had occurred in the timing device that was supposed to fire the motor. Hughes Aircraft Company, builders of the satellite, decided to pay NASA US$10-million to mount a full-scale repair effort, which took place on Mission 51-I in August, 1985, and would come to be known as the "jump-start" rescue. Astronauts James van Hoften, an EVA veteran, and rookie William Fisher, a former surgeon, performed two spacewalks in as many days, including a seven-hour effort on the first day that was the longest EVA ever done by U.S. astronauts in earth orbit. Two EVAs were required because a malfunction in the Canadarm prevented its being operated in a computer-aided mode; arm operator Michael Lounge instead had to use a more time-consuming manual back-up mode that allowed the arm to be positioned only one joint at a time. Precise positioning of the arm during the retrieval and repair operations was essential.

Capture of the slowly rotating satellite was the first order of business and the manual handling techniques developed for the Westar/Palapa rescue stood the astronauts in good stead. Commander Joe Engle flew the shuttle to within 10 metres of Leasat. Van Hoften was anchored by a foot restraint to the end of the Canadarm, which was being maneuvred by Lounge to within inches of the satellite. Fisher, who would do the repair work, was standing in another restraint on one side of the cargo bay.

Van Hoften approached cautiously and pulled the arming lever that had been opened on Mission 51-D to the off position. Next he was to attach to the satellite a bar equipped with a grapple fixture for the Canadarm, but he ran into difficulties attaching the bar. At the same time, the relative positions of the satellite and the shuttle were becoming less favorable. To offset these problems, van Hoften decided to attach a simpler capture bar; it did not have a grapple fixture but it gave him greater manual control over the satellite. Clutching Leasat by hand, he was lowered into the cargo bay by Lounge, who positioned the satellite so that Fisher could reach the side opposite from van Hoften. The satellite was so big that neither astronaut could see the other.

Fisher attached another manual handling bar on his side of Leasat and then grasped the satellite, balancing it above his head as van Hoften let go. Van Hoften then replaced the manual bar on his side with the one with the grapple fixture so the arm could grab the satellite. He then climbed off the arm and Lounge maneuvred it over to pick up Leasat from Fisher. Because Lounge could move the arm only one joint at a time, Fisher was required to hold the seven-tonne satellite for more than hour while receiving instructions every 15 seconds on how to position it to provide Lounge with a steady target.

Once Leasat was securely in hand, Lounge maneuvred it so that Fisher could perform a variety of "safing" operations. First, he shorted out the faulty sequencer to prevent a sudden, unexpected revival of the satellite. Then he removed two panels and attached a new command unit to the outside of the satellite, hot-wiring it to bypass the inoperative sequencer. Finally, he connected a remote power box to the outside of the satellite.[11] These devices would allow command signals from the ground to be received by the satellite. The astronauts then called it quits for the day, seven hours after they'd started the EVA. Leasat was left sitting on the Canadarm for the night.

The next morning at 8:15 a.m., the two astronauts went back outside to launch Leasat into space for the second time. This, too, involved some risky manual operations. First, Fisher grabbed one handle on Leasat, allowing Lounge to release it from the arm, which he then used to pick up van Hoften, who would actually release the satellite into space. While Fisher balanced Leasat from below, van Hoften replaced the arm's grapple bar with another manual handhold device. Both astronauts were now holding the satellite manually. Fisher unlatched his handle bar, retaining only a light grasp on the satellite. This is when they ran into trouble that threatened the success of the whole operation and even put the shuttle and crew in potential jeopardy. The shuttle was firing small thrusters to maintain its position, but this was making it extremely difficult for van Hoften and Fisher, who could not see each other, to hold onto Leasat. "I'm trying to keep it from hitting the spaceship," van Hoften said at one point. Things stabilized enough for Fisher to let go of the satellite but van Hoften continued to experience considerable difficulty. "If something happens and I'm about to lose it, I'm going to give it a heck of a push and bail out," he told Mission Control. At that point ground controllers told Engle he could let the shuttle drift and this solved the problem. Van Hoften's next task was to spin the satellite up to at least two rotations per minute so that all the solar cells covering its cylindrical surface would be exposed to the sun's energy; he did this by grasping the bar and giving it a lifting push. In the riskiest EVA exercise done up to that time, van Hoften performed this rotating toss maneuvre five times, while Engle moved the shuttle up each time to chase the satellite and Lounge pulled the arm back to protect van Hoften from being hit.

Finally, van Hoften watched the spinning satellite sail off into the darkness of space as he stood on the end of the arm while the shuttle backed away. "There that bad boy goes," he said. A few hours later, ground controllers confirmed that Leasat was responding to commands from the ground. The satellite would be monitored for about two months before an attempt was made to fire its booster motor; there was concern that the propellant had frozen, possibly damaging the fuel lines, and that the satellite might explode when the rocket was commanded to fire. However, the firing occurred without mishap in early November.

Just before the Challenger accident temporarily shut down the U.S. manned program, the arm played a key role in yet another important space task. On Mission 61-B in November, 1985, astronauts Jerry Ross and Sherwood Spring earned themselves the title of "the first hard-hats in space" as they practiced for the first time the on-orbit construction techniques that will be used to build the U.S. space station in the 1990s. It was a scene that any child who's ever played with Tinkertoys could relate to — except that the Tinkertoys were giant-sized and were being assembled by white-suited astronauts floating 200 kilometres above the earth. During two six-hour space walks, Ross and Spring, working out of the shuttle cargo bay, assembled and tore down two structures — a 3.6-metre upside-down pyramid made of aluminum struts and a 14-metre metal beam constructed from 99 snap-together metal rods — and practiced accurate positioning, modification and repair of the structures. The capabilities of the human hard-hats were also being evaluated during the tests. The space suits were wired to record the heart rate and oxygen consumption of the astronauts, to give an indication of how hard they were working at various tasks, information that will help space station planners assess what human construction workers can be expected to accomplish in building, repairing and maintaining the station.

The first EVA focussed on assembly tasks. The astronauts worked both with their feet clamped in foot restraints and floating free. It is believed that free-floating construction will be necessary on the space station because it may not be possible to use foot restraints in all locations.

The arm, controlled by astronaut Mary Cleave, was used during the second EVA, which was devoted to a variety of space construction tasks. Anchored by a foot restraint on the end of the arm, Spring assembled part of the tower structure and then practiced stringing a simulated cable along its side as Cleave moved him up a metre at a time. Then Ross hoisted the entire 14-metre truss in his hands for a positioning test; he was able to control it precisely enough to reinsert it into its support structure in the cargo bay — a crucial task in space station construction. Later, Spring was held by the arm while he disassembled part of the structure, performed a simulated repair and practiced holding and positioning it by hand. TV pictures showed him standing on the end of the arm, hoisting the tower over his head like a barbell. "I could balance this thing on my nose," Spring remarked.

The dramatic TV pictures that were transmitted to earth carried an important subliminal message, conveying, for perhaps the first time, the increasing *reality* of the space station as a permanent home and workplace for human beings. Even though the space structures Spring and Ross assembled did appear to the 1-G mind to be almost ridiculously flimsy, seeing hardware actually being put together in space had a way of giving substance to an idea that many people still regarded largely as science fiction. At one point during the highly successful tests, Ross radioed to Mission Control: "Let's go build a space station. We're ready." Later, during a press conference from the spacecraft, he added that he and Spring will be assisting and advising space station designers. (Later, the astronauts and space station managers concluded that their original construction plans called for an unreasonable amount of EVA and the role of unmanned robotic systems was greatly increased. See Chapter 7.)

The success of the Canadarm in these varied operations was obviously a source of great satisfaction to those who built it, but they had known for some time that, in this early incarnation, it was basically not ready for a future that included a permanently manned space station, a variety of new space vehicles and greatly increased requirements for on-orbit servicing, repair and construction. For all its successes, the arm was basically only metal and motors; what it needed for the future was a set of "eyes," hands that could "feel" and, most important, a computer brain. In fact, a major reason for Canada's interest in building a servicing facility for the U.S./international space station was the role that such a project would play in promoting research and development in the fields of automation and robotics (A&R), including artificial intelligence and "expert" systems.[12]

Although humans are expected to play a major role in space construction and servicing, automated systems and intelligent robots will nevertheless be extensively used. The objective is to optimize the division of labor between human beings and machines, allowing each to do what they do best. To free humans as much as possible from mundane tasks, many routine and repetitive functions will be performed by computers and robotic devices. Space construction, assembly, servicing and repair in particular will depend greatly on smart robotic vehicles and servicing systems equipped with advanced remote manipulators. Free-flying robotic vehicles will be used to retrieve disabled satellites and return them to the station for refurbishment, or to repair and refuel satellites in orbit, under remote control by humans on the space station or on earth. This remote control — known as teleoperation — will become increasingly important because putting humans outside the pressurized modules is both hazardous and expensive and will be done only when it offers a significant advantage.

For Canada, the first step along the A&R path is the development of a machine vision system for the Canadarm. It will be used to provide astronauts controlling the arm with better information on the relative position, orientation and motions of the payloads they are trying to grab. In the past, the astronauts have used camera images, their own eyesight and judgement honed by intensive training to maintain precise control of the arm, and their success rate in the space retrieval and repair missions discussed above demonstrates that they have performed these tasks extremely well. In future, however, the workload will be much greater and the astronauts will be manipulating larger and more difficult payloads.[13] In many cases, they may not be able to "eyeball" the operation very easily since viewing conditions in space are often unfavorable. Frequently there are no reference points to help them gauge distances and speeds, and the flat, harsh lighting in space can complicate grappling procedures a great deal. The lighting changes that occur as a spacecraft moves from sunlight to darkness can also drastically alter the visual cues used to approach and grab a payload.

The space vision system is designed to overcome these problems and make grappling operations faster, safer and more accurate, particularly when large payloads are involved. In ground-based tests, a prototype reduced the time required to berth a large payload from five minutes to one.

The SVS system was developed by Lloyd Pinkney and Charles Perratt of the National Research Council, who started work on the system in 1976. The CDN$4-million contract to build the system was given to Spar Aerospace as prime contractor, with Leigh Instruments of Ottawa as the major subcontractor.

Pinkney says this type of vision system is "well suited to a number of applications, especially those in which you want to know *where* something is, rather than *what* it is." The key to the system is a process known as "real-time photogrammetry," which involves extremely rapid computer processing of TV images of the payload.[14] The term "real time" refers to the fact that the operator of the arm needs the information fast enough to execute the job at hand. For example, Pinkney said, if the RMS operator is performing a task in which the payload moves the length of a table in one minute, but the SVS information is being updated only every two minutes, "the thing would have moved twice the length of the table and he wouldn't be able to control it at all. It's very important that the operator's update rate is much faster than the dynamics of the [RMS] system."

The computer generates a screen display, in both numbers and graphic images, that enables the astronaut controlling the arm to quickly and accurately determine the payload's relative position, orientation and motion with respect to the arm. The system can tell how fast the payload is moving in any combination of the six degrees of motion — up or down, right or left, back and forth — or rotating around any of its three axes (pitch, yaw and roll). It can measure the distance to the payload with an accuracy of one in 2000 (i.e., if the payload is 200 metres away, the system can tell its distance to within 10 cm). The computer performs millions of calculations per second and updates the information supplied to the astronaut 30 times a second.

The payload is outfitted with special reflective targets — either black dots on a white background or white dots on a black background — arranged in a rectangle known as a "target cluster." The closed-circuit TV images of this target cluster are fed into the computer, which analyzes the position of each circle in the cluster. The computer is programmed with the exact position of the dots relative to each other and with the target cluster's exact location on the payload, relative to a fixed reference point. It is also programmed with relevant information concerning the optical characteristics of the cameras taking the pictures. From this, the computer can calculate the position, orientation and velocity of the payload by analyzing the geometry of the dots. For example, if the target cluster is close, the dots appear more separated from each other than if the cluster is further away. Or, if the payload is turning or tilting, the dots will appear as shapes other than the rectangle that appears when the target cluster is aligned upright and face-on to the camera. (See Figure 2.)

The distance over which the SVS system will work depends on the lighting available to illuminate the target. With only ambient or conventional lighting (i.e., natural lighting conditions in space or the shuttle's cargo bay lights), an object up to 200 metres away can be seen. In future, however, it is expected the system will have its own laser lighting system, which will enable it to pick up payloads several kilometres away. Since Steve MacLean was doing research on lasers when he was selected for the astronaut program, this is an aspect of the SVS development that particularly interests him. "That's why I thought I was hired, actually. But they're not doing that right now — maybe in a couple of years. I feel we should be doing stuff like that — improving the engineering prototype — but there was so much training involved in getting up to speed on the shuttle, getting the mission-related training and the orbiter-related training done. We have had such a crash course there, that there hasn't been time."

For the foreseeable future, the SVS system is primarily intended to assist astronauts controlling the arm. Although the computer can provide precise numerical data, Perratt said, human beings are better at evaluating what type of information is most valuable at any given time. It is possible, however, that this technology will eventually be incorporated into a fully automatic system in which the computer will both process the images and control the movements of the arm.

Preliminary tests of the SVS system were conducted on Mission 41-G. The prototype photogrammetry unit was not flown; instead it was located in Mission Control and processed images relayed to the ground from the shuttle's TV system. The purpose of the test was to gain experience with the real space environment, particularly its harsh lighting conditions; no attempt was made on this first mission to provide real-time assistance to astronaut Sally Ride, who operated the arm. Using closed-circuit TV cameras on the Canadarm and in the cargo bay, Ride took pictures of a target cluster of black dots that had been painted on the solar panels of the ERBS satellite.[15] This information was videotaped and then transmitted to the SVS processor on the ground, which analyzed the release of the satellite by the arm and monitored its position relative to the shuttle orbiter as the two separated. There were

Figure Two

1. WHAT THE COMPUTER SEES

The computer, which guides the robot, knows exactly where the moving object is by using a camera to follow the target attached to the object. The position of the dots as they are imaged by the camera is measured by the computer. The camera takes 30 pictures per second and measurements are made for each picture.

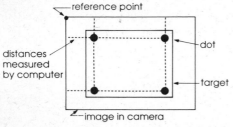

The computer measures the position of each dot with respect to a reference point.

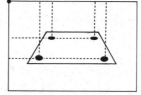

As the object is tilted backwards, the positions of the dots change.

2. TARGET MOVEMENTS—
WHAT THE COMPUTER CAN MEASURE

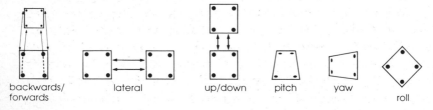

backwards/ forwards   lateral   up/down   pitch   yaw   roll

3. HOW THE COMPUTER DETERMINES POSTION

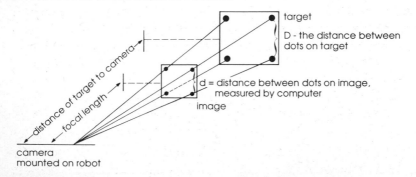

target

D - the distance between dots on target

d = distance between dots on image, measured by computer

image

camera mounted on robot

Because the ratio of d to the focal lenght is equal to that of D to the distance of the target from the camera, and the values of focal lenght, d and D are known, the exact distance of the target to the camera is calculated by computer.

Using the same kind of geometric relationships, the computer can also determine whether an object is rolling, moving sideways or up and down, and at what angle, to a fraction of a degree, the object is yawed or pitched.

some problems, however. First, the Canadarm blocked one of the target dots during the release of the satellite and it had only begun to move away from the target when Ride switched to using another camera — something the Canadian team had not anticipated. As a result, only four seconds of data were obtained in which all four dots could be seen in the images. However, Doetsch said after the mission that "even with that small amount of data, we were able to identify how fast the ERBS was moving relative to the orbiter. We generally have high confidence in the data."

As the shuttle moved away from the satellite, another problem arose — ERBS was bathed in brilliant sunlight, which created a "blooming" effect in the camera images that literally washed out the dots. However about 35 seconds of useful data were obtained by "corner-tracking" — that is, tracking the sharp edges of the light-colored solar panels, which contrasted sharply with the dark background of space. This required some rather frantic juggling by Pinkney and Perratt, who were operating the ground-based SVS prototype in Mission Control. "They just worked flat out," said Doetsch. "There had to be some ad-hocery in all of this. Instead of taking the target information ... they used the corners, the edges ... and they came up with a solution that gave good data; we were able to work out the separation velocity [of the ERBS satellite]."

Despite the problems, enough data were obtained to test the system adequately and even the trouble-shooting provided valuable experience. So did the extreme lighting conditions, and the problems they created, said Steve MacLean, who will perform more detailed experiments using a flight version of the SVS on his shuttle mission.

Doetsch said that the results of these preliminary tests helped refine MacLean's SVS experiments and the design of the SVS system in general. They particularly demonstrated the importance of being able to switch quickly from one data-collection method to another to adapt to changing conditions. He said the results also suggested that lighting of the satellite must be better controlled, both by illuminating the targets and by improving the camera system — perhaps by the use of special filters — so it can make these kinds of measurements more competently. "If you have a light source which is very closely aligned with the camera, the light you send will bounce right back into the camera," he said. Research is also being done to enhance the light-reflecting characteristics of the material used to make the dots.

The tests planned for MacLean's mission will be much more elaborate than those done on Mission 41-G and will involve placing a great deal more hardware on the shuttle. A flight version of the SVS system, including the photogrammetry unit and a display and control panel (weighing 98 kg), will be installed at a payload station located just behind the commander's seat on the flight deck. The Canadian Target Assembly (CTA), a payload carrying the target dots, will be located in the cargo bay where it can be manipulated by the Canadarm. During some six to eight hours of testing, MacLean will use the SVS to track the movements of the CTA as it is maneuvred by the arm in the cargo bay and later released to fly free.[16] The tests are expected to include the use of the SVS to aid in berthing the payload and in a simulated space construction task. It will also be used to track the CTA at ranges from 9 to 90 metres and beyond. The shuttle's closed-circuit TV system will be used to feed images of the target to the photogrammetry unit. The computer analysis can then be displayed on screens at the RMS operator's control station and at MacLean's panel.

During the tests, MacLean will work at a computer keyboard, performing a variety of tasks to control the operations of the SVS system. For example, to instruct the computer to lock on to the four dots on the target, he will use a light pen to point at the images of each of the dots on the TV screen. He will also control the videotape recording of the test runs.

The SVS tests call for close collaboration between MacLean and the NASA mission specialist who will be operating the arm. "They'll be very much a team," said Bruce Aikenhead, program manager of the Canadian astronaut office. "The RMS operator will be serving the experiment by positioning the target where we'd like it to be and moving at desired rates and doing various tasks for us. And, on the other hand, the RMS operator will also be a test subject — we'd like to see how these space vision system displays will ... serve to make the RMS operator's task easier."

Because the operator of the Canadarm is located in the aft part of the flight deck, looking out on the cargo bay, it was considered essential that MacLean also operate the SVS from the flight deck. However, it is rare for anyone to request equipment room on the flight deck and Aikenhead said that it proved "a bit of an uphill struggle" to persuade NASA to allow the SVS to be installed there, rather than in the mid-deck below. "There was a point of view that said the place for payload specialists is down in the mid-deck — they stay down there and keep out of the way. The flight deck is for real astronauts."

Putting MacLean in the mid-deck would not do, however. This "would have essentially disconnected our Canadian payload specialist from what was going on up in the flight deck," said Aikenhead. "He would be getting his information essentially by hearsay. He would have little way of appreciating how the RMS operator was using the displays and he would not have any sense of the operational atmosphere." NASA eventually agreed.

Figuring out what Canada will be charged for the flight was another extremely complicated matter. Canada will have to pay to put hardware on the flight deck and in the cargo bay and possibly also for crew training. And since maneuvring of the orbiter will be required to do the SVS tests, Canada may be charged for the gas. Finally, said Aikenhead, "if it should be necessary for some contingency EVA because our target gets hung up, then we'll get the bill for that too." He estimated that, if Canada is charged for everything, the total could amount to between CDN$2- and $3-million.

MacLean's flight had been scheduled for Mission 71-F in March, 1987, but was put on hold after the Challenger accident. However, development of the hardware and the experimental protocols for the mission were held to the original deadlines, in part to maintain momentum and morale and in part to be ready for the earliest flight opportunity that presents itself. By summer of 1986, both the flight model of the SVS and the ground-based system that would be used for simulations were ready. The flight model would later be taken to the Johnson Space Center for tests of its compatability with the shuttle's electrical and closed-circuit TV systems. After that, it will go through safety checks and then be returned to Ottawa for mothballing, if necessary, to await resumption of shuttle flights and the assignment of MacLean to a mission. "One of the nice things about doing it this early is, if we do get into any trouble — let's say that it flunks one of these tests — then we've got some time in which to arrange the necessary re-tests," said Aikenhead. He was finding the second time around a lot easier than preparing for Garneau's mission, not only because there's more time, but because the team now has experience with the NASA system and "I've got more people helping me this time."

The flight unit won't be installed aboard a shuttle until about three months before flight. Aikenhead said they hope MacLean can fly within a year after shuttle flights resume, but this is complicated by the fact that Canada is asking not only for two mid-deck lockers[17] (as opposed to one for Garneau's mission), but also for room in the cargo bay and on the flight deck. The mission will not go until all three can be accommodated, he said. An added factor is that the Canadian experiments are considered secondary payloads, lower in priority than many other payloads, particularly military ones.

There is much more to the development of the SVS experiments than preparing flight hardware, however. During the first half of 1986, MacLean, Tryggvason and Garneau were deeply involved in all aspects of the SVS project, including development of the hardware, the computer software and documentation. They developed the procedures and checklists for using the SVS system, particularly the tasks that will be performed on MacLean's mission, and were also involved in the development of a ground-based testing and simulation facility at the NRC. MacLean and Tryggvason developed computer programs and training videotapes that will be used to generate visual scenes in the simulator. These scenes will enable astronauts to practice the SVS procedures required for scheduled tasks and also learn how to cope with a variety of potential malfunctions.

Tryggvason was also a member of the working group that was overseeing the development of the CTA. From the beginning, he had believed it was important to the success of the SVS test that Canada fly its own target payload, rather than riding piggy-back on someone else's, as had been done with ERBS. He felt that this would give the research team far greater latitude in using the kind of targets needed to fully demonstrate the SVS system's capabilities. Tryggvason also worked on developing the specific tests the SVS will be called on to perform in space. "We want to push it, test it to the limits," he said.

Garneau, meanwhile, was writing the SVS operator's manual, which he described as "the bible. [It] will have all the information available that explains what each of the buttons does." This work is also expected to help in the development of the detailed procedures and checklist for MacLean's mission. Garneau also developed a computer data base that will be used in generating the graphic images that will appear on the RMS operator's display screen.

Remote manipulator technology is destined to play an increasingly important role in space with the development of a permanently manned station and the wide range of commercial and scientific activities that will be associated with it. Indeed, Canada's major role in the coming era of permanent human habitation of space will centre on the use and further improvement of this technology. Foreseeable advances will include the addition of a tactile sense, expert systems and, ultimately, artificial intelligence. The tactile sense would allow the arm to "feel" how much force is being applied and how much resistance it is meeting. (In humans, this sense tells you, for example, how firmly an egg can be grasped without breaking it.) Jim Middleton of Spar Aerospace said that a tactile sense will be important for space construction activities because many space structures will be built of lightweight, thin-walled hollow tubes that manipulators must be able to handle without squeezing too hard.

The combination of artificial intelligence with robotic arms will ultimately result in manipulator systems capable of automatic operation and even perhaps some independent decision making. However, no one is seriously talking — yet — about taking human beings out of the picture. Savi Sachdev, engineering director for Spar Aerospace, said that tasks in space fall into four broad categories: manipulation, information transfer, information processing and decision making. Machines largely handle the middle two, an area ripe for developments in artificial intelligence. Both humans and machines handle manipulation tasks and humans will likely be needed for "fine manipulation" — such as delicate repair tasks — for a long time. The final category, decision making, is entirely the province of humans at present and "will remain so for the foreseeable future," Sachdev said. "Artificial intelligence and expert systems will eventually help in this decision-making process but they cannot replace man's ability to perceive, understand, redefine, take initiative, adapt to unforeseen circumstances, supervise machines and interpret data." (Le Roy Nelms, associate chief of research and development for the Department of National Defence, has commented that " the human is the most versatile expert system that we have at present.")

Sachdev said the trade-off between using humans or machines is becoming increasingly complex, but some of the factors that have to be considered include safety, cost and the frequency of the task; for example, humans are best for infrequent contingency or emergency operations; machines for frequent but routine operations. Productivity is also a factor and the productivity of human beings will be increased with the use of robotics and automated systems. "For now, man and machine will continue to live in a symbiotic relationship."

NOTES

1. As Nelson began his return to the shuttle, Crippen maneuvred Challenger slightly. To a nonplussed Nelson, already frustrated by the failed rescue attempt, this appeared as though his backpack was beginning to act up. "I'm not flying right either, Crip. I don't believe this," he remarked as his heartbeat increased to about 90-100 beats per minute. Then he realized that Challenger was moving.

2. This did not present any problem regarding the shuttle's return to earth because the forward RCS thrusters were not required to kick the shuttle out of orbit for re-entry.

3. It was later determined that the rates had gone up to about two degrees per second in all three axes. In a subsequent eight-hour run in the simulator, astronauts were able to grapple a payload moving that fast only once. "The task was not possible," Middleton said.

4. Later NASA did ground-based simulations of the feasibility of using the MMU to rescue stranded or disabled astronauts. One scenario would require an astronaut wearing an EVA suit and the MMU to carry crew members in what NASA, with its penchant for technical circumlocution, calls a "personal rescue enclosure." This is a glorified beachball, less than a metre in diameter, into which each crew member would be stuffed in a fetal-like crouch, clutching a life support box. In this manner, the crew could be transported through the deep freeze and deep vacuum of space by one of the space-suited astronauts. It may be undignified, but it sure beats the alternatives. Since only two EVA suits are carried aboard each shuttle, the rescue balls would be used to transfer other crew members. Other scenarios involved the rescue of conscious or unconscious astronauts wearing both suits and MMUs. These methods would be used in EVA situations in which an astronaut was incapacitated by illness or accident, or if he or she came untethered and drifted off, or if an MMU was disabled while the astronaut was flying away from the shuttle.

5. Middleton said that Crippen "knows more about the orbiter than any human alive" and that his decision-making skills were so highly regarded by the flight controllers that they gave him an unusual amount of personal control over the mission. "The flight directorate quite often says: 'Let Crippen do what he wants to do.' "

6. Through 1970 and 1971, DSMA did studies funded by the Department of Industry, Trade and Commerce and visited NASA to promote Canadian expertise in the development of remotely controlled manipulators operating in hazard environments. DSMA later worked on the Canadarm project and on preliminary studies for Canada's space station program, but was closed down in 1986.

7. There were some in Canada who weren't too happy either. Solar energy proponents were angered when $750,000 was lifted from the NRC's renewable energy program to help pay for the arm.

8. Everything is, of course, weightless in space; NASA was concerned here with the design problems and costs associated with lifting the whole package off the launch pad.

9. Four years later, in the wake of the Challenger accident, Truly would take over as shuttle manager with a mandate to put the devastated program back on its feet.

10. Even so, *Time* magazine, in its wrap-up article after the mission, neglected to mention the arm at all, despite the fact that the RMS test was one of the major objectives of the flight. (It did mention a sunflower-growing experiment that failed.)

11. Since Fisher had been a surgeon before becoming an astronaut, it was considered particularly appropriate that he would perform this "bypass surgery."

12. An expert system is a computer system that incorporates a specialized body of knowledge and a degree of artificial intelligence that permits it to make assessments of information fed into it. Expert systems are used, for example, to assist doctors with medical diagnoses. The system is programmed with information about signs and symptoms of disorders or diseases, and with certain "rules" (for example, "If the results of a lab blood test are X, this means Y"). Medical diagnosis systems are only one of a great number of expert systems that are expected to be used in space; others would be developed for guidance, navigation and control, communications, flight planning, fuel control, monitoring malfunctions and many other uses.

13. Although a large payload does not weigh anything in space, it still has mass and inertia. If it is moving fast when the arm grabs it, it will tend to keep on going, which could stress or damage the arm.

14. Pinkney said that, from the beginning, they knew they had to work with the existing closed-circuit camera system used on the shuttle, rather than trying to have a specialized camera put on board. "Any little modification on that orbiter costs a fortune. You're not going to take over control of those cameras."

15. MacLean had responsibility for overseeing the placement of the targets, which is far from as easy a task as it might seem. The satellite's designers were concerned about anything that might cause thermal problems for the solar energy cells. A special material that MacLean wanted to use for the targets was vetoed, so he reverted to using space-rated black paint.

16. The CTA is essentially a small, flat piece of metal. It is a passive device, with no attitude control system of its own. It will not be retrieved by the arm, but will be left in orbit and eventually will re-enter and burn up in the earth's atmosphere. Canada has requested a shuttle flight with a relatively low orbit, so the CTA would re-enter fairly quickly. NASA is always unhappy about debris left in the orbital region in which the shuttle operates; although the CTA is small, it could still cause serious damage if it were to collide with a shuttle at some future date.

17. Each of the items that will go into the two lockers must also go through safety checks; they include an apparatus to study the separation of biological materials in liquids in zero gravity and a tiny furnace to be used in a zero-gravity materials processing experiment. "This is going to be on the mid-deck, so we don't want any nauseating fumes coming off this thing ... we don't want it catching fire or nasty things like that," said Aikenhead. "And it has to be capable of unattended operation because Steve can't just sit there and watch it."

CHAPTER SEVEN

The
Space Station

*D*ecember 11, 2005,
6:30 a.m. orbital time:
A low but persistent beeping noise
issues from the computer-communications unit
located near the "ceiling"
of a personal crew compartment
aboard the international space station
orbiting 460 kilometres
above the earth.
Astronaut-engineer Karen Jenkins
rouses from sleep and,
grasping a handhold above her,
pulls herself out of the sleeping-bag-like bed
attached to one wall.

With one hand, she pushes it flat against the wall and the cover instantly stretches taut, giving the bed a neatly made-up appearance. Jenkins muses, not for the first time, that as a child she'd have given half of her construction set for just such a self-making bed. She floats up to the computer and turns it on. The screen reveals the duty roster and directives about space station activities from the crew commander and Mission Control. She grimaces at the reminder that it's her week for laundry duty.

Jenkins presses a key on the computer and finds there are several messages from earth in her electronic mailbox, including one from her parents, which reminds her that she has to do some computer shopping for Christmas. Other messages include a reminder from Mission Control about a lecture she's scheduled to give on space engineering that will be viewed live by 100 university engineering classes around the world, and a note from her boss at Solar Power Systems Inc., who wants to extend their weekly teleconferenced briefing session later in the day to discuss her planned space walk to repair one of the station's solar power panels. After tapping out a brief affirmative and dispatching it to SPS's electronic box, she switches the unit to receive an earth-side news show while she prepares to start the day.

After dressing, Jenkins is ready to climb aboard the stationary bicycle for her morning "ride." At least two hours of exercise is needed every day to maintain muscle tone in zero gravity. She flips a switch on the control panel, which lowers a screen in front of the bike, and then inserts a video cassette into the VCR unit. The image of a tree-lined bicycle path appears on the screen and, as she starts to pedal, the picture moves, giving her the feel of riding through the park.

"Where are you this time?" asks her crewmate, NASA mission specialist Ron Harkness, who is strapping himself down to the treadmill beside the bicycle.

"I finally got that videotape of the park near my parents' home where I used to ride as a kid. How about you?" she asks, pointing to the screen descending in front of the treadmill.

"Boston Marathon." He grins sheepishly. "It's a lot easier in zero-G."

An hour later, Jenkins floats down the corridor containing the eight crew compartments to the shower stall at the end. She attaches her robe to the wall in the small ante-room and enters the cylindrical shower compartment, hooking her toes around the little metal "mushrooms" on the floor to stabilize herself. She flips a switch to start first a downward air flow and then the water. Getting water to fall down in zero gravity was quite an engineering challenge — and so is cleaning up afterwards; as Jenkins leaves the shower compartment, she flips another switch that causes a plunger to descend slowly within the cylindrical chamber, sweeping the water clinging to the walls down into the drain.

After a quick breakfast, Jenkins prepares for her first major task of the day — a final evaluation of the damage to the solar panel prior to briefing her company's earth-based engineers that afternoon. Sitting at her computer terminal, she remotely controls a camera-equipped robot vehicle on an inspection tour of the panel. The section needing repair was one of the first to be *installed and has been suffering the ravages of the harsh space environment for nearly ten years.*

By noon, Jenkins has reaffirmed her initial impression that the repair work will require both an EVA and the use of the space station's "smart" robotic manipulator arm. Jenkins goes in search of Gilles Lemieux, a Canadian astronaut who is her frequent partner on these outings. Lemieux, who is responsible for the operations of the Mobile Servicing Centre built by Canada, is an expert in the use of the arm for repair EVAs. Jenkins finds him in the galley/dining area of the station. He's pulled KP duty this week and is grumbling good-naturedly as he prepares lunch for the members of the crew on the "day" shift. "A PhD in electrical engineering and they put me to work as a short-order cook," he mutters as he launches a ham sandwich her way frisbee-style.

"Yeah, but what a great greasy spoon to work in," Jenkins remarks as she deftly fields it.

Most of the afternoon is taken up with a video teleconference between the space station, Mission Control and two SPS centres on earth. After dinner, the crew participates in an audio-visual game of advanced Trivial Pursuit (the Space Version). It is the final match against the defending champions, the Mission Control team, and the space station crew, which snatches the title for the first time in three years. Afterwards, Jenkins and Harkness once more review procedures for the next day's EVA and agree to meet early the next morning near the airlock, where the bulky EVA suits are stored, to inspect their suits and prepare for the six-hour space walk. Jenkins then puts in another hour on the bicycle before getting ready for bed. As she finishes her exercise, two crew members who are on the "night" shift — a Japanese researcher doing experiments to produce new drugs in zero gravity and a European doctor doing zero-G physiology studies— arrive to start their work day.

To the chronically earthbound, scenes like this may still belong in the realm of science fiction, but, by the turn of the century, they will become a day-to-day reality for a growing number of people who will be living and working aboard the permanently manned space station being built by the United States, Canada, Europe and Japan. The station, which is scheduled to go into operation in the mid-1990s, will support rotating international crews of up to eight people for tours of duty lasting about three months at a time.

At first, the crews will consist largely of career astronauts, technical experts, and scientists and engineers from government agencies, universities and private industry. But eventually, a wide range of people with other skills — journalists, educators, artists, photographers, dancers and film makers, for example — will also be going into space.

The concept of the space station is not new — it has long been a staple of science fiction stories. What is new is that we are on the verge of transforming the fantasies of centuries past into the realities of the 21st century. We have been going about the business of learning to live and work in space on a long-term basis since the early 1970s. The Soviet Union turned its attention to manned operations in low earth orbit in the 1960s when it realized the United States would beat it to the moon; the first of the Salyut space stations was put in orbit in 1971 and soon the Soviets had set the record for long-duration flights with their 237-day mission. By the mid-1980s, the Soviet space station program was considerably more advanced than that of the United States; and the Soviets are currently in a much better position, at least in the near term, to capitalize technologically and scientifically from using the space environment, particularly after the Challenger accident forced suspension of shuttle flights in 1986. In fact, the Soviets will probably beat the West in this latest round of the space race; in hindsight, it appears that losing the race to the moon may turn out to be the best thing that could have happened to the Soviet space program.

By 1985-86, the Soviets were moving aggressively toward the goal of a permanently manned space station. In September, 1985, for the first time in either the Soviet or the U.S. programs, a partial change of crew took place and Salyut remained manned during the exchange, whereas previously Salyut had been left empty for days or weeks at a time while crews were rotated. Also, a new 13-metre module was attached to Salyut 7, nearly doubling its size. The module included a habitable compartment and an unmanned re-entry vehicle, which can return hundreds of kilograms of research products and military intelligence to earth without requiring the crew to return as well. In February, 1986, the Soviet Union launched the MIR (Peace) space vehicle, widely regarded as the first step toward a full-scale, permanently manned facility.[1] By mid-1986, the Soviets had clocked more than 4300 days in space, compared with about 1770 for the Americans, and had spent a much larger proportion in long-duration missions, prompting *Jane's Space Flight Directory* to claim that the Soviet Union has taken an "almost frightening" ten-year lead over the United States in the aftermath of the Challenger accident. However, NASA administrator James Fletcher challenged this, saying the Soviet shuttle program is years behind and the U.S./international space station will be much more advanced than Salyut or MIR.

The U.S. program, dominated first by the Apollo program and then by the trouble-plagued development of the shuttle, has had only one brief experience with operating a space station. In 1973, NASA mounted the US$554-million Skylab project, an experimental, short-term space station, using a converted third stage of the Saturn V moon rocket to house crews of three men each for three missions lasting more than five months in total. A major objective of the program was to demonstrate not only that human beings could live and work in space, but also why it might be worth their while to do so. Skylab provided researchers with both the time and the room to do space research projects that had not been feasible before; nearly 300 biomedical and scientific investigations were carried out on the missions. Following Skylab, NASA was preoccupied with getting the troubled shuttle program off the ground. Technical problems and cost overruns beset the development program — which in the end cost about US$10-billion, about twice the original projection — and this put space station plans on hold for more than a decade.

By the mid-1980s, however, both the United States and the Soviet Union were getting really serious about putting humans into space to live and work on a permanent basis. We are, in fact, poised on the brink of the next major migration of the human species. By the turn of the century, barring a catastrophic war on earth, space will have become a base for commercial, industrial, scientific and military activities; a staging area for eventual assaults on the moon and the other planets; and, for an ever-growing number of people, a new home and a new way of life. "We expect to see extensive population and utilization of low earth orbit early in the 21st century," says Thomas Paine, a former NASA administrator and chairman of the U.S. National Commission on Space.

The human migration into space is often compared with the discovery and colonization of North America and, in some ways, the comparison is apt. The quest for new territory was very much dominated by the politics of the day and the prospect of economic return. Certainly there were many doubters and nay-sayers back then and they too complained about the cost of the adventure, just as today's critics of the space program do. But there are also some important differences, the most critical being that space is an environment that the human body is not inherently equipped to survive. It is characterized by extremes of temperature, an almost total vacuum, high levels of radiation and almost non-existent gravity forces. There are no native plants or animals to provide food, clothing and shelter, no streams or rivers for water; there isn't even any air to breathe.

In fact, it is the profoundly alien quality of this environment that makes us forget that the distance to be travelled — a mere 460 kilometres to the space station, for example — is far less than that generally covered by explorers and trail-blazers on earth. The difference, of course, is that in order to cross this seemingly trivial distance, we must climb out of the deep well of the earth's gravity and take a complete and virtually foolproof life support system with us. This is what requires billions of dollars worth of firepower and high-tech equipment. Fortunately, however, space does provide one very important commodity in virtually unlimited amounts — energy from the sun — and this provides the prospect of ultimate freedom for the space colonies from perpetual dependence on supplies from earth.

The move into space differs from past colonization efforts on earth in another important respect. This time, those who go will be in constant communication with those left behind; indeed, people on earth will be able to participate vicariously in this new wave of colonization to an extent never before possible. Although Soviet space projects and the space activities of the military will continue to be largely shrouded in secrecy, just about everything else undoubtedly will be photographed, televised, videotaped, written about and commented upon in excruciating detail. When the space station is operational, it is anticipated that researchers and scientists will use the elaborate audio-visual communications systems on board to conduct "open university" courses that will be beamed directly from space to the general public and to schools, universities and educational TV outlets around the world.

Of course, as with every other space project, the space station program has attracted its share of critics. Some question the cost of the program and the political priorities that permit it to co-exist with pervasive unsolved social problems such as crime, poverty and hunger. Others are wary about the projected economic return; the station has already been dubbed "Blind Faith 1," on the grounds that no one knows for sure whether the gamble will pay off. Nevertheless, the United States, Europe, Japan and Canada are collectively betting billions of dollars that it will indeed pay off exceedingly well — not only by providing humans with a base of operations in space, but also by priming the pump for the advancement of major high-technology programs and providing jobs on earth. As a result, the U.S./international space station project has begun to dominate the space programs of all Western industrial nations, lending substance to a growing perception within the scientific and industrial aerospace community that, for better or worse (and some are not sure which is the case), it has become pretty much the only game in town.

NASA started planning for a space station in the 1960s, even before the Apollo moon program was completed. In 1966, before the Apollo fire, the space agency was talking big: an operational station by 1972, a manned moon base by 1975 and a landing on Mars by 1986. These goals demonstrate how far we've come from the technological, fiscal and social optimism of the Sixties; indeed, from the perspective of the "cutback" Eighties, they appear almost laughable. But then, part of what the space program is all about is reaching beyond our grasp; this is, in fact, one of its most important and least-appreciated roles.

In this first dazzling conception of the human migration into space, the shuttle was viewed as only one small, though essential, part of a much larger picture; it was then intended solely as a workhorse vehicle to ferry people and supplies to and from the space station. But by the early 1970s, the political ambience in the United States had changed dramatically. The euphoria from the first landing on the moon had dissipated and, worse, had been supplanted by a series of bleak economic and political distractions — the world oil crisis, Vietnam and Watergate. NASA scaled down its dreams of the station, but scaled up the shuttle concept — it would not only be a ferry vehicle but it would be used to launch commercial and military satellites. The argument was that, because the shuttle was reusable, it would ultimately be much cheaper than expendable rockets and, in fact, would eventually become the sole American launch vehicle. This was a pivotal concept, for it set the United States on a course of putting nearly all its eggs in one basket, an ultimately disastrous strategy that left it vulnerable to the devastation of launching capability caused by the loss of the Challenger orbiter in 1986. However, at the time, NASA had an understandable goal in pushing the shuttle as a reusable cargo carrier; the prospect of making the shuttle pay for itself in a relatively short time was appealing to an increasingly tightfisted Congress. One persuasive study done at the time projected that the shuttle would achieve a schedule of nearly one flight a week and that it would turn a profit at 30 flights a year. As it turned out, these projections were almost ridiculously optimistic; NASA was pushing hard to manage 15 flights in 1986, and it was widely believed that the pressure to increase the frequency of launches contributed, at least in part, to the Challenger accident. In the aftermath, NASA was directed to leave commercial satellite launches to the expendable launch vehicles and to concentrate on carrying humans and special payloads that required the shuttle's unique qualities and, ultimately, on servicing the station. It was back to square one.

But in the early 1970s, Congress bought NASA's all-things-to-everyone scenario and approved the shuttle as a stand-alone project. Even so, they lopped the requested budget in half, to about US$5-billion, which resulted in a vehicle that was no one's ideal design and was widely regarded as a space-age camel. Under the circumstances, plans for the space station were mothballed, although NASA never lost interest in the program. It continued to lobby strongly for the project for many years, arguing, correctly, that the US$10-billion investment in the shuttle made little sense if the U.S. did not proceed with the station. Despite its successes, the shuttle was still essentially only a high-tech truck and it would never be suitable for long-term missions.

It was not until 1984 that NASA received the official green light from President Reagan to dust off its plans for a permanently manned station. It was a hard-fought battle. Not only was the space station project fighting for life within a climate of severe financial restraint, it inherited all the opposition that had been levelled at the manned space program for nearly three decades. The 1980s version of this argument was typified by a letter in the *Globe and Mail* in February, 1984. It asked if Reagan was not being "... irresponsible to promise the American people a station in space, when back here on earth acid rain, together with other pressing environmental issues, is ignored?" and concluded by wondering whether there will be "sufficient space stations to house the American people when Mother Earth can no longer sustain life."

Ironically, in view of the widespread public misconception that the space station program was promoted primarily by the military, the U.S. Defense Department lobbied strongly against the project, since it anticipated having little use for the station and was concerned that funds would be diverted from shuttle operations that were important for military programs.

Within the scientific community, much of the criticism has been focussed specifically on the manned space program. Unmanned communications and remote-sensing satellites and robotic probes, such as those that explore the planets, have had undeniable successes and performed spectacular feats. They do not involve a risk to human life and are generally less expensive than manned missions, although the cost of an unmanned mission is by no means trivial; for example, the Viking Mars landing missions cost US$1-billion. Many space scientists decry both the expense and the danger inherent in putting humans into space, believing that there is a much better scientific return on investment in unmanned programs. (See Chapter 8.)

Despite the considerable opposition to the space station from various fronts, U.S. President Ronald Reagan was adamant that the program go ahead. In fact, he surprised many people by embracing the project more enthusiastically than expected in his State of the Union Address in January, 1984. In a speech very reminiscent of, though far less eloquent than, the one given by President John F. Kennedy in 1961, in which he committed the United States to landing on the moon before the end of the decade, Reagan declared that "America is too great for small dreams," and directed NASA "to develop a permanently manned space station and do it within a decade."[2] The theme of his speech was "America is back" and in it, he exhorted the people of the United States to rise above the crisis of confidence that had characterized the 1970s and to "make a new beginning." Reagan did say that the space station project would create new industries and jobs, would promote "quantum leaps" in scientific and technological research and development. But in large part he relied on an emotional appeal to patriotic sentiment and pride. The project would "build on America's pioneer spirit," he said.

"America has always been greatest when we dared to be great. We can reach for greatness again."

Like Kennedy, Reagan intended to use the space station project as a dramatic and highly visible symbol. It could provide the nation with some psychological bootstrapping in the face of economic troubles at home, its apparent helplessness against anti-U.S. terrorism abroad, and unsatisfactory relations with the Soviet Union. Once again, a key aim was to use technological achievement to revitalize a sense of destiny in the American people; in a 1983 speech, then NASA administrator James Beggs said that the U.S. had achieved its position of leadership in space "because we had the imagination to dream great dreams and the national will to fulfill them."[3] Robert Freitag, then director of policy and plans in NASA's space station office, described the project as "primarily a leadership program to set the pace for the next 25 years."

But the project is expected to produce more than political brownie points; in fact, one major advantage it has over the moon program is that, in a political climate dominated by the "bottom-line" school of national dreams, it offers the prospect of a significant dollars-and-cents return on investment. Whatever else the space station may become, it is intended to be the first profit-generating industrial park in space. The importance of this idea in selling the station concept to President Reagan, the U.S. Congress, the American taxpayer and other governments around the world cannot be overestimated (although projections of the economic returns have, at times, probably been overly optimistic). It was never anticipated that the moon program would generate a direct economic return or would, in itself, pay back the more than US$30-billion invested in it — although, of course, it did, as intended, give a tremendous shot in the arm to the U.S. aerospace industry and ultimately to several other high-technology industries as well, particularly the computer industry.[4] The space station, on the other hand, is fully expected eventually to earn its keep by providing the infrastructure needed to support a wide range of industrial and commercial activities. (See Chapter 8.)

There are other important distinctions between the two programs: unlike the moon program, the space station is to be permanently manned. As Freitag put it, if the Apollo program was designed to put man on the moon and return him to earth, "we are now charged with sending man into space and, in a sense, leaving him there so that he can return benefits to earth." Moreover, this time, the project is not strictly a national showpiece; indeed, the U.S. aggressively sought the participation of its allies in building and operating the station. In his speech, Reagan said: "NASA will invite other countries to participate so we can strengthen peace, build prosperity and expand freedom for all who share our goals. We want our friends to help us meet these challenges and share in the benefits." What he carefully didn't say, of course, was that the U.S. was particularly interested in having them share the costs, not only of building the station but also of operating it.

In the mid-1980s, the total cost of the 10-year program was projected to be in the range of US$10- to $13-billion, of which the U.S. share was expected to amount to about US$8-billion. However, as the shuttle program demonstrates, mammoth aerospace ventures can be dogged by technological setbacks, program delays, cost overruns — and, in the extreme case, human deaths. Few aerospace industry experts expect the space station's final price tag to come in at the projected US$8-billion. Still, barring a major and unexpected turnaround in U.S. space policy, the project will go ahead — although not without continuing criticism, delays and redesign — and will dominate the aerospace industry through the turn of the century, not only in the United States, but also in Canada, Europe and Japan, all of whom have made plans or commitments to participate.

Canada plans to spend about CDN$800-million to the turn of the century to build and operate a Mobile Servicing Centre (MSC), which will be used first in the assembly of the station itself and, thereafter, in the servicing and maintenance of the station, the shuttle and payloads attached to the station. (In its various incarnations, the servicing centre has been referred to in the media as "Pit Stop Canada" and the "Petrocan of space.") Japan is planning to build its own multi-purpose pressurized research and development laboratory with an attached Japanese-built manipulator arm to service a nearby unpressurized work platform exposed to the space environment. The Japanese contribution is expected to be in the range of US$1- to 2-billion. NASA has also been involved in protracted negotiations with the European Space Agency, which is expected to build one of the manned laboratory modules (and two unmanned free-flying platforms) at a cost of about US$2.5-billion.

NASA's plan for assembling in orbit what it calls the "space station infrastructure" was to have the basic system — known as the "initial operating capability" — in operation by the mid-1990s, in time to meet Reagan's 1994 deadline. However, in 1986, severe budgetary problems and program delays resulting from the Challenger accident were causing serious problems with both the space station schedule and its design. (These developments are discussed in more detail later.)

The station is intended to evolve in size and capability after the turn of the century. "We are talking about a space station that has a permanent and indefinite lifetime and therefore must accommodate all kinds of growth and reconfiguration of payloads and customers who want to come and go," said John Aaron of NASA's space station program. As space exploration gives way to space exploitation, the system will ultimately consist of the following major elements:

• *The "core" station:* The hub of the station will consist of four pressurized modules with life support systems to permit human habitation. The two supplied by the United States will be for crew quarters and materials processing research. The European-supplied module will be for life sciences research (and possibly materials processing research) and the Japanese module will be for advanced technology research. The mobile servicing facility for refurbishing and repairing satellites, instruments and spacecraft will be an integral part of the core station. There will also be docking bays for transportation vehicles, beams for mounting scientific instruments and large solar power panels to provide energy for the station.

The core station is too large and complex a structure to be launched as a whole from earth, so its major elements will be transported into space in pieces and assembled over a period of several years. In late 1986, NASA projections indicated that about 15 shuttle flights would be needed over two to three years to assemble the station, and additional "logistics" flights would be required to ferry equipment and supplies once astronauts started to live and work on the station.[5] A Canadian-built manipulator system, which will be used in the assembly of the station, will be launched on an early shuttle flight.

The station will circle the earth at more than 28,000 kilometres per hour, in an orbit about 460 km high, inclined 28.5 degrees north and south of the equator. This means it will fly over areas no farther north than the Kennedy Space Center in Florida and no farther south than about the middle of Brazil. This orbit is the easiest and least expensive to achieve because launching into a higher inclination orbit requires much more energy. NASA's studies have indicated that most of the requirements of the station's potential customers can be met with this orbit; however, there are some applications, primarily remote-sensing and military surveillance, that are better served with high-inclination orbits.

• *Co-orbiting and polar-orbiting space platforms:* There could be a number of unmanned or "man-tended" platforms or modules associated with the station. These platforms would carry scientific instruments, sensors for observing the earth or the stars or equipment for producing new materials in zero gravity. Some would be in the same, nearly equatorial, orbit as the station itself, while others would have a north-south or "polar" orbit that would cross high latitudes not covered by the station's orbit. Canada has a particular interest in a polar-orbiting remote-sensing platform, because neither the space station nor co-orbiting platforms would cover the Canadian land mass or northern ocean areas very well. Europe plans to build a polar-orbiting platform. The military is likewise interested in higher-inclination orbits, which would cover more territory of strategic interest.

• *Space transportation and communications system:* The elements of the space station infrastructure will be linked with each other, and with earth, by an elaborate computer-communications network and by a varied transportation system that will include the space shuttle and probably unmanned cargo vehicles for earth-to-low-orbit operations; the orbital maneuvring vehicle (OMV) for low-orbit operations centred on the station; and the orbital transfer vehicle (OTV), which will ply the spaceways between the station and geosynchronous orbits. These vehicles, equipped with smart robotic devices, will be used for transporting satellites and other spacecraft to their proper orbits, for periodically refuelling, resupplying or servicing them and, when necessary, for returning them to the station for repair or refurbishment. Eventually, other spacecraft will also form part of the transportation system of the station; these could include unmanned heavy-lift launchers for hauling large amounts of cargo and smaller shuttles, such as the manned spaceplanes being planned by France and Japan.

The space station infrastructure is intended to serve a multitude of purposes. It will provide scientific and industrial research laboratories and serve as a base for observing the earth, the solar system and the stars — in the last case providing astronomers with a permanent vantage point above the obscuring effects of the earth's atmosphere. The station will also be a manufacturing and commercial centre, providing pressurized modules for continuous human supervision of experiments and unpressurized automated facilities that will be periodically monitored and resupplied by astronauts or by remotely controlled robotic servicers. (See Chapter 8.)

One of the most important functions of the station will be to provide facilities for the repair, servicing, maintenance and assembly of spacecraft, satellites and other large space structures (e.g., gigantic "antenna farms" that will eventually replace communications satellites). Given the cost of lifting things off the earth, on-orbit construction and upkeep is essential if the space station is to be cost-effective, so virtually all assembly, repair and maintenance of the station infrastructure will be done in space. On-orbit servicing could become a billion-dollar business after the turn of the century, according to some economic projections.

As described in Chapter 6, the feasibility of space servicing was dramatically demonstrated in 1984 and 1985. Satellite refuelling was tested for the first time and several disabled satellites were rescued and repaired. These achievements were all the more remarkable because not one of those satellites had been designed for recovery in space. As a result, the design of future satellites will likely be modified to permit in-orbit servicing and refurbishment; for example, important components will be in the form of removable "black boxes" that can be replaced by astronauts or by a robotic arm. Radarsat, an advanced remote-sensing satellite, was to be one of the first of this new generation of satellites[6] and eventually most space systems will be designed for extensive repair and refurbishment.

Finally, the space station will be a transportation hub, the focus of space activities in low earth orbit and a way station to higher orbits. Ultimately, it will also serve as a staging base for manned and unmanned missions to the moon, the planets and other regions of the solar system, such as the asteroid belt. In April, 1986, President Reagan's National Commission on Space, headed by former NASA administrator Thomas Paine, recommended an ambitious program that would result in human colonies on the moon by 2017 and on Mars by 2027. It is significant that these recommendations were made after the shuttle explosion occurred — the report was, in fact, dedicated to the Challenger crew — because they represented a strong endorsement of the view that the accident, tragic as it was, should not imperil the long-term goal of permanent human habitation of space.

The shuttle accident soon began to affect planning for the space station, even though the program had no requirement to use the shuttle until the mid-1990s. The loss of Challenger compounded the already serious financial problems NASA was facing in the spring of 1986 as it went to the U.S. Congress with its US$7.7-billion budget request for Fiscal 1986-87. This budget included the first "big money" for the space station — about US$410-million — since NASA planned to start hardware development in the spring of 1987. But the space agency was now also asking for an extra US$2.8-billion to build a new shuttle. In fact, the Congressional budget office estimated that NASA would need an extra US$1-billion a year for five years, not only to cover the replacement of Challenger, but also to pay for more costly launch operations after shuttle flights resumed and to offset expected increases in the cost of constructing the space station.[7] Additional costs were expected to result from the measures taken to correct the management problems that contributed to the accident.

These requests for extra funds could not have come at a worse time; Congress had passed the Gramm-Rudman-Hollings Bill, which mandated massive across-the-board cuts in government spending to balance the U.S. federal budget by 1991. For NASA, the only way out of this financial box was to persuade Congress to exempt it from Gramm-Rudman-Hollings — a proposition that became politically more difficult the longer the time elapsed since the Challenger accident. As one Congressional staff member pointed out, politicians on the receiving end of constituents' complaints about cutbacks in child vaccination programs were going to have trouble accepting a big increase in the space budget.

All of this — plus an expected slow start in the pace of shuttle flights when they resumed — raised doubts that NASA could have the station assembled and operating within the ten-year deadline set by President Reagan in 1984. By mid-1986, the accumulation of technical and financial problems had already forced a "stretch-out" of the program. Still, sceptics were reminded that similar gloomy predictions in the dark days after the

Apollo fire were disproved when NASA landed Apollo ll on the moon just 2 1/2 years later and within the decade deadline set by President Kennedy.

Work on the actual design of the space station continued at a rapid pace throughout 1985 and 1986. The two-year "definition" phase (Phase B), which began in April, 1985, involved a large number of international studies to define the basic "look" of the station and the major technical elements that would comprise the initial operating capability.

The major elements of the station were divided into four "work packages," each of which was assigned to a different NASA centre to manage. Initially, the Johnson Space Center in Houston was designated the "lead" space station centre. (After the Challenger accident, NASA began a major reorganization of the space station program to centralize authority at Headquarters and to lessen the independence of the centres. Some of the proposed changes to JSC's role sparked a political row and a great deal of internal in-fighting.)

NASA received bids on the packages from 13 industry teams involving more than 100 top U.S. aerospace companies. In April, 1985, eight teams were awarded 18-month design contracts, worth about US$145-million in total; the contractors expected to spend as much of their own money doing the studies as they received from NASA. In addition, the Kennedy Space Center in Florida awarded contracts worth more than US$100-million to three more industrial teams to study various aspects of ground processing and launching the space station components and payloads.

At the same time, NASA was engaged in intensive negotiations with Canada, Europe and Japan to determine the nature of the contributions these international partners were prepared to make to building and operating the station. Initially, NASA tended to view the station as a self-contained U.S. project with international "add-ons," but as negotiations with the international partners progressed, a concept of "functional allocation" gradually evolved. Functional allocation meant that each of the partners would provide certain essential facilities and services to everyone using the station, that each partner would in turn have access to all the facilities and services provided by the others and that all the partners would have a role in the management and day-to-day operations of the station. This was done for a number of reasons:

it would make the whole undertaking more truly international in nature; it would reduce costs by avoiding costly duplication of facilities; and it would help minimize the transfer of cash across borders, which was important to all the international partners. However, conflict with the international partners occurred when NASA came under pressure from the U.S. Congress to protect some of the most important technology development and commercial research activities for the U.S.

NASA aggressively promoted international co-operation. James Beggs, then NASA administrator, issued invitations to foreign governments to participate during visits to Canada, Japan and Europe in early 1982 and again, more formally, in early 1984. Shortly after Beggs' 1984 visit to Ottawa, concerns were voiced in a House of Commons estimates committee that the government "will drag its feet and we will lose out on opportunities that would appear to be golden for Canada in high-technology and aerospace work." Donald Johnston, who was then the science minister, said: "I do not think we will miss that window of opportunity," but he added the government wanted to be sure there would be economic and technological benefits before Canada climbed on board the station. "We clearly have to ensure that there are applications of the space station that make sense for this country industrially." Johnston added that his discussions with Beggs indicated that the U.S. was "very anxious to have our participation ... I think they would be very unhappy if they were to proceed without our participation."

There was a two-fold rationale behind NASA's strategy: not only would it provide much-needed funding for the project, but the increasing entanglement of most of the United States' major allies would also, it was thought, provide an important measure of security against political faint-heartedness and potential budget cuts at home. (This was before the dreaded Gramm-Rudman-Hollings bill had even appeared on the horizon.)

In response to NASA's invitation, the government commissioned studies to determine the potential costs and benefits to Canada. The National Research Council gave a contract to Spar Aerospace Limited of Toronto, builder of the Canadarm, and Philip A. Lapp Limited, a Toronto consulting firm, to determine the interest within Canadian industry in building and using the space station. The reponses covered the entire spectrum, from enthusiasm for an immediate start to the view that nothing should be done because of a perceived lack of return on investment. However, nearly half of the responses were in the form of proposals for specific projects, some of which were already in advanced stages of planning. These proposals covered a broad base and "in light of the long time period which will elapse before the user will have routine access [to the space station], very encouraging," according to Karl Doetsch, who was then in charge of Canada's preliminary space station studies as well as the astronaut program.

The survey indicated that Canadian needs could be best served by four major elements of the space station system: a manned research and development laboratory for commercial and industrial experiments; an unmanned remote-sensing platform for observing the earth, in a polar orbit to cover Canada's northern and Arctic latitudes; satellites co-orbiting these facilities to serve special needs;[8] and finally, a transportation system and other technologies to service these facilities. The study also concluded that Canada's existing space industry could contribute to the construction and servicing of a space station, to the building of large solar power arrays and other space structures and to the development of space sensors.

Sufficiently encouraged by the results of this study, the NRC commissioned two further studies in 1984. Spar and a team of six subcontractors[9] received a CDN$1.6-million contract to investigate ways in which Canada's aerospace industry might become a supplier of technology to the space station. Six more contracts, worth CDN$600,000, were awarded for studies of the potential industrial and commercial materials processing experiments Canadian industry might do in space.[10]

These studies concluded that Canada could benefit technologically and economically from involvement in the space station. On March 30, 1985, just as NASA was awarding its Phase B contracts, the Canadian government made a commitment in principle to participate and in mid-April signed a Memorandum of Understanding with NASA. Thomas Siddon, the science minister at the time, said that Canada's participation "ensures that we will be a partner in one of the most complex and visible technological achievements in history." It was estimated that the potential economic benefits for Canada could exceed CDN$2-billion by the year 2000.[11] The European Space Agency and Japan had also embarked on their own Phase B studies, so the project seemed to be off and running as a truly international undertaking. The plan was that, throughout 1985, the international partners would identify which elements of the station they would like to build. Then, in early 1986, just as the final baseline design of the station was being frozen, decisions would be made concerning the allocation of space station elements among the partners and, during the second part of Phase B, between April, 1986, and April, 1987, detailed design studies of the selected projects would be done.

The Memorandum of Understanding between NASA and Canada spelled out their relationship in conducting space station design and definition studies. NASA promised to provide the information necessary to integrate Canadian-built hardware with the space station and to provide Canada with access to NASA facilities, such as the space shuttle, to support development of the Canadian technology. The NRC was designated program manager for the Canadian work. In addition, a program co-ordination committee, composed of NASA and Canadian officials, was set up to ensure that NASA would be kept aware of Canada's planning, to avoid potential misunderstandings or rude surprises along the way.

As it turned out, there were some surprises, many of them rude, on both sides when bargaining on the details commenced. Between the summer of 1985 and the fall of 1986, the behind-the-scenes story of the quest for Canada's particular niche aboard the space station read like a high-tech version of *The Perils of Pauline*, and some of those privy to the discussions had doubts on occasion that the heroine could be saved. Political forces, both at home and in the United States, combined with the preoccupation of governments in both countries with deficit-cutting to create a very tense year for those negotiating Canada's position. At the same time, NASA was embroiled in fractious negotiations with Europe and it was undergoing considerable internal upheaval. In late 1985, there were a number of major changes in senior management, including the departure of administrator James Beggs, who left under a cloud because of fraud charges related to his tenure in industry before taking over at NASA. The management crisis was further exacerbated by the Challenger disaster in early 1986 and the subsequent revelations about NASA's serious internal problems. "It was a very rocky period for everybody," said Mac Evans, director-general of the space policy sector of the federal Ministry of State for Science and Technology and Canadian co-chairman of the Canada/NASA program co-ordination committee.

The Canadian government's commitment in principle to the space station project in April had been a crucial first step, but it neglected one small detail: it did not spell out what, exactly, Canada proposed to build for the station. This was a direct result of the stated intention of the new Conservative government, then in office less than a year, to develop a long-term space plan that would cover not only the space station project, but also the Canadian astronaut program, M-Sat and Radarsat and all other Canadian space activities to the turn of the century. In a paper released at the time, the government espoused what has become conventional wisdom within Canadian industry: in order to succeed in the world of expensive high-tech ventures, Canada must develop expertise in specialized "niches" — little bite-sized bits that Canada can do well enough to survive in fierce competition against international industrial giants. The development of the Canadarm was a prime example of just such a strategy. "Canada does not have the financial or human resources required to be at the forefront of all areas of space technology," the paper said. "Our success in the past has stemmed from our ability to focus our resources in a few areas where the probability of achieving substantial benefits was the highest."

The government indicated that, by the end of 1985, the long-term space plan would be announced and Canada would specify what part of the space station it wanted to build. This timing was dictated at least in part by the important program milestones that had been set by NASA for early 1986. In the meantime, interim funding of CDN$8.8-million (out of a total 1985/86 space budget of CDN$195-million) was provided for space station definition (Phase B) studies during the remainder of 1985. Of this, CDN$4.7-million went to Spar and its subcontractors[12] to continue Phase B studies on a proposed servicing facility for the station. In announcing the interim funding, the government did say it intended to "maintain and develop Canadian capabilities in space" — a statement that gave some comfort to the aerospace industry because it came just before the release of the first federal budget by a government preoccupied with reducing the national deficit. (The government had severely cut the National Research

Council's budget and killed the rocket and balloon research program, giving rise to serious alarm within the scientific and industrial community that many of Canada's space activities might all but cease.)

Officially, the studies during 1985 focussed on three potential options:

• *A free-flying remote-sensing platform* in a polar orbit to provide coverage over all of Canada, including the far North.

• *Solar power arrays* to provide electrical power for unmanned polar-orbiting platforms associated with the station.

• *An Integrated Service and Test Facility (ISTF)* that would provide a centralized capability for servicing and repairing satellites, scientific instruments mounted on the station, space vehicles and the station itself. The ISTF concept was originally developed by Spar and its subcontractors over a two-year period starting in 1984. It featured advanced versions of the Canadarm, sophisticated computer-control systems, "smart" manipulators and a range of special repair tools.

From the beginning, the servicing facility was the front-runner, although it would encounter fierce opposition before it emerged victorious. It was also almost self-evidently Canada's best option, for several reasons:

• *The project would enable Canada to capitalize on the money and research already invested in the Canadarm.* The servicing facility is a logical extension, not only of the original CDN$100-million Canadarm project, but of NRC's CDN$4.7-million project to create a computer-controlled machine vision system for the arm.

• *Building the servicing facility would give Canada a highly visible presence on the space station.* This was a major objective of the Canadian space officials involved in the negotiations and was a direct legacy of the experience with the Canadarm. The PR payoff in having built a distinctive, recognizable "technological nugget" — something on which it was possible to stamp Canada's name and the maple leaf — had become increasingly obvious during 1984 and 1985. Every time dramatic images of the arm appeared on TV, Canadians received a host of subliminal messages: this is technological success, this is the big league, this is value for your tax dollar. "The arm remains ... the best-advertised piece of Canadian technology ever," according to Christopher Trump, Spar's vice-president of public and government affairs, who said the arm's visibility also enhanced Canada's international reputation as a maker of high-technology products.[13] Drawings of the proposed servicing facility always feature a large Canadian flag painted on the side.

• *The facility would enable Canada to develop highly marketable products and skills in on-orbit servicing, repair and construction operations — services that would help pay our way on the station and provide access to space for Canadian industrial and scientific researchers.* The servicing facility is "going to be used all the time," Evans said. "Every time there's a fix-it job in space, Canada would be part of it." Such "fix-it jobs" will be a common occurrence. The significant long-term impact on the entire space business of developing the ability to construct, service and repair systems in space was underscored by Robert Freitag, who pointed out that the space station will be "dramatically different from anything we've ever done before" because it will have to be maintained in space. "It's not going to be brought back to the shop. So the subject of design for maintenance and maintainability is closely associated with the servicing question." He said that Canada's studies on space servicing and repair will be an "important stepping stone" to space operations in the next decade. The very nature of the next generation of space systems — how they will be designed and operated — will be significantly affected by current studies on space servicing. Freitag predicted that by the next decade, these efforts could result in the establishment of a world standard in space systems that would apply not only to space station servicing operations, but to the space shuttle, to free-flying platforms and robotic vehicles and to a new generation of serviceable spacecraft.

Building the servicing facility would give Canada the chance to develop knowledge and skills that will be much in demand in the future, not only by Canada and the United States, but also by the Europeans, Japanese and possibly even the Soviets.

• *The servicing facility would be an integral part of the core space station and would give Canada access to advanced space station technology.* "The technology of the space station will have to be known to us in order for us to [build the servicing facility]," said Evans. "A whole new set of technologies are going to flow out of this thing that will affect the design of satellites, design of robotic systems, control systems. Artificial intelligence will be a major part of all this. By being in this major program we will have access to those technologies. We'll be able to learn about them, use them and be totally familiar with them."

• *The project will promote research and development in new high-technology fields with large potential applications on earth, particularly robotics and artificial intelligence.* A study by the Canadian Institute for Advanced Research (CIAR), a university-based private think tank, strongly recommended Canadian participation in the space station project because it would create an "exploitable knowledge base" within Canadian universities and industry, spin off new technologies (particularly advanced robotics and artificial intelligence) into earth-based industries and encourage the establishment of new space-related commercial ventures. The space station project "has the potential to be a major — perhaps *the* major — driving force in a number of key technologies for the next quarter century," the report said. It noted that the space station project will "lead to the development of increasingly intelligent machines" and the servicing facility would represent a "singular opportunity for Canada to carve out a 'niche' in what promises to be key technologies of the future. It will create a long-term technological 'pull' in [these] fields ... for a significantly long period of time. The technologies developed for the space station can and will be applied on earth." Therefore, the project should be viewed not just as a space project but as a "way of spurring technological innovation in industry ... It is, at least in part, an economic development project. It would be possible to establish new knowledge-intensive industries that could compete effectively in the international marketplace. If that effort is successful, there would be a very handsome return on the government's investment."

• *The space station is a civilian space program.* The Mulroney government had earlier rejected official participation by Canada in the U.S. Strategic Defense Initiative ("Star Wars") program, although some Canadian high-tech companies were interested in bidding for SDI contracts. (They were told they could do so privately.) Helping to build the space station would give Canada's aerospace industry a boost while avoiding the sticky domestic political problems posed by entanglement in a controversial military project.

Following the government's commitment in principle, Canadian space officials began a series of discussions with NASA on two levels. On Level A, which involved policy discussions, Canada was represented by Mac Evans. On Level B, which involved negotiations on technical matters, the Canadian representative was Karl Doetsch, supported by Jim Middleton, space station project manager for Spar Aerospace. Ed Shaw, director of the Radarsat project for the Department of Energy, Mines and Resources, was also a member of the team involved in the discussions and he made a number of presentations to NASA on Radarsat.

The team spent the better part of a year navigating the shoals of international negotiations to reach agreement on Canada's contribution to the space station program. They ran into heavy weather on both technical and political fronts, both at home and in the United States, and continuing delays in promised public statements on Canada's long-term space policy and its contribution to the space station gave testimony to the fact that some hard bargaining was going on behind closed doors.

During the summer of 1985, Canada presented its concept of an integrated servicing facility to NASA. The ISTF was then conceived as a centralized, fixed service bay, although the large manipulator arm would be capable of moving around the beam structure of the station to collect payloads for transport to the bay for servicing or to do repair work on the station itself. The concept of an *integrated* facility was crucial, Middleton said. "It wasn't a bunch of subsystems like an arm here and a screw there. It all had to be in a neat package that could have a Canadian flag on it and had a unique task." This not only made sense technologically, he said, but would provide a high profile for the project, an identifiable return on the taxpayers' investment. Given that the size of the investment would be in the hundreds of millions of dollars, visibility was a prime Canadian requirement.

The Canadian negotiators had to tread carefully in presenting the ISTF proposal. They knew the servicing facility was an important technological plum; it was part of the core station and considered a "mission-critical" item essential to space station operations. It was not possible for NASA to simply hand it over to Canada because there were many competing U.S. interests to contend with; not only could the Canadian project potentially step on the toes of three NASA centres[14] that had been assigned work packages related to servicing, it also ran up against NASA's mandate from Congress to use the space station program to promote the development of automation and robotics (A&R) in U.S. industry.

"What we had done was cross all the boundaries," said Middleton. The Canadian proposal would take "little pieces or major chunks" out of the NASA work packages and "we were heading into an area that was very sensitive to the United States — robotics and automation."

In April, 1985, in response to Congressional concerns, a NASA committee, the Advanced Technology Advisory Committee (ATAC), recommended that A&R should be a significant element of the station's technology and that the project be designed to accommodate future advances in this fast-growing field. NASA then set up a major new A&R program and it was estimated that between US$800-million and US$1-billion of the space station budget eventually would be spent in U.S. industry on the development of expert systems, robotics and other forms of automation for the station. A&R technologies would be used for far more than just the servicing function on the station — the ATAC report outlined a great many applications[15] — but it was clear that robotic servicing systems would play an important role in the day-to-day operations of the station and in the repair and maintenance of the station, the shuttle, satellites, free-flying platforms and scientific and commercial instruments and equipment.

That Canada shared the United States' interest in using the space station servicing project to push R&D in robotics and artificial intelligence on the ground was no secret; however, NASA seemed rather taken aback by how much work the Canadians had done on the ISTF concept when it was presented in the summer and fall of 1985. The U.S. space agency had been understandably preoccupied with the larger picture and NASA officials acknowledged at that time that Canada was about nine months to a year ahead of them in developing servicing concepts. "At that point, I think, NASA came to life on this servicing issue," said Mac Evans. "They realized that they had to come to grips with some of the questions we were asking and they were going to go into high gear and try to catch up."

NASA was not wholly comfortable with the idea that Canada would take a major role in servicing or that its operations would be integrated "so deeply into the core of the space station," Middleton said. But this was one of things that Canada most wanted. The study by the Canadian Institute for Advanced Research recommended that unless Canada played a "meaningful, long-term role" in both the development and the evolution of the station by building and managing an integral part of it, Canada should not participate in the project at all.

New studies on space station servicing were quickly commissioned by NASA and by the Congressional Office of Technology Assessment. The Canadian negotiating team tried to smooth ruffled feathers by emphasizing that Canada was not trying to take over all servicing functions, nor was it trying to corner the market on automation and robotics on the station.

If NASA wasn't entirely happy about what Canada wanted to do with the ISTF, it had a few of its own ideas about what Canada should do. For example, it wanted a large shelter built around the service bay, to provide thermal protection and special lighting for satellites (especially space telescopes) that would be serviced in the bay. NASA also wanted Canada to build the mobility system for the manipulator arm — a kind of flatbed carrier that would crawl along the beam structure of the station. Canada was frankly not the least bit thrilled with either suggestion. The shelter was not a technologically interesting project and "we felt that the number of satellites that would really require shelter of that nature was too small to justify the fairly large expenditure on our program," said Doetsch. The cost — an estimated US$100- to 120-million — would be a serious problem. "We were running into difficulties with how much money we would be requesting the government put into this if we accepted all the things that people would like us to accept," Doetsch said. Middleton concurred: "There was no benefit to Canada in developing that shelter. The cost … was going to blow us away."

Building the arm's mobility system also lacked appeal. To minimize the potential for technical problems, Canada wanted a "clean interface" between the Canadian-built servicing system and the NASA-built beams and trusses that would comprise the external structure of the station. NASA's design of the beam structures on which the system would move (indeed, the design of the entire station) was constantly changing and "we just felt a lack of control over that interface that would cause us some potential, unknown headaches in the future," Doetsch said. What Canada wanted was to simply plunk the arm and its control system on top of whatever moving flatbed NASA came up with.

As summer turned to fall, these technical issues remained unresolved. At the same time, political problems were brewing at home. Some were not directly related to the space program. For example, when the Mulroney government was beset that fall by a series of political scandals and embarrassments, all programs were temporarily affected by the resulting paralysis of a government completely diverted by the effort to protect itself politically.

Other political developments struck closer to home. The most notable was a proposition by the managers of the Radarsat program that their project be considered an alternative to ISTF as Canada's contribution to the space station. It is clear what prompted this move: the government had three very expensive new space projects on its plate — Radarsat, ISTF and M-Sat[16] — each of which would cost hundreds of millions of dollars. In the deficit-cutting climate that prevailed in Ottawa at the time, the budget battle was clearly shaping up to be a bloody one. Since the government was already committed in principle to making a contribution to the space station, the strategy of trying to protect Radarsat by tying it to the station was understandable. It just didn't make any sense. Radarsat would be a free-flying platform in an orbit that was both higher in altitude and more polar than that of the station; its relationship with the station would be passing indeed — they wouldn't even be within waving distance of each other at the two intersection points of their respective orbits.

Notwithstanding its own considerable merits as a remote-sensing project, the Radarsat proposal was completely out of keeping with Canada's major objectives in climbing aboard the space station — to be an integral part of the station, to be involved in its ongoing operations and to promote R&D in automation and robotics. In this respect, it simply could not offer the same kind of tangible and intangible long-term benefits as an integrated servicing facility. In any event, NASA soon informed Canada that, while they were interested in the Radarsat project (they would be providing a free launch for the satellite), they did not consider Radarsat a suitable contribution to the space station program. This left Radarsat to fend for itself in the upcoming budgetary dogfights.

In October, another major development occurred, this time on the technical front. Just a few months before NASA intended to freeze the design of the space station, it adopted a radical change in the basic or "reference" configuration. For more than a year, NASA and its contractors had been evaluating several different concepts and one known as the "power tower" had emerged as the front runner. This design involved a single 91-metre mast, crossed by a 61-metre beam, with the habitable modules located at the bottom of the vertical mast, attached end-to-end in a "race-track" pattern. This concept and all others were summarily scrapped in favor of a new design known as the "dual keel" concept, a more box-like structure than the power tower. It consisted of two vertical masts, traversed in the middle by a horizontal beam; the beam structure was to measure about 110 metres by 150 metres. Smaller crossbeams across the top and bottom of the twin keel would create two open box-shaped areas, allowing much more room on the beams for commercial and scientific users to mount instruments and equipment, conduct space servicing operations and provide docking facilities for orbital vehicles. In the "power tower" design, the lower part of the station was dominated by the pressurized habitable modules. In the new design, the modules were located on the central crossbeam — closer to the station's centre of gravity and therefore better situated for commercial materials processing work because they will be less affected by minute changes in gravity forces as the station orbits the earth.

John Aaron of NASA's space station program office said: "We are talking about a space station that has a permanent and indefinite lifetime and therefore must accommodate all kinds of growth and reconfiguration of payloads and customers who want to come and go. When we ... looked at all the customers and tests, the hardware and experiments that we would need to put on it for the next 20 or 30 years, we found that we needed additional area to mount things."

Changes were also made to the configuration of the pressurized modules for safety reasons. The previous design, involving end-to-end attachment of the modules, was criticized for not permitting individual modules to be sealed off in case of emergencies. The new design called for a figure-eight arrangement of the modules, each of which would be attached to external airlocks that would act as central hubs. This would allow individual modules to be sealed off while the others continue operating.[17]

As the process of fixing the baseline design continued throughout the fall and winter of 1985, the bargaining between NASA and the international partners intensified. In many ways, the negotiations resembled a high-stakes poker game. NASA wanted the financial and political support that the international partners could provide and none of the partners could afford to build its own space station complex, so collaboration was in everyone's interests. Still, each player was angling to obtain the best possible returns — economic, technological, industrial and political — for a very large investment of taxpayers' money, and their diverse objectives were not always compatible.

By mid-December, however, Canada was closing in on an agreement with NASA on the configuration of the ISTF. On December 19, a preliminary accord was reached, spelling out what both sides had agreed to in general terms. NASA recognized and accepted Canada's interest in having "visible, meaningful participation" in the space station program and said that Canada would have a "significant, ongoing role" in the management and operations of the station. But perhaps the most significant clause, in light of later developments, was the following: "NASA and Canada agreed to Canada's provision of a *robotic servicer* [my italics] in addition to the flight telerobotic system to be provided by the United States, and also agreed to Canada's providing a remote manipulator system." There were some outstanding issues — for example, Canada had still not agreed to build either the shelter or the mobility system for the arm — and it was agreed that the two sides would try to hammer out the details by the end of January, 1986.

Then, in mid-January, NASA received the "Boland letter."

Congressman Edward Boland was the chairman of a powerful subcommittee of the House of Representatives' Committee on Appropriations, one of four that oversees NASA's budget. This committee had previously expressed strong views during budget hearings about the need to promote the development of advanced automation and robotics within U.S. industry; it had been responsible for a bill requiring NASA to use space station contracts to do this and had earmarked US$5-million of NASA's 1986 space station budget specifically for this purpose.[18] Attention was focussed particularly on the robotic servicer, a crab-like device that features small, "smart" manipulators capable of doing fine repair and servicing tasks under the control of an advanced computer incorporating "expert system" technology and artificial intelligence (AI). The robotic servicer was an important "technological nugget."

The servicer, sometimes also called a "smart front end," could be attached to the station's main remote manipulator arm, or it could be attached to the orbital maneuvring vehicle (OMV), a fetch-and-carry device NASA is planning to build, which would do servicing and repair work away from the station. The OMV system was the "flight telerobotic system" referred to in the December 19 agreement between NASA and Canada. Canada's ISTF proposal contained provision for a Canadian-built version of the robotic sevicer to operate on the end of the station's main remote manipulator arm. "It's distinguished mainly by its dexterity and its increased ability to do things without human intervention," said Doetsch. These included "not just routine pre-programmed things," but the kind of diagnostic and decision-making tasks that are the province of expert systems and AI devices.

Canada's proposal caused alarm in some circles in Washington, if the strongly worded Boland letter was any indicator. It expressed concern that "NASA could be tempted to make compromises with potential foreign partners in order to gain a short-range financial benefit that may have a negative long-range impact on U.S. high technology development." The letter emphasized the committee's view that "U.S. industry be able to make maximum use of the space station as a vehicle for vital spin-off benefits in the automation and robotics field" and noted that the US$5-million specially earmarked for this purpose had been given to NASA under "extraordinarily difficult budget conditions." The letter went on to address the matter of the robotic servicer or "smart front end" in considerable detail. It noted that NASA was reviewing whether one or two such devices would be built — one of "a more robust variety" that would be used primarily for assembly, and a second, more advanced device capable of more "delicate and sensitive" tasks such as repair and replacement. The letter stated unambiguously that if only one was to be built, the United States would build it. If two were to be built — and the committee wanted to review such a decision — "then it is our belief that the U.S. should develop, through an advanced automation and robotics program, the primary end effector for space station payload servicing."

This was a bombshell and it got everyone's immediate attention. "It was very clear that NASA could not accept a turn-key operation from Canada to do all of the servicing," Doetsch said. "Clearly, the area we've chosen is very attractive; everybody's vying for it. We would be naive to think the U.S. industry would not take some steps to try and make sure it gets that type of activity."

At a crucial meeting on February 4 in Washington,[19] NASA put forth a proposal that outlined how Canada and NASA might share the servicing function. Canada would build the space station manipulator system — characterized as the large-scale effector — which would be used for assembly, maintenance and evolution (growth) of the station, and for servicing external "attached payloads" (that is, scientific instruments and commercial equipment mounted on the station's beam structure). The satellite shelter and the mobility system for the arm were still part of the package. NASA would build a small-scale telerobotic servicer that would be used on the end of a manipulator arm to service visiting spacecraft (that is, free-flying satellites and platforms that would be brought to the station for servicing). Eventually, this robotic servicer would also be put on the orbital maneuvring vehicle, which would work on satellites away from the space station. (NASA had indicated from the start that it would take responsibility for the OMV's front-end servicer. The Canadians gained the impression that national security concerns at least partly accounted for this, because the OMV would be used to service U.S. military satellites.)

NASA's proposal was in keeping with its emerging philosophy of "functional allocation": dividing responsibility for specific services and tasks — and the relevant hardware — among the international partners. It was clear that the concept of a robotic servicer was commanding a great deal of attention — perhaps, it could be argued, a disproportionate amount. True, the servicer was an important element of the station, but it was only one of many A&R components discussed in NASA's ATAC report, and it was relatively small when compared with some of the major systems. Doetsch suggested that the amount of attention paid to the servicer was partly due to the fact that it is "such a visible thing and it's easily recognized as robotics." Again, the lesson of the Canadarm.

The Canadians were not at all unhappy with NASA's proposal, because it indicated that "there was room for us to move," said Evans. It was becoming apparent by this time that "the servicing job was larger than had been originally anticipated, that there was going to be a need for a lot of servicing equipment." This provided both sides with a way out of the dilemma; if there was enough work for Canada and the United States to share, the negotiations could focus on defining a suitable division of labor rather than getting bogged down in an either/or stand-off.

Doetsch commented later that "if we had not found this path that allowed both parties to sort of move in the directions they wanted to, I think the agreement would have been in jeopardy." The challenge for the Canadians was to see if they could come up with something that worked within the framework proposed by NASA, but still satisfied Canadian technological aspirations and remained within the budget submitted to the government. In the end, the team even called for some assistance from experienced Washington hands, including industrial lobbyists and the Canadian embassy, to reinforce Canada's position. "We brought the diplomatic levers to bear very quickly to ensure that the United States understood Canada's objectives in participating and understood that we weren't just going to do the nuts and bolts stuff, but had to do something that was of benefit to us," Evans said.

NASA asked for a response to its proposal from Canada within a week. During the rather frenetic days that followed, the ISTF was figuratively torn down, repackaged and rebuilt.

On the afternoon of Thursday, February 6, Jim Middleton was in his Toronto office pondering NASA's proposal. Although he initially wasn't happy about Canada's being restricted to servicing attached payloads, he ultimately concluded that this wasn't such a bad thing because "there's a lot more work in attached payloads than there is in visiting spacecraft. Those spacecraft only come back once in a while when they run out of fuel or need repairs, and ultimately they're all going to be serviced *in situ* with the OMV, so we'd lose that business in the long term." That afternoon, he had a sudden flashback to the concept of a mobile servicing facility that had been considered and discarded several years before in favor of the ISTF. He immediately turned Spar's engineers loose on the idea and by the time he went home that evening, he felt the team had found the concept that could break the logjam. Working feverishly on Friday and over the weekend, Middleton and the Spar engineers filled in the details and Middleton presented the concept to Spar's senior management on Monday morning. "So I got the idea on Thursday afternoon and we had the whole program rebuilt by Monday," he remembered.

On Monday afternoon, Middleton and Terry Ussher, director of Spar's space station program, flew to Ottawa for a round of meetings with Karl Doetsch, Mac Evans and other government officials. On Tuesday morning, Middleton and Doetsch worked out the technical details of the presentation that would be made to NASA and Evans promptly reviewed it to ensure it embraced Canada's objectives. Evans and Doetsch then flew immediately to Washington and Doetsch presented the proposal to NASA right on deadline on the morning of Wednesday, February 12.

NASA and Canada verbally agreed on the technical elements of the Canadian contribution to the space station that day. Evans said that NASA officials indicated they were impressed with the Canadian proposal, not only because it had been restructured so quickly but because it was technically clever. "They had no real basis to object because it was really an ingenious proposal." Spar and the NRC, he said, had done "a tremendous job in repackaging the ISTF."

What they had repackaged it into was the Mobile Servicing Centre (MSC). According to the agreement worked out by NASA and Canada, the MSC would consist of two large remote manipulator arms (which would permit "two-handed" work, including using one arm for positioning)[20] and a base structure with a cradle-like bed to carry payloads. There would be control stations both inside and outside the station's habitable module, which astronauts could use to operate the arms, and a positioning mechanism to hold astronauts doing EVA repair work. There would also be a small fixed-base site on the station's beam structure for storing tools, equipment and supplies.

This was a reversal of the ISTF concept; instead of using the mobile unit simply as a "fetch and carry" device to deliver payloads to the "garage" for servicing, it would carry out the work on location. Doetsch said Canada would, in effect, be building "a sophisticated service truck instead of the service station" it had originally proposed. This option was made even more attractive by an increase in the size of the station's beam trusses from three metres square to five metres square; this would enable Canada to build a mobile servicing unit big enough to accommodate any payloads carried in the shuttle's cargo bay, which is 4.6 metres wide.

The servicing system would perform a large number of important functions. Although NASA is still trying to determine the appropriate roles for humans and robotic systems in space construction, it is expected that the manipulator system will play a major role in the initial assembly of the space station. Then, after construction is completed, the MSC would trundle around the beams, performing maintenance tasks on the station and servicing the attached payloads, such as astronomical and remote-sensing devices and materials processing equipment. The arm would also be used to transport equipment and supplies around the station — for example, moving payloads from one location to another — and it would be used to assist astronauts during EVA. Finally, the arm would be used for deploying and retrieving satellites and loading and unloading payloads and supplies from the shuttle. Canada also proposed that the arm could be used to assist in docking the shuttle and other spacecraft to the station.[21]

Canada stood firm in its refusal to build the mobility system for the arm (it will, however, provide a turn-table device that will permit the arm to swivel on its base) and there was no requirement for the large shelter on the mobile servicing system; neither of these items appeared in the final agreement.[22] Nor was there any reference to the robotic servicer as such, but the MSC would include what was referred to as "special purpose dexterous manipulators, end effectors and servicing tools" and Canada had made it clear to NASA that these special manipulators would incorporate advanced robotics technology — such things as machine vision, tactile sensors and advanced computer-control systems. It was also anticipated that a sophisticated computer system would be developed to orchestrate simultaneous operations of the two manipulator arms. "It's not just a Canadarm over again because we now have to have these two arms working co-operatively together," Evans said. "It is the interaction between these arms which brings in the important aspects of automation and robotics."

"I really think that as far as space robotics are concerned, we're in a lead position," Doetsch said. "We've got a pretty good track record with the Canadarm. I think because of that we can stand tall. Now ten years down the road, who knows? But one of the reasons for being in this program is to make sure that ten years down the road we're still there."

Once the basic technical elements had been agreed to, it remained for the Canadian government to formally give the go-ahead and, more important, to commit the funds necessary to carry out the project. NASA wanted an answer by March 10 because it had scheduled the "systems requirements review" for late that month. This was an important milestone; it marked the end of the first half of the space station definition phase and NASA wanted some firm answers about the hardware each of the international partners planned to build so that the final design of the station's initial configuration could be established by the end of 1986 and the hardware development phase (Phase C) could begin by April, 1987.

The credit for the February 12 agreement must go to Evans, Doetsch and Middleton. It was a "very good team effort," said Doetsch. "Karl and Spar were doing an admirable job keeping our technical credibility intact," said Evans, who was carrying the ball at the policy level. Considered an extremely skilled negotiator, he was credited with finding the "right path" through what could easily have become a quagmire of incompatible goals and unresolvable differences. For all his affable and easy-going manner, Evans later acknowledged that it had all given him a few very tense months. "It was a hyper period of time."

But credit for the agreement goes to NASA Headquarters, too. It would not have been difficult for the U.S. space agency to resolve the political complications at home simply by killing any hope of an agreement with Canada. Despite the difficulties, however, NASA remained steadfast in its commitment to international participation.

The Canadian negotiators were very happy with the agreement. They were relieved to find a way for Canada and the United States to share the servicing function, while allowing Canada to achieve all of its essential technical objectives. But there was an edginess beneath the elation, a sense of waiting for the other shoe to drop. "It was more than I expected to get," one senior government official said of the agreement. A pause. "We may have got more than they intended." The reason for this wariness was that NASA would be going through Congressional budget hearings during the summer and fall of 1986 and questions on the subject of automation and robotics were almost certain to come up. (NASA is "micromanaged to death by the Congress," said one U.S. space analyst.) With what turned out to be prophetic insight, one person who was privy to the behind-the-scenes maneuvering characterized the upcoming hearings as "The Empire

Strikes Back." Another said: "The battle's not over yet."[23]

In fact, at that point, the battle wasn't even entirely over at home. The February 12 agreement had spelled out hardware details and functional responsibilities — who would build what to do what — but now it was time for Canada to ante up. The ball was tossed back into the court of the Canadian government. In Cabinet, the MSC was facing a fierce challenge from the Radarsat program, sponsored by the federal Department of Energy, Mines and Resources. Rumors filtering out to the aerospace community had it that Pat Carney, then the energy minister, had become Radarsat's vigorous champion and had garnered a great deal of influential support on behalf of the project.

Observers close to the action described it as "tough going — really tough." One bemusedly characterized the ongoing battles over Radarsat, M-Sat and the space station as "three kids fighting over the Hallowe'en candy." Another who followed the fate of the space station closely admitted that at one point, "I thought it was lost."

The fight was not about the intrinsic merit of the respective projects; it was about money, pure and simple — or, rather, the lack of it. "The bill is staggering," said one observer. The conflict was exacerbated by the political and financial climate that prevailed in the early months of 1986. In January, just as the government was beginning to emerge from the paralysis caused by the political scandals of the previous fall, it was beset by a seemingly endless stream of bad economic news. Oil prices had started to fall sharply; the value of the Canadian dollar was dropping to record lows on international markets, forcing large cash outlays to prop it up; interest rates were climbing. These events were seriously undermining the government's stated intention to hold the federal deficit to CDN$33.8-billion for 1986, and they were wreaking havoc with the federal spending estimates and the budget, which were then in preparation. By February, with the dollar still managing to drop to new record lows almost daily, speculation abounded that the budget, due at the end of the month, would be savage. Early that month, the government imposed a freeze on departmental discretionary spending until the end of the fiscal year on March 31. At the end of February, the federal budget was brought down — it was not quite as savage as had been predicted — and the Nielsen review of government spending was released shortly after, amid renewed government vows of a continuing assault on the deficit.

All of these events conveyed a strong sense that the government was unlikely to look kindly on new projects carrying large price tags. Any hope that the aerospace industry might find special favor seemed futile in light of the government's determination to proceed with the controversial CDN$155-million sale of de Havilland Aircraft of Canada to the U.S. aerospace giant, Boeing Commercial Airplane.

At the same time, the government was under pressure from various sources to make an unequivocal decision on Canada's space station contribution. NASA and Canadian space officials were pressing for an answer because of program deadlines, and the media had been asking about the promised long-term space plan since late 1985. A combination of financial problems at home and protracted bargaining in Washington conspired to make a decision impossible before mid-February. "Certainly, in the December-January time frame, I could not tell the government that we had a reasonable deal," said Evans. "In parallel with this, the government had in front of it the long-term space plan and all the proposals on space and they were having to come to grips with the financial requirements."

This was the climate that prevailed when the final decision on Canada's contribution to the space station landed on the federal Cabinet's plate in mid-February.[24] It was already known that the space station project would be a big-ticket item; figures ranging from CDN$200-million to $600-million had been bandied around for nearly a year. Few people believed the lower figure would buy any meaningful contribution for Canada; but given the financial problems, there was considerable speculation that the government might try to get away with a nickels-and-dimes approach, or that it would make only a limited commitment to continue with Phase B studies and worry about the rest of the program later. Concerns such as this reflected the fact that, with some notable exceptions, Canada has a bad habit of, as one Canadian government official put it, "chickening out at the last minute." But a half-hearted commitment to the space station would have been worse than none at all; NASA had to be assured that Canada really meant business before it would entrust Canada with building such a vital element of the station.

Evans said that the Mobile Servicing Centre is a "mission-critical item" and NASA had to be convinced that the Canadian government was fully behind the project before it would accept Canada as a mission-critical supplier. "It is different with the Japanese and the Europeans. They're building modules that can be attached whenever and the whole space station project doesn't come to a grinding halt if they don't come through with those things."

The decision rested with the Cabinet. The interdepartmental fight over money was fierce; in the end, the resolution stemmed in large part from a conviction at the highest levels of the government that, after all, Canada's already-announced commitment in principle to the space station program had to be honored.

Although the decision was made before NASA's March 10 deadline, it was not publicly announced until March 18, during Mulroney's "Shamrock Summit" with U.S. President Ronald Reagan in Washington. Later that day, at a hastily called news conference in Ottawa, science minister Frank Oberle revealed the details of the program, including the news — surprising to even the most optimistic space advocates — that the government had bought the deluxe package. Canada would spend CDN$800-million over 15 years mostly to build and operate the Mobile Servicing Centre.[25] Of this, $220-million would be spent in the first five years — which works out to an average of $44-million per year in a national space budget that, in 1985-86, ran to CDN$158-million.

"Canada's participation is designed to lead Canadian space activities into the 21st century," Oberle said. "Our contribution will give Canada a highly visible role ... in the most important international civilian space program of the century." The minister estimated that the project would create 80,000 person-years of work and generate CDN$5-billion in revenues.

The non-military, international nature of the space station program and its expected spin-off effect on Canada's high-technology aerospace industry were what ultimately sold the government on the project, despite the steep price tag. A. E. Collin, then Secretary of the Ministry of State for Science and Technology, said the government recognized that other industrialized nations were making a major commitment to the project, that the cost of participation "was tolerable within Canadian budgets" and that the opportunity for Canadian industry "was measurable and can be presented with some level of credibility."

Ultimately, he said, the decision to go ahead resulted to a large extent from a major reorientation of the Canadian space program toward collaborative international projects. In the past, Canada tended to pursue more strictly national goals in space — a series of projects run by government departments in support of their particular responsibilities. The two most obvious examples are Canada's communications and remote-sensing satellite programs, and new initiatives in both areas — Radarsat and M-Sat — were being considered by the Cabinet at the same time as the space station project.[26] Historically, international projects were a small and relatively low-priority component of the Canadian space program, but the Canadarm project and the Canadian astronaut program had begun to alter this balance and the magnitude of the commitment to the space station project tipped the scales. In this respect, Canada is following what has now become a world-wide trend; many other industrialized Western countries now spend half or more of their space budgets on large international programs, not only to share the burden of high costs but to avoid wasteful duplication of effort. No one can afford to do it alone any more, so the marriage of convenience has become the norm.

A desire not to be left out of the biggest international space effort of this generation was quite a strong motivator for the government. Science minister Frank Oberle said that it would have been "terribly unfortunate, if not irresponsible" to deny Canada a future role in the exploitation of space. "Much of the future prospects of mankind will be linked to space," he said, adding that this is a view shared by Prime Minister Mulroney. The opportunity to participate in building the space station was unique — a chance that would not come around twice — and this is ultimately what gave the project the edge over Radarsat. In remote-sensing, Oberle said, Canada could continue to do what it has always done — buy the satellite signals and interpret and translate them for Canadian purposes. "Once you lose your contact with the space station, it's gone forever. We felt that we could not afford to lose contact."

The government's decision to go with the space station — and to do so from the beginning, so that Canada could influence how it was built and managed — was the right one. It was also surprisingly visionary for a country too often given to attacks of technological faint-heartedness. Moreover, it was a decision that would be more popular than not with the Canadian public, which had been primed by the highly publicized successes of the Canadarm and the sterling performance of Marc Garneau and the other Canadian astronauts.

Despite this, the government went about informing the Canadian public about its decision in an oddly diffident way. The whole thing was curiously paradoxical, combining, as it did, a fairly high-profile public announcement with an almost calculated effort to downplay the news or, more specifically, the financial aspects of the news. Mulroney said only a few words on the subject in his Washington statement — admittedly, he was rather preoccupied with free trade and acid rain at the time — and in Ottawa, the media were given barely two hours' notice of Oberle's on-again off-again news conference. In fact, a bit of a cat-and-mouse game had been going on for weeks before the announcement: Mulroney would say something in Washington, no he wouldn't, maybe he would; there would be a press conference in Ottawa, no there wouldn't, no one knew whether there would or not.

The government, still conscious of its promised war on the deficit and stung by earlier scepticism from the business community about its resolve on this score, was evidently trying to soft-pedal the $800-million figure. In the news release issued by Oberle's office, it was not mentioned until the last paragraph. Inevitably there were questions about where the cash would come from; Oberle said the funds would not be new money — they would have to come from a "re-arrangement of priorities" within the government and the transfer of money from other programs. (Asked when a new research effort would receive funds under the space station program, one scientist wryly observed: "They haven't stolen it yet.") In late 1986, the government announced another round of budget cuts at the NRC and, at the same time, mandated the NRC to contribute CDN$74-million over five years out of its existing funds to the space station program. The move created bitter dissension inside the NRC and caused a major controversy to erupt in the scientific community. This resulted in the unedifying spectacle of scientists taking potshots at each other instead of addressing the real issue — the seriousness of the government's commitment to improving Canada's performance in scientific and technological research. There seemed also to be a widespread misconception that Canadian space station dollars would end up in the United States.

In fact, the space station funds would be spent in Canada, mostly in industry. As expected, the agreement with NASA was a no-cash-across-the-border deal. A space station project office was established within the National Research Council, under the directorship of Karl Doetsch, and the prime contract went, not surprisingly, to Spar Aerospace. The subcontracting team consisted of CAE Electronics Ltd. of Montreal; Canadian Astronautics Ltd. of Ottawa; and SED Systems Inc. of Saskatoon.

Many people, even some of those closest to the action, were surprised that the government had gone for the whole $800-million package. Middleton, for example, saw the figure for the first time when he glanced at the news release before the press conference in Ottawa. Doetsch admitted to some tense moments during the months of negotiating and deliberation but he remained optimistic. He believed the space station project was "a powerful package" both technologically and politically and the $800-million was "the sort of dollar level you need" to be an effective partner in a project of that magnitude. Compared with the total cost of the space station, "it's not a vast amount of money. In fact, $800-million for what is being done — including an operation in space to the year 2000 — isn't a tremendous amount."

For Doetsch personally, the decision meant assuming stewardship of yet another very challenging space project. It would be his third major project in rapid succession, after the Canadarm and the astronaut program, with barely time to catch his breath. The latter had gone from a standing start to a smoothly running operation in less than two years under very demanding conditions (Doetsch's hair getting noticeably greyer in the process), and while he did have personal regrets about handing it over to someone else, he said managing the astronauts' shuttle flights and negotiating with NASA about their future would be a major effort in itself.

Getting the space station project launched prompted such a sigh of relief among all concerned that the loose ends of Canada's space program were left to dangle for a while. There was the small matter of the still-unannounced long-term space plan, but the urgency had dissipated with the announcement of the show-piece program. The Canadian astronaut program was clearly in no danger of termination and Oberle said that Canada expected the right to have at least one Canadian among the space station crew "on a continuing basis." He indicated that the role of Canadian astronauts on the station — and the possibility of training them for mission specialist duties, including EVAs — was among the issues Canada would put on the table in further discussions with NASA. There were also strong hints that Canada would seek more flights for Canadian astronauts, in addition to the three already committed, when the shuttle resumed flying.

Oberle's official announcement of the continuation of the astronaut program came in mid-May, along with most of what remained to be settled of the promised long-term space plan. The government committed an additional CDN$476-million to various projects, including M-Sat, Radarsat and space science; it was estimated that this funding, plus the space station project, would provide 100,000 person-years of employment and generate revenues of some CDN$8-billion by the year 2000. M-Sat received an additional CDN$50-million in research funds and a commitment that the government would lease CDN$126-million worth of capacity on the satellite. Radarsat was the biggest loser. Although no one disputed the merit of the project, the misfortune of bad timing had left it essentially orphaned as far as federal funding was concerned. When last seen, it was dependent for survival largely on its ability to attract a new coalition of supporters, including provincial governments, the private sector and possibly other international partners.

One of the loose ends not addressed in the second announcement was the question of establishing a Canadian space agency. By 1985, there were increasing signs that this was an idea whose time had finally come, particularly in the new era of increasing international collaboration. The Science Council of Canada, the Aerospace Industries Association of Canada and the Canadian Institute for Advanced Research all released reports urging the establishment of a single Canadian space agency.

The Science Council's report, issued in October, 1985, said that it "unhesitatingly opts" for the establishment of a space agency. It said that "a major reorganization of government space activities is needed ... Individual departments naturally have difficulty in justifying space expenditures *per se* since none is concerned primarily with space. They use space expenditures as a way to satisfy or justify their particular departmental mission. The result is fragmentation of space related interests and activities, which in turn creates a difficult planning problem, not just for the federal government but even more acutely for the domestic industry ... What is needed is the political will to make this shift, painful though it may be in terms of some entrenched interests within the existing government structure."

The space station project appeared to be just the thing to break the logjam; the level of Canadian industrial participation would be higher than ever before, relative to government participation, and beyond the technological challenges, Canada would have to meet schedules set by others. The project's international character introduced "several new levels of complexity," said A. E. Collin, Secretary of the Ministry of State for Science and Technology. "We have to move to put a management structure in place." The move was finally made in October, 1986, when the government announced in the Speech from the Throne that it would set up a Canadian space agency.

The ink was barely dry on the March space station agreement between NASA and Canada when the "Empire" did, as prophesied, strike back. In May, NASA started running a gamut of budget hearings before four Congressional committees, including two headed by Senator Jake Garn and Representative Bill Nelson, both of whom had flown shuttle missions.[27] The Canadian negotiators did not expect major problems with three of the four committees, but the Boland committee remained particularly concerned about automation and robotics and it did, as it had promised, subject the agreement with Canada to considerable scrutiny during hearings in the spring and summer of 1986. Members of the Canadian negotiating team kept close tabs on these hearings, trying to sort out the technical and political complexities involved. For a time, it appeared that protectionist sentiment in the U.S. Congress might be playing a role, and the outbreak of the much-denied trade war between Canada and the United States in June did not particularly help the situation.

The major problem, however, seemed to stem from the fact that Boland wanted assurances that NASA would not be tempted to abandon its space station A&R program, while an embattled NASA, swamped by the problems resulting from the Challenger accident, simply didn't have the wherewithal to concern itself with what was, after all, not an immediate priority. "We're caught a bit by NASA's not having its own A&R program in a state where they can convince Congress that they're serious about it," Evans commented at the time.

In the period just before the release of the Challenger inquiry report, NASA seemed to be drifting without firm leadership. The morale problems and management morass seemed to be worsening as the agency braced itself for the Challenger report due in June. One observer described NASA as having assumed a "fetal position." In mid-May, however, James Fletcher, the former NASA administrator who had been asked by President Reagan to resume leadership of the agency, began his attempt to restore NASA's tattered credibility and sense of direction. Because his views concerning the agreement with Canada were unknown, Canada insisted on an early meeting with the new administrator. Fletcher met with Evans, Collin and Canadian ambassador Allan Gotlieb in Washington on June 5 and indicated he would stand firmly behind the international agreement.

However, Fletcher had far more to worry about than Canada's space station problems. A battle was raging in Congressional and White House circles over whether to fund a replacement shuttle and NASA was in the middle of hard bargaining over its budget. In fact, it was trying to fend off a proposal to pay for a new orbiter by cutting the space station budget. In the middle of all this, the Challenger accident report was released in mid-June. It concluded that a faulty seal on the shuttle's right solid rocket booster had caused the accident and it did, as expected, criticize not only NASA's "flawed" decision to launch the Challenger, but also its overall management of the shuttle program. It said that NASA had played "a kind of Russian roulette," staying with the faulty seal design, failing for years to fix it, and finally making it an "acceptable" flight risk.[28] It said NASA's management system permitted safety problems to "bypass key shuttle managers" and that NASA was "stretched to the limit" by an overly ambitious launch schedule. "There was pressure to conform to a launch schedule that perhaps NASA should never have set," said former astronaut, Senator John Glenn. "There was economic pressure; there was social pressure."[29]

Fletcher did not try to duck the criticism. "There's enough blame to go around; the fault is not with any single group, but was NASA's fault...We are going to behave like a family which has suffered a tragic event. We are going to deal responsibly with our loss without needless recrimination and we are going to move

282

forward, facing and conquering the challenges that face us." He pledged that "where management is weak, we will strengthen it. Where engineering design or processes need improving, we will improve them. Where our internal communications are poor, we will see that they get better."

Toward the end of June, Fletcher and Boland exchanged letters on the matter of the space station automation and robotics program. Boland asked NASA to advance its A&R program so that their dextrous manipulator would be available on the space station first. (Canada planned to provide the main "workhorse" manipulator system in time for an early shuttle flight dedicated to assembling the station, but the Canadian dextrous manipulator was not scheduled to fly until about two years later.) In his June 25 letter to Boland, Fletcher agreed to accelerate NASA's A&R program and said that this could be "accomplished simultaneously with the meaningful co-operation with Canada" under the existing agreement. Fletcher said he was pleased that Boland's directives "do not alter the roles assigned to Canada" and added that NASA "remains fully committed to the agreement with Canada." Fletcher subsequently sent a letter to the Canadian government reaffirming his support for "shared U.S. and Canadian roles in space station assembly, servicing and maintenance."

In late June, NASA announced that it was investigating the idea of a joint venture with the private sector to develop the U.S. servicing system for the space station. This was described as a dextrous robotic device that would consist of several arms, tools and camera, and a powerful computer-control system employing artificial intelligence. The manipulator's functions would include assisting astronauts during EVA in performing station assembly, maintenance and servicing. The private company would retain ownership of the system and could sell its services to other space station customers. NASA planned to evaluate industry interest in the idea during the summer of 1986 and subsequently decide whether to proceed with the joint venture.

Evans said Canada has been told this does not alter the functions assigned to Canada in the March agreement. The Canadian MSC is supposed to play the chief role in station assembly. However, the U.S. dextrous manipulator will be compatible with the Canadian arm and Evans said it is possible that the U.S. system could be used on the end of the Canadian arm to assist in assembly tasks. (The U.S. dextrous manipulator will be designed to operate with the shuttle arm, the MSC arm, the arm in the U.S. payload servicing bay on the station and, finally, on the orbital maneuvring vehicle.)

During the late summer of 1986, NASA's situation seemed to get messier by the day. Despite protracted wrangling with the White House and Congress, it remained uncertain that a fourth orbiter would be funded; the space agency could not get its budgetary house in order and was embattled during its Congressional budget hearings. Its attempt to reorganize the management of the space station program resulted in almost open mutiny by the Johnson Space Center, and the space station program was facing potential funding problems and delays. NASA was being "battered from all sides," said one Canadian observer. "We've been a crisis-a-day organization for the last few months," one senior NASA official admitted.

The turn of events of greatest direct interest to Canada concerned changes in the construction and assembly schedule for the space station. Serious questions were raised about the feasibility of building the full dual-keel station with the limited launch capacity resulting from the Challenger accident, and concerns were expressed (particularly by the NASA astronaut office) that the station was too complex for assembly and continuing maintenance by astronauts doing EVA from the shuttle. There was pressure to greatly reduce EVA and to put up a simpler station, consisting of two habitable modules and only one beam in the initial stages and work toward the more complex box-like beam structure over a period of years. In part, this was to ensure manned operations as early as possible, at least in a "man-tended" mode (i.e., the crew would come and go with the shuttle, which would provide their life support system, rather than staying with the station.)

The Boland committee in particular expressed concern that the assembly sequence be guided by a requirement to "produce *useful* results at the *outset* of station activity … The Committee believes that the space station should be assembled and funded in such a manner that both external and internal payloads are producing useful scientific results as soon as possible."

The committee also had concerns about international participation in the program, saying that, since the United States would be paying for about 80 per cent of the station, it should derive an equivalent percentage of the benefits. It stated that none of the international facilities was to be launched before the entire U.S.-built infrastructure was up and operating, except for "the Canadian-furnished mobile arm."

The changes in the space station assembly plan naturally had a big effect on the Canadian MSC program. By late 1986, it appeared that deployment of the MSC would occur in four phases over about two years — a strategy dictated in large part by competing demands for space aboard the shuttle, but also to some extent by politics. The plan is to launch only those tools absolutely necessary to do each step of the job; thus, it calls for a remote manipulator arm and a rudimentary transporter systems to be launched on the third assembly flight to start putting the truss structure together. This will be followed by the launch on subsequent flights of the second arm, the fixed servicing and maintenance depot, and finally, the full-capability transporter system, the special purpose dextrous manipulator and the full complement of tools and equipment needed for servicing payloads. The entire package — the MSC, the fixed depot and associated space- and ground-based equipment — will be known as the Mobile Servicing System (MSS).

The detailed design of the system will undoubtedly continue to evolve to keep up with changes to the overall space station design, but "the basic requirement is still there," said Mac Evans. "I don't believe this changes what we're trying to do."

There is no question, however, that toward the end of 1986, the NASA was becoming far more aggressive in its pursuit of a space station robotics program than it had been before, largely in response to Congressional concerns. NASA proposed to fly its own flight telerobotic system (FTS) very early in the program — before the Canadian dextrous manipulator will fly. The FTS, which is expected to include a vision system, a computer-control system and dextrous manipulator arms, could be used as a "smart front end" on the MSC arms or on the shuttle's arm (and in a variety of other ways). NASA assured Congress that the FTS would be used in early station assembly and servicing tasks — that it will, in fact, be used for the first "telerobotic manipulation of an attached payload." NASA requested an additional US$160-million to $210-million from Congress to build the device.

It is clear, then, that political exigencies have forced a technological overlap in the Canada and U.S. space station robotics programs. Since both countries see it as a means of promoting large spin-off benefits on earth, neither was prepared to abandon the field entirely to the other. It was fortunate, therefore, that other factors conspired to force a much-increased emphasis on the use of robotic systems in assembling, maintaining and operating the station, which helped to ease what might well have become a political crisis between Canada and the United States.

"As long as there's enough work for everybody and as long as the tasks are challenging enough, everybody's satisfied," said Karl Doetsch.

The new U.S. aggressiveness on the matter of space station robotics did raise concerns in some quarters in Canada, however. For example, it prompted the Canadian Institute for Advanced Research to issue a follow-up to their first report, in which they urged the government to ensure that the $800-million Canada would be spending on the project would generate spin-off technological benefits in advanced automation and robotics in Canadian industry. Noting that the U.S. is moving quickly to exploit this opportunity, the CIAR report said Canada "should take a similarly hard-nosed approach."

"The true significance of Canada's participation in the space station will be measured, not in what occurs in space, but rather in what happens on earth," the report said. The major goal of the Canadian program should be "to stimulate the development and diffusion of advanced technologies that will strengthen the competitiveness of Canadian industry" and provide Canada with new knowledge-based products and services to compete in international markets. The CIAR report said that "delivery of a component" should not be the only goal of Canada's space station program. The "real opportunity" is to help Canada develop a capability for long-term applied research, which it described as one of this country's "most pressing challenges."

In response, Mac Evans said technology diffusion *is* a major objective of the space station program and the government is working with industry and universities to develop a way of managing the process. "The government went into this program with the expectation that it would create an advanced technology capability within the country in A&R that would flow into a wide range of industries," he said. All three sectors — government, industry and the universities — "agree it has to be done, but this is new to us. There is a concerted effort by all three to manage that process." He said this would be one role for the new Canadian space agency.

The CIAR report recommended establishing a "coherent management structure," including something similar to the federal granting agencies to ensure that "an exploitable knowledge base" is established and that diffusion of A&R technology into Canadian industry and universities takes place. Finally, it recommended that no more than half of the space station budget should go into the production of the space-based servicing facility and that three-quarters of the remaining funds—nearly 40 per cent of the total — go into a ground-based industry/university program of technology development and exploitation. These budgets should be separate and, if the cost of building the servicing facility increases, the technology program should not suffer, the report said.

But Evans said that the costs cannot easily be divided this way, because a significant amount of basic technology development will occur in designing and building the servicing facility. The question, he said, is how much extra money will be needed to adapt and extend the technology into Canadian universities and industry. This is "a judgement call, which we are studying."

By late 1986, NASA was beginning to have some success in putting its managerial house in order and space station planning started to move forward again. In October, administrator Fletcher carried an upbeat message to Congress: "The United States remains committed to the development of a permanently manned space station," he said, noting that the fiscal 1987 budget included a request for funds that would formally initiate development of the station. This event was important for several reasons, he said. "It will signal to our international partners that the U.S. commitment to the space station is firm and that their own budgetary and intellectual resources can safely and productively be devoted to a co-operative space station program. It will signal to the private sector here in the United States that future investments in commercial space activities can be planned with confidence. It will signal to U.S. industry that the space station program is on track and that its own investment of money and talent is justified. In addition, moving foward as planned will signal the Soviets, who how have an operational space station, that their current advantage will not remain unchallenged. Perhaps most importantly, (it) signals America's intention to look confidently to the future."

Difficult as it was, obtaining agreement on the hardware items and services that Canada would provide did not end the negotiations with NASA. A formal decision whether to proceed to the next phase (Phase C/D) — otherwise known as "cutting metal"— would not be made until the spring of 1987. In the meantime, negotiations continued on Canada's role in the on-going management and operations of the station. The March agreement stated that Canada would have a significant role, but the details remained to be worked out by an operations working group.

All of the international partners had concerns about their operational and management responsibilities, especially about how operational costs would be calculated and shared. Operational costs were a matter of growing concern to NASA as well. The U.S. space agency had earlier been criticized by a panel of outside experts, who noted that operational costs were not being included in the Phase B definition studies and said these costs must be considered early in the planning or they might be so high as to scare off potential commercial users.

At the end of 1985, NASA estimated that operational costs over the expected 25-year lifetime of the station would be about 150 per cent of the original hardware costs. If building the station cost US$11-billion, this would come to US$16.5-billion in total, or US$660-million a year. However, one European estimate put the annual cost at US$1- to 2-billion, of which Europe's annual share was estimated to be US$250- to 500-million. Canada's commitment of $800-million was intended to cover Canada's share of operating costs over 15 years.

NASA had indicated from the start that it expected its partners to help with the expenses, but the other countries were adamant about not simply paying rental or service fees to the United States. At an international meeting of space station project members in November, 1985, Jean Arets, then chief of international affairs for the European Space Agency, made very clear what they wanted instead: "What we envision is to provide services to the station, and not to pay cash." There were good political and economic reasons for this — it would permit the international partners to spend their space dollars developing marketable skills and technologies within their own countries.

Canada took this position as well. "If the Canadian government is going to pay for operations ... they want to pay for jobs here in Canada rather than for somebody in the United States or Europe," Evans said. The March agreement between Canada and NASA explicitly stated that costs would be "structured so as to minimize the exchange of funds across the border."

By the spring of 1986, it looked as though some kind of high-tech barter system was shaping up, with each partner accumulating brownie points for services rendered, which could then be applied against their use of the other partners' facilities. "What we expect," said Evans, "is that all the partners will be responsible for owning, maintaining and operating the equipment they supply. All partners will have access to all parts of the station and the overall operational costs ... and the utilization time will be partitioned among the partners in some way."

This 'some way' was open for negotiation during the rest of 1986 and it represented a potentially tricky apples-and-oranges kind of problem, not only because different countries were providing different facilities and services, but also because certain basics — the use of electrical power and "consumables" (such as air and water), and transportation of people and equipment to and from the station — also had to be factored into the equation. "One can see that there'd be some difficulties in coming to common agreement as to the value of a particular contribution," Evans said. He said Canada was "taken by surprise" by NASA's proposal to allow private industry to charge customers for the use of the U.S.-built remote manipulator system on the station. Canada had previously been told it could not charge for the use of the MSC, because all facilities would be shared among space station partners; Evans said it appears this policy will remain in effect for the international partners who contribute to the station.

The involvement of non-American nationals in station management and operations was a major aim for all of the international partners. Doetsch said Canada would expect to have a representative in Houston and "to be closely involved in any of the mission planning using the MSC." And it wanted a place for Canadian astronauts on board the station. Since Canada couldn't afford its own pressurized module, it wanted its contribution of the MSC to open the airlock to the habitable modules for Canadians, not just as scientific payload specialists doing Canadian experiments, but as mission specialists involved in running the station, operating the MSC and even performing EVAs. A major objective here, said Doetsch, is to assist Canadian industry in improving the servicing facility. "It's very important to have one of our astronauts telling us what the headaches are, getting feedback into our industry so that we don't stop dead with our development once we've delivered the first set."

In fact, Canada had been talking to NASA about mission specialist training for Canadians even before the March agreement. It was too soon for a program to be established, both because of the hiatus caused by the Challenger accident and because the Canadian government had not officially given the go-ahead, but "our NASA colleagues indicated that a mission specialist role was not inappropriate for Canada," Doetsch said. A Canadian mission specialist on the station would not work only for Canada; slots will be at a premium and everyone on board will have to perform multiple duties. By the same token, astronauts from other countries would sometimes be in charge of MSC operations, since "it's very unlikely that we will have one astronaut on the station all the time." Nevertheless, Doetsch believes it is feasible for a Canadian to be on board for at least one 90-day tour of duty a year.

NASA's negotiations with the European Space Agency were, if anything, even stormier than those with Canada. They were so contentious, in fact, that ESA failed to meet the March 10 deadline by which the international partners were to define the hardware elements they would build for the station. By mid-April, NASA officials said that if agreement were not reached soon, planning on the space station would proceed on the assumption that Europe would not be involved.

The two groups had been engaged in a wary gavotte throughout 1985 and they often seemed to be working at cross purposes to each other. European political leaders initially had been reluctant to make a commitment to develop hardware until the ill-defined operational cost-sharing arrangements were resolved. They were also concerned about the cost and availability of shuttle flights, even before the Challenger accident. The major stumbling blocks were the technical nature of the module that Europe was planning to provide for the station, its function, and the degree of autonomy ESA would have over its operations.

The European module, called Columbus, was to be a pressurized manned module, one of four habitable modules that would form the core of the station and serve as living quarters and laboratories for the astronauts. ESA wanted to build a module that would remain attached to the core of the station for most of the time but that could detach itself for brief periods to operate as a "man-tended" free-flying laboratory, away from the minute gravity effects that would be produced by the station itself. West Germany was particularly keen on having a free-flying "quiet" lab for materials processing research.

NASA insisted that if Europe wanted to be a full partner in the project, its module must form part of the long-term core structure of the station. Moreover, NASA was unalterably opposed to having a free-flier in the initial stages of the station's development, believing that the available resources (such as astronaut time, docking facilities and computer and communications systems) would not be adequate to support a free-flying module during the early years of operation.

There were serious policy issues underlying the positions of both NASA and ESA. For its part, NASA had adopted the concept of functional allocation and felt that if the proposed European, Japanese and U.S. systems were considered independently this would be a waste of space station resources and would miss taking advantage of the international character of it.

Interestingly enough, the Europeans were caught in a rather contradictory bind, see-sawing back and forth between their desire to be an equal partner in a truly international undertaking and their desire for control and autonomy over their own operations. Early in the negotiations, the Europeans had criticized NASA for viewing the project as "a U.S. station with foreign participation," as Jean Arets put it. "What we want is not just to add a piece to a U.S. station. I think that ideally it should be an international station."

At the same time, however, ESA was fiercely protecting its independence. Its interest in a free-flying module was prompted to a large extent by the desire eventually to develop a completely autonomous European space station, a goal that had been strongly endorsed by the ESA member nations at a meeting in Rome in January, 1985.

But although Europe had already established its own facilities for ground control of space missions by late 1985 — indeed in

November of that year the German Space Operations Centre near Munich collaborated with NASA in the actual control of shuttle mission 61-A — Europe still lacked capability in several essential areas required for completely independent operations in space. For example, ESA did not have a reusable space transportation vehicle and a launcher capable of lifting heavy loads into orbit, nor the technology and skills needed to perform EVAs. However, programs to fill these gaps were already underway by 1985, including the development of a heavy-lift Ariane launcher and a shuttle-like spaceplane called Hermes. Europe was always concerned about sole dependence on the shuttle and these concerns intensified after the Challenger accident. Hermes is not expected to be ready until at least the mid-1990s and initially may have about two flights a year. The missions are expected to be somewhat longer than the typical shuttle mission of seven to 10 days.

ESA has also started studies of space station EVA operations and the possibility of using remote-control robotic systems for outside work. In all, European officials believe they can develop the technology needed to operate independently in space, but expect this to take at least 15 to 20 years.

For its part, NASA has been less than completely enthusiastic about the European emphasis on independence. NASA officials expressed concern that Europe was essentially using the U.S. space station program as a stepping stone to its own station — that ESA might pull out of the U.S. project after only a few years, leaving NASA to carry the entire cost of running the station. "Sometimes Europe sounds more like a short-term user than a long-term partner," said Kenneth Pedersen, then NASA's director of international affairs. By late 1985, he was saying that "it's not clear that we have the basis for an agreement. An agreement would require that each partner accept a degree of dependence. We hope that Europe's concern for autonomy and independence is not inconsistent with the concept of integration."

As 1985 drew to a close, Neil Hutchinson, then NASA's space station project manager, said that they were working to achieve a delicate balance that combined fair cost-sharing and avoidance of duplication with a degree of autonomy and "a semblance of national uniqueness" for the international partners. But he conceded that these objectives were not easily reconciled.

European officials said it was all a big misunderstanding. "We didn't mean to suggest we'd hook up to the station one day and then decide to sail away three months later," said Frederik Engstrom, ESA's space station director. "NASA saw only our dreams about autonomy," said one German space official soothingly. "Columbus provides both the opportunity for co-operation and for a version of autonomy." For all that, ESA officials remained firm in their commitment to eventual independence. In mid-April, 1986, the issue remained unresolved, but, on the basis of unofficial communications, NASA included a European module — permanently attached — in its baseline design of the station. In May, ESA formally proposed that it contribute an attached module but said it would also pursue studies on a man-tended free-flier to satisfy Europe's desire for eventual autonomy. It also proposed to contribute a polar-orbiting remote-sensing platform and to study the idea of a co-orbiting unmanned platform.

Europe and NASA continued to discuss Europe's desire to use its space station module for materials processing research; NASA, under directives from the Boland committee, insisted on retaining primary responsibility for the space station materials processing lab. The continuing problems resulting from the Challenger accident also boosted the fortunes of the Hermes spaceplane project within ESA and reinforced the sentiment in favor of eventual European space autonomy.

NASA did reach agreement with Japan on the design and definition phase by March 10. Japan's proposed contribution would include a pressurized multi-purpose research and development laboratory attached to the space station, an unpressurized open work deck that would expose experiments and instruments to the space environment, an airlock, and a "local" remote manipulator arm, which would be controlled by Japanese astronauts inside the module and used to move equipment on the open work platform. The Japanese have a major interest in doing life-sciences, materials processing and biotechnology research in the microgravity environment.

In a report focussing on Japan's burgeoning space industry, *Aviation Week and Space Technology* noted that Japan wants to participate in the space station "because the commercial opportunities are enormous and Japan is determined that those opportunities must not be missed. The pity is that this determination is no longer shared in the U.S. or has been blunted by the more immediate problems at hand."

In fact, for all the international partners, NASA's travails in the aftermath of the Challenger accident were increasingly worrying; the U.S. at times seemed incapable of pulling its space program back together and providing the firm leadership that everyone continued to expect of it. As *Aviation Week* noted, in an editorial entitled "Who's in Charge?", the U.S. "is at an historic juncture with its space program and is in critical need of positive action to end the indecision blocking definition of a coherent policy that will reassert the U.S.'s leadership in space. The trouble is no champion has stepped forward to seize the initiative, and the ensuing confusion leaves even casual observers wondering whether anyone is in charge of setting the nation's space goals." After going through an agonizing period, the U.S. needed to "pull up its socks and get on with the job."

In late 1986, the government announced that another round of severe budgetary cuts would be imposed on the National Research Council, in part to cover the cost of Canada's participation in the space station project. The NRC was mandated to contribute CDN$74-million over five years out of its existing programs to the project. Many scientists were dismayed by this move, which reportedly caused bitter dissension on the NRC's governing board. One board member, who described the space station program as Canada's Roman circus, said this country had "no business wasting money in space when it is destroying a part of our national heritage."

NOTES

1. In May, 1986, crew members on board MIR transferred to the Salyut station to perform some housekeeping tasks left undone by a previous crew, which had to return to earth hurriedly because one of the cosmonauts became ill.
2. The text of his statement originally referred only to a "permanent" station, but on the morning of his speech, Reagan reportedly was persuaded by space station supporters to change the wording to "permanently manned." They were concerned that ambiguous wording might be interpreted to mean that the president did not fully support the project.
3. NASA officials always seemed conveniently to forget that the Soviets had had, in effect, an operational space station for more than a decade.
4. In fact, a strong case can be made that the demand for small advanced computer systems generated by the moon program provided one of the essential sparks that resulted in the microelectronics revolution of the 1970s.
5. Even before the Challenger accident, there was concern that a four-shuttle fleet would be inadequate to build and supply the space station and to meet the demand for launching commercial satellites and foreign, military and scientific payloads. The job would have been virtually impossible with a three-shuttle fleet, which is a major reason why NASA lobbied the White House and Congress so strongly for the nearly US$3-billion needed to build a replacement for the Challenger. It is expected that, in the post-Challenger period, the shuttle's role in launching commercial satellites would be greatly reduced, if not virtually eliminated. Nevertheless, NASA still anticipated difficulties meeting the space station's requirements after shuttle launches resumed, for several reasons: a slow, cautious approach would be taken in building up the frequency of launches, a large back log of payload would have to be dealt with (including many high-priority military payloads) and the shuttle probably would not carry the maximum weight of payloads for which it was originally designed. It seemed increasingly likely that expendable launch vehicles would be needed to supplement the shuttle's role in supplying the station and NASA was also considering development of an unmanned heavy lift vehicle as a workhorse cargo carrier.
6. Radarsat, an international project headed by the Canadian federal Department of Energy, Mines and Resources, was being redesigned so that batteries, tape recorders and solar panels could be replaced, fuel tanks refilled and sensors updated. If a problem is too serious to be repaired in space, the satellite could even be stowed in the shuttle's cargo bay and returned to earth. The design changes were expected to cost about CDN$40-million, but it was estimated this would double the satellite's lifetime from five to ten years and increase the economic returns by about CDN$500-million. Although planning for Radarsat had been going on for several years, the project was facing an uncertain fate by mid-1986; its federal funding was greatly reduced in favor of participation in the international space station and it was left to seek resources elsewhere.
7. There was considerable debate whether it might be wiser to fund the development of a new generation of space vehicles, rather than simply replicate to another shuttle with 1960s technology.
8. Interestingly, the industry in which Canada first made its mark in space — communications — had little immediate interest in the space station, in

part because it is already commercially mature and also because it requires geosynchronous orbit, 36,000 km up, far above the approximately 300-km to 500-km operating orbits of the shuttle and the space station. By the turn of the century, however, the station may be used for assembling and testing very large communications platforms or "antenna farms" that will replace today's communications satellites.

9. The subcontractors were: CAE Electronics Ltd., Montreal; Canadian Astronautics Ltd., Ottawa; DSMA Atcon Ltd., Toronto; Dynacon Ltd., Toronto; MacDonald Dettwiler & Associates Ltd., Richmond, B.C.; and Moniteq Ltd., Concord, Ontario.

10. The contractors on these studies were: DSMA Atcon Ltd., Toronto; BM Hitech, Collingwood, Ontario; Canadian Astronautics Ltd., Ottawa; MPB Technologies Inc., Dorval; T. A. Croil Ltd., Toronto; and Spar Aerospace Ltd.

11. There were objections to Canada's involvement in the project. Some scientists feared it would drain funds from space science programs and there were expressions of concern that this would provide a "backdoor" route for Canadian involvement in military space activities. These issues are discussed in Chapter 8 and the Epilogue.

12. CAE Electronics, Canadian Astronautics, DSMA Atcon, SED Systems Inc. of Saskatoon and Dynacon.

13. Trump said that the arm's reputation helped export sales directly in at least two cases — the sale of fire trucks in the United States and mechanical tree planters in China.

14. The fact that NASA was having serious difficulty controlling its centres was revealed during the investigation of the presidential commission into the Challenger accident, which cited poor internal communications as a major cause of the accident. Over the years, these operational arms had become very decentralized and NASA Headquarters had all but lost control of them. *Aviation Week and Space Technology* said in an editorial that "NASA's fractious centers have to be pulled back into line and the agency transformed into a tightly run unit with strong central government."

15. Some examples of space station functions in which artificial intelligence or "expert" systems could be used include: guidance, navigation and control of the station, the shuttle and other vehicles; communications and tracking; information and data management; electrical power control; environmental control and life support; propulsion and fuel control; flight planning; "habitability" (medical diagnosis, physiological monitoring and health maintenance); and managing processes aboard scientific and commercial orbiting platforms. One expert system being developed, which would be used to detect malfunctions in the system that removes carbon dioxide from spacecraft cabin air, is called FIXER (a self-conscious acronym for "Fault Isolation Expert for Enhanced Reliability").

16. Radarsat was expected to cost CDN$520-million (plus another $40-million if redesigned for in-orbit servicing.) Of that, about $300-million was to come from Canada; the U.S., Britain and other international partners were to contribute the remaining amount. M-Sat is a new-generation communications satellite designed to enhance communications from mobile sources (e.g., ships). It was expected to cost more than CDN$300-million, but CDN$260-million was expected to be raised by Telesat Canada from the private sector, so the project did not figure as strongly in the competition for federal space funds.

17. A panel of non-NASA space experts, including a group of retired astronauts, which was asked to review plans for the station, expressed concern about the vulnerability of the station to collision with debris in orbit and about the role of the shuttle in station safety. "Panel members from areas outside the manned space field felt that an attached simple return vehicle might be an expedient thing to have," according to a NASA summary of the panel's critique. The explosion of the Challenger also raised questions about how the station would be resupplied if shuttle flights should be suspended in the future. France and Japan are planning to build small manned space shuttles, which could potentially be used as back-ups for the U.S. shuttle. NASA is also studying the development of a crew escape or "lifeboat" system to be attached to the space station.

18. The committee's concern that the high-tech spin-offs from the space station project benefit the United States was also reflected by the fact that it instructed NASA to retain responsibility for the station's materials processing laboratory module, something both the Japanese and the Europeans were interested in. The Japanese module was designed for "advanced technology" research and the European module for life sciences; however, European space officials were very unhappy about this and it became a source of continuing conflict in their negotiations with NASA.

19. The fact that this was the week after the Challenger accident did not noticeably slow planning for the space station at this stage. Although NASA as a whole was still reeling in shock, the people in the space station program were clearly taking a long-term perspective. "From what we could see, the program was just carrying on," Evans said.

20. This was similar to a concept Spar had worked on a few years earlier to provide a short second arm, called the Handling and Positioning Aid, for use on the shuttle.

21. If the shuttle orbiter uses its own small thrusters to dock with the station, this raises the possibility that it could crash into the station if the thrusters malfunction. "You can get control of the docking much better with the arm than you can if you're using the jets on the orbiter," said Middleton. "You reach out and grab ... with the arm and you pull the whole thing in." The shuttle has a much greater mass than the current Canadarm is designed to grapple so "we have to develop the manipulator system to be able to handle a whole orbiter."

22. The United States is planning to build a service bay with a shelter to handle visiting satellites and it is likely that a small special-purpose manipulator arm would be located inside this bay. The U.S.-built robotic servicer could be used on the end of this arm.

23. In fact, Canada had acquired an unusually high profile in the U.S. Congress that spring as a result of a great deal of controversy over free trade and acid rain. Although none of this had any direct relationship to the space program, this argumentative visibility was an unfortunate coincidence, given Congressional concerns about Canada's role in the space station project.

24. The Challenger explosion at the end of January did not have a negative impact on these deliberations; in Canada, as in the United States, it was generally felt that human habitation of space was too important a long-term goal to be abandoned, even in the wake of a tragic accident.

25. A portion of this was earmarked for concurrent "user development" projects supporting scientific, commercial and industrial R&D in fields that ultimately could create profitable new high-technology opportunities for Canada. These opportunities are examined more fully in Chapter 8.

26. During the first half of the 1980s, communications and remote-sensing together took up more than three-quarters of the government's space budget. It is anticipated that, in the last half of the decade, each of these two areas will account for about a quarter of the annual space budget and the space station program, negligible before 1986, will also take about a quarter of the budget.

27. One of the tragic ironies of the Challenger accident was that Gregory Jarvis, a Hughes Aircraft payload specialist on the ill-fated flight, had been bumped from not one but two previous missions to make room for the two politicians.

28. One of the commission members, Richard Feynman, characterized NASA management as a child who refuses to listen to its parents (that is, the engineers who had warned of problems with the O-ring seals on the solid rocket boosters) when told not to run into the street. "The parents are very upset and say, 'It's very dangerous' and the child says 'But nothing happened' and he runs out on the road again, several times. If the child's view that nothing happened is a clue that nothing was going to happen, then there's going to be an accident. Sooner or later, the child gets run over. Is it an accident? No, it's not an accident. I don't know how to assign blame, or whether it does any good. You can blame the child for being a little foolish, but it's very difficult. The question is, how do we educate the child?"

29. Members of Congress often neglected to mention that a large fraction of this pressure came from Congress itself.

CHAPTER EIGHT

Living, Learning and Working in Space

In
the early 1960s,
U.S. President John F. Kennedy
was able to propose
sending men to the moon
largely to satisfy the imperatives of Cold War
politics and national glory.
The anticipated return on investment was
measured in terms of international prestige,
technological oneupmanship,
and to a certain extent,
industrial spin-offs back on earth,
but no one really expected the trip
to pay for itself directly in dollars and cents.
In contrast, the 1980s saw a far more pronounced "bottom line" approach to new endeavors in space, reflecting a growing sense that it was time for the 25-year-old manned space program to grow up and start earning its keep. In the same State of the Union address in which he announced a commitment to building the space station, U.S. President Ronald Reagan also stated that the Administration would introduce measures to promote private investment in space, saying that "the general welfare of the United States requires that [NASA] seek to encourage ... the fullest commercial use of space."

This perspective is implicit in the way in which the space station has been pitched to political leaders and the public. True, it is cut from the same "New Frontier" cloth as the Apollo program, but it is also characterized as "the gold rush in outer space." Various economic estimates suggest that space-based commercial and industrial ventures — the production of very pure drugs and high-quality electronic materials, for example — could generate annual revenues in the billions of dollars by the turn of the century. The total space industry is expected to be in the hundreds of billions of dollars, rivalling the electronics and aviation industries. Moreover, it is expected that there will be many earth-based industrial applications of new technologies developed for the space program, particularly in the fields of robotics, artificial intelligence and new materials and processes. Peter E. Glaser, vice-president of the Cambridge, Massachusetts, consulting firm Arthur D. Little, has said: "I believe that space in the 21st century will probably be what aviation, electronics and computers were, together, in this century. It is the next evolutionary step for humanity."

With the notable exception of communications satellites, making space pay for itself has proved frustratingly elusive. The space shuttle is an instructive case in point: as the first reusable space vehicle, it was intended to dramatically reduce launch costs, but its continuing technical problems have forced a hard re-examination of the whole concept of a multi-purpose, reusable space vehicle that must be all things to all people. The fact that the shuttle could serve as a launch vehicle, spacecraft, airplane, cargo-hauler, scientific laboratory, observation platform, repair truck and human life support system was touted as one of its big plusses, but the Challenger accident dramatically exposed the extreme vulnerability inherent in putting all your eggs in one basket.

Even before the accident, the U.S. National Commission on Space identified continuity of launch services and a drastic reduction in space transportation costs as the two most important imperatives for opening up the space frontier. Its recommendation for the development of several new launch and space transportation vehicles reflects a growing sense that diversification is necessary to ensure the permanent human habitation of space. "We expect to see extensive population and utilization of low earth orbit early in the 21st century," said Thomas Paine, chairman of the commission. "To do that, our one paramount goal is easy, low-cost access to space." Depending on how you do the calculations, the estimated cost of launching something in the shuttle ranges from about US$3000 to US$9000 per kg. The objective is to cut costs to about one or two per cent of that.

The shuttle and the space station have one important thing in common — they are designed to allow humans to live and work in space, and their high costs are largely a reflection of this fact.

All of the international partners share the major goal of wanting to put their own astronauts and scientists on board the space station, not only for the economic and scientific benefits this would create but also for the visibility this would give to the project back on earth. It is anticipated that scientists, technical experts, engineers, space construction workers and other specialists will live, learn and work in space continuously, performing a wide variety of functions: conducting research and development programs, overseeing the repair and refurbishment of the station, scientific instruments, satellites and other spacecraft; constructing and assembling large space structures, including more and larger space habitats, laboratories, automated factories and manufacturing facilities; and finally, monitoring and resupplying these facilities. As we have seen, humans will bring to these tasks an ability to deal with the unexpected, to apply on-the-spot diagnostic and "fix-it" skills, and generally to provide a degree of flexibility that machines cannot (yet) duplicate.

If going into orbit 25 years ago was humanity's first step out of the cradle of our earthbound existence, then building the space station is the equivalent of putting up a tree-house in the backyard.

If human beings are going to work productively in space, they need more than protection from the elements and the bare essentials of life. Mere survival will not be good enough; creature comforts will be necessary if working in space is not to become an endurance test or an ordeal. Given the high cost of training space workers, it will be important to keep down the turnover in skilled personnel that might well occur if people are disgruntled or depressed by their experiences on the station. "We want to be extremely efficient because it's costing a lot of bucks to keep people up there," said Chris Perner, deputy of the Man/Systems Division at the Johnson Space Center. Larry Bell, a University of Houston architect and NASA consultant, adds that, in space, "any errors are expensive errors. We're talking about some very expensive time by people who can do a lot of damage if they screw up."

Thus, more attention will have to be paid to psychological factors and crew morale than in the past. People with the Right Stuff are willing and able to put up with a lot of frustration and inconvenience during a seven-day shuttle mission, but even they would not appreciate a steady diet of it on a three-month tour of duty on the space station. After several months in space, crew members may be tired, bored, yearning for their families and possibly worried about family problems that have cropped up during their absence. They may also be frustrated by technical problems, equipment breakdowns or scientific experiments gone awry. Giving crew members living amenities won't solve all the problems, but it will help them cope. In the past, if there was any spare room, the engineers automatically stuffed in another black box. "Now we're realizing that the person to fix the black box is as important," Bell said. He noted that the space station will be a small, confined environment that must be all things to all people all at once. Various crew members will be simultaneously sleeping, working, preparing meals, exercising, relaxing and doing household chores. The challenge, he said, is to permit each crew member as much control as possible over his or her environment without interfering with the activities of others.

There will, moreover, be a greater potential for personality differences aboard the station because crews will be a more heterogeneous mixture than in the past. Shuttle crews, for example, have consisted largely of career astronauts who have trained together as a team for long periods of time and who operate under an almost military chain of command. Teamwork is everything. This is a system designed to minimize personality conflicts or at least weed them out before a mission is launched. But the pattern had already started to change with the addition to shuttle crews of payload specialists from private industry, international scientist-astronauts and citizen-observers. The question to ask, says NASA mission specialist Tony England, is whether a potential crew member is "someone you think you would be comfortable going camping with for a long time." The payload specialists who were willing to work as part of a team "got a lot more out of the orbiter crew than other payload specialists would have." Others have been "very eccentric and very difficult to work with."

As the space station era approaches, crews will increasingly include rather mixed collections of independent scientific and engineering types. In some ways, the social conditions aboard the space station will be similar to any situation in which a disparate group of people is forced to share confined quarters for long periods of time in a difficult and potentially hazardous environment. The Antarctic research stations provide a particularly useful model, especially because they involve rotating teams of scientists and technical experts, often from different countries, conducting their own research programs under the auspices of different institutions.

Given the complex international crew rotation system that will likely prevail, the people on board at any one time may not have trained together and may not even know each other very well. The potential for conflict and psychological problems will be great and would undoubtedly be exacerbated by deficiencies in the living conditions. Thus, while the engineers are pondering how to build the station and the scientists are trying to figure out what they want to do with it once it's built, the human factors experts are worrying about how to prevent it from becoming a dirty, dilapidated hotel and how to keep its inhabitants happy and healthy. As John Frassanito, an industrial designer from San Antonio, Texas, and a NASA consultant on space station habitability, said, the station must not become a "rundown hotel. We need to make sure this thing is a clean, cozy place rather than a dirty, dingy place. Things have a way of getting very dirty very fast in zero gravity."

In its effort to make daily life aboard the station manageable and pleasant, NASA is studying the development of gadgets such as zero-gravity clothes washers, dishwashers, showers, personal microcomputers, self-making beds — even, perhaps, housekeeping robots. The effects on mood and productivity of color, lighting, privacy, exercise, entertainment and communications with earth are also being studied.

Cleanliness and neatness will be of paramount importance, Chris Perner said. Unlike the shuttle, which returns to earth after about a week in space and can be thoroughly cleaned on the ground, the space station won't be coming back, so "you've got to build it so you can clean it up there very well." This will not be as easy as it might seem; the station will have a closed, filtered and recycled environment and many traditional methods will be unsuitable. "Can you imagine finding a cockroach?" Perner asks. "What would you do? You can't just get the aerosol and spray him; you'd contaminate the whole works."

In designing equipment for the station, some of the greatest challenges will come from items taken very much for granted on earth: clothes washers, dishwashers and showers. At present, astronauts carry enough clothing and utensils to see them through their week-long shuttle flights, but this clearly is not feasible for the space station. Literally tonnes of supplies would have to be carried up to see a six- to eight-member crew through a three-month tour of duty. "We don't want to carry up a million forks," Perner said. There is a problem, however: "We don't know how to manage fluid in zero gravity very well yet. A sealed enclosure and a method of reprocessing the used water is needed," Perner said, adding in his laconic Texas drawl: "You can't just set the old Maytag up, pour the soap in, fill it full of water and turn it loose. It'd just be everywhere."

Developing a zero-G shower also poses problems. A shower ought to be an enjoyable, relaxing experience, but removing water from the walls is not a simple matter. "It doesn't just fall to the floor and down the drain," said Perner, pointing out that the Skylab astronauts gave up using their shower — a folded canvas cylinder pulled up around the body — because wiping it down became such an ordeal. Some intriguing concepts have been proposed: a syringe-like plunger or a revolving door that could be used to wipe cylindrical walls clean; or a vacuum-driven shower-cleaning robot, similar to earthbound pool sweepers.

The really important thing, according to Frassanito, is that the space station should be self-cleaning as much as possible. After all, the station's personnel will be highly trained experts who are unlikely to appreciate being turned into high-priced window washers. One of Frassanito's contributions to the cause of maximum neatness with minimum effort — an idea that will appeal to children everywhere — is a self-making bed. His premise is that "an unmade bed is a depressing thing to look at." When in use, the bed — or "sleep restraint" — is rather like a semi-rigid sleeping bag that expands to assume the shape of the sleeper; otherwise, it collapses flat against the wall with its covering automatically stretched taut.

Actually, since sleep preferences in space are highly individual, it remains to be seen how many crew members will use sleep restraints at all. On the shuttle, some astronauts not only use a sleeping bag, but strap even their heads down; others sleep in their chairs or just tie a strap around one wrist and float free. Still others, like Marc Garneau, don't even bother to tether themselves. Aboard the space station, each crew member will have an individual enclosed sleep compartment about the size of a large closet, which will contain the bed, personal storage lockers and possibly a small desk and room for a microcomputer. This will afford an essential measure of privacy that astronauts don't currently enjoy.

The quality and variety of food will be another major factor affecting productivity. "Good food is a real morale builder," Perner said. "A meal ought to be something you enjoy, not endure, or we'd just use pills." The food aboard the shuttle leans toward camping trip cuisine, consisting mostly of pre-cooked, plastic-wrapped freeze-dried foods that are "rehydrated" by adding water. It's not exactly four-star fare and planners are hoping to offer a somewhat more appealing menu aboard the space station. Certainly, a much larger selection of food can be stored in the space station's supply module. "We can't expect people to live out of a tin can or a plastic jug for 90 days, so we need to learn to cook in space," Perner says. Among other things, this means developing the first space stove, but it is expected that an off-the-shelf microwave with a few modifications will do the job.

Experience on the shuttle has shown that, except for liquids, most foods manage to stay on the plate reasonably well in zero gravity, especially with a little help from a sticky sauce or gravy. Crumbs can be a real nuisance, though. The crew of the second Spacelab mission discovered this in a rather unorthodox way. This was a mission that carried two squirrel monkeys and 24 rats, and tiny bits and pieces of their food and feces ended up floating all over Spacelab. "The crumbs are all over. Please give instructions," Commander Robert Overmyer plaintively asked Mission Control. When the debris managed to migrate all the way through an eight-metre tunnel with two elbow bends into the shuttle cockpit, Overmyer was heard to grumble, with magnificent understatement, that "it's really discouraging to get monkey feces in the cockpit."

Greater variety in clothing, particularly in color, will also be permitted aboard the space station — one of the things the Skylab astronauts complained about was the "unimaginative wardrobe" — but NASA will probably always maintain some control over the clothing allowed on board, to minimize the risk of fire and environmental contamination. There are, of course, some special requirements for zero-gravity clothes: for example, they should have many pockets to store small items that would otherwise float away. They should also be adjustable to allow for the changes in body measurements that occur in zero-G. As for footwear, heavy shoes aren't needed and could be dangerous with people floating around. Many of the shuttle astronauts go barefoot or wear socks, but it may be necessary to design footwear that can be used for gripping and anchoring the body. Frassanito has designed a sock-like shoe with a lightweight aluminum sole; the toe section of the sole separates from the sock, providing a kind of "thumb" that can be used to grip things and to anchor the body to the floor. Frassanito has also designed little metal "mushrooms" on the shower floor that astronauts can slip their toes around to hold themselves down.

In the past, concerns about flammability and contamination have resulted in pretty drab space vehicles, but designers hope to use color, lighting and textures more imaginatively on the space station. "We'd like to liven [it] up a little," Perner said. Movable, multicolored walls and different colors and intensities of lighting are being studied, as are the effects these factors might have on task performance and on spatial perception. As for furnishings, chairs obviously aren't required in zero gravity, but an efficient method of anchoring the body will undoubtedly be needed from time to time. Although shuttle astronauts can perform many tasks floating free, they sometimes need the greater stability achieved by inserting their feet into loops attached to the floor. Aboard the space station, foot loops may not be suitable for long stretches in front of a microcomputer work station, but some method of restraint will be necessary to keep the user from floating away. "You either have to have your feet restrained — and, if that's the case for a long time, your legs and ankles start tiring — or your rear end has to be restrained," Perner said. Designers are studying a variety of foot restraints, waist tethers and even a kind of modified bicycle seat with a lap belt.

The work stations themselves must be designed to accommodate the "zero-gravity slump" — a position half-way between sitting and standing that the human body naturally assumes in weightlessness. Zero-G effects must also be considered in the design of the keyboards. Perner notes that, in zero gravity, the arms want to float up and apart, so keyboards designed on earth may seem too narrow in space. Splitting the keyboard in the middle and separating the two halves might be one solution, Perner said. "Keyboards as we know them now are a little bit too narrow; the keys are too close together." At least one preliminary microcomputer concept involves a machine that has a "mouse" input device in addition to the keyboard. Of course, the mouse must also be kept from floating free — probably with a magnet to hold it to a flat surface.

However, zero gravity does offer some advantages to computer users. For one thing, it gives new meaning to the term "portable computer" — you don't have to worry about the "weight" of the machine and you can literally use it anywhere, even on the "ceiling." It is expected that the microcomputers on the space station will be moved around and plugged in at various handy locations, including crew compartments.

NASA is giving a lot of attention to computer work stations because it plans extensive use of advanced microelectronics to make the station more "user-friendly" than other spacecraft. Even the shuttle was originally designed 10 to 15 years before the most explosive growth in microcomputer technology and its cockpit is literally covered with complicated switches and gauges. "When you go into any one of our spacecraft, it's just wall to wall switches," said Perner. "We don't want that any more; we want clean walls. We just don't have the room or the weight capability to use old concepts." Microelectronic systems are ideal because they are lightweight and portable, require little power and are "efficient and accurate and easy to learn," he said.

The computers will be multi-purpose machines, used not only to interact with the station's technical systems — for example, to control temperatures or turn valves off and on — but also for personal entertainment and communication with family and colleagues on earth. Frassanito, who designs computer systems, says that information flow will be one of the most important aspects of space station life. "You'd like to be able to have face-to-face conversations with your boss or your kids as though they were in the next room." Medical experts can be "beamed up" by teleconferencing for consultations. Sponsors of experiments being done in space will be able to use telecommunications systems to monitor the progress of work in space and to talk regularly to their space-based employees.

The units could also be used to monitor the status of the station itself. For example, Frassanito envisions crew members being able to use the computer, in combination with a free-flying robotic camera, to examine the exterior of the station. "You can go out and check the south forty or the bumps in the night, all from your bunk."

Frassanito noted that the space program has always been a driving force behind the tremendous technological advances in computing. The need to reduce the size of circuits for satellites and deep space systems "is why we have small computers today." During the launch of the Saturn V rocket, "more information was transmitted in digital form in the first 15 to 20 seconds than had been written by all mankind for all of time." He predicts that the space station program will continue this tradition and strongly reinforce many existing trends in computing, such as the integration of functions and the combination of different technologies — business and scientific computing, computer communications, digital compression and transmission, video and TV images, graphics, teleconferencing, speech synthesis, voice recognition, robotics and artificial intelligence. Over the next decade, the space program will accelerate the development of systems that can do it all and this should — as it has in the past — push the growth of the technology here on earth.

Computer communications, including video teleconferencing, will play a particularly important role in space station life. They will be essential not only for scientific, engineering and commercial activities but as a morale booster for the crew, to alleviate the sense of isolation crew members are likely to experience. Computer users on the station will likely become part of a global computer networking system. In fact, one NASA study has suggested that scientists on the station could use the on-board communications system to give lectures and conduct classes from space.[1] The two lectures that teacher Christa McAuliffe was going to broadcast during Mission 51-L would have been the progenitors of this concept.

All the attention being paid to human factors aboard the space station is to try to ensure that highly trained people will find long-term living in space pleasant and rewarding enough to sign up for repeat tours of duty. Because space station missions will last much longer than shuttle missions, entertainment and recreational activities will assume a greater importance and space station planners would like to link these activities as much as possible to the intensive exercise regime that astronauts will have to maintain. On long-duration missions, several hours of exercise a day may be needed to maintain muscle tone and combat the physical deconditioning of the human body that occurs in zero gravity. The objective is to make this exercise as enjoyable as possible, Perner said. For example, he said, the bicycle and treadmill could be positioned in front of one of the station's windows so that astronauts can watch the world go by — an activity that most shuttle astronauts have reported as a source of continuing fascination. Frassanito has also suggested that sophisticated audio-visual aids could be used to bring a little bit of earth up to the space station. "You've got the birds chirping, the whole bit," Perner said. "That has really got to be an incentive to get on the bicycle and do a little hard work."

On the whole, however, designers do not anticipate that most people will have trouble adapting psychologically to life in zero-G. Experience on the Skylab missions and the shuttle has demonstrated that many early concerns did not materialize. Most people come to enjoy weightlessness, even those who initially suffer from motion sickness. In fact, Frassanito commented, astronauts returning to earth often resent having to carry around a body — "a 170-pound bag of concrete" — again. "You watch these folks spinning around and they are obviously enjoying themselves. It's apparent that zero gravity is preferable in many ways to one gravity. It's not only better, it's fun."

Designing things for zero-G does pose some difficulties for earthbound engineers, who may suffer from what has been referred to as "geo-chauvinism" — a sense of the "right" way to do things based on a life lived in 1-G. The trick is to learn to "think zero-G," says Larry Bell — not an easy thing to do for people who have never experienced the real thing. Bell said that many common tasks are easier in space — you don't need stairs, you don't have a problem moving "heavy" objects, you don't have to worry about access to out-of-the-way places, you can use all the available space and people can even work upside down with respect to each other. On the other hand, there are unique problems — people have to find "clever ways to anchor themselves. You don't put things in drawers — you put them in bags and pockets." You build gadgets with latches and hinges instead of using screws that will float off.

Chris Perner said that a certain amount of "geo-chauvinism" will be necessary in the training program. Many aspects of the space station must be replicated in ground-based simulators which, of course, must operate in 1-G; thus a true zero-G design could hamper the people who train astronauts on the ground. "When we build our mock-ups and trainers, we'd like something that people can walk in. But we're going to try very hard not to let training and the ease of using mock-ups on earth be a design constraint." The shuttle should be available for testing some equipment in zero-G before the station is built and a great deal of training will likely take place on board the space station itself once it's in operation, particularly after NASA builds up a cadre of experienced astronauts who have done repeat tours of duty.

The exact nature of space station life is difficult to predict at present, but in the initial stages, the major activities will likely fall into three main categories: maintenance and continuing construction of the space station infrastructure, scientific research and commercial and industrial materials processing research and development. Materials processing — the manufacturing in space of products such as drugs, optical fibres, semiconductors and new alloys — has been described as the infant of commercial space activities. Certainly, it is still very much in the pre-commercial stage. Yet much of the justification for spending billions of dollars on the space station infrastructure rests on the expectation that commercial space activities will generate billions of dollars in annual revenues after the turn of the century.

As with all crystal-ball gazing, however, these projections must be viewed with considerable caution, particularly since operating experience with materials processing in space is still quite limited (and nearly non-existent in Canada). The private sector was slow to develop a serious interest in space materials processing, put off by the high cost and difficulty of operating in space, by the lack of an immediate return on investment, and by the possibility that improvements in earth-based processes could overtake space-based processing techniques. Doing R&D in space remains expensive, time-consuming and fraught with technical setbacks even under normal conditions — and the prospect of utter disaster is still with us, as demonstrated by the extraordinary series of launch explosions, including the Challenger accident, in the first half of 1986.

Even if the estimates of vast profits from space processing prove to be true, the 10- to 15-year pay-back period will be much longer than the three- to five-year time frame most investors generally prefer. The space manufacturing industry is likely to require at least two or three decades to reach maturity. Judith Rosenblum of Coopers & Lybrand, a large management consulting firm that has done several studies on the prospects for business in space, said in 1984 that "it would be extremely difficult for anyone to lay out an economic analysis that proves the space station is a good investment." But she added that "what we always come around to in our analysis is the question of whether we can afford not to build the station." The situation has been compared to the days when governments built transcontinental railways to open the West. Brad Meslin of the Center for Space Policy Incorporated, a Boston-based consulting firm that specializes in business in space, said that no one in 1840 "could imagine a fraction of the economic potential that would eventually be realized by opening up the West." Leonard David of the U.S. National Space Institute has suggested that an appropriate name for the first station would be "Blind Faith 1."

In view of these realities, industry analysts warned of the dangers of too much hype and of the backlash that might occur when the inevitable technical troubles and setbacks start happening. "We believe that space commercialization will happen, will be strong and will work ... [but] some people are going to get burned financially and some businesses are going to fail," said one analyst. *Aviation Week and Space Technology* magazine has noted that, "as with any newly emerging field of enterprise, there is a wide range of opportunities open to early entrants. One of these is the opportunity to go bankrupt."

Projections of the economic returns from space processing by the turn of the century are being revised downward in the aftermath of the Challenger accident and it is still difficult to determine what the long-term impact will be. Certainly, the timing could hardly have been worse. Industrial interest in materials processing in space had only just begun to pick up, parallelled, in a kind of chicken-and-egg fashion, by the necessary development of new technical facilities needed to carry out processing experiments in space. By 1985, such experiments were becoming

311

a regular feature of shuttle and Spacelab missions and 1986 had promised to be the first really big year for research in this field. The Challenger accident put everything on hold; the suspension of flights for a minimum of two years halted, at least temporarily, a number of promising commercial projects just as they were beginning to gain momentum.

Two of the most enthusiastic corporate supporters of space commercialization, McDonnell Douglas Astronautics and 3M, had several major shuttle experiments planned for 1986. Both companies have made a serious long-term commitment of their own resources — both money and research personnel — to doing research in space, but it is uncertain how long these commitments can survive the delay in shuttle flights. Perhaps even more serious for the long-term picture, 3M was forced to suspend negotiations with NASA for 72 flight opportunities over ten years. The company said it must have assured access to microgravity in order to continue its long-term commitment to space research, but NASA is re-examining its ability and willingness to commit so much shuttle space to a single company. This is unfortunate, because 3M has been one of the most forward-looking companies and, even more unusual, one willing to take risks. "The greatest risk, in our view, would be a lack of timely progress on the learning curve for space," said Lester Krough, 3M's vice president of R&D. "A wait-and-see posture could endanger a company's competitive edge considerably more, in the long run, than its attempt to move out ahead."

David Lippy, president of the Center for Space Policy, believes that companies that have already made a serious commitment will ride out the delay. Their reasons for getting involved in space "have not changed one iota. They hope that there will be a technical solution to solve the problem and that we will move forward. I don't think that this will cause them to waver one bit." Geraldine Kenney-Wallace, a professor of chemistry and physics at the University of Toronto who has been working with U.S. industry on space projects, agreed that such companies have made commitments that will "take them far into the 1990s and beyond, and it seems to me that they're going to hang in and keep the faith." Evidence of this was provided by the Boeing Aerospace Company of Seattle, Washington, which, in May, 1986, entered an agreement with NASA to fly materials processing experiments on three future shuttle flights. Coming before the Challenger accident report was released and before there was any realistic idea of when shuttle flights would resume, this was a much-needed demonstration of faith in NASA and in the future of manned commercial operations in space.

Kenny-Wallace said that many companies involved in shuttle projects would not find a short delay in shuttle flights entirely unwelcome; the need to analyze the results from one set of experiments in time to prepare for the next flight was putting a lot of pressure on them. "At this stage, you must build on your previous measurements each time. These are very expensive flights; you're not just going to send up many different experiments and see if one works. The breathing space is appreciated — but they don't want too much breathing space." Roy VanKoughnett, director of space research operations for the NRC's space division, agreed that "a lot of experiment development activity can usefully profit from more time on earth, more thinking it through" and this will increase the probability of later success in space. "On the other hand, the downside is that people are less interested in and enthusiastic about something that's going to happen three years away."

The reaction of companies that had not yet entered the game, and of the business community generally, was more difficult to predict. Lippy said that the accident had the potential to create a "severe and negative impact" among what he called the "sideline observers." "These are people whose corporate board of directors can only react to what they read in the press. They would shy away from spending money because it's always a difficult chore to convince people up and down the corporate ladder to move in a new direction." Unfortunately, these companies had just begun to think about a potential investment in space research. "It looked like a banner year working with those typical non-aerospace Fortune 1000 companies who were looking to a new market, new ideas ... new opportunities."

Kenney-Wallace said uncertainty about the future is likely to deter companies not already firmly committed to doing space research. "It's really an enormous commitment of manpower and time. You've got to pull your staff off what they're normally doing; you have to essentially set up a separate space agency within your company."

Interestingly enough, the worst damage to NASA's reputation within the business community was caused not so much by its technical failures as by revelations of the serious deficiencies in its management procedures and its attention to safety. A pervading sense of disappointment — a sense that NASA had let everyone down — grew steadily through the months of investigation into the accident, culminating in the strongly worded report of the presidential inquiry. At the same time, there was a strong feeling that NASA could ultimately correct and rise above its technical and managerial setbacks and that the program would move on. Both the inquiry report and President Reagan endorsed this approach.

The future of space commercialization projects obviously was seriously affected, at least in the near term. When flights resume — NASA hopes by early 1988 — undoubtedly a very conservative approach will be taken for safety reasons. This means shuttle crews will be small at first and probably restricted only to NASA career astronauts. It may be some time before payload specialists from industry and from other countries are allowed to fly again and the backlog of competing demands for shuttle space will be considerable. Further restrictions will be caused by the priority that will be given to military payloads. The Air Force has an almost pre-emptive claim on shuttle flights and Major General Donald Kutyna, a member of the Challenger inquiry panel, estimated that some 45 shuttle military flights would be needed before 1992, which works out to an average of nine flights a year in the five years from 1988 to 1992. Even if NASA resumes flying in 1988, it will be hard pressed to achieve nine flights a year in the early stages; if the military had its way, it could easily take up all available shuttle launches well into the next decade. On the other hand, in the wake of the Challenger accident, there was strong sentiment in the United States to move to a mix of shuttle and expendable launches for both military and commercial payloads. Expendables will undoubtedly take some of the load off the shuttle's back.

However, NASA will be operating with only a three-shuttle fleet until about 1992, when the replacement oribiter is to be delivered. In mid-1986, Isaac Gillam, NASA's associate administrator for commercial programs, said that NASA had not determined the priority that commercial payloads would receive or which companies would be offered the first flight opportunities. "We have to assume there'll be empty lockers" for commercial payloads, said Gillam. One U.S. Congressman has expressed concern that the limitations of operating a three-shuttle fleet will force NASA to choose "the biggest, most conservative aerospace operators now in place, guys with fairly limited visions of what can be done, not the dreamers and thinkers toward the future that exist in small, entrepreneurial-type businesses."

Space offers several potentially exploitable environmental variables — including extremes of temperature and a nearly complete vacuum — but its unique feature, and the one most useful for materials processing, is what is commonly referred to as zero gravity. The term zero gravity is actually a misnomer — objects in orbit are actually in "free fall" and still under the influence of earth's gravity. At the altitude of the space station, gravitational effects are only about one-millionth of those on earth. For most purposes, this can be considered essentially zero gravity; however, even minute gravity forces can have important effects on materials processing experiments, so the term *microgravity* is more commonly used in reference to space processing.

Throughout all of human history — indeed, during the nearly four billion years the earth has existed — the force of gravity on earth (by definition one-gravity or "1-G") has been virtually unvarying. For most of that time, it has been impossible to reproduce microgravity conditions on earth, and even now, modern technology permits this to be done for only seconds at a time. Thus, all industrial processes have been developed with 1-G as a constant. Many of them, especially those involving fluids, are significantly and often adversely affected by gravity, often in subtle ways that have proved difficult to understand properly without the *absence* of gravity.

Space processing programs focus on two different kinds of research: developing and eventually manufacturing new products in space that are difficult or impossible to produce on earth; and using the microgravity environment to gain a better understanding of gravity effects to improve earth-based processing. The Soviet Union, the United States and European countries, notably West Germany, have been doing materials processing research since early tests in the 1970s demonstrated that space processing could offer many advantages.

On earth, convection currents, sedimentation and other effects due to gravity cause imperfections, impurities and inefficiencies in the processing of many materials, such as molten metals and alloys, glasses and ceramics, biological substances and crystals used to make electronic components. A major problem on earth is convection, circular flows that occur in a fluid when warmer (less dense) fluid rises and cooler (more dense) fluid settles under the influence of gravity; this inhibits the uniform mixing of different substances. In any situation involving molten materials with widely different densities, the effects of gravity can make uniform mixing virtually impossible. Sedimentation — the tendency of solid particles to settle out of a liquid — can also cause problems. In other cases, the separation of useful substances from contaminants in a solution can be frustrated by gravity on earth, making it difficult and expensive to produce such things as drugs, crystals and semiconductor materials with desired levels of purity and uniformity.

In microgravity, these problems are greatly reduced and many important materials can be produced in much larger quantities or sizes, more quickly and/or in a much purer form than on earth. Crystals, which are used in optical and electronic devices, can be grown tens to hundreds of times larger in microgravity and with fewer imperfections. New alloys that could not be made at all on earth can be produced in space. "Containerless" processing is also possible in microgravity, eliminating another source of impurities — chemical reactions with the walls of containers. Biological separation techniques in microgravity can produce much larger and purer quantities of some important drugs than are possible on earth. Basic research has also been done to study the solidification of molten materials in space and to gain a better understanding of the behavior of various fluids in microgravity. These experiments are intended both to improve earth-based processes and research and to develop or improve technologies used in space.

Research efforts to date have begun to demonstrate what may be technically feasible in space processing, but while such feasibility is a necessary condition to establish a viable space manufacturing industry, it clearly is not a sufficient condition. There is no getting around the fact that space processing is extremely expensive at present, in part because entirely new technologies must be developed for operating in microgravity and also because the cost of transporting people and equipment into space is still very high.

In order to entice private companies and investors into this new high-risk form of business, at least in the R&D phase of their ventures, NASA was forced to develop new strategies to minimize the costs and share the risks. In late 1984, the agency announced that to reduce technical risks, NASA would perform its own research to develop new space technologies and transfer them to industry. And to reduce financial risks and institutional obstacles, NASA established a variety of R&D incentive programs. For example, under its technical exchange program, researchers can use NASA's ground facilities at no cost to determine if doing experiments in space is justified. And under its Joint Endeavor Agreement (JEA) program, NASA shares in the costs and risk of doing the space experiments by providing space on shuttle flights free of charge and by training industrial personnel to fly as members of the shuttle crew to perform space processing experiments. In return, NASA obtains the use of any space processing hardware developed and access to the data obtained and it expects to be reimbursed for later shuttle flights if the venture proves profitable. NASA also tried to streamline the procedures — and therefore the amount of time — required to get experiments aboard the shuttle. Finally, NASA established a policy to buy new space-made products, as long as the agency has a need for the products and the private company producing them has put its own resources at risk in doing the space research.

One of the most important trends is the teaming of aerospace companies, which have the expertise to build new space hardware, and non-aerospace "user" companies, such as pharmaceutical or electronics firms, which might be interested in manufacturing their products in space. Lippy said that teaming between large corporations and smaller, more entrepreneurial companies is also important. "I used to think it was going to be the entrepreneurial kinds of guys that would be the trail blazers. I don't believe that any more. It'll be what I call a Big Brother relationship, where the small guy has the enthusiasm and the energy ... [and] the big company has the technological abilities and the deep pockets."

The universities are also playing an important role, especially since much of this research, even though ultimately aimed at commercial development, is still at a basic research level. To promote teaming arrangements between industry and universities, NASA has given five U.S. universities about US$1-million each for up to five years to establish new Centres for Commercial Development of Space, which then attracted corporate backers to match the NASA funds. By May, 1986, NASA had received

317

applications from 25 universities, research institutes and government and industry laboratories and it planned to establish as many as seven more centres before the end of the year.

As Kenney-Wallace said, space research "ends up stirring up an awful lot of activity on earth." In many cases, scientists who want to understand how a process works in space realize they "don't even know the answer to this question on earth. For every project that stimulates space-based activity, it is not at all uncommon for maybe two or three earth-based projects to be stimulated to match it."

With time and experience, the cost of materials processing in space will decrease, as new technologies are proved out, permanent facilities are established and processes become more routine and automated. Nevertheless, in most cases, space manufacturing is likely to remain quite expensive for some time, and in order to attract private investment, it must offer significant advantages over earth-based processing. Initially, at least, this is most likely to occur with products that are already extremely expensive, difficult or impossible to produce on earth.

Because of the transportation costs, actual manufacturing in space may be limited to low-weight, low-volume products. For example, the first commercial space-processed materials produced are highly uniform microscopic latex spheres; some 15 million can fit in a vial the size of a little finger. NASA produced the spheres for the U.S. National Bureau of Standards and they are being sold to industries that use them as measuring standards — essentially very tiny rulers. The very smallest of these can be made on earth, but gravity effects prevent the formation of larger perfectly formed spheres (ten-millionths of a metre, about the size of a red blood cell). It is expected that space processing will be used to produce spheres ranging from 10- to 100-millionths of a metre.

But weight and volume are not the sole considerations. Given the high costs of doing R&D in space, it has been estimated that a product must be worth at least $20,000 per kilogram to justify manufacturing it in space. Products that offer the greatest potential include biologicals and pharmaceuticals; crystals and other semiconductor materials; ceramics and glasses; and metals and alloys. Large U.S. corporations have already started research on these materials, often in joint ventures with universities and with

NASA's research centres. Although much of this work is proprietary, it is possible to give an overview of emerging trends.

•*Biologicals and pharmaceuticals:* Microgravity processing can be used to produce large and extremely pure quantities of important drugs, such as interferon and monoclonal antibodies (experimental drugs used in the treatment of cancer), insulin, urokinase (an enzyme that dissolves blood clots), human growth hormone and others. Because pharmaceuticals are so valuable — single drugs have produced revenues in the billions of dollars — they are considered likely to be the first space-produced materials to pay off. Brad Meslin of the Center for Space Policy has said that "in the long term, the first pharmaceutical product developed on the shuttle that results in a significant advance against disease will all by itself justify forever the economic investment in the shuttle."

Drugs are particularly good candidates for space processing because in many cases, producing them on earth is already very expensive and they have a very high value-to-weight ratio. Some candidate drugs are estimated to be worth millions of dollars per kilogram; interferon has a market value estimated at about US$250,000 per *gram*. In some cases, drug processing in space may actually be less expensive than on earth; one study estimated that the production cost of urokinase could be reduced from US$1200 to US$100 a dose. (One researcher commented that producing a single dose of urokinase on earth requires "88 man-urine days.")

Several space experiments to date have employed an important biological separation technique, called electrophoresis, which involves separating biological substances in solution into different streams by subjecting them to an electrical field. The process has been used for many years, but convection and gravity forces limit its effectiveness on earth. Shuttle experiments have demonstrated a seven-hundred-fold increase in the quantity of drug produced in microgravity, and a four- to five-fold improvement in purity, compared with earth-based electrophoretic processing.

There is also a great deal of interest in using electrophoresis to produce monoclonal antibodies in space. Though still largely experimental, these substances, which are produced by living cells, are believed to have great potential in the early diagnosis and treatment of cancer and other diseases. However, producing the large quantities that would be needed for extensive research and therapeutic use is difficult and expensive; at present it would cost hundreds of thousands of dollars to produce a kilogram by conventional earth-based methods. A large number of research institutions and companies are investigating both new bioengineering techniques and the potential of space-based processing to increase antibody production. Space experiments have already demonstrated that the volume of cellular products produced by live cells in microgravity can be hundreds of times greater than on earth.

Another field that is creating a great deal of excitement is the production of protein crystals in microgravity. These organic crystals are believed to be the key to developing a whole range of powerful new drugs to combat cancer, high blood pressure and rejection of transplanted organs. However, earth's gravity makes it nearly impossible to grow protein crystals large enough to characterize their atomic structure. Detailed knowledge of protein crystal structure is a vital piece of information needed in order to bioengineer new drugs that work either with or against the atomic structure of bodily proteins to combat disease. On earth, gravity effects prevent the laboratory production of all but 100 of the estimated half-million proteins involved in human diseases. "If the proteins at the heart of most viruses and bacteria can be enlarged to reveal their structure, then these dreams of treating diseases from arthritis to influenza are real," says Richard Halpern, NASA's director of microgravity sciences.

In a West German experiment on the space shuttle, one type of protein crystal grew 1000 times larger than it did on earth, and another grew 30 times larger. In another test a protein crystal grew, within four days, to a size that normally takes six to eight weeks to grow on earth. Three large U.S. pharmaceutical companies — SmithKline Beckman Corporation, Schering Corporation and Upjohn Company — working in conjunction with U.S. universities flew protein crystal growth experiments aboard the shuttle in 1985.

Space processing of drugs does, however, face competition from earth-based bioengineering techniques. When it entered the space processing field in a big way in the early 1980s, McDonnell Douglas projected annual sales of US$1-billion for pharmaceuticals before the turn of the century. McDonnell Douglas and the Ortho Pharmaceutical Division of Johnson & Johnson, in a joint venture with NASA, performed pioneering drug processing experiments on half a dozen shuttle flights in 1984 and 1985, including three missions in which McDonnell Douglas engineer Charles Walker was a member of the crew, making him the first privately employed person to fly on the shuttle. Ortho had planned to start marketing the first space-processed drug[2] by 1988 and had identified half a dozen other biological products they believed could be profitably produced in space. However, in a surprising turnaround in September, 1985, Ortho suddenly dropped out of the space project because it believed that new ground-based bioengineering methods might lead to a marketable product 12 to 18 months earlier than if it went with the space-produced product. McDonnell Douglas believed that space processing would pay off in the long run because it would produce a cheaper and much purer form of the drug — factors that will make it competitive because it must be taken in repeated doses — and pursued the space project with a new partner, the Riker Laboratories Division of 3M Corporation. After the shuttle disaster, these negotiations fell through due to "timing and competition" but McDonnell Douglas continued to seek a partner to test and market the drug. These events came as a disturbing setback to the industry and have inevitably prompted some re-evaluation of the economic prospects for space commercial activities.

• *Crystals and Semiconductors:* In microgravity it is possible to grow large, pure crystals for use in manufacturing a wide variety of important high-technology products: semiconductors, computer chips, high-density electrooptical data storage devices, high-density, high-speed recording devices, lasers, microwave systems, solar cells, sensors, radiation detectors and many more. Silicon has been the mainstay of electronics to date, but now attention is turning toward new materials such as gallium arsenide (GaAs), germanium, cadmium mercury telluride (CMT), iridium phosphide, mercuric iodide and a variety of others. It is expected that these materials will play a vital role in the next phase of the electronics revolution.

Gallium arsenide in particular is commanding a great deal of attention. In 1984, worldwide sales of GaAs amounted to about US$75-million, a distant second to silicon's US$1-billion. But it has been estimated that by 1990, the world market will reach about $1-billion for bulk GaAs and $5-billion for GaAs semiconductors. GaAs has been described by one expert as "by

321

far the most technologically mature of all leading edge semi-conductor materials." It has several superior features — it conducts electricity more than five times faster than silicon, it has better optical properties, it can operate at higher frequencies and is more resistant to radiation. GaAs is expected to become increasingly important for use in high speed data processing systems, in fibre optic data transmission systems, in optical devices such as lasers and photodetectors and in circuits that combine optical and electronic components on a single chip. The faster computing speed and radiation tolerance of gallium arsenide makes it of particular interest to the military, which requires radiation-"hardened" space technologies. This material is considered essential for the Star Wars program.

The molecules in a crystal are organized in an orderly structure, a lattice pattern; the more regular the pattern, the better the crystal. This orderly structure gives crystals important qualities, such as strength and ability to conduct electricity. Crystals can be grown in several different ways. One method involves mixing different solutions in a way that forces organic chemicals to crystallize out of the solution. "On earth, crystals are affected by gravity and fall to the bottom of chemical reactors where they cluster like lumps of coal in a pile," said Christopher Chow, manager of 3M's space research lab. "In space, crystals grow separately without falling and the molecules that make up the crystals position themselves as precisely as tiny ceramic tiles." Thus the space crystals not only grow to much larger sizes, but are much more uniform than earth-grown crystals. 3M Corporation has used this method in experiments aboard the shuttle to grow crystals that have important potential electrooptical applications.

Another method of crystal growth that can be improved in microgravity involves depositing material in vapor form onto a small "seed" crystal so that it grows larger. On earth, gravity effects cause imperfections to occur during crystal growth, limiting the size of high-quality crystals. Contamination from containers is also a problem. Experiments on the shuttle have shown that these problems can be reduced in microgravity; tests with mercuric iodide have shown that the crystal grows five to ten times faster in space than on earth and that space-grown crystals have fewer imperfections. One space-grown mercury iodide crystal, about the size of a sugar cube, was estimated to be worth millions of dollars; it was sliced into thin wafers to be used in earth-based research projects. These crystals can be used in space telescopes and they could also have military and industrial applications. For example, they are used in X-ray and gamma-ray detectors to reduce radiation exposure in patients receiving X-rays and CAT scans.

• *Glasses and Ceramics:* Research on microgravity processing of glasses and ceramics is not as far advanced as that on pharmaceuticals and crystals. However, it has been estimated that, by the turn of the century, there could be a multi-billion-dollar annual market for ultra-pure glasses and ceramics produced in space. Potential applications include fibre optic communications systems, lasers, power generation systems, fusion energy systems, insulating foams, and high-speed computers. Space-produced ceramics — long-wearing, self-lubricating and almost indestructible — might be used in new automobile engines.

Glasses and ceramics are non-metallic materials that are typically processed at very high temperatures. Containerless processing in microgravity offers the potential for creating very pure, bubble-free glasses and ceramics and it is possible that entirely new types of specialty glasses that cannot be made on earth at all can be produced in space. "The range of glasses with useful properties can be expanded significantly," said S. E. Prasad of B.M. Hi-Tech Incorporated, an Ontario company that has done studies on the potential of glass processing in space for the National Research Council.

• *Metals and Alloys:* Convection and gravity effects cause imperfections to occur when molten materials solidify. But in space, these effects are greatly reduced and completely uniform mixing of the molten materials is possible, resulting in the production of much less flawed metals and alloys. Microgravity also makes it possible to create new alloys using materials of widely different densities; these often cannot be manufactured at all on earth. On one Spacelab flight, a strong but lightweight aluminum-zinc alloy was made in which the two metals were much more uniformly mixed than would be the case on earth, where gravity would cause the aluminum to fall out while the molten mixture was cooling.

Containerless melting and solidification of metals could be employed to reduce impurities. It isn't necessary to put molten materials into a container in microgravity because they will remain suspended. But they can't be allowed to simply float free either; they must be confined in some way. One method being investigated involves the use of acoustic levitation to keep the molten materials in place. In another Spacelab experiment, liquid drops were suspended and spun into different shapes by an acoustic levitation system. The results of this test were used to improve ground-based fluids research and to prepare for further experiments in metal and glass processing in space.

NASA has been attempting to interest the aviation and auto industries in the potential for developing strong but lightweight metals and composite plastics. General Motors and 3M have started a multi-million-dollar joint venture to produce test samples of a common automotive plastic in microgravity. (The first flight of this experiment, which had been scheduled for July, 1986, was yet another casualty of the Challenger accident.)

At present, much of the research on space processing of metals and alloys is focussed primarily on improving ground-based processing of metals. For example, John Deere & Company, a farm equipment manufacturer with US$4-billion in annual sales, planned iron processing experiments aboard the shuttle to improve its ground-based iron foundry processes and to increase the service life of components in the machinery it sells. Deere has been negotiating with General Motors to enter into a joint project to conduct shuttle experiments on solidification of iron to further enhance earth-based processing techniques.

Metals are less likely to be actually manufactured in space than drugs, glasses or crystals; they generally do not sell for a high enough price to justify the cost. However, metals manufacturing in space may be feasible in the future for some types of alloys that cannot be produced on earth and that prove useful in the construction of large space structures, such as the space station.

Industrial interest in materials processing in space has started to pick up worldwide. Efforts in both the U.S. and the Soviet Union accelerated during the mid-1980s and Europe and Japan also began to move into the field in a big way. Through ESA, several European countries have started to do space experiments, particularly aboard Spacelab. West Germany has shown the greatest interest. It committed nearly US$200-million to buy the entire cargo bay for two space shuttle flights and much of this money was put into materials processing research. The first mission, Spacelab D1, was completed in November, 1985; it carried equipment for a large number of materials processing experiments in fluid physics, crystal growth, separation of liquids and the solidification of glass, metals, alloys and composite materials. The second mission had been scheduled for late 1988. In addition the French national space agency (CNES) flew a mercuric oxide crystal growth experiment on the Spacelab 3 mission in April, 1985.

In October, 1985, a new European marketing organization, Intospace, was established to promote commercial space activities. The biggest shareholders, from both the aerospace industry and non-aerospace "user" companies, are German and Italian. Intospace, which is based in Germany, is expected to lose money for the first five years and its founding companies have agreed to cover losses up to US$2.6-million. However, it is hoped that the company will generate much more than this in space business — for example, promoting the purchase of Spacelab missions at tens of millions of dollars a shot. The Europeans are also exploring the potential of marketing pressurized modules of the type being developed as part of the Columbus space station program.

The Japanese have been described by U.S. space processing experts as "really aggressive" in the materials processing field. Japan had bought shuttle cargo space on a flight originally scheduled for January, 1988, and it has shown a great deal of interest recently in space-based pharmaceutical production. McDonnell Douglas has signed Mitsubishi as its representative in Japan.

It is estimated that the Soviet Union has performed more than 1500 materials processing experiments in space and that its program is three to four times larger than NASA's. In October, 1984, Vladimir Solovoyov, one of three Soviet cosmonauts who set a record of 237 days in space, said that the Soviet Union is "approaching the stage" of putting space factories into orbit. A year later, in October, 1985, the Soviets launched a large new module, which was attached to the Salyut space station, nearly doubling its size. The module includes a vehicle capable of returning to earth on its own, which will allow Soviet cosmonauts to remain in space while sending to earth several hundred kilograms of military intelligence data or research products, such as materials from space processing experiments.

Canadian industry has been considerably slower off the mark on space materials research than the other major players. The reasons for this include the high costs and risks, the conservatism and risk-aversion of Canadian industry and investors and their lack of awareness of new developments in the space processing field, and a lack of government programs to promote and support the entry of Canadian industry into this field. It is clear that a great deal of public funding will be needed in the early years to prime the pump. Canadian companies will, in any event, be hampered by their small size, limited financial resources and lack of R&D experience, compared with many U.S., European and Japanese companies.

Only a handful of Canadian materials experiments had been done in space before the Challenger accident and none was sponsored by Canadian industry. The experiments — two designed to investigate how materials are degraded by the space environment and one that involved the separation of biological materials in microgravity — were developed by university and government scientists.

Researchers at the University of Toronto, the federal Department of Communications and the National Research Council investigated the damage done by the space environment to materials used for spacecraft structures and insulation. These include new composites — strong but lightweight materials, typically consisting of various types of fibres imbedded in a glue-like resin — which are being widely used in the automotive and aviation industries on earth as well as for space hardware.[3] Until the advent of the shuttle, these materials were never returned to earth, so it was difficult to evaluate the extent and nature of long-term damage.

One of the Canadian experiments involved putting such samples aboard an unmanned satellite, known as LDEF, which was left in space by the shuttle and has yet to be recovered. The other — the advanced composite materials exposure experiment (ACOMEX) — involved samples strapped on the Canadarm during Marc Garneau's shuttle mission. When the samples were subsequently analyzed, the results were rather shocking: they showed that the environment in low earth orbit seriously damages and alters the properties of these materials. The Canadarm was pointed in the direction of the shuttle's flight to expose the materials to the most aggressive environment; total exposure time was 38 hours and the fact that the materials were so badly damaged in such a short time was very disquieting, since they will likely be used on space structures intended for long-duration missions. "Clearly the materials problem will be a key issue with the space station," said ACOMEX principal investigator David Zimcik of the Department of Communications. "In 30 years, there are a lot of 38-hour periods."

The samples included: carbon-epoxy and kevlar-epoxy composites, potential structural materials; a thin film of kapton, an insulating material; and several protective paints and coating films. Also included was material that might be used as SVS targets on spacecraft. The kapton lost 60 per cent of its mass and its thermal properties were altered. Its normally smooth-looking surface took on an irregular "rug-like" appearance. Specimens of epoxy resin, used as a matrix to hold fibres in composite materials, were riddled with holes. The fibres in carbon-epoxy composites had been attacked and the samples were so severely eroded that they were "nothing more than porous remnants" when they were returned to earth, according to Zimcik. "It's just devastating. I am amazed at the aggressiveness with which these things have been attacked." Rod Tennyson, a professor of aerospace engineering at the University of Toronto's Institute for Aerospace Studies, said the samples "look like Swiss cheese."

Researchers believe the damage is caused by atomic oxygen in low earth orbit. Although the oxygen is not very dense at the shuttle's orbital altitude — usually between about 200 and 300 km — the shuttle plows through it at nearly 29,000 km per hour, resulting in a high rate of flow across exposed surfaces. Zimcik added that even satellites that normally operate in higher orbits could be affected because they will be put into low orbit by the shuttle before being boosted to their operational orbits; in future they may also be returned to lower orbits for repair and refurbishment. "Even the short time spent in shuttle orbit ... may have serious effects on exposed materials," he said.

Another member of the research team, Paul McLean of the National Research Council, questioned whether atomic oxygen alone is responsible and he suggested that chemical reactions, not impact damage, may be the cause of the problem. Laboratory tests indicate that an electrically charged surface suffers twice as much weight loss as an uncharged surface, he said, suggesting that it's possible the shuttle may perturb its own immediate environment in such a way that insulating surfaces become charged.

Research is continuing to assess the protective abilities of various coating materials. Some coatings used in the ACOMEX experiment did protect the materials. Zimcik said, "We're reasonably optimistic that we will be able to overcoat and protect these materials from attack without increasing the weight or changing the properties of the materials."

"We know we cannot fly these materials in the bare state; [they] have to be protected," said Tennyson, who participated in the ACOMEX experiment and was the principal investigator for the LDEF experiment. He said that NASA is projecting recovery of LDEF sometime in 1988 or 1989. If it is not retrieved by 1990, its orbit will begin to decay and it may be lost for good; at some point, it will start tumbling too much to be grabbed by the Canadarm and will eventually re-enter the earth's atmosphere and be burned up. If the recovery is made on time, the materials samples will have been exposed to the space environment for three to four years; Tennyson hopes they'll still be in fairly good shape and says the longer exposure may provide even better data than expected. In any event, there will be a record of what happened to the samples during the first 14 months because a data-collecting system was installed aboard LDEF.

Tennyson has used the results of the ACOMEX experiment to develop a simulation facility for screening materials on the ground to pick the most promising ones for use in satellites and other space hardware. It is critical that the simulator accurately reproduce the effects of the real space environment and the data collected on Garneau's shuttle mission has helped Tennyson to do this. Previously, damage in the simulator occurred far too slowly, because the atomic oxygen was not moving as fast past the materials as it does in space. Now, with improvements to incorporate the velocity factor, a day in the simulator can match a day in space, and in fact the process can be accelerated so that a day in the simulator can be made to cause the same amount of damage as months in space. This is particularly important for testing materials intended to survive the space environment for years or decades. Tennyson is particularly interested in the effect the damage has on the response of composite materials to the extremes of heat and cold in space. Materials can be designed not to contract or expand under extreme temperatures, but the loss of mass and the degradation of fibres now known to occur may change these properties.

This type of research has been characterized as research on materials *for* space, as distinguished from research on materials *in* space. One example of the latter type was a Canadian experiment on the separation of biological substances in microgravity done on shuttle mission 51-D in April, 1985. Developed by Donald Brooks, a chemistry professor at the University of British Columbia, the experiment was designed to determine whether a technique called "phase partitioning," used to obtain pure samples of cells, works better in microgravity than it does on earth. This research is expected to have implications for the treatment of diseases such as cancer and diabetes. For example, it would be useful for separating tumor cells from healthy "stem" cells in bone marrow; this would produce "clean" stem cells that would be injected into a patient receiving a bone marrow transplant.

The process involves the use of two solutions (phases) that do not mix with each other but separate into different layers (similar to what happens with oil and vinegar). If small particles of other substances are added, some will attach to one of the solutions and will be separated from the other materials in the mixture. (For example, pepper added to a mixture of oil and vinegar will preferentially attach to the oil.) This technique can be used to separate biological cells, but the efficiency of the process on earth is affected by gravity. In the case of cancer of the blood system, for example, all cells from bone marrow (where both good and cancerous cells replicate) would be extracted; the cancerous cells would then be separated out and the normal cells reinjected. This treatment requires an extremely good separation process and is far from being a reality at present. Scientists are currently trying to find solutions that will attract biological cells on the basis of certain specific features — for example, the electrical properties of their surface membranes. Brooks said being able to separate cells according to a variety of different properties would be very useful; it might, for example, permit separation of two kinds of tumor cells that have no physical differences but may differ in their degree of malignancy.

The experiment on Mission 51-D required a payload specialist[4] to shake a clear, cigar box-sized container with several chambers containing different solutions. The subsequent separation of the test solutions was then photographed, and it was discovered that they separated more quickly than anticipated.

Brooks is planning a similar experiment for Steve MacLean to do on his shuttle mission. Different test solutions will be used and the effect of electrical fields on the solutions will also be assessed.

Zimcik, Tennyson and McLean also plan a follow-up to the ACOMEX experiment on MacLean's flight, to explore further the effect of atomic oxygen in degrading materials that will be used on satellites and solar panels. Some samples will have protective coatings and one sample will contain NRC-developed fortifiers, which improve the strength, stiffness and other physical properties of composite materials.

The interest of Canadian industry in doing materials processing research in space has been slow to pick up, but a beginning has been made. Between 1984 and 1986, the NRC sponsored a series of seminars and workshops to raise the level of awareness in Canadian companies and to bring them together with university and government scientists already doing fundamental research in this field. At this stage, there is considerable involvement on the part of university scientists who are more interested in basic research than in direct commercial applications. "I think that is where all of this is starting in any event," said VanKoughnett. "The companies by and large don't have the research expertise and the university is the obvious place to find it." He said that the real challenge is finding which applications really make sense to do in space.

The process of trying to determine what Canadian industry might usefully be able to do in space processing began in 1984. In conjunction with its space station studies, the NRC gave CDN$600,000 worth of contracts to Canadian companies to do preliminary studies to identify areas offering potential opportunities for Canadian industry in space materials processing and to investigate ways to promote industry teaming between aerospace companies and "user" companies.

These studies identified a number of areas of potential interest and the contractors subsequently submitted several further proposals for continuing research. The NRC earmarked nearly CDN$1-million in fiscal 1985-86 to support earth-based research that could lead to space processing experiments before the end of the decade and the NRC awarded several contracts for further research on crystal growth, glasses and ceramics, pharmaceuticals, metals and alloys.

The proposals for crystal growth experiments include both gallium arsenide and germanium, materials that had annual sales of, respectively, US$75-million and US$65-million in 1984. It has been estimated that Canada could potentially capture about 10 per cent of the world market for GaAs semiconductors (projected to be worth about US$5-billion by 1990). Cominco Limited is a producer and exporter of GaAs, and the NRC and Bell-Northern Research (BNR) Limited of Ottawa have started a CDN$14.4-million co-operative research effort to develop the capability to produce gallium arsenide integrated circuits by 1987. In June, BNR completed construction of a CDN$3.5-million laboratory to build such prototype circuits. This is a ground-based program, not directly related to the potential space-based research. It is possible that the two lines of research may end up competing with each other, but it is also possible that new insights gained in space research may result in improvements in earth-based techniques.

MBP Technologies Incorporated of Dorval is another Canadian company interested in gallium arsenide crystal growth experiments; it received NRC contracts for preliminary ground-based experiments. MPB does research on laser, microwave and digital systems, all of which require integrated circuits, and thus is interested in the development of superior new semiconductor materials. A team consisting of Noranda Incorporated, Honeywell Canada, T.A. Croil and the Ontario Research Foundation has also studied space-based GaAs processing under NRC contract. Honeywell, a manufacturer of computer systems and sensor systems for the aerospace and defence industries, is interested in the use of GaAs in optical electronic systems and is already doing research to develop GaAs semiconductors. Honeywell is also exploring the possibility of becoming a supplier of instrumentation and control technology for space materials processing operations. Noranda is involved in the production of high-purity compounds and optical electronic materials and the Ontario Research Foundation is doing research on optical electronic materials processing.

Although it is a major producer of gallium arsenide, Cominco has given a low priority to space processing of this material, saying that the most important advances over the next 15 years will come from improvements in earth-based processing techniques. Cominco has, however, been doing research on space processing of another kind of crystal — cadmium mercury telluride (CMT). The average selling price of CMT wafers is about US$1-million, compared with $20,000 for GaAs and $1300 for silicon. This material is widely used as a high-performance infrared detector material; new devices require larger and more uniform CMT crystals than can be grown on earth. Cominco is also studying containerless processing of germanium crystals in space; germanium crystals used in gamma radiation detectors "are required to have a purity and crystal perfection unsurpassed by any other material," said Brent Bollong of Cominco's electronic materials division.

Queen's University has established an Experiments in Space Technology (QUEST) program and is doing research in a variety of fields, including alloys, crystals and the degradation and repair of materials in space. Queen's researchers have developed two furnaces that will be used for space materials processing experiments aboard the shuttle and eventually the space station. One of these furnaces, a six-inch cube, will be flown on Steve MacLean's mission to study diffusion in microgravity. Diffusion — the rate at which atoms or molecules move around and between each other — is an important factor in many industrial applications, especially those involving solidification of liquids. Experiments to obtain accurate measurements of diffusion on earth "tend to be bedevilled with unwanted convection," said principal investigator Reg Smith, of Queen's department of metallurgical engineering. The experiment is designed to measure the diffusion rates of several molten metals in microgravity at a variety of temperatures. Smith said that research such as this may one day lead to the production of materials that can't be made on earth, but it will also help scientists gain a better understanding of the fundamental properties of materials that are of great importance on earth.

The Queen's researchers are also planning to fly several experiments relating to crystal growth and the solidification of alloys on the Hitchhiker, an unmanned platform that will be carried in the shuttle's cargo hold. These are part of a group of 11 experiments sponsored by the former Canada Centre for Space Science (now part of the NRC's new space division); others include a glass formation experiment by BM Hi-Tech Incorporated and crystal growth experiments by the NRC and the University of Toronto. These experiments were expected to have been on a shuttle flight in 1986 or 1987; it is unknown when they will be rescheduled.

Canada may eventually become involved in drug processing in space through a research project being done by Connaught Laboratories Limited of Toronto, which is working on "microencapsulation" — a technique of putting insulin cells, known as "islets," into tiny semi-porous plastic-like capsules.

In healthy humans, these islets are little factories that vary the production of insulin to match the body's daily requirements; since these requirements are constantly changing, it is often difficult to find just the right dose for a diabetic's daily injections. The companies hope that injecting islets into diabetics will essentially provide a cure for the disease by mimicking the body's natural demand-and-supply system. However, the injected cells must be encapsulated in a plastic-like membrane to protect them from the immune system, which attacks them as invaders. These capsules are semi-porous, so that insulin can get out but the immune cells can't get in. It is hoped that these capsules, filled with insulin-producing cells and injected by needle, could provide diabetics with more accurate doses of medication, thereby reducing the incidence of harmful side effects — such as blindness, kidney failure and heart trouble — believed to result from over- or under-dosages. Diabetics are 25 times more likely to go blind and 17 times more likely to suffer kidney failure than the average healthy person and it has been estimated that their life expectancy is reduced by one-third. There are about 580,000 insulin-dependent diabetics in North America and it costs an estimated US$120,000 in lifetime health care costs for each, about half of which goes to treat complications of the disease.

Connaught is currently studying earth-based methods of producing the capsules, but may later conduct space-based experiments when access to shuttle flights resumes. Producing the capsules in space is expected to improve the effectiveness of the cells and reduce the likelihood of triggering an immune response, says A. M. Sun, senior research scientist with the Connaught Research Institute in Toronto. Space-produced capsules will be more perfectly spherical and will have smoother walls with a more uniform thickness. The islet cells will be more centred inside the capsule, rather than clustering near the bottom as they do on earth. And, finally, the capsule size will be smaller and more consistent. Sun said he hopes this technology will eventually result in a once-in-a-lifetime injection for diabetics; however, even if more frequent injections are required, diabetics will receive great benefit from the reduction in side effects due to incorrect dosages.[5] It has been estimated that even once-a-year injections would cost no more than diabetics now pay for insulin injections.

Several Canadian projects fall more into the category of research *for* space than research *in* space. Given the plans for building the space station by the mid-1990s, the former may in fact be the more urgent. The Queen's researchers are interested in research on techniques for joining materials in space (e.g., adhesive bonding, welding, etc.) Alcan Aluminum Limited of Montreal has expressed interest in the possibility of supplying aluminum-lithium alloy for building structures in space. This material, already used to build aircraft, is both lighter and stiffer than other structural materials that might be used in aerospace applications.

Another firm, Electrofuel Manufacturing Company of Toronto, is developing a new high energy-density battery that combines a long operating lifetime with low weight and volume. It has potential applications in spacecraft as well as in electrical vehicles on the ground. The battery's electrodes are made of lithium-aluminum alloy and Electrofuel had to develop a new boron-nitrite ceramic fibre to separate the positive and negative posts. The separator is attacked chemically and "very few materials survive in that environment," said Sankar Das Gupta, a partner in the company. Electrofuel is the only manufacturer in the world of the boron-nitrite fibres; the company hopes to use the product to find a niche in the US$12-billion worldwide market for advanced ceramics. The company has also manufactured a small furnace that will be used for Canadian materials processing experiments in space.

In a slightly different vein, P.C. Hughes of the University of Toronto's Institute for Aerospace Studies has started a research program on controlling the form, shape or orientation of large structures in space. Once the ability to build structures in space is developed, and it is no longer necessary to launch the structures from earth, there is theoretically "no limit to the size things can be," Hughes said. Size is not itself so much the problem; however, in microgravity, even very large objects can be extremely flexible and flimsy. Giant antennas, which could be used on advanced communications or remote-sensing satellites, are prime examples; not only must they be accurately pointed, but their shape must be maintained to prevent distortions in the beams they transmit. In order to conduct tests on earth before doing research in space, Hughes has built a ground-based facility in which the behavior of a structure in space can be simulated and studied.

Most of the Canadian work being done on space materials processing is still at a very fundamental level; it will be quite a while before commercial products are produced and even longer before automated factories are set up in space. Parvez Kumar, head of the user development program for the NRC's space division, said he doesn't believe there will be "big money" to be made in space manufacturing before the turn of the century. The space station will be "essentially a research facility" and the early benefits will come from improvements in earth-based processing. VanKoughnett agreed: "That's where you're going to get the largest potential economic return in the short period. It's not necessarily what you produced in space but what you learn in space that can be applied to processes on earth."

By pursuing its traditional strategy of selectively seeking "niches" in which to excel, Canada's space industry can be part of the "gold rush in space," despite its limited financial resources. However, careful choices will be necessary, because of the high cost of doing business in space. Even the enthusiasts of space commercialization have warned of the dangers of overselling the benefits of space manufacturing and of raising expectations too high too soon.

VanKoughnett said that Canada doesn't really have a demonstrated strength in any field of space processing. Canadian industry does have some expertise in semiconductors and metallurgy, but very little pharmaceutical research and development is done in Canada and this has hindered the entry of Canadian industry into this field of space research. Kumar said that Canadian industry is still "lifting itself up by its own bootstraps and educating itself, so what they're doing now is primarily research." He cited crystal growth experiments as an example, but said that since much of this work is proprietary, Canadian scientists don't get much feedback from researchers who have been working in these fields in other countries.

At an NRC-sponsored seminar on space materials processing, Brent Bollong of Cominco said that "we must not be too short-sighted in our approach to space commercialization. Short term benefits cannot be measured in economic terms; they must be of scientific value. Space processing of commercial products may show unexpected progress, but for now basic research should be emphasized." But he added that "a future trend toward space processing is inevitable" and said that Cominco views the prospects with "cautious optimism."

Much of the government support for research in materials processing in space will come from the CDN$800-million committed to the space station project. Of the $220-million earmarked for the first five years of the program, about $50-million will be for "user development" — i.e. microgravity materials processing research by potential users of the space station. However, the program was put on hold for several months after the announcement while the government grappled, none too rapidly, with the problem of finding the promised funds, which were to come from other government programs. Funding of CDN$3-million for 1986-87 and CDN$6-million for 1987-88 was approved, but Kumar said it was likely that less than $2-million would be spent in the first year — money that would have to come from the existing NRC budget.

Kumar said the projected Canadian investment in materials processing represents about the same ratio (approximately 20 per cent of the amount put into building new space hardware) that is being spent in other countries, although the dollar amount is much lower. He said the funding will be modest at first — an estimated CDN$3-million in 1986-87 and working up to about CDN$11-million annually — because it will take time to build up the expertise of Canadian industry to levels similar to those in the U.S. and European industries. "Right now, if you did give me all the money I needed, I would never be able to spend it because we don't have the infrastructure out there in industry that could usefully absorb that money. I mean, they'll take it, but it won't be usefully spent."

Education is one of the immediate objectives of the program, he said. Workshops and seminars will be sponsored to increase the awareness of both industry and the public. Kumar said he hopes to encourage proposals and new ideas on space research from industry, universities and government agencies and to promote teaming among these groups. Such teaming arrangements, which have proved very successful in the United States, have only just begun to happen in Canada. Kumar is also particularly interested in encouraging the involvement of small companies with good ideas; in larger companies, it is often difficult to get good ideas through the bureaucracy. Kumar said he would even be receptive to ideas from school children and the general public, although such proposals would need industry backing to go very far. "If they make sense and they're part of the whole strategy of the user development program, we'll fund them."

Although government involvement is clearly necessary to support basic research in materials processing in space, Kumar said it is nevertheless important that companies be willing to invest their own resources, whether in the form of cash or expertise. "What one has to do is take a step back and say, 'Suppose we weren't funding it. You think it's such a hot deal; would you still go with it?' What we have to do right now, with the small amount of money we have in the early years, is to ensure that we're building up the expertise in industry, giving them the confidence that they can go into space and do useful work. We're trying to encourage them to start spending some of their own funds in later years." He said it is also important to increase the awareness of the general business community and venture capitalists as possible sources of funding down the line.

He admitted, however, that "it has been a long slog over the two years we've been pushing this thing." Companies need proof that there's "a pot of gold" in the sky. "They need to see somebody who's gone up there and done something. It's going to be very slow until they actually start selling something, either a service or a new material or some product."

"It's early days" for private investment, said John Graham, head of space station and microgravity programs for Canadian Astronautics. But he said that, although the time scale of commercial development in space is still uncertain, "the general feeling throughout the whole community is that it is inevitable. It's going to happen."

Kumar said it is an important priority of the user development program to establish a mechanism whereby those who gain experience in space research are obliged to pass on what they've learned to other researchers just entering the field. "If we don't get the feedback, then the new users don't get any benefit from [our] having been into space." To this end, it is hoped that several centres of excellence in materials research can, at some point, be set up in universities and in industry across Canada.

This can be a difficult proposition because of the proprietary nature of much of the research done by industry. When government funds are involved, a certain amount of leverage can be brought to bear, but even so, some compromises are necessary to avoid scaring off private industry. No company is going to make a large investment in high-risk research in space if it faces the prospect that competitors can snatch the goods right out from under its nose for practically nothing. For this reason, NASA has been forced to modify a longstanding policy that all data acquired during space missions must be made publicly available. Although there were considerable qualms about using NASA's technology — representing an investment by the American taxpayer of some US$200-billion in total — to promote the profit-making activities of private companies, the U.S. space agency has taken steps to provide some degree of protection for the proprietary rights of companies doing research in space. At present, exclusivity and data and patent rights can be negotiated between NASA and a private company as part of a joint endeavor agreement. At the same time, the U.S. government has taken aggressive legislative steps to ease the way for space research. In mid-1984, the Reagan Administration introduced a new national space policy to update laws and regulations to take space operations into account, to encourage and expand industry's role in space R&D and to establish consistency in policies and provide the long-term commitment needed for space research. One result of this is new legislation introduced to extend the 10 per cent investment tax credit to space products, which had been denied because of the IRS view that anything that went into space was an export. The legislation is also intended to ensure that space products being returned to the United States will not be taxed as imports, and it provides for 100 per cent depreciation on research related to space processing.

Needless to say, these measures are intended to give U.S. companies an edge; it will largely be up to the governments of other countries to support and encourage the entry of their own industries into commercial space activities. Europe has established programs to encourage industrial teaming and co-operative

338

funding of major projects and to promote commercial uses of space. Japan is fully expected to tackle the mobilization of its space industry in much the same way as it has managed to terrorize the automotive and consumer electronics industries. In June, it established a special space station R&D unit within its national space agency, which was expected to spend more than US$3-billion on research before the station even flies.

Canada, on the other hand, has barely begun to come to grips with some of the financial, legislative and management issues related to commercial exploitation of space. Nursing the nascent space manufacturing industry through its growing pains without succumbing to too many pitfalls will be a challenge. Kenney-Wallace said that without government incentives "nothing will happen. It's too expensive to get into just for the fun of it." VanKoughnett agreed: "Companies are not going to go through an extensive company-funded period when they're searching. They can't survive the search."

Asked why tax dollars should be spent to promote the activities of companies whose objective is to make a profit, he said that there are precedents for government support of industrial development for the general good of the country. Kenney-Wallace said that the tax dollar should not have to pay for everything, but in the initial stages, the government has to set the climate and offer enough incentives to get industry started. "When it looks as though it's going to be profitable, then those who are going to make a profit can take the risks. But because we don't exactly have a history of people doing that in this country, you can't expect attitudes to change overnight." What Canada does have a history of doing is "dabbling, getting the feet wet. I think we have to be the world's expert at trying the temperature of the ocean, but we don't swim enough. Now is the time to swim. We've got to create new research, new science, new technologies that are going to take us into the future. Nobody will be asking why we should be in space in about 20 years' time."

During the next decade, one of the most significant factors pacing the development of materials processing in space will be access to the microgravity environment and to the types of facilities required to do space-based experiments. Even before the Challenger accident, capacity was limited and line-ups were long.

The accident was a devastating blow, not only because it temporarily eliminated the shuttle as a microgravity laboratory, but because many other facilities, such as Spacelab and various free-flying platforms, also depended on it. Western researchers have no alternative facilities for providing microgravity on a long-duration, continuous basis. Earth-based facilities, which include "drop tubes" and aircraft like NASA's KC-135, typically provide less than half a minute of microgravity and sounding rockets provide no more than several minutes. However, this is often long enough to check out equipment and do some preliminary experiments. Kumar said that a small T-33 jet is being converted into a microgravity aircraft, giving Canadian researchers access to their own facility of this sort for the first time. It will "give confidence to these companies as to whether the equipment's going to work, whether their ideas are going to work. It's a cheap way of trying it out on earth."

Earth-based tests such as this are useful, but only up to a point. Many important materials processing experiments require much longer periods — hours or days — of continuous microgravity. The shuttle provided several alternatives. Experiments inside the pressurized crew compartment (in the "mid-deck") could be tended by humans. However, there were power limitations and severe safety constraints put on any equipment carried in the mid-deck. Also, locker space was a prized and scarce resource, especially when the personal effects and housekeeping requirements of a large crew had to be accommodated. ("Every time you put a Senator on board, you lose two lockers," one space scientist commented acerbically.) By the fall of 1985, a considerable backlog of mid-deck experiments had accumulated and was doubling every year. A Washington company called Spacehab is offering a solution — a pressurized module, three metres long, which would fit in the cargo bay immediately next to the crew compartment and connected to it by the airlock that astronauts use to exit during EVA. The first module, which had been scheduled to be available for flight by the end of 1987, would contain up to 100 additional lockers for storage, experimental equipment and astronaut sleep stations. Later modules would contain more complex equipment and be designed to permit experiments and testing of systems ultimately intended for the space station. Spacehab estimated that leasing a complete module would cost about US$5-million per flight; however, individual lockers could be rented for a fraction of this cost. Since a Spacehab module would take up no more than a quarter of the shuttle cargo bay, the rest of that space would be available for other commercial payloads.

In the cargo bay, automated experiments requiring little or no human intervention could be accommodated in small cannisters called Getaway Specials (GAS), which could be leased for a relatively low cost (less than US$10,000 in some cases). However, the cut-rate prices had a few strings attached — the GAS cans were self-contained units that received virtually no support from the crew or the shuttle's power supply and they were low-priority "payloads of opportunity," tucked into available corners of the cargo bay. Researchers wanting to fly experiments were backed up for months or years. This situation will be even worse when shuttle flights resume because of a big backlog of high-priority military and commercial payloads. NASA is also developing a larger structure called Hitchhiker, an unmanned payload carrier that would be carried in the cargo bay, on which GAS cannisters or larger, more complex instruments and equipment could be mounted. Unlike the GAS cans, the Hitchhiker would be plugged into the shuttle's power and data recording system, so it naturally costs quite a bit more — in the quarter-million-dollar ballpark. "It's an expensive plug," VanKoughnett conceded, but, he said, the Canadian experiments on the Hitchhiker can be monitored and controlled from the ground during flight and "by chucking out all of the batteries and control electronics, we were able to more than double the number of experiments."

Another major facility for materials processing research was Spacelab, the European-built module that fits into the shuttle cargo bay. It flew four missions before the Challenger accident and three more were in the planning stages. Spacelab consists of both a pressurized module for manned operations and an unpressurized pallet for unmanned experiments. In the pressurized module, astronauts can work in a shirt-sleeves environment, tending the experiments and trouble-shooting if necessary.[6] However, Spacelab flew relatively infrequently and it required a long lead time to prepare experiments, so even before the shuttle accident, there were long line-ups of researchers waiting to get aboard.

Long-duration exposure to microgravity is also provided by shuttle-launched free-flying unmanned platforms. The U.S.

Spartan and West German SPAS [shuttle pallet satellite] platforms are designed to be deployed and retrieved during a shuttle flight; SPAS was flown during missions in 1983 and 1984, the first time in a free-flying mode and the second time attached to the Canadarm. In April, 1984, another free-flier, the long-duration exposure facility (LDEF) was deployed from the shuttle. LDEF carried 57 experiments developed by some 200 researchers in eight countries; it has several dozen trays for exposing various materials (ranging from tomato seeds and electronic and optical materials to paints and advanced composite materials) to the space environment. The original plan was to leave it in space for close to a year but its recovery is not anticipated before 1988 or 1989.

During the next two to three decades, a variety of space manufacturing modules will be developed. Some, like the laboratory modules of the space station, will be pressurized to allow for continuous human supervision of experiments. Others, such as free-flying platforms, will be "man-tended"— that is, visited periodically. The Europeans are planning to build a free-flying platform called Eureca that would be deployed and retrieved by the shuttle after about nine months in space. The first Eureca mission was scheduled for late 1988. A Houston firm, Space Industries Incorporated, is planning to build a free-flying space factory called Industrial Space Facility, at an estimated cost of about US$250- to $500-million. NASA agreed to launch the factory, which will offer rentable lab space, with no up-front launch fee, in return for 12 per cent of the annual revenues until the launch costs were recovered, and to resupply the factory from the shuttle three times a year. McDonnell Douglas has been considering development of a drug processing factory that could fly alone or attached to the space station, in the latter case providing a shirt-sleeves working environment for humans. The Japanese have also shown a great deal of interest in free-flying space factories.

All of these projects have been affected by the suspension of shuttle flights. And at least one proposed project to build a free-flying commercial materials processing facility was put on indefinite hold even before the Challenger accident. Fairchild Space Company backed away from its plan to build a free-flier called Leasecraft, because the company was unable to obtain enough commercial customers or sufficient commercial insurance for the project.[7]

The Canadian astronaut office has put forth a proposal for a Canadian Space Carrier (CSC) that could be deployed and retrieved by the shuttle and remain in space up to several days. Having their own space carrier would give Canadian researchers a greater measure of protection from being bumped from foreign-owned facilities. A report on the proposal, prepared by Bjarni Tryggvason, Marc Garneau and Steve MacLean, said that "the CSC would allow Canada to form and control its own series of experiments and thus maintain control over its own space science."

Kumar said the project will not receive immediate funding, but the concept will not be abandoned. "There is a need for this thing. I'm trying to ensure that we have repeated, regular access to space ... and that, if there are proprietary processes, they remain in Canada." He said Canadian researchers will need a space-based microgravity facility in the period before the space station is built; afterwards, the carrier might evolve into a free-flying platform co-orbiting with the station. A major objective would be to "impress industry that we mean business and here is something they can use."

The availability of such a device would allow researchers in Canadian industry and universities to "know that there is a flight with a certain amount of space at such and such a time every year and a half or so," said Tryggvason. Without such "long-term, secure planning ... it's going to be hard to get them to commit to anything."

The price of security is not trivial and it is not confined to development costs alone: the carrier would cost about CDN$3- to $4-million over four years to build, and launch costs are estimated at about CDN$6- to $9-million per shuttle flight. It would be possible for Canada to buy a platform from someone else, but Kumar said it would be difficult to justify spending the $3- to $4-million outside Canada and, in any event, the Canadian aerospace industry should be developing more space hardware. Ideally, Canadian industry would also develop the skills necessary to integrate all the experiments on the carrier and check it for safety so that Canada can put a stamp of approval on the whole package and simply hand it over to NASA for launch. In the past, Canada has paid NASA for these services. "We want to push it out into the private sector," Kumar said. "I want them to get out there and make money on running this thing." Telesat Canada has expressed interest in running the CSC as a commercial enterprise.

A major issue relates to how to get samples back to earth. "It's very expensive to get up there and it's even more expensive to get the things down," said Kumar. Experiments done on the shuttle can be returned with the vehicle, of course, and the shuttle and other manned spaceplanes could also pick up samples from unmanned free-fliers. But it would not always be necessary to have a manned vehicle for the job. The Soviets have already attached an unmanned re-entry module to their Salyut space station, and for the space station era, scientists are urging development of a "space mail" system for rapid delivery of samples to earth. This would involve ejecting small (one-kilogram) packages that would re-enter the earth's atmosphere to be intercepted by recovery aircraft, much the way film from military satellites is currently retrieved.

Eventually, there will be highly automated factories in space. It has been estimated that the annual leasing market for such facilities could be in the billions of dollars after the turn of the century, but the accuracy of these projections over the near term will depend on how successfully the shuttle program recovers from the Challenger accident.

Access to the space environment is only one requirement for materials processing research; the other is having the right equipment to do the experiments. This includes various types of automated furnaces for doing experiments with fluids, metals, alloys and glasses; devices for growing crystals; electrophoresis and other machines for processing biological materials; and acoustic levitation devices for containerless processing. A number of these devices have already been flown and many more are under development by companies around the world. For example, McDonnell Douglas has been working on a drug processing apparatus designed to operate on a continuous basis in the shuttle's cargo bay; it has a production capacity about 24 times that of the unit it has flown on the shuttle mid-deck. This device was scheduled to fly in mid-1986, but has been put on hold. McDonnell Douglas has tried to minimize the impact by shifting some drug production activities to earth-based processing. "If we had to depend entirely on space processing for early commercial-ization, we would have been dead in the water," said James Rose, director of space electrophoresis operations.

In Canada, the thrust is to build "single-discipline, multi-user" devices — that is, equipment that would be used by a number of different experimenters, but for only one type of material processing operation (e.g., crystal growth). This is intended to avoid a proliferation of a variety of similar devices. The NRC has funded the development of several types of furnaces that can be used for metals, crystals and glasses.

The ultimate key to success in microgravity processing is the development of hardware capable of routine, continuous and highly automated operations in space. The difficulties in doing this should not be underestimated. Since even experienced aerospace companies, such as McDonnell Douglas, have encountered substantial hardware development challenges, how much more difficult will this sort of development work be for "user" companies that have little or no expertise or operating experience with space-rated hardware? This is one reason why teaming arrangements between user and aerospace companies are so important.

Astronauts — particularly payload specialists with engineering and scientific expertise — have played an extremely important role in this early phase. The failure rate of these experiments undoubtedly would have been much higher if it had not been for frequent on-the-site applications of brainpower and the ability to wield a screwdriver. On the first Spacelab mission in late 1983, payload specialist Byron Lichtenberg saved some of the fluid physics experiments endangered by malfunctioning equipment. During the trouble-plagued second Spacelab mission in mid-1985, payload specialist Taylor Wang spent more than two days rewiring around a short-circuit to revive a sophisticated device designed to suspend liquid drops in weightlessness using sound waves, thereby salvaging an experiment he had been working on for 12 years.[8] The McDonnell Douglas electrophoresis experiment that flew on the shuttle encountered technical problems that could be overcome only because engineer Charles Walker was on board to troubleshoot. His in-flight monitoring of the experiment also proved crucial in determining that the experiment had worked properly after samples returned to earth were found to be contaminated by bacteria. In these and many similar cases, experiments costing millions of dollars to develop and representing years of effort by many researchers would have been lost without the presence of humans to perform fix-it jobs.

Even in non-crisis circumstances, the presence of an astronaut can provide a degree of flexibility and responsiveness to the unexpected, which is not currently possible with automated systems. The Queen's University diffusion experiment scheduled for Steve MacLean's shuttle flight is a case in point: the ability of the astronaut to change the materials means that 60 different samples, instead of only a few, can be tested in the tiny furnace.

MacLean said that having humans on board means that the maximum amount of scientific information can be obtained on each flight; this is especially important because the lead time to prepare for a flight is very long and there are often long periods between flights. The presence of a human experimenter permits "the next scientific step to be taken on the same flight, instead of waiting for the next chance." As Karl Doetsch said, astronauts are "the most sophisticated form of robot we have."

On the use of humans generally, however, the position of the scientific community can be described as ambivalent. ("Schizophrenia might be the best word," said VanKoughnett.) On the one hand, space materials processing is at such a preliminary stage that it is providing valuable opportunities for scientists doing fundamental or basic research on materials, particularly fluids. On the other hand, some of the loudest objections to the manned program have come from space scientists doing fundamental rather than commercially oriented research — e.g., space physics, astronomy, planetary science, upper atmospheric research, earth observations, etc. — who believe their programs suffer in the budgetary wars with programs designed to promote the commercialization of space and the development of new space hardware. "The problems with the shuttle have delayed, postponed or terminated a lot of interesting science," said solar physicist Richard Willson of the Jet Propulsion Laboratory in California.

Pure science has always been something of a poor relation in the space program, typically commanding only about 10 to 15 per cent of the total space budget.[9] Even the extremely successful planetary exploration program has been decimated in recent years — largely because of the financial drain caused by the troubled development of the shuttle — despite the fact that it has often provided spectacles to equal those of the manned space program.

Shortly after Canada's commitment to participate in the space station was announced, University of Alberta space physicist

Gordon Rostoker grumbled that "science is being pushed aside. The space community is a very disillusioned group of people because they know that every bit of what has happened is dictated not by science but by trying to provide Canada with an industrial base for earning money."

He is right that the prospect of industrial benefit drives the space program far more than science does; this has characterized the program since it began and it isn't about to change. Space technology, industrial development programs and the political and PR benefits of manned extravaganzas in space offer far more tangible returns to politicians and the public, who generally have little understanding or appreciation of the role of basic research. Many space scientists have been politically naive in assuming that, if a given number of billions of dollars was not spent on landing men on the moon or building a space station, it would flow instead into pure space science projects. They ignore the fact that, to governments, large projects like the space station are not solely, or even primarily, scientific undertakings, but rather exercises in technological bootstrapping and instruments of national prestige. "Space presence is a means of political power," said one European space official. "A presence in space makes your views more influential on world events." One of the Canadian government's prime objectives in committing itself to the space station program was visibility — visibility in the form of Canadian-built hardware with the maple leaf stamped on it and visibility in the form of Canadian astronauts living and working on the space station.

Political forces dictate the nature of the "grand plan" for space, which "has not been put together just to keep scientists happy — I mean, why should the public pay for our hobbies?" said Ralph Nicholls, director of the Centre for Research in Experimental Space Science at York University, chairman of the space science working group that advises the Interdepartmental Committee on Space. "The space station isn't just a scientific thing, though parts of it are going to be. The principal rationale is not science at all, it's technology." This is not say, however, that scientists shouldn't try to influence the program. Nicholls, who was Canada's official observer on NASA's task force on scientific uses of the space station (TFSUSS), pointed out that the task force played a major role in persuading NASA to revamp the design of the station completely to accommodate microgravity

347

materials research better. It was also instrumental in thwarting an attempt by NASA engineers to reduce the atmospheric pressure and to change the oxygen-nitrogen mix of the atmosphere on the station. If they had done so, all the human physiology data gathered on earth by life scientists would have been rendered useless as a baseline against which to compare the long-term physiological responses of people living in space. "Our committee hit the roof," Nicholls said. "We sort of took that apart ... so now we're back up to 14.7 psi [atmospheric pressure at sea level on earth]. "

The manned space program has been made the whipping boy in this debate, in large part because keeping people alive in space is very expensive and many space scientists believe machines can do a better job at lesser cost. These scientists argue that the only time you really need humans in space is to study humans in space — to do physiological research on the adaptation of the human body to the zero-gravity environment. A number of prominent critics of the manned program — notably astronomer Thomas Gold and physicist James Van Allen — have been very vocal in their disparagement of the manned program. Van Allen has said that the diversion of funds to the shuttle program decimated the space science program, resulting in "a slaughter of the innocent: massive cuts, postponements and cancellations ... The progressive loss of U.S. leadership in space science can be attributed largely to our excessive emphasis on manned space flight." Several years ago, the U.S. National Academy of Sciences issued a report that argued against the space station project, saying that the money should be spent on unmanned spacecraft and instruments.[10]

To some extent, NASA had only itself to blame for this hostility. Throughout the Mercury, Gemini and Apollo programs, science took a back seat to technology development and much the same was true for the shuttle program until recently. The astronaut program, dominated by the Right Stuff test-pilot types, was never particularly welcoming to scientists; the first group of scientist-astronauts, chosen in 1967, were so low on the flight pecking order that they took to referring to themselves as the XS-11 (Excess Eleven). Over the years, a number of the scientist-astronauts left the program in disgust, often without ever having flown a mission, and some, like astronomer Brian O'Leary, became unrelenting critics of the manned program. It took

Congressional arm-twisting to get a scientist, geologist (later Senator) Harrison Schmitt, on the final Apollo moon mission, and even then, the highest accolade accorded him by the test-pilot astronauts was that he had learned to become one of the better pilots among the scientist-astronauts.

The Challenger accident only served to rekindle this long-running debate over the scientific value of the manned program, especially when contrasted with the spectacular success of the unmanned Voyager 2 mission, which coincidentally made its closest approach to the planet Uranus the same week the accident occurred. But many scientists are coming to realize — and to accept, though often only reluctantly — that the manned program is what "sells" space to the public and politicians. "It's very hard to sell it on the basis of space science by itself, particularly in Canada," acknowledged Ian McDiarmit, former head of the NRC's Canada Centre for Space Science. "What we've been trying to sell is that a certain fraction of the total that goes into the space program should go to science." If the fraction is, say, 15 per cent, the total pot for space has to be quite large to make the 15 per cent worthwhile, he said. For this reason, he believes Canada's involvement in the space station program could benefit space science.

It would be misleading, in fact, to suggest that all scientists involved in space research are arrayed against the manned program; they are not monolithic in their views. And in any case, many scientists appear to have adopted the motto "If you can't beat 'em, join 'em."

"You can't damn the only game in town," said Nicholls. In its 1986 report, TFSUSS said that, with proper organization and resources, the space station "can become an active, vital part of the U.S. and international science establishment. The possibility has excited the task force and led us to actively support the space station project." It said the station has the potential to overcome the problems associated with doing research on the shuttle — short duration missions, rigid timelines and long periods between flights.

Hundreds of scientists around the world have now become personally involved in the manned space program — most as ground-based investigators and a small but growing number as scientist-astronauts. The prospect of having a permanent manned laboratory in space is exciting to them. West German physicist

Ernst Messerschmid, who flew on the Spacelab D1 mission, said: "I am convinced that the space station is the thing to do and I think we will all benefit from it."

"It's very important for us to try to keep the momentum up," said Roberta Bondar, who has made it her particular mission to encourage Canadian life scientists to submit ideas for experiments that Canadian payload specialists can do in space. She has also been working with the federal granting agencies that fund university research in Canada, which have not had to deal with research proposals of this kind before.

In the near term, many space science projects will be hampered by an expected major reduction in spacelab misions resulting from the Challenger accident. However, the space station era will provide many more scientists with the opportunity to go into space themselves, and for others, there is the prospect of "telescience" — a close, almost minute-by-minute collaboration between researchers on the ground and those in space. The model for this was the Spacelab D1 mission, during which the principal investigators on the ground were allowed, for the first time, to talk directly to the astronauts on the shuttle, without having to route every conversation through Mission Control in Houston. The old system is simply too slow and unwieldy for the true give-and-take needed on scientific missions and it will undoubtedly be greatly modified during the space station era.

In its report, TFSUSS made a number of recommendations on how to improve the station as a research facility. It said that the management of science operations should be separated from the operational management of the overall station (i.e., there should be a "vice-president" for science). It urged a flexible approach to space station design, so that facilities can be changed and modified to adapt to new scientific requirements at a reasonable cost. (NASA has said that the habitable modules will be designed to allow such modifications.) The report also said that both free-flying platforms and attached payloads (i.e., instruments for observing the earth, sun, planets and stars) must be an important part of the space station core structure.

Perhaps most significantly, the report came out strongly in favor of a permanent human presence, saying that "a truly long-term manned capability" is necessary to do science in space. The spectrum of experiments that could be done in the automated mode is "greatly restricted," the report said. It recommended a crew of at least ten people on the station — larger than the six NASA had originally envisioned. Another committee said that a crew of six would be "grossly overcommitted" in terms of their workload. In the end, NASA said the station will support up to eight people in its initial operating configuration. "Crew time will be by far the most precious commodity aboard the space station," said Nicholls.

This is not to say that having humans around doesn't present some problems. Even slight movements on the station — slamming a locker door, pushing off a wall — can upset sensitive astronomical instruments or delicate materials processing experiments that require near-perfect zero-gravity conditions. In fact, astronauts are told that if they feel a sneeze coming on, they should try to avoid touching any equipment, or even the walls of the spacecraft. Even typing on a computer keyboard could make a telescope jitter. On one Spacelab mission, once the materials processing experiments were started, astronauts had to stop doing a physiology experiment that required them to bounce up and down on the end of elastic cords.

On the space station, the docking and undocking of the shuttle and the firing of the station's positioning jets will cause even larger gravity effects. This is one reason why the Europeans, the West Germans in particular, are so anxious to have a free-flying "quiet lab" operating in a man-tended mode for microgravity materials processing research.

The competition for limited space station facilities and crew time is one major reason why Canada, like all the other partici- pating countries, wants to have its own scientist-astronauts on board along with a say in managing the station's day-to-day operations.

According to Nicholls, one major problem with this type of research is that it is what he calls "big science," which is not only costly but very time-consuming. Kenney-Wallace said that much frustrating time is spent meeting NASA's safety regulations, which "were always, if anything, too conservatively applied." It generally takes years to get an experiment on a shuttle flight and a major project can easily consume a decade of a researcher's time. Nicholls points to the experience of York University physicist Gordon Shepherd, who has been working for many years on a major experiment called WAMDII, which was scheduled to fly on a Spacelab mission in 1989.[11] "There's a decade or more of his career and imagination," said Nicholls. "How many people are willing to put decades of their career on the line? How many decades are there in a person's career?"

This situation is having an even more severe impact on the training of young scientists. The time required for "big science" is "far too long to do high quality graduate work. We are running out of the ability to train the people," Nicholls said. "Medium science" — such as that carried out as part of the now-defunct Canadian rocket and balloon program — is ideal for training graduate students, he said, because experiments could be designed and carried out over no more than two to three years. He said abandonment of the rocket and balloon program was "foolish."

This view was echoed in a report by NASA earth and planetary scientists, who pointed out that the 10 to 20 years it takes to mount large projects like the US$1.1-billion Space Telescope or planetary exploration missions do not dovetail very well with typical university graduate and postdoctoral programs lasting four to five years. "There was a time when a student could plan an experiment, design hardware, build hardware, fly a mission, collect data and evaluate the results," said Jeffrey Rosendhal of NASA's space science and applications office. "They had hands-on experience with all aspects of the process." Now, an entire career can be consumed by a single mission and students often are involved only in isolated aspects. "Educators are getting very worried about the kind of students they are turning out."

This situation has, of course, been exacerbated by the Challenger accident. NASA had billed 1986 "a year for space science" because the shuttle was to launch a large number of important scientific payloads, including the Space Telescope, the Galileo mission to Jupiter, the High-Energy Astrophysics Laboratory, the European-built Ulysses solar observatory, a satellite to study Comet Halley and an ultraviolet telescope observatory. Before the shuttle explosion turned all these plans to dust, Burton Edelson, NASA's associate administrator for space science and applications, said: "1986 may well be remembered as the year that mankind learned more about the vast reaches of our universe than any other year in recorded history."

The coincidence of these projects — all involving the use of machines — with an equally large array of experiments that require the presence of humans demonstrates dramatically that there is no longer an either/or choice between humans and machines in space; rather, the issue is determining the appropriate mix.

Whether the skills that humans bring to these missions are worth what it costs to keep people alive and functioning efficiently in space — and worth the inevitable loss of human life — is still a hotly debated issue and the debate will go on, probably indefinitely, especially if tight money continues to force hard choices between manned and unmanned space projects. But there is little prospect of a retreat from the goal of permanent human habitation of space, short of a disaster on earth that forces total abandonment of the space program. Quite aside from any argument about the superiority of human decision-making skills, the fact is that it's in our nature to do these things ourselves. We *want* to go out there where the action is. No doubt a robot could be built that could climb Everest without any risk to human life, but what would be the point?

This is not to say there won't be room for machines in space. The new generation of intelligent machines, expert systems, remotely controlled robotic devices and sophisticated computer-control systems will be part of a new partnership with humans in which the strengths of each are used to offset the weaknesses of the other. The symbiotic relationship that is being forged will play a pivotal role in opening up humanity's latest "New World."

NOTES

1. This proposal was not entirely altruistic in its intent. The report stated that it would be necessary to keep the activities of the space station alive in the public mind in order to garner continuing political support. This is not a job that can be left to the mass media alone; it noted that the media tend to report only spectacular and disastrous events and pointed out that the scientific activities of the long-duration Skylab missions were rapidly relegated to oblivion. "Most of the public forgot that crewmen were orbiting overhead. Space station will suffer a similar fate unless its communications are not limited to the commercial press but are expanded into the educational system generally."

2. Much of this type of work is proprietary. However, *Aviation Week and Space Technology* reported that the drug involved was erythropoietin, which is used to stimulate the production of red blood cells. This drug is not widely used at present because conventional production methods leave impurities that cause harmful side effects. It would be used by people whose bodies have lost the ability to produce red blood cells naturally; many now require regular blood transfusions to stay alive. It could also be used to reduce transfusions in surgery, thereby avoiding many possible complications.

3. Many parts of the Canadair Challenger aircraft and the de Havilland Dash-8 STOL aircraft are made of composite plastics. These materials are also being used increasingly in consumer products, such as cassette players, tennis rackets, bicycles, watches and fishing rods.

4. "We got Jake," Brooks said, in reference to the fact that Senator Jake Garn was the only crew member available for the job.

5. If microencapsulation works for insulin, it is possible this technology could be used for a variety of other medical applications, such as encapsulation of liver cells for treatment of liver failure.

6. The second Spacelab mission, in April, 1985, was plagued by so many technical problems that the astronauts spent most of their time trouble-shooting. The difficulties included a faulty fuse on a crystal-growth experiment, a plumbing malfunction that resulted in urine from a biomedical experiment being released into the cabin, a mysterious "glitch" that kept a fluid experiment from functioning, a faulty laser that hampered operation of an earth-observation telescope, and not least, crumbling rat food that ended up flying around the Spacelab in bits and pieces.

7. The insurance problem was a direct result of the loss of a number of satellites during 1984 and 1985. Despite successful repair and recovery efforts by shuttle astronauts, the losses plunged the commercial space insurance industry into a crisis that was exacerbated by the explosions of the shuttle and other launch vehicles in 1986. "We can no longer sell underwriters on the idea that the shuttle phase is safe," said one U.S. space insurance broker, who added that matters have not been helped by the negative image with which NASA has emerged from the investigation into the accident. The fallout from this situation is likely to plague space commercialization projects for many years.

8. When the device failed to operate, Wang kept urging ground controllers to diagnose the problem and send up repair instructions. At one point, he apologized for his persistence, but added: "You know, there's a lot at

stake." After the fix-it job was done, he said: "I'm going to connect everything up, bolt it down and if anybody's religious, please go find a church chapel and pray." Moments later, he turned the device on and jubilantly reported: "It's working, it's working!" This announcement was greeted by whooping and hollering in Mission Control.

9. In the first half of the 1980s, space science accounted for about 14 per cent of the total Canadian space budget; during the last half, it is projected that this will be reduced to less than 10 per cent.

10. The cost of the unmanned program is by no means trivial, however. The two Viking Mars missions, which cost about US$1-billion, carried instruments designed to search for microbes on the planet — and failed to detect any signs of life. "That was a very, very expensive mission," Doug Watt pointed out. "Some of our best brains got together and decided what key experiments should be done to see if there is life on Mars. The machine landed, everything went fine — *and the question was not answered.* Some very interesting data came back, but they lead immediately to new questions. It was a machine, it couldn't think, it couldn't recognize the importance of those answers." Asked if the question of life on Mars would have been answered if humans had been on the flight, Watt said: "We'd be closer than Viking was. Unquestionably."

11. WAMDII — which stands for Wide Angle Michelson Doppler Imaging Interferometer — is a device for measuring the wind velocity of the thin, electrically charged portion of the atmosphere between 80 and 300 km above the earth. This is an extension of Shepherd's long-time research on the earth's upper atmosphere and the interaction of the solar wind with the earth's magnetic field. Another version of the instrument, called WINDII (Wind Imaging Interferometer), will be flown aboard NASA's US$650-million Upper Atmospheric Research Satellite. A large team of scientists from York University and the universities of Western Ontario, Calgary and Saskatchewan are working with Shepherd on the WINDII project. Before the Challenger accident, both experiments had been scheduled to fly in 1989.

"We Will Go On"

Nineteen
eighty-six
was a year of paradox
for the manned space program
of the Western industrial world —
a year in which optimism about the future
co-existed with disillusionment
and even despair about the present.
On one hand,
the long-term fate of the program
appeared brighter than ever before —
the result of major international commitments
to build an orbiting home
that would serve as a base for permanent human habitation of
space. On the other hand, the near-term future had never appeared
bleaker — the result of the Challenger disaster and the subsequent
crisis of confidence in NASA.

This paradox was neatly captured in the reports of two U.S.
presidential commissions on space, which released their findings
within two months of each other. One was the report of the
National Commission on Space and the other was the report of
the presidental commission on the Challenger disaster. The
former, called *Pioneering the Space Frontier — Our Next Fifty
Years in Space*, called for a US$700-billion five-decade grand plan
that would carry human habitation beyond low earth orbit to bases
on the moon by the year 2017 and to Mars by 2027. It described a
panoply of new space vehicles to ply the spaceways, ferrying
humans and cargo from earth to and among these new outposts. It
recommended that 1992 — the 500th anniversary of Columbus'
discovery of North America — be declared International Space
Year. This would serve to rekindle flagging spirits in the
aftermath of the Challenger accident and would reinforce the

commitment to long-term human exploration and habitation of space.

Coming in the midst of the Challenger mess, the report was seen by some as wildly unrealistic, but Thomas Paine, the former NASA administrator who chaired the commission, claimed that 15 years hence, the report would be viewed as not visionary enough.

Yet the near-term realities were undeniably grim. Most of the problems stemmed from the loss of launch capability. (The difficulties faced by the industrial community were discussed in Chapter 8.) The space science community, particularly the part of it concerned with planetary exploration, was in even worse straits. NASA dropped a program to develop a US$1-billion booster rocket called Centaur, designed to be deployed from the shuttle's cargo bay to carry payloads farther into space. The Galileo mission to Jupiter, the Magellan mission to Venus and Europe's solar satellite Ulysses were all intended to be boosted by Centaur. (Galileo and Ulysses had already been scheduled for 1986.) This leaves the planetary program with few alternatives, especially after the launch pad explosions of two of the trustiest unmanned expendable boosters in the U.S. arsenal; the Galileo mission, for example, could be delayed for six to ten years.

It is open to question whether the planetary probes will be launched aboard the shuttle in future. The U.S. National Research Council has called for a change in policy to reintroduce the use of expendable launchers for many of the space science missions. Using the shuttle "deprived the nation of launch vehicles for major scientific payloads for almost a decade [and has] been devastating for space science," the NRC said. The last major planetary probes, the two Voyager spacecraft to the outer planets, were launched in 1977. In a major policy shift, NASA decided in mid-1986 to move to a "mixed fleet" concept that would involve launching space science missions on expendable boosters wherever possible.

However, the cost of reverting to expendable launchers will not be trivial; this, plus the delays in planetary program launches that are now inevitable, will likely increase the cost of some projects by hundreds of millions of dollars. It is a sad state of affairs for a program that had, during the 1970s and early 1980s, produced some of the most dramatic and exciting scientific findings in human history. In 1986, the near-term fate of the planetary exploration program remained extremely uncertain.

Still, there are some potential bright spots on the horizon. The Soviet Union, which has recently taken a great interest in Mars, has proposed an international unmanned mission to return soil samples from the planet as a precursor to an international manned expedition. Roald Sagdeev, director of the space research institute of the Soviet Academy of Sciences, has said that the manned mission "would not be realistic without international co-operation." He said that the Soviet experience with long-duration missions on the Salyut and MIR space stations will provide important data on the physiological effects of such a mission, which would likely take at least three years.

Enthusiasts of the soil sample mission suggest it would be the perfect way to inaugurate International Space Year in 1992.

The other major sector of the space community significantly affected by the loss of U.S. launch capability is the military. The military presence in space is expected to expand rapidly during the next two decades; the placement in orbit of the first elements of the Strategic Defense Initiative ("Star Wars") system is projected to occur in the mid-1990s, although technical and political factors might delay this schedule. The debate over the technical and strategic advantages or disadvantages of the Star Wars system cannot be discussed in detail here, but the program does have an impact on the civilian manned space program, particularly the space shuttle and the space station.

The impact on the shuttle — and all who use it — may be substantial, particularly over the next five years as NASA picks up the pieces after the Challenger accident. The political decision made by the Nixon Administration in the early 1970s (largely for financial reasons) that the civilian and military programs must share the shuttle has returned to haunt everyone. NASA was never very happy about the sharing arrangement but was critically dependent on the Pentagon's financial and political support for the shuttle. The Pentagon wasn't happy about sharing with a civilian program either, but it wasn't able to persuade a tight-fisted Congress to approve a separate military shuttle program. NASA's push to make the shuttle the sole U.S. launch vehicle made the military nervous from the beginning and it fought to retain the capability of launching satellites on unmanned expendable boosters — a strategy that seemed to be a godsend in the aftermath of the Challenger accident, until the unmanned boosters also started blowing up. In April and May, 1986, two workhorse expendables, a Titan 34D solid rocket booster and a Delta rocket, exploded shortly after launch.[1] The Titan rocket was carrying a "Big Bird" spy satellite. Its failure, the second in less than a year, was expected to result in a six- to nine-month delay in launching, which, in combination with the suspension of shuttle flights, effectively eliminated the U.S.'s ability to launch large military payloads and raised concerns about its ability to maintain its space reconnaissance system. For example, the Air Force has only one operational KH (Keyhole) spy satellite left in space and the satellite is expected to reach the end of its normal three- to four-year lifetime by the end of 1987. The KH satellites are designed to be launched either by the shuttle or on the Titan.

The Titan explosion was bad news for civilian as well as military users of space because it will exacerbate the fight over access to the shuttle when it starts flying again. In any showdown between civilian and military users, the civilians are likely to come out the losers — possibly the big losers. As we have seen, the military may require 45 shuttle flights by 1992 to clear its backlog of payloads. Nor will the demand lessen after that. Estimates of the sheer amount of material that has to be lifted off the earth in the 1990s to accommodate even a modest Star Wars system are staggering: 1.2 million kg in the first year of deployment (more than four times the amount of military hardware previously lifted annually by the shuttle and expendables) and nearly two million kg a year by the turn of the century. Other estimates, particularly those that include the weight of protective armor for the system, are 10 to 50 times higher, and in the words of John Pike of the Federation of American Scientists, "quickly become bizarre as opposed to just daunting." A report to Congress has estimated that it could cost US$60-billion just to lift the necessary hardware into space — more than twice the approximately US$25-billion it is expected to cost to develop the weapons. (All this for a system that many technically knowledgeable SDI critics claim, with considerable credibility, will never work.) In the 1984 issue of *Jane's Space Flight Directory,* editor Reginald Turnbill said that "the battle for space-based laser weapons is settling down to be grimmer and much more expensive than the race to the moon 20 years ago."

The demand for shuttle flights that the military will undoubtedly place on NASA will present the space agency with some image problems in the civilian space community and among the public generally. NASA has always staunchly defended its role as a civilian agency that operates in the open, and to a large extent this has been true (although its reputation for candor and openness was seriously damaged during the hearings into the Challenger accident). Still, NASA has been forced by financial realities to co-exist with the military. Secret shuttle missions have been flown, and one of the shuttles, Discovery, was scheduled to be based permanently at the Vandenberg military launch complex in California.[2]

Perhaps even more important, however, is the matter of appearances. Over the years, key NASA officials have moved freely back and forth between the civilian space agency and the military program. A few examples:

• James Fletcher, the present and former NASA administrator, was head of a study team that urged President Reagan to proceed with the SDI program.

• Lt. Gen. James Abrahamson, formerly head of the NASA shuttle program, is now director of the SDI program.

• William Graham, who was acting NASA administrator at the time of the Challenger accident, was a former chairman of the President's General Advisory Committee on Arms Control and Disarmament and a former weapons researcher. His appointment was opposed by senior NASA officials on the grounds that it might compromise the agency's civilian character.

• Rear Admiral Richard Truly, a former NASA astronaut, was head of the Navy Space Command before he returned to NASA to take over the shuttle program in the wake of the accident. Many NASA astronauts on active duty are also in the military.

In addition, NASA has trained astronauts and flight controllers who later became members of the U.S. Air Force and Navy space commands and it instituted strict security measures in its own flight simulators and Mission Control rooms to accommodate the military presence, a move that Turnbill said has eroded NASA's tradition of openness. He maintained that these developments were leading to the formation of "a new breed of military astronauts" and that the establishment of the military space commands reflected the belief of U.S. defence officials that, in the next 25 years, "contests in space are not only possible but almost inevitable."

Thus, despite NASA's oft-stated desire to maintain an arm's length relationship with the military, it cannot avoid giving the appearance of having very close ties with the military. Certainly, it would appear that many of the people in top positions within NASA are knowledgeable about, and presumably sympathetic to, the military's goals in space. This is perhaps one reason why there seems to be a pervasive public belief that the space station will be largely run by the military — a concern that has been particularly strongly voiced in Canada. At the time Canada announced it would study participation in the space station project, questions were raised by politicians, scientists and the public about the possibility of Canada's becoming entangled in a military research venture. The critics were all the more watchful after the controversy over whether Canada should participate in the Star Wars research program (an option the government ultimately rejected in September, 1985, although it said that private companies could bid on SDI contracts if they wanted to).

In March, 1985, New Democrat Michael Cassidy called for a Parliamentary committee to review the proposed project on the grounds that it might be "used as a back door to get Canada on-side with President Reagan's Star Wars research." His concerns were echoed by Liberal science critic David Berger, who said, "There is a question over what kind of controls we would have in an American project."

Tom Siddon, then the science minister, said that Canada was convinced the station would be used for peaceful purposes and that it had "no military implications." Mac Evans said that Canadian participation would be "entirely consistent with our international treaty obligations on the peaceful uses of outer space."[3] James Beggs, then the NASA administrator, who was in Ottawa to sign the agreement, told reporters that the U.S. military had no plans to use the station and that if in future they did want to go into space, "I expect ... they will go on their own."

A year later the same questions arose when the government committed Canada to spending CDN$800-million to develop the servicing facility for the space station. Frank Oberle, who succeeded Siddon as science minister, said that he didn't foresee a situation in which it would be used for military purposes.

All of this is true, but there are some subtleties involved. The station is a civilian project and it will not be run by the military. In fact, the Pentagon has never been a big fan of the project, saying that it had no use for the station and expressing concern that it might drain funds from shuttle projects in support of military missions. The station will not be of much use for military

361

reconnaissance because of its low-inclination orbit, which does not cover high-latitude territory (for example, the Soviet Union) that would be the target of such surveillance. And the station is unlikely to be used for highly classified weapons development work because of all the U.S. and foreign civilians who will be running around on board.

This is not to say, however, that research of interest and importance to the military will not be done on the station. In all likelihood, it will be. Researchers working directly on military contracts can use the station — NASA has said they will be treated like any other customers — and it is likely that much of the civilian zero-gravity research program will prove to be of interest to the military. The development of new electronic materials and glasses is a case in point; the military will be a major market for products like gallium arsenide semiconductors and high quality optical fibres. These are both areas of interest to Canadian researchers. The question — as usual — is, how pure is pure research? The fact is that it's often impossible to draw an absolute dividing line between military and non-military research, whether done in space or on earth.

The same can be said for space technology development. The Canadarm, for example, was developed as part of the civilian space program, but because the shuttle had to be shared with the military, the arm has undoubtedly been used to handle military payloads and will continue to be used in this way. Canadian peace activists have suggested on occasion that Canada demand restrictions on the military uses of Canadian-built technology in the agreements it negotiated with NASA. These suggestions were — rightly — rejected as naive and unworkable; Canada never had the clout to enforce such a policy. Kenneth Pederson, formerly NASA's director of international affairs, was once asked how NASA would respond to a Canadian request that the arm be used only for civilian peaceful purposes. He said: "I would hate to have to structure a deal with Canada saying the arm will never touch a military payload. It just doesn't seem realistic — why get involved in making promises everyone knows are silly?"

The same principle applies to the European-built Spacelab, which is expected to be used on a flight dedicated to SDI research when shuttle launches resume. It is expected that laser weapon pointing and tracking tests will be done on that mission.

In some respects, the effort to open space to permanent human habitation is not a new challenge. In one form or another, the problems and promises have all been encountered before. Whenever an assault on a new frontier has been made, the cast of characters has been the same: there are always the doubters, the penny-counters, the dreamers, the trail-blazers and the heroes. The circumstances are always the same, too — triumph and tragedy, technical set backs and spectacular successes, escalating costs and great financial rewards. In all such ventures, two kinds of failure are possible: there is the failure to finish and there is the failure to start. Of the two, the failure to start is the easier mistake to make. When the choices are tough and the dollars scarce, failing to start is a deceptively simple and tempting option. Who can put a value on what might have been?

Examples of such shortsightedness abound in history. Isaac Gillam, head of commercial programs for NASA, has pointed out that when Congress was asked to fund the exploration and settlement of the United States west of the eastern seaboard, "no lesser person than Daniel Webster voted against the idea saying that it would be a waste of the taxpayer's money because the territory, as everybody knew, had nothing but barren scrub cactus, deserts, high mountains and uncivilized savages."

And there were these words of wisdom from the Talavera Commission in Spain in 1491, which rejected a proposal for expedition funding from one Christopher Columbus: "The committee judged the promises and offers of this mission to be impossible, vain and worthy of rejection: that it was not proper to favor an affair that rested on such weak foundations and which appeared uncertain and impossible to any educated person, however little learning he might have."

It does not appear that the Western industrial world will make the same mistake, despite the shock and disarray in the wake of the Challenger accident. As *Aviation Week* put it in an editorial, the United States has "a lot of work to do in pulling [its] space act together before we take it out on the road to the stars. But take it out we must." U.S. President Reagan has pledged that "we will go on." Canada, Europe and Japan are still preparing for the space station era.

Columbus made it to North America despite the naysaying of the members of the Talavera Commission, and humanity will make it into space despite the naysaying of their spiritual

363

descendants. With any luck, it will not be too long after the 500th anniversary of Columbus' discovery that humans will be able to look down on the continent he found — from a permanent home nearly 500 km above the earth.

NOTES

1. In late May, a European Ariane rocket with a communications satellite on board failed shortly after launch and had to be blown up by the safety officer. It was the fourth Ariane failure in 18 months.
2. However, in the aftermath of the Challenger accident, consideration was being given to postponing the use of the Vandenberg launch site or even shutting it down altogether. This was partly because of the two-year delay in resumption of shuttle flights and the reduced flight schedule that would follow, but there were also technical problems with the Vandenberg launch pad that would have delayed its use until 1988 anyway. The decision to build a fourth orbiter revived the prospect that the Vandenberg site would be used as planned.
3. The 1967 Treaty on Outer Space, which has been ratified by Canada, declares that the exploration and use of space should be the "province of all mankind" and that space is not subject to claims of national sovereignty or appropriation. Nuclear weapons and weapons of "mass destruction" are prohibited and bases for military maneuvres are also forbidden. Star Wars proponents argue that the laser weapons that would be used are a defensive system and not weapons of mass destruction. In his 1982 address to the United Nations Special Session on Disarmament, former Prime Minister Pierre Trudeau called for a treaty "to prohibit the development, testing and deployment of all weapons for use in outer space."

370